Our
Social World

**An Introduction
to Anthropology, Psychology
and Sociology**

Wayne Sproule

PEARSON

Prentice
Hall

Toronto

National Library of Canada Cataloguing in Publication Data

Sproule, Wayne, 1944-
    Our social world : an introduction to anthropology, psychology and sociology

For use in grade 11.
Includes index.
ISBN 0-13-041068-3

1. Sociology. 2. Anthropology. 3. Psychology. I. Title.

HM586.S67 2001   301   C2001-930297-5

ISBN 0-13-041068-3

Publisher: *Mark Cobham*
Product Manager: *Anita Borovilos*
Managing Editor: *Elynor Kagan*
Developmental Editors: *Chelsea Donaldson, Jenny Armstrong, Kelly Ronan*
Contributing Activities Editors: *Jenifer Borda, Rachel Powell*
Copy Editors: *Susan Ginsberg, Mary Kirley, Kelly Ronan*
Proofreader: *Laurel Bishop*
Production Coordinator: *Zane Kaneps*
Art Direction: *Zena Denchik, Alex Li*
Page Layout: *Jack Steiner*
Cover Image: *Sheena Land/Stone*
Illustrations: *Kevin Cheng/Supercat Illustration*
Photo Research/Permissions: *Michaele Sinko, Amanda McCormick,
    Jane McWhinney, Karen Hunter*

The publisher has taken every care to meet or exceed industry specifications for the manufacturing of textbooks. The spine and the endpapers of this sewn book have been reinforced with special fabric for extra binding strength. The cover is a premium, polymer-reinforced material designed to provide long life and withstand rugged use. Mylar gloss lamination has been applied for further durability.

Printed and bound in Canada

8 FR 11

Contents

Skill Focus Features

Preface

This book is about enlarging our understanding of people through the social sciences that strive to find out more about how we think and behave. In particular, the book applies the disciplines of anthropology, psychology and sociology to investigate human thought and behaviour. These social sciences are relatively new—they have developed over the last hundred years or so. Yet, in that period of time, they have produced a great deal of information about human beings.

People have always been curious about human thought and behaviour. They observe and draw conclusions in everyday life about themselves and others. What can the social sciences add to our understanding? They can offer new ideas resulting from research and can show us how to find out more. In our personal lives, in our work lives and in our social encounters, the ideas and methods of the social sciences can increase our ability to understand ourselves and others. Some of the students who take this course may be interested in taking more social science courses in college or university. They may wish to further their study of anthropology, psychology or sociology. The contents of this book will give them a sense of what such courses will be like.

Those who worked to produce *Our Social World* have this primary goal in mind—we wish to present the most recent social science information as clearly as possible and to provide opportunities to practise the methods of discovering and using this information. We also hope that we have made this search enjoyable and exciting.

Features of *Our Social World*

- **Key Terms** appear at the beginning of each chapter to provide an overview of the major concepts in the chapter.

- **Case Studies** describe actual examples to show how the social sciences can be used to study real problems and situations.

- **Social Science Live** activities encourage students to participate in ways that test and investigate ideas about thought and behaviour.

- **Skill Focus** activities introduce new learning, inquiry and communication skills, which students can practise by applying them to material related to the chapter.

- **Society Matters** excerpts focus on real-life social concerns, often presented in the form of newspaper or magazine articles.

- **Activities** allow students to deepen their understanding and to practise the skills of thinking and evaluating, applying information, researching and communicating.

- **Key Points** at the end of each chapter summarize major ideas in capsule form for easy reference and review.

- **Build Your Research and Inquiry Skills** and **Demonstrate Your Learning** sections at the end of each unit allow students to review and apply what they have learned.

Acknowledgements

A number of people worked hard to make *Our Social World* and the accompanying Teacher's Guide the most effective resources possible. Publisher Mark Cobham ensured that all supporting efforts were well coordinated. Product Manager Anita Borovilos provided the vision. Managing Editor Elynor Kagan made sure that everything was done on time and that the material was of the highest standard. Her efforts were invaluable. Developmental editors Chelsea Donaldson, Jenny Armstrong and Kelly Ronan worked professionally and carefully on the editorial details. Others who contributed significantly are copy editors Susan Ginsberg and Mary Kirley; proofreader Laurel Bishop; production coordinator Zane Kaneps; photo researchers Michaele Sinko, Jane McWhinney and Karen Hunter; art directors Zena Denchik and Alex Li; page formatter Jack Steiner; and marketing manager Barbara Webber.

A special note of appreciation goes to the reviewers for their comments and suggestions at various stages of development of the text: Tony Coccimiglio, Vince Dannetta, Kelly Fotinos, Robert Gellner, Julie Hunt Gibbons, Ardis Kamra, Kim Lynch-Johnston, Patrick Mahoney, Lisa Skinner, Terri Slack, James Terry and Wendy Wilson. Special thanks go also to Jenifer Borda and Rachel Powell for reviewing and editing the activities.

I would like to take this opportunity to thank those I have had the pleasure and privilege to work with in education over the years. The enthusiasm and curiosity of my students have always provided me with motivation and desire to provide the best materials and instruction. Both teachers and teachers-in-training have been an inspiration. They have all taught me so much about human behaviour and about the potential inherent in young people.

I would especially like to acknowledge the importance of my family in this undertaking. I want to thank Lottie and Shirley for their constant support. And of course, thank you, Beverly, for your patience and encouragement throughout.

Wayne Sproule
March 2001

1

Social Sciences: Self and Others

Unit Overview

ow can we understand ourselves better? How can we learn to understand others? These are questions most people ask themselves at one time or another. Social scientists, who also ask these important questions, are committed to finding the answers. This unit introduces three disciplines: anthropology, psychology and sociology. Throughout this text, these three social sciences will provide ideas and methods for understanding the forces that shape us as individuals in a social world. The central question you can keep in mind as you read is, How can anthropology, psychology and sociology help us understand ourselves as individual human beings and as members of society?

Anthropology, Psychology and Sociology in This Unit

Anthropology, the physical and cultural study of humanity in the widest sense, will provide "the big picture" in order to discover who we are as human beings. Think, for a moment, how you would describe human beings to a visitor from another planet. What physical and cultural characteristics would you include in this description? How would you explain how cultures have adapted over time? As you can see, your anthropological description would encompass a very broad scope.

Psychology is the study that examines human thought and behaviour. Through the eyes of the psychologist, you will look at such human characteristics as how we experience and perceive the world around us; how we think, learn and remember; the role of emotions; and how we deal with life's demands and problems. Often psychology concerns itself with the individual's mental processes, but it also draws conclusions about how the individual behaves in a social setting.

Sociology, providing a third view of humanity, is the study of people in groups and within the social structures they create. Using the ideas and methods of the sociologist, you will continue your investigation of why and how individuals become part of groups and societies. Human beings have often been called "social animals"; sociology can help us understand this description.

Introducing the Social Sciences

Key Terms

social sciences

anthropology

psychology

sociology

inquiry

hypothesis

case study

sample surveys

unstructured observation

structured observation

participant observation

Workers Rebelling After "Decade of Pain"

Horrifying, but is it a crime?

4300-YEAR-OLD TOMB FOUND

Is Stress Hurting Teens Today?

OLD AND WISE? FORGET IT!

Workplace stress takes toll on families

Human beings are naturally curious about the thoughts and actions of others. This curiosity has prompted people over the ages to investigate human thought and behaviour in a scientific way. Although their methods have been scientific, their subject matter often starts with ordinary people and everyday life. You can start your own investigation of human thought and behaviour by surveying the newspaper headlines above. Choose the headline that interests you the most, and write two or three sentences speculating what you think this headline is about. Then discuss the following questions with the class. Your answers will provide a preview of the sorts of issues and inquiries you will conduct in this course.

- How many headlines are questions? How many are statements?

- How might you either answer these questions or test these statements?

- Why is it important to think about these statements and questions?

Three Social Sciences

Over the centuries, people have turned to science to explore human societies and social relationships. This category of science is known as the **social sciences,** and it includes the study of people as individuals and as members of groups such as families, tribes and communities. The social sciences include branches such as history, civics, economics and politics. In this text, we will look at three social sciences that add to our understanding of what it means to be human: anthropology, psychology and sociology. These social sciences are sometimes known as behavioural sciences, the scientific study of human behaviour.

Anthropology is the study of human beings as a species and as members of different cultures. There are two major branches of anthropology: physical anthropology and cultural anthropology. Physical anthropology looks at the ways in which humans are similar to, and different from, other species; it also examines how humans have developed biologically over time. Cultural anthropology explores how culture shaped the way people lived in the past and how they live in the world today. For example, a cultural anthropologist would be curious as to why the structure of families or how children are raised varies from one culture to another.

Psychology is the study of human mental processes and behaviour. Theoretical psychologists try to understand general rules that guide our thinking and behaviour. They examine both overt actions (those that can be seen) and mental processes, which may be harder to discern. Overt actions include how people behave in certain situations; mental processes refer to how people think, feel, remember and learn. Clinical psycholo-

Focus Questions

What is social science?

What are anthropology, psychology and sociology?

What will we learn in this text?

culture—the shared values, beliefs, behaviours and material objects of a group of people

Figure 1–1

An anthropologist might ask, "How does education in Canada differ from education in other cultures?" A psychologist might ask, "How do teenagers feel in specific situations at school?" A sociologist might ask, "How do girls and boys respond differently in the classroom?"

gists use this understanding to study emotions such as anger, anxiety or depression in order to help individuals who are experiencing psychological problems.

Sociology is the scientific study of people in groups. It examines the relationships between people and the social structures they develop. A sociologist studies the actions and responses of individuals within a group in order to detect general patterns of human behaviour. Although each of us is unique, we also belong to different categories, such as students, teenagers, males or females, brothers or sisters and so on. Sociologists explore how the categories we belong to shape our experiences of the world. Sociologists also try to understand how society as a whole can influence our thoughts, feelings and actions.

Social Science Inquiry

Focus Questions

What is the purpose of social science inquiry?

What are the steps in the inquiry model?

Why are anthropology, psychology and sociology known as "sciences"? It is because all three disciplines attempt to investigate human thought and behaviour in a scientific way. That is, they all follow a process of **inquiry**—an investigation that follows a formal procedure. This process can lead to answering questions about people and the world around us.

The Inquiry Model

As outlined below, a scientific inquiry has five steps. Follow the process and then read on to learn more about some of the key stages.

1. **Identify a problem or question.** The starting point for all inquiry is a question or a problem. This problem provides a reason for the inquiry and indicates a plan of action. For example, a social scientist might be wondering about the impact of driving on teenage life. The first step in any social science inquiry is to put the problem in the form of a question. The question in this case might be "Do students who own or have regular access to a car have lower grades in school?"

2. **Develop a hypothesis.** A hypothesis is a possible answer to a question and a starting point for further investigation. This step is crucial because without a hypothesis an inquirer can waste a lot of energy looking for information that may not be relevant to the answer. A hypothesis indicates what needs to be tested and which research method to use. For instance, the social science inquirer might hypothesize that owning or having regular access to a car has a negative effect on school grades.

data—facts, figures or other information from which conclusions can be drawn

3. **Gather data.** The inquirer must determine how to gather data or information. The method of research used should be appropriate to the question and the hypothesis. In the social sciences, a number of

research methods may be used: case studies, sample surveys, experiments, interviews, or observation (see pages 8–13). For example, the inquirer might conduct a survey to find out how many teens own cars or how often and what time of day they have access to a car, and what grades these teens are getting at school.

4. **Analyze the data.** Collected data is not meaningful unless it is organized, interpreted and analyzed (see pages 14–16). In our example, the inquirer might organize the information gathered from the survey into the form of a graph that shows a relationship between having access to a car and school grades. This type of graph would allow the inquirer to see any trends, or general patterns, that would help to answer the question.

5. **Draw conclusions.** At this point, the inquirer determines whether the hypothesis is supported or not. Should the hypothesis be accepted, rejected or revised? What kind of an answer can be provided for the question asked? The researcher might determine that there is, in fact, a relationship between having access to a car and school grades, but that it does not support the hypothesis. Based on analysis of the data, the researcher might find that having access to a car during the daytime does not harm grades, but having unlimited access to a car during evening hours does have an impact. (See page 16.)

Figure 1–2

Although some researchers might choose to investigate the impact of car use on student grades, what other problems related to car use could be used for a social science inquiry? Would you classify your problem as anthropology, psychology or sociology?

Activities

Understand Ideas

1. What is the purpose of the social and behavioural sciences?

2. Compare and contrast the disciplines of psychology, sociology and anthropology.

3. Make a flow chart showing the stages in a social science inquiry. In your chart, provide an example of your own for each stage.

Think and Evaluate

4. Which behavioural or social scientist would be concerned with
   - your personal problems?
   - how you relate to your friends?
   - how your group spends its spare time?
   - the educational system?
   - how chimpanzees find food and make tools?
   - how families differ from one culture to another?

5. Rearrange the order of the following sentences so that they follow the model of inquiry:
   - The doctor gathered the notes from her observations and added them to the test results she had obtained.
   - The patient walked into the doctor's office, complaining of fever and lack of energy.
   - The doctor concluded that the patient had the flu.
   - The doctor thought the patient might have the flu that was going around.
   - The doctor prescribed rest, aspirin and plenty of liquids.
   - The doctor inspected the patient's eyes, nose and ears and ordered some tests.

Apply Your Learning

6. **a)** Pose a question based on each of the following situations:
   - repairing a car
   - choosing courses

- buying a CD player
- looking for a part-time job

b) Choose one question from Activity 6a and outline in point form how the steps in the inquiry process can be applied to the question you have selected.

c) Identify a new question or problem of your own choosing and follow the same process you used in Activity 6b.

Research and Communicate

7. Review the definitions for anthropology, psychology and sociology. Identify a question or problem for each social science and record a possible hypothesis for each question. Keep these hypotheses for further inquiry. You may wish to begin collecting information related to one or more of these issues.

Focus Questions

What research methods do social scientists use?

What steps do researchers use to conduct experiments?

What is a sample survey?

How do researchers conduct interviews?

Why do researchers use the method of observation?

Research Methods

Social scientists have a range of methods they can use for the third step in the inquiry process—gathering data. The research method chosen will depend on the question or problem and the field of study. Anthropologists, psychologists and sociologists often prefer different approaches.

Case Studies

A **case study** is the observation of an individual, a situation or a group over a period of time. A psychologist may work closely with one individual in order to understand and help that particular person. A sociologist may observe and interview the students of one class. An anthropologist may study people in one culture.

Why study one example or case? By studying one situation in depth, a lot of detail can be unearthed, and hypotheses about similar situations can be developed. Researchers may then use these hypotheses to study and understand other individuals, social groups or cultures. For example, if

Figure 1–3

An anthropologist might conduct a case study of child rearing in Mexico, using it as a basis for comparison with child rearing in other countries. A psychologist might conduct a case study of a parent and child to better understand their relationship. A sociologist might conduct a case study to find out more about the role of parenthood.

you were to study the case of one student whose marks seem to be falling as a result of having a car, you might be able to apply what you have learned to other students who are not doing well in school.

Experiments

The essence of an experiment is to determine how one factor is related to another—for example, could one factor be caused by the other? What happens if one factor is changed? How does this change appear to affect other factors?

In the natural sciences such as physics, biology and chemistry, experiments are widely conducted. However, in the social sciences, this method is used with great care due to the ethical questions involved in experimenting with human beings. For example, it might be possible to measure the impact of car use on grades by encouraging one group of students

ethical—pertaining to the accepted principles that govern the conduct of a profession or practice

Conducting an Experiment

Here's How

1. **The question:** Like other forms of inquiry, experiments begin with a question or a problem.

2. **A testable hypothesis:** The purpose of the experiment is to determine whether there is evidence to support the hypothesis.

3. **Independent variable:** This is the factor to be changed in the experiment. For example, if the experiment is to determine the impact of car use on school grades, the independent variable might be the number of hours a week that students have access to a car.

4. **Dependent variable:** This is the factor affected by the change. In the car-use inquiry, the dependent variable would be the grades.

5. **The control group:** In order to measure the impact of the independent variable, experiments will often have a control group—that is, a group that is monitored as a standard for comparison with the experiment. For example,

to study the impact of car ownership on grades, the researcher must compare the grades of car owners with grades from a control group of students who do not own cars.

6. **Control of other factors:** The researcher must ensure that other factors are not causing the observed effects. For example, if all the car drivers in the experiment also belonged to a gym team and were committed to long hours of practice, there would be no proof that car use caused the falling grades.

7. **Observation:** The experiment requires some method of observing, measuring and recording the change that takes place. For example, in the car-use inquiry, the researcher would have to measure the hours of car use—perhaps the time of day and the number of hours the car was available.

8. **Conclusion:** This statement indicates whether the hypothesis is supported by the evidence provided in the experiment.

to spend every evening over the next few months driving around, while a control group spent several hours each evening doing homework. Would this be ethical? Probably not—it's likely that the grades of the students in the experimental group would fall, and the students would suffer the consequences. It would be ethical, however, to record how many hours car-owning students do homework per week, compare this number with students who do not have access to a car, and then observe their grades. In this case, the social scientist would not be intruding or harming the students.

Sample Surveys

Sample surveys are used to obtain information about the thoughts or behaviour of a large group of people. They are called "sample" surveys because researchers ask questions of a fairly limited number of individuals who represent a larger group; then they draw conclusions about that larger group. For example, a researcher might investigate the impact of car use on grades in the entire school by surveying several teens from different classes. Sample surveys are often used by sociologists because they provide a general idea of trends and responses. The tool used to gather information is usually a questionnaire—a series of formulated questions aimed at collecting information for research or statistical study. Many questionnaires use a multiple-choice format, which allows researchers to collate the results easily.

polling companies—organizations that conduct and assess opinion surveys

How many people must be sampled to have a reliable result? The sample should be large enough to include a range of characteristics that might affect the result. For example, a car-use survey should include students with different levels of academic achievement. In political surveys, when polling companies ask 1000 people whom they will vote for, they must make sure that they question a cross-section—a range of people representing different aspects of the population with respect to age, sex, occupation, region, culture and other characteristics. From this representative sample, they will draw conclusions about Canadians in general. One drawback is that sample surveys do not allow people to explain their thoughts or opinions beyond responding to the questions themselves.

Figure 1–4

Using a questionnaire, a student conducts a survey of classmates, recording answers as they are given.

Conducting a Sample Survey

Here's How

1. **The problem:** First focus on your main question.

2. **The hypothesis:** As in all social science inquiries, develop a hypothesis to guide your research.

3. **The questionnaire:** Prepare a questionnaire that will allow you to collect enough evidence to test the hypothesis. Use a multiple-choice format if possible.

DO:

Phrase questions so that there is no doubt about the answer.

Use questions that will help you quantify your data.

1. Do you own your own car?
   a) Yes   b) No
2. Do you have access to a car owned by someone else?
   a) Yes   b) No
3. How many hours a week do you have access to a car?
   a) Never   b) 5 hours or less
   c) 6–10 hours   d) More than 10 hours

DON'T:

Ask questions that can be interpreted in different ways.

Ask questions that are not needed to test the hypothesis.

1. Do you own your own car or have access to a car owned by someone else?

2. Do you enjoy driving?

4. **The sample group:** Decide the size of the sample you need to get a meaningful result and who will complete your questionnaire. The people you actually select to respond to your questionnaire are called your sample group. If your respondents are chosen by chance, you have what is called a random sample. For example, to get a random sample of students in your school, you could put everyone's name in a hat and pull out a certain number of names.

5. **Analyzing data:** Using a blank questionnaire, record the number of responses to each question. Convert the raw scores to percentages:

Size of sample: 40
1. Do you own your own car?
   a) Yes   **10/40 = 25%**
   b) No   **30/40 = 75%**
2. Do you have access to a car owned by someone else?
   a) Yes   **20/40 = 50%**
   b) No   **10/40 = 25%**

Interviews

Interviews are used when a researcher requires detailed information from a few people and is looking for explanations or descriptions of thought and behaviour. An interview takes the form of a dialogue between the interviewer and the subject. Generally, a number of questions are prepared before the interview; the interviewer may stay with these questions or allow the interview to develop according to the discussion that follows. Interviews are a useful tool for anthropologists, psychologists, and sociologists alike.

Conducting an Interview

Here's How

1. Preparing for the interview

- Write down your purpose for conducting the interview. This purpose is often the central problem of your inquiry. Example: Does car use affect student grades?
- Write down specific things you want to find out. For instance, you might want to know about accessibility to a car, rules imposed by parents and reasons for using the car. Now convert these areas of interest into a list of questions you will ask. Begin with straightforward questions; move on to questions that may require more thought or longer answers.
- Contact the person you wish to interview. Explain the purpose of the interview, and arrange a time and place for your meeting. Remember that you are asking the person to do you a favour, so be courteous.

2. Conducting the interview

- Arrive on time. If possible, bring a portable tape recorder, and ask permission to use it. Check that it is working properly before you begin. Check the spelling of the person's name. Have your interview question sheet with you; leave space between questions to jot down notes.
- Ask your questions, but be prepared to ask additional questions that come to mind as the interview proceeds.
- After completing the interview, check that you have asked all the questions you prepared.
- Thank the respondent for helping you with your research.

3. Analyzing the results

- If you are doing more than one interview, analyze the first one before conducting the second. Decide whether you learned information from the first interview that will help you ask better questions. If so, reword or change your questions.
- In writing up your findings, explain the purpose of your research. Discuss the findings in a logical way and include quotations from each interview. Longer segments of the interview may be put into an appendix at the end of the report. Sum up the main findings of the interview in a conclusion. Indicate further research that needs to be done.

Observation

In everyday life, we use observation to learn about how people respond in certain situations. Observation techniques are also important in the social sciences—in psychology, sociology and anthropology. Methods that rely on observation have the advantage of helping researchers learn about people in their normal surroundings, or "in the field," as social scientists say.

There are several methods of observation. **Unstructured observation** involves studying people without a predetermined idea of what to look for. A researcher may sit in a cafeteria or on a park bench and note what people do and say, open to anything that might occur. Unstructured observation allows for fresh insights and ideas, and provides new hypotheses for further research. **Structured observation** involves planning beforehand what will be observed and noted, and keeping a list of things to look for. For example, a researcher studying the effect of car use on grades might observe a class and look for signs of fatigue or restlessness in students known to be car owners. The observer might also use content analysis, which is a particular kind of structured observation. In content analysis, a researcher will examine an area of interest—perhaps written materials, television shows or segments of a conversation or debate. For instance, a researcher may watch television commercials for cars to see how they appeal directly to young people. Usually a checklist is used to help the observer make notes and draw conclusions. You will learn more about content analysis in Chapter 17, Culture, Communication and Computers.

Participant observation is a technique used mainly by anthropologists. The researcher not only observes the group but also participates in the group's activities—for short periods of time in one's own society or for longer periods in other cultures. Anthropologists may live with people in another culture or country for as long as one or two years.

Figure 1–5

If you were to observe this situation as a social scientist, which form of observation would you choose? Why?

Skill F●CUS

Conducting Observation Research

Here's How

1. **Choose** the method that best suits your purpose: unstructured observation, structured observation or participant observation.

2. **Describe** the physical setting of your observation, including the surroundings and any objects that are being used (e.g., tools, equipment or furniture).

3. **Observe** the behaviour of the people involved and how they interact with each other. Note what they do and say.

4. **Analyze** what you have observed. What do your observations reveal about the scene you have studied? What further questions do they raise?

Activities

Understand Ideas

1. Create a chart showing the research methods used by social scientists. The five research methods will be your column headings across the top of your chart. Below each heading, write in point form two important characteristics that describe each method.

2. a) What steps are involved in conducting an experiment?

b) Why is it important to have a control group?

c) What type of problem or question is best suited to this research method?

3. How would you prepare to conduct an interview?

Think and Evaluate

4. Which research method would you use to test each of the following hypotheses? Give reasons for your choices.

- Teenagers have more leisure time than their parents.
- Teachers ask more questions of the students in the front of the class than at the back.
- Over 75 percent of students you meet in the school corridors will return a smile.
- All school facilities are wheelchair accessible.
- Students in the cafeteria tend to sit with people of the same culture.
- Students who sit in the front row of the class get better grades than those in the back.
- Girls in secondary school get better grades than boys.

Apply Your Learning

5. Develop a hypothesis for each of the following questions. Suggest a research method that would be most appropriate for testing your hypothesis in each case. Why did you choose those particular methods?

- Will students work harder for marks or for free time?
- Are women better drivers than men?
- Does more education bring higher income?
- Are older or younger students more willing to follow school rules?
- Do Canadian television shows reflect the cultural diversity of Canadian society?
- Do most seniors in your community live independently, with their families or in retirement homes?
- Do parents allow daughters less freedom than they give their sons?
- Is there a relationship between school grades and having a part-time job?

Research and Communicate

6. a) Select one of the topics listed in Activity 5 above and conduct your research based on the method you have chosen.

b) Present your findings to the class. Be sure to describe the method you have used as well as your findings.

Focus Questions

What are the three steps in analyzing data?

Why is analyzing data so important?

Analyzing Data

The research methods we have discussed will all yield data that takes a variety of forms depending on the method chosen, for example, numbers and statistics from a survey questionnaire, a description of a structured observation or notes from an interview. The data, in itself, will not be useful unless it is organized and analyzed. It must be changed into a format that helps test the hypothesis and answer the question being asked—it must be turned into evidence.

Analyzing Data: How Much Do Students Spend?

Follow the procedure below to put your social science skills into action.

Question: How much money does a high-school student spend per day, on average?

Hypothesis: Most students spend more than $4.00 per day.

Research method: Use a sample survey questionnaire. Conduct a random sample survey of students in the school. Make sure your sample includes at least 15 people. Ask the following question: "On average, how much money do you spend in a day? Consider daily expenditures (such as bus fares) and exception expenditures (such as going shopping for clothes or going to a movie on the weekend)."

Data analysis: Start by listing your findings. Your findings might look like this:

Fatima	$0.00
Robin	$4.00
Vasily	$70.00
Abiba	$4.50
Tara	$5.00
Jeanne	$3.00
Rasheed	$14.00
Kirsten	$20.00
Bill	$5.50
Lana	$20.00
Liam	$3.00
Mara	$14.00
Dee	$4.50
Tommy	$3.00
Zachary	$80.00

Now organize your data to make sense of your findings. One way is to determine the median, which is derived from ordering the statistics from lowest to highest. The median is the mid-point, or the point at which half the numbers are above and half are below. In the example above, $5.00 appears to be the median:

$0.00
$3.00
$3.00
$3.00
$4.00
$4.50
$4.50
$5.00
$5.50
$14.00
$14.00
$20.00
$20.00
$70.00
$80.00

Another way to organize your data is to determine the mean average. To do so, you take the total amount spent and divide it by the number of people surveyed. In the example above, the total is $250.50. When the total is divided by 15, the result is $16.70 per person.

Which of these methods of organization do you think would be best for your purposes? Choose one and draw a conclusion based on your survey. Compare your findings with others in the class.

Steps to Analyze the Data

Analyzing data is a process that involves three steps:

1. **Data should be separated into two categories: relevant and irrelevant.** Some of the data that has been collected may not have a bearing on the question or the hypothesis. This data can be discarded as irrelevant. The only data that is retained and used is whatever will address the question and support or negate the hypothesis.

2. **Data should be organized in a way that makes it clear.** Unorganized information can become a random collection of facts and figures. Data can be organized in several ways: divide the data into information that either supports or negates the hypothesis; convert numbers into percentages; or put the data into a chart or a graph to determine whether it reveals any trends over time.

3. **Data should be analyzed in terms of how it supports, or fails to support, the hypothesis.** This is a crucial step in research. Once the information has been organized, the researcher has to determine the extent to which it supports the hypothesis. This process involves dividing the data into three categories: information that supports the hypothesis, information that provides evidence against the hypothesis and information that neither supports nor negates the hypothesis.

random—having no specific pattern, purpose or objective

Focus Questions

What are the four categories of conclusions?

How can you verify that a social science study has value?

Drawing Conclusions

In the social sciences, a conclusion is an answer to the question being asked. It is also a statement of the degree to which the hypothesis is supported. Based on the hypothesis, conclusions can be divided into four categories:

1. The evidence supports the hypothesis.

2. There is some evidence in support of the hypothesis.

3. The evidence does not support the hypothesis.

4. The evidence supports an alternative hypothesis.

Figure 1–6

Data can help you draw conclusions only if it is organized and analyzed.

Which of these conclusions best fits the findings of your survey on student spending?

Social scientists should not be overly cautious when considering warranted or reasonable conclusions. On the other hand, they must never go beyond what is supported by the evidence. There are three general tests to check that a social science study has value: objectivity, relevance and validity. To be objective, the findings should not be coloured by the personal opinions of the researcher. To be relevant, the findings must relate directly to the problem. To be valid, all results must be accurate and reliable.

Previewing a Textbook

Before you go any further, take a few minutes to preview the text so that you will have a better sense of what and how you will learn in this course. A preview will allow you to become familiar with the format of the book and it will whet your appetite to learn more about society in general as well as specific topics.

Here's How

- Turn to the Preface and read the author's orientation to the book.

- Turn to the table of contents and see how the author has organized the information into units, chapters or other subsections.

- Leaf through the book, rapidly scanning the contents. You might wish to read the occasional paragraph or heading that interests you. Try to get the feel of the book.

- For each section that interests you, skim the text and notice the visual material. In a phrase or short sentence, answer the question, "What is this material about?"

- Put the book down and write three questions concerning matters you have become curious about as a result of this preliminary examination.

Practise It

1. Follow the steps above for this text.

2. Share your questions with a partner. Identify the topics or features that you think will interest you most in the text.

Figure 1–7
Previewing a textbook will give you a sense of what you will learn in the course.

Activities

Understand Ideas

1. **a)** List and describe the three steps of data analysis.
   b) Why is analyzing data such an important step in the inquiry model?

2. **a)** What are the four categories of conclusions? Provide an example of each.
   b) Refer to your own survey in Social Science Live (page 15). In which category does your conclusion belong?

   c) Why is it useful to divide conclusions into categories?

3. What tests can you use to confirm the value of your study?

Think and Evaluate

4. How do you decide whether data is relevant?

5. In your opinion, which step in data analysis is most important? Why?

Key Points

- All of us wonder why people act and think the way they do. The social sciences of anthropology, psychology and sociology study human thought and behaviour.

- These disciplines use scientific inquiry to ask and answer questions about how people think, feel and behave.

- To conduct this inquiry, social scientists can choose from various research methods such as case studies, experiments, surveys, interviews and observation.

- Researchers must collect and analyze the data in order to draw reasonable conclusions.

- In this book, social and behavioural sciences will provide some of the tools we need to explore questions about people and the world around us.

Activities

Understand Ideas

1. How can the social sciences help people understand themselves and others?

2. Provide an example of a problem or question for which the most effective research method would be a) a case study; b) an interview; and c) a sample survey.

3. **a)** What steps would you follow to do observation research? (See Skill Focus, page 13.)
   b) Why would some situations be better suited to structured versus participant observation? Provide examples to illustrate your reasons.

Think and Evaluate

4. Which step in conducting interviews do you believe is most important? Give reasons for your choice. (See Skill Focus, page 12.)

5. How would you determine the validity of your data?

6. What is the difference between stating a problem and developing a testable hypothesis?

Apply Your Learning

7. Develop a questionnaire to check one of the following hypotheses. Test your questionnaire on five people; be sure to use a cross-section of the population (see Sample Surveys, page 10). Use their responses to help you improve your questionnaire before distributing it to a wider audience. Illustrate your final results on a graph.
   - A higher percentage of males than females participate in high-school sports.
   - Students in the upper grades are more involved in school clubs and activities than students in lower grades.
   - Most students have a part-time job.
   - Most students would prefer to go to school 12 months a year and graduate sooner.
   - Most students know what career they wish to pursue after graduation.

Research and Communicate

8. **a)** Return to Activity 7 on page 8 where you recorded a hypothesis for each branch of social science. Select one of your hypotheses and apply the appropriate research method in order to arrive at a conclusion.
   b) To what degree did your conclusion support your hypothesis?
   c) Be prepared to share your findings with your class.

2

Anthropology, Human Beings and Culture

Anthropology aims to describe what it means to be human, in the broadest possible sense. At one time, anthropologists studied only people in cultures other than their own, especially traditional societies that had existed for a long time but seemed on the verge of disappearing. More recently, anthropologists have begun to examine all cultures. Start your study of anthropology by thinking about your own tradition or culture.

Draw a diagram similar to the one below, with examples in each category from your culture. Compare your diagram with those of at least four other students. List the similarities and differences among them.

Beliefs
1. Personal: _____
2. Community: _____
3. National: _____

Food
_____
_____

Culture
_____

Traditions
1. Old _____
2. New _____

Clothing and Accessories
_____
_____

In this chapter, we will explore different branches of anthropology. In general, **anthropology** is the study of human life throughout history. The two major branches of anthropology are physical and cultural anthropology. **Physical anthropology** strives to understand and define the physical or biological nature of human beings. **Cultural anthropology** is the study of human beings in different cultural settings around the world.

In This Chapter

- What are the major branches of anthropology?

- What biological and social developments led to the evolution of human beings?

- What is culture?

- What is the "nature-nurture" debate?

- How do cultures adapt?

Key Terms

anthropology

physical anthropology

cultural anthropology

culture

nature-nurture debate

subcultures

ethnocentrism

cultural relativism

archaeology

ethnology

ethnography

evolution—the theory that organisms change structurally and genetically over time, resulting in the gradual development of new species

artifacts—an object of historical interest that has been produced or shaped by human craft

Figure 2–1

Raymond Dart holds the tiny skull of a child, approximately three million years old. ▼

Physical Anthropology

Physical anthropology examines human beings as biological organisms and tries to differentiate them from other species. Some physical anthropologists trace the origins of the human species; others study biological similarities and differences among human beings today. More than any other social science, physical anthropology uses the research methods of natural or physical sciences. Physical anthropologists work with fossils, bones and other remnants of human life. Some may also measure, record and compare physical information about living individuals.

At the root of the discipline of physical anthropology are the theories of Charles Darwin. In 1859, Darwin published *On the Origin of Species,* which described his theory of evolution. Although the idea of evolutionary change was not new, Darwin introduced new data and a different explanation of how evolution came about. Darwin proposed that no two members of a species are exactly alike, and that this variation is a result of biological inheritance and adaptation to the environment. Members of a species that survive pass on their unique characteristics to their offspring. Over time, successful variations will produce a new species. Darwin called this process "natural selection."

In his book, *The Descent of Man,* Darwin discussed the origins and nature of humanity. He concluded that, although there is variation within the human species, human physical and mental characteristics are so similar that all human beings must have originated from one ancestor. Recent genetic studies support this conclusion, tracing all humans back to a common African origin. The date of this common origin and the way humans dispersed throughout the world, however, is still debated.

Over the decades, anthropologists have looked for evidence of early human origins in the bones, tools and other physical evidence that humans left behind. Anthropologists who search for bones and artifacts must look in accessible places where they believe early humans lived and where the remains may have been preserved. Some remarkable finds have added to our knowledge of early human beings. Just a few are described here.

Raymond Dart was an anthropology teacher in South Africa. In 1924, one of his students reported seeing what he thought was a baboon skull on the mantelpiece of a home he was visiting. When Dart saw the skull, he immediately recognized it as an extinct form of baboon. He asked the owner, the director of a quarry, to send him any interesting bones he dug up. Soon after, other remains were delivered to Dart's home. Among them were a skull and fossilized brain of a human child who had lived up to three million years ago. Dart recognized the skull as a previously unknown species that had many traits of a human being but a brain the size of a primate's. He named the species *australopithecus africanus.*

Louis and Mary Leakey worked at a site on the ancient rock of the Olduvai Gorge in the African country of Tanzania, searching for evidence of our earliest human ancestors. One day in July 1959, Mary Leakey

noticed a small bone fragment partly buried in rock. When the Leakeys carefully uncovered the fragment, they found a nearly complete fossil skull lying on what appeared to be the floor of an early Stone Age home. Nearby were stone tools flaked to sharp edges. These fossils were important in establishing that the earliest human beings lived in Africa.

The anthropologist Donald Johanson was digging in Ethiopia in 1974 when he found almost 40 percent of a skeleton eroding out of a hillside. That night, as he and his team listened to the Beatles' song "Lucy in the Sky with Diamonds," he decided to name the find Lucy. Lucy was the first early skeleton of its type that could be reconstructed. Since then other fossil finds have added to our knowledge of early humans. The search to fill in the missing pieces of the puzzle, however, is far from over.

How Do Humans Differ from Other Species?

One branch of physical anthropology seeks to define what it means to be human by comparing human beings with other living creatures. However, such comparisons must be made with care. Physical anthropologists are wary of equating similar behaviour patterns with similar intentions. It is fine to talk about your pet dog or cat as if it were human, but this anthropomorphic approach is not scientific enough for anthropologists.

anthropomorphic—giving human attributes to animals

Primates and Humans

Humans belong to the biological group called primates, the highest order of mammals. While we are not directly descended from chimpanzees or gorillas, we may have had a common ancestor. Evidence seems to indicate that the genetic make-up of primates and humans varies by only 1 to 2 percent; we also share many physical and some social characteristics. For this reason, physical anthropologists look to primates for clues that may shed light on the evolution of humans and their behaviour.

Human Diversity: Myth or Reality?

Anthropologists speculate that physical differences among human groups develop in response to various climatic, geographical or cultural conditions. For example, over the period of tens of thousands of years, skin pigmentation has changed according to climate. Dark skin provides survival value in hot climates, since it is more resistant to ultraviolet radiation. In colder climates, where the sun's rays are weaker, lighter skin captures more sunlight needed to produce vitamin D. Anthropologists continue to study how other physical variations developed.

The Myth of Biological Superiority

In the past, physical anthropologists used to divide humans into three distinct racial groups, Caucasoid, Mongoloid and Negroid, based on external physical characteristics. Today, while the concept of race is still in common use, most social scientists question its validity. In 2001, the human genome project revealed that every person shares 99.9 percent of the same genetic code, indicating that all humans have a common ancestor and that variation among us is minimal.

Not only is the concept of race inaccurate, it can also be dangerous. For example, in the nineteenth century it was widely believed that certain races were superior to others. Social Darwinists applied Darwin's theory of natural selection to the social world and set forth the doctrine of the "survival of the fittest." They believed that those they considered less intelligent, or less aggressive, would ultimately be replaced or conquered by those they believed were fit to survive. This theory was used to justify the view that certain races (and classes) were inferior to others, and that their "superiors" had a right and even a duty to dominate them.

Such ideas of racial superiority have often been used to justify exploiting and annihilating peoples around the world, such as the Aboriginal people of North America; Africans who were brought to North America as slaves; and Jews, Slavs and other ethnic groups killed by the Nazis in the 1930s and 1940s. In South Africa, the policy of apartheid granted rights and privileges to individuals based mainly on skin colour.

The Benefits of Diversity

Nowadays, reputable anthropologists accept that no group of people is superior to any other—mentally, physically or morally. Most agree that all human beings are descended from the same ancestor and that we share more similarities than differences. The "success" or dominance of one group over others at a particular time or place is considered to be the product of greater opportunities, education or other cultural factors, rather than an indicator of biological or genetic superiority. Moreover, anthropologists have found that diversity among humans has contributed greatly to the success of the human species. If this millennium brings environmental changes, diversity may mean that some people will have the physical traits necessary to adapt. These characteristics may give future humans an edge that will allow our species to continue.

What Do You Think?

1. How has physical anthropology added to our understanding of human diversity?

2. If you were debating social Darwinists, what arguments would you use to convince them that their ideas are wrong?

Why Are Opposable Thumbs So Important?

Spend a couple of hours living without opposable thumbs. First devise a way to stop yourself from using your thumbs. You might use duct tape to tape them down alongside your index finger, or wear socks on your hands to prevent you from opposing your thumb to your other fingers (no cheating!).

At the end of the experiment, write a brief report. What tasks were most difficult? What techniques did you use to get around these problems? What conclusions can you draw about the importance of opposable thumbs in human development?

Among the more significant features we share with other primates are opposable thumbs, which make it easier to manipulate objects, and we have three-dimensional, or binocular, vision that allows us to judge distances. We also share a highly developed brain with a large capacity to learn and think, although humans obviously outperform primates on this count. Socially, our children, like those of other primates, remain dependent for a long period of time and require a lot of care in order to learn and develop into self-reliant, independent adults. Humans and other primates are social creatures, depending on the group for survival; but we also share a capacity for aggression and defence of territory. Anthropologist Jane Goodall recorded her observations of a group of chimpanzees that divided into two communities. Over the next few years, Goodall watched as one group attacked the other, killing isolated individuals until the weaker group was exterminated. Goodall speculated that this "warfare" may have been a fight for territory.

One human trait that primates and other animals do not share is "bipedalism," the ability to walk upright over long distances, allowing humans to carry objects and perform tasks while standing. Chimpanzees can also walk upright, but not for long distances and not while performing tasks. In addition, humans have developed the ability to communicate complex and abstract ideas through language. While many animals use calls or gestures to signal others, humans use language in many different forms—to teach their young, to develop and share ideas and to pass on ideas to the next generation. Some anthropologists believe that

Figure 2–3

Jane Goodall was one of the first anthropologists to study the behaviour of chimpanzees at close quarters. When she started in the 1960s, no research of this type had ever been done, so she had to develop her own observation techniques. Goodall was the first to observe chimps making and using simple tools, an activity that, until then, was thought to be uniquely human.

Raising Questions

As you saw in Chapter 1, all research begins with raising questions and identifying problems. The ability to raise questions determines the value of the research and clarifies the problem to be solved. In fact, asking good questions about what you are reading is one of the best ways to study and learn.

Here's How

Use the following types of questions to get started:

1. **W5 plus H:** Journalists use these questions to determine the facts of a situation: Who? What? Where? When? Why? and How?

2. **Analytical questions:** In the social sciences we need to ask questions that go beyond simply what happened. Usually we want to dig deeper into some aspect of human or social existence. Here are some questions that help:

- What is...?
- How is...different from...?
- What causes...?
- What is the effect of...?
- What can be done about...?
- What is important to understand about...?

Practise It

1. Review the section on physical anthropology.
   a) Write six questions about this section using W5 plus H.
   b) Write six questions about this section using the examples of analytical questions in the list above.

2. Choose one of the analytical questions you have written. Suggest a research method that would help you answer your question. Explain why you have chosen this method.

the capacity for language is what finally separates humans from all other species.

These unique and shared human characteristics combine in a way that has enabled our species to survive and prosper. Their importance is obvious when we observe the behaviour of young children. Children inspect the world around them, first by looking at shapes and colours, then by reaching out to touch them. An inquiring mind, good eyesight and adept hands provide powerful tools for understanding the world.

How Did Humans Become Human?

While a study of primates is useful in uncovering what traits set humans apart from other primates, anthropologists disagree as to how evolution to the human species took place. Some anthropologists say that aggressive, warlike traits encouraged early humans to develop the first tools, which they used to kill both enemies and prey. Hunting in groups required effective communication, which encouraged the development of language. According to this view, the combination of using tools, hunting in a group and communicating with language led to the rapid growth of the human brain.

However, other research suggests that the tool-hunting-language connection may have accelerated brain development but was not the driving force. This view holds that our social skills—our ability to get along in groups—may have been crucial in the development of our ability to think. Anthropologists and other social scientists point out that daily living within a group calls for a special kind of intelligence: a good memory, the ability to recognize and learn from others and the capacity to act on that knowledge. According to anthropologist Jane Lancaster, learning to share may have been the most important step in human development: "It is the rock upon which all human culture is built; it is what makes us human."

Figure 2–4

Some researchers think that our ability to get along in groups is a distinctively human characteristic.

Activities

Understand Ideas

1. Explain the difference between Darwin's theory of natural selection and the social Darwinist theory of survival of the fittest.

2. According to Darwin, what is the significance of variation in the natural world?

3. With a partner, create a chart to show what characteristics humans share with other primates and what characteristics are unique to humans.

Think and Evaluate

4. "Human beings are more alike than different." Do you agree or disagree with this statement? Explain your answer in a paragraph. Support your answer with at least three reasons.

5. **a)** In a group, discuss how extraterrestrial visitors might perceive the human species.
   b) Working on your own, use the ideas you discussed to write a report that describes what a human is like from an extraterrestrial point of view.

Apply Your Learning

6. In your opinion, can the results of Jane Goodall's work with chimpanzees be applied to the study of human behaviour? Provide reasons and examples to support your answer.

7. In a small group, discuss ways you have personally experienced the benefits of diversity.

Research and Communicate

8. Conduct your own research to find out more about the life and work of one of the following anthropologists:
   • Raymond Dart
   • Mary and Louis Leakey
   • Richard Leakey
   • Donald Johanson
   • Jane Goodall

   Present your findings to the class in a brief oral presentation. Be sure to include the following information: date and place of birth, early years, major accomplishments and what you believe is your subject's most important contribution.

nature—(in the social sciences) the influence of inherited biological characteristics on human behaviour

nurture—the process of training and influencing a child through learning

CASE STUDY

1. What observations did Margaret Mead make in her comparative studies?

2. What conclusions did she draw?

Connections

Which of the four categories of conclusions describes Margaret Mead's research results? (See Chapter 1, page 16.)

What Is Culture?

What is culture and where does it come from? Over the decades, there has been an ongoing debate about the factors that influence human behaviour, attitudes and other aspects of culture. At one time, it was believed that inherited characteristics, or "nature," directed human behaviour—people in a specific culture behaved in certain ways because they inherited these behaviours from their parents. This school of thought linked culture closely to race, as you saw on page 22. As the discipline of anthropology evolved, however, anthropologists began to believe that culture is based, not on inherited characteristics, but on the way people learn to adapt to their environment in order to survive. In other words, culture is the result of "nurture" rather than "nature." So anthropologists now define **culture** as all the learned behaviours, beliefs, attitudes, values and ideals of a particular society or population.

As you will see in later chapters of this book, the **nature-nurture debate** has shaped the thinking of social scientists not only in the field of anthropology, but also in the fields of psychology and sociology.

Margaret Mead and the Nature-Nurture Debate

Margaret Mead (1901–1978), one of the most widely known anthropologists of the mid-twentieth century, was a student of Franz Boas, an early developer of cultural anthropology. Boas encouraged Mead to study the gender roles of men and women. Mead conducted field work in New Guinea, Polynesia and other Pacific Islands. Her findings supported Boas' view that learned culture, not biology—nurture rather than nature—largely determines human behaviour.

One of Mead's studies involved a comparative look at gender roles in three different cultures: the Arapesh, the Mundagumor and the Tchambuli. Among the Arapesh, she found that children were treated warmly and that both men and women participated actively in child care. Consequently, both genders grew up to view the world in a trusting way. Aggression was not acceptable.

The Mundagumor revealed very different cultural patterns. There, both girls and boys were treated harshly and left to fend for themselves. They learned to view others as potential enemies. As a result, both men and women grew up to be hostile and aggressive. The gentle, co-operative and responsive individual—whether male or female—was seen as maladjusted.

In the Tchambuli culture, gender roles were reversed; women were tough and hearty, while men were passive and looked after the households. As children, girls were trained in handicrafts and were absorbed into the women's way of life. Boys, however, were given no training for their future roles. As a result, adult women formed a cohesive group, while boys were excluded from major ceremonies, standing around in everybody's way.

Margaret Mead concluded that most of the personality traits we associate with "masculinity" and "femininity" are the result of early learning, not heredity. In other words, nurture rather than nature was determining human behaviour. In the mid-1900s, Mead's findings were revolutionary. People had accepted that men and women had roles defined by nature. Today, most social scientists accept that nurture plays a very important part in shaping aspects of a culture, such as gender roles.

Characteristics of Culture

Culture can be broken into non-material and material aspects. Non-material culture consists of thoughts and behaviour we learn and share with others. Our values, beliefs and ideas about the world are part of our non-material culture, and so are our language, rules, customs, skills, myths, family patterns and political systems. Material culture consists of all the physical objects that humans create and give meaning to, including clothing, cars, wheels, schools, books and everything else we have and use. A stick lying in the forest is not, in itself, an example of material culture, but if a hiker picks it up to use as a walking stick, it instantly becomes part of the hiker's culture.

What Do Cultures Have in Common?

Individual cultures can vary greatly, but all cultures share some common characteristics:

Figure 2–5

Margaret Mead shows items of clothing from the Pacific Islands. In addition to carrying out extensive field work, Mead also popularized anthropology, appearing on talk shows and writing articles for magazines.

BEHAVIOUR PATTERNS

Politics
- government
- law
- judicial system

Economics
- exchange of goods and services
- production of goods and services
- forms of property

Family
- marriage
- sex
- child rearing
- family relationships

Communication

Recreation and Leisure

War

KNOWLEDGE AND BELIEFS
- science
- myth
- attitudes
- religion
- philosophy
- values

MATERIAL CULTURE
- food
- dress
- tools
- transportation
- shelter
- art
- weapons
- industry

Figure 2–6

Identify several cultural elements that could be placed in either the material or non-material category.

Culture is learned. We learn most of our thoughts, behaviours and values, and we continue to learn throughout our lives. But not everything shared by a group of people is cultural. For example, we inherit physical characteristics such as hair colour, and biological characteristics such as the need for food. We may, however, learn to colour our hair or to eat the kinds of food that are popular in our culture.

Culture is shared. If only one person has a recurring thought or repeatedly performs a certain act, this behaviour becomes a personal habit, not an aspect of culture. If a group or society thinks or acts in particular ways, those ways become part of a culture. For instance, in North American culture it is commonly accepted that marriage involves only two people. On the other hand, if a small group of people share a cultural value or behaviour, such as a love of motorcycles or a commitment to a vegetarian diet, they may belong to a subculture. **Subcultures** share characteristics of the overall culture but also have important distinctive ideas and behaviours. Some subcultures are voluntary, while others are not. For example, few homeless people, for example, really choose to belong to the subculture of homelessness.

Culture defines nature. Culture can limit, fulfill, expand or in other ways influence our biological needs and inherited tendencies. For instance, all people need to eat—that is "nature." But what we eat—grasshoppers or pork, rice or potatoes—is shaped by culture, or "nurture." All people have an innate need for the company and support of others, but how we relate to families and friends varies, depending to a great extent on culture.

Culture shapes how we perceive and understand the world. The northern Inuit people developed numerous ways to describe snow because these distinctions were important to their survival. Perhaps you know just as many computer commands because they are important to your school work or to your job.

Figure 2–7

What subculture is shown here?
Why is it considered a subculture?

Culture has patterns. Cultures are not random collections of beliefs and behaviours. If one aspect of a culture changes, so will others. Underlying any culture are certain core values and world views that are usually taken for granted by members of that culture. Often we are not even aware of the values we hold because they seem self-evident. For example, many people in Canada share core values such as progress, education, equal opportunity, democracy and technology. Such values define our culture and set it apart from others.

Activities

Understand Ideas

1. Make a web diagram to identify words and ideas you associate with the word *culture*. Identify which of these associations relate to the modern anthropological view of culture and which do not.

2. **a)** Explain what is meant by "Culture defines nature."

   b) Identify three needs that all humans have. Show how each of these needs is fulfilled differently in different cultures. Describe one other trait that all cultures have in common.

Think and Evaluate

3. **a)** In the case study describing Margaret Mead's observation of three cultures, Mead concluded that nurture, rather than nature, was determining gender roles. What other traits or behaviours could be attributed to nurture rather than nature? Provide reasons for your answer.

   b) During Mead's stay in the communities described in the case study, which research methods do you think she used? What qualities can you imagine she must have possessed in order to obtain information from such diverse cultures?

Apply Your Learning

4. Identify at least two subcultures in your school or community. Explain why you consider these groups to be subcultures.

5. Copy the diagram about material and non-material culture (Figure 2–6) into your notebook. Fill in each category with as many examples from Canadian culture as possible. Compare your list with others. How closely do your lists agree?

Cultural Anthropology

Cultural anthropology is the study of how culture shapes human ideas and learned behaviour. Anthropologists of the early twentieth century usually studied non-industrial, non-Western cultures. Their goal was to record the practices of these cultures before they were absorbed by colonial and industrial nations. Today, however, anthropological methods are used to study all cultures. Anthropologists conduct research in urban and rural settings around the world as well as in their own societies.

Historically, travellers and explorers have written about different cultures all over the world. However, their descriptions were not always scientific; sometimes they showed sympathy toward the people they met and at other times they were highly critical. Like other scientists, cultural anthropologists base their knowledge on observation. They try to be objective and to draw reasonable conclusions from data, without imposing value judgments on unfamiliar ways.

One major goal of cultural anthropology is to combat **ethnocentrism**—the tendency to judge other cultures by one's own values. An ethnocentric view is to look at another culture as strange or inferior. Anthropologists believe that all cultures should be respected for developing ways to survive and for meeting the challenges of their environment. This attitude of respect and acceptance is known as **cultural relativism.** It

Focus Questions

What is the scope of cultural anthropology?

What are the main branches of cultural anthropology?

Chapter 2: Anthropology, Human Beings and Culture

does not mean that anthropologists have to approve of everything they observe; it does mean, however, that they will strive to understand and record cultural ways as honestly and as accurately as possible.

Branches of Cultural Anthropology

Archaeology is cultural anthropology of the past, especially prehistoric times. Archeologists analyze material and human remains left by ancient cultures to discover what early humans were like, and where and how they lived. They look for evidence of tools, shelter, clothing, vessels and other materials. Archeologists also search for clues that indicate how early humans provided for their needs and what changes these different methods brought.

Usually, archaeologists, like physical anthropologists, must work from fossilized remains. Occasionally, however, they are given a more complete glimpse at early life. Such was the case with Ötzi, the Ice Man, uncovered in the Tyrolean Alps of southwestern Austria.

CASE STUDY

1. How were Ötzi's date and manner of death determined?

2. What conclusions can we draw about the Ice Man's culture?

Ötzi, the Ice Man

One day, as autumn threatened the sudden, brutal storms that pound the high country, a short, stocky man trudged through the Alps. Alone in harsh country, he probably was fleeing enemies who had flushed him from a farming settlement some weeks before. Perhaps those enemies were responsible for the broken ribs that made breathing painful as he struggled across the glacier.

At some point, he lay down in the modest protection of a rocky gully. And there he died—alone, cold, and in pain. The snows began soon after he died, hiding his body from carrion-eaters that would have picked it apart. Frozen and snow-covered, his body remained locked in the gully as the glacier moved ponderously overhead. Then, one unusually warm summer more than 5000 years later, the ice melted briefly. Ötzi, the Ice Man, was discovered—and he would illuminate the day-to-day life of ancient Europeans in ways a century of archaeological excavations could not.

The Man in the Ice was discovered by two German tourists on September 19, 1991, in the permafrost of the Ötz valley on the border between Austria and Italy. Not only was the body preserved, but so was his remarkably complete kit of clothes, tools, and weapons—mostly perishable items that rarely survive for archaeologists to examine.

Once free of the ice and protected in refrigerated storage, Ötzi faced the full weight of modern science. He was examined, measured, X-rayed and dated. His tissue was examined microscopically, as was the pollen found on his gear. Five laboratories developed radiocarbon dates for the remains, producing consistent ranges for Ötzi's death of about 5100 to 5350 years ago.

The real treasure trove, however, was the clothes he wore and the gear he carried. Ötzi clearly was a man familiar with the mountains and well prepared for them. His clothes, including a grass cloak, were surprisingly warm and comfort-

able. His shoes were remarkably sophisticated: Waterproof and quite wide, they seem designed for walking across the snow. They were constructed using bearskin for the soles, deer hide for top panels and netting made of tree bark. Soft grass went around the foot and in the shoe and functioned like warm socks.

His weapons, tools and stock of replacement materials would permit him to survive away from his home village without regular supplies. He carried an axe with a copper blade and a flint dagger with a scabbard made of plant fibres. The remnants of what apparently was a pack-frame for a knapsack were found. Plant fragments show he had been in a settlement during the time when a grain crop was being harvested and threshed, shortly before his death.

Yet it is also clear that critical parts of the Ice Man's equipment were in extremely poor shape or missing altogether—and that he was trying desperately to replace them. He carried a damaged quiver, for instance, with an unfinished bow, two arrows and 12 rough arrow shafts. He must have been working on them as he made his doomed crossing of the Alps.

All this suggests Ötzi left somewhere in a great hurry, without taking all his equipment, and that he was trying to elude his pursuers by taking a route over the main Alpine chain. He failed. But Ötzi's lonely death gave him an immortality of sorts. An ambassador from the past, he put a face on our ancestors that changed forever our view of the people of prehistory.

Connections

How did archaeologists use the inquiry model to study the Ice Man? (See Chapter 1, pages 6–7.)

From "Ötzi: The Man in Ice: A Human Face from the Late Stone Age" by Konrad Spindler

Applied anthropology is the action-oriented branch of cultural anthropology. Anthropologists specializing in this approach use the information they gather to solve practical problems. For example, applied anthropologists might share with one culture another culture's method of providing health care or cultivating crops. Also, evidence of how the environment influences human beings could be applied to issues such as waste disposal and pollution.

Anthropological linguistics is the study of languages. Linguists use documents, existing research or tape-recorded interviews to study changes in language over time, how different languages may be related and the meaning language has for the people who speak it. The linguist wants to know why you say "Hi!" to your friend and "Good morning, Ms. Reynolds" to the school principal.

Ethnology is the study and comparison of past and contemporary cultures. Ethnologists want to know about cultural beliefs, practices and patterns of thought and behaviour, such as marriage customs, family relations, politics, industry, religion, art and music. They often gather their information through observation and interviews, and by referring to published research on specific cultures.

Ethnography is the in-depth description of a particular culture. The ethnographer may live for a year or more within a culture, observing, talking with people and recording their thoughts and behaviour. This whole process is called field work. In order to be good participant observers, anthropologists must learn the language, gain the trust of the people and take part in everyday life. At the same time, they must remain objective and disturb the culture as little as possible. An important source of information in ethnographic field work is the informant, or teacher, who will explain the meaning of events and help the anthropologist integrate into the community. Margaret Mead is an example of a well-known ethnographer.

The account that follows shows how difficult it can be for an anthropologist to participate and fully understand the customs and behaviour of another culture.

Connections

What are the pros and cons of structured and unstructured observation for linguists, ethnologists and ethnographers? (See Chapter 1, pages 12–13.)

CASE STUDY

1. Why did the Bushmen act as they did toward Lee and his gift?

2. What did Lee learn about his own behaviour from this experience?

Gift Giving Among the !Kung

Canadian ethnographer Richard B. Lee has done extensive ethnographic field work with the !Kung Bushmen of the Kalahari desert. Since the 1930s the !Kung have celebrated Christmas by slaughtering an ox and sharing it with others. Lee thought that this would be a good opportunity to thank those who had been helpful to him during the year. He bought a large, well-fed ox, enough to feed everyone, he believed, but was surprised when most people reacted to his plan with ridicule, claiming that the beast was too thin, too old and practically unfit to eat. Lee describes what happened next.

At dawn Christmas morning, the great beast was driven up to our dancing ground, and a shot in the forehead dropped it in its tracks. I asked /gaugo to make the breast bone cut. This cut, which begins the butchering process, allows the hunter to spot-check the amount of fat on the animal. A fat game animal carries a white layer up to an inch thick. The first cut opened a pool of solid white in the black skin. The second and third cut widened and deepened the creamy white. Still no bone. It was pure fat; it must have been two inches thick.

"Hey /gau," I burst out, "that ox is loaded with fat."

"Fat?" /gau shot back, "You call that fat? This wreck is thin, sick, dead!" And he broke out laughing. So did everyone else. Grinning broadly, men packed chunks of meat into the big cast-iron cooking pots and muttered and chuckled all the while about the thinness and worthlessness of the animal.

We danced and ate that ox two days and two nights; we cooked and distributed fourteen potfuls of meat and no one went home hungry and no fights broke out. But the "joke" stayed in the mind....

Finally, Lee asked /gaugo to explain what had happened.

"Why did you tell me the black ox was worthless, when you could see that it was loaded with fat and meat?"

"It is our way," he said smiling. "Say there is a Bushman who has been hunting. He must not come home and announce like a braggard, 'I have killed a big one in the bush!' He must first sit down in silence until I or someone else comes up to his fire and asks, 'What did you see today?' He replies quietly, 'Ah, I'm no good for hunting. I saw nothing at all...just a little tiny one.' Then I smile to myself because I know he has killed something big."

"But...why insult a man after he has gone to all that trouble to track and kill an animal and when he is going to share the meat with you?"

"Arrogance," was his cryptic answer.

"Arrogance?"

"Yes, when a young man kills much meat he comes to think of himself as a chief or a big man. We refuse one who boasts, for someday his pride will make him kill somebody. So we always speak of his meat as worthless. This way we cool his heart and make him gentle."

Figure 2–10

!Kung children examine a book. Why would a book be a special item for them?

"But why didn't you tell me this before?" I asked.

"Because you never asked me," he said, echoing the refrain that has come to haunt every field ethnographer.

The pieces now fell into place. I had known for a long time that in situations of social conflict with Bushmen I held all the cards. I was the only source of tobacco in a thousand square miles, and I was not incapable of cutting an individual off for non-cooperation. Though my boycott never lasted longer than a few days, it was an indication of my strength. I was a perfect target for the charge of arrogance and for the Bushmen tactic of enforcing humility.

From "Eating Christmas in the Kalahari" by Richard Borshay Lee

Activities

Understand Ideas

1. **a)** Define ethnocentrism, using an example.
   b) How might you use cultural relativism to overcome the ethnocentric attitude of a friend or classmate?

2. Describe three branches of anthropology and formulate a question for each that could open the door to further research.

3. **a)** Briefly indicate the research methods used in ethnography.
   b) To be effective and well accepted by the host culture, what attitudes and personal qualities should ethnographers possess?

Think and Evaluate

4. In the case study about !Kung culture, we saw that Lee learned a valuable lesson. Would you recommend that Lee try this tactic on his Canadian friends? Why or why not?

Research and Communicate

5. Imagine that an ethnographer from another culture is doing field work and wants to observe a Canadian celebration that involves gift giving. What attitudes or behaviours might he or she find puzzling? With a partner, write and role-play a dialogue between you and the ethnographer in which you explain the gift-giving customs of your culture.

How Cultures Adapt

How cultures obtain and distribute material goods is regarded by many anthropologists as a form of adaptation. Cultures that adapt to their surrounding by having the same type of economy tend to be similar in other cultural ways. The major culture types based on economy include foraging, horticulture, agriculture, pastoralism, industrialism and the communication-based economy.

Foraging Cultures

Until about 10 000 years ago, all humans were foragers. Both men and women hunted game and gathered roots, berries and fruits, depending on what was available in their region. For many, starvation was a distinct possibility. Foraging bands tended to be small since game supported only a limited population and decisions were usually made informally by the group. The band moved regularly, carrying few possessions and following the animals and plants in season. Shelters were temporary; the Inuit, for example, could build an igloo in a matter of hours, and Aboriginal people of the Canadian plains used hides to make portable tents. Few foraging cultures still exist—those that do have been pushed to less habitable deserts and other barren places. Also, most cultures have changed over time through contact with other groups.

Horticultural Cultures

About 10 000 years ago, a revolutionary change transformed food gathering to food production as people began to cultivate plants and domesticate animals. Using hand-held tools such as hoes and digging sticks, people found that they could produce more food. Usually this change occurred where temperatures were warm and there was adequate rainfall for crops. This early farming, called horticulture, is sometimes referred to as "slash and burn cultivation" because the existing foliage is burned to fertilize the soil. Horticulturists farm the land for a few years until it is no longer fertile, then they move on to another location. In the past, the Iroquois people of the Great Lakes region farmed in this manner. Even today, the Yanomamo of the Amazon rain forest still practise horticulture.

Life became more settled with horticulture. Although hunting was still important, it was no longer necessary to follow the game. People made and kept more personal possessions such as pottery, woven cloth and tools. Abundant food produced by horticulture allowed populations to grow, and as a result, more complex forms of decision making developed. Respected and important leaders would call formal meetings to discuss community issues and relations with other villages and tribes.

economy—the wealth and resources of a community; the production, distribution and consumption of goods and services

foraging—searching for food

Figure 2–11

An Inuit hunter. Contemporary foragers are limited to a small part of the world. While they tell us a little about our early ancestors, they do not live in exactly the same way; they, too, have changed over time. In the Arctic, for example, many of the Inuit use snowmobiles and other modern equipment.

Agricultural Cultures

Connections

Why would an anthropologist, a psychologist and a sociologist each have a different reason for studying agricultural and pastoral cultures? (See Chapter 1, pages 5–6.)

A natural extension of horticulture is agriculture, which began to develop in Africa and Asia about 8000 years ago. Agriculture involves working the land intensively and continuously, using techniques that horticulture had not yet developed. Essential nutrients are returned to the soil through manure or chemical fertilizers. Irrigation is used to store and supply water during dry periods, and plows are pulled by non-human energy such as animals or tractors.

Gradually, agriculture produced surpluses for storage or sale elsewhere. Towns and cities grew, and large populations led to a high degree of work specialization. Political organizations became more complex, and differences in wealth and power became more apparent. In the nineteenth and early twentieth centuries, Canada was primarily an agricultural society.

Pastoral Cultures

Pastoralism emerged in the Middle East at about the same time as horticulture. Pastoral societies make their living by domesticating herds of animals such as cattle, sheep, camels or goats. They use the meat, milk or wool of their herds or sell the livestock to nearby farmers for other needed products. They move with the herds in different seasons, searching for fertile pastures. Sometimes the entire group travels together, while at other times only those looking after the herd move from place to place, leaving the rest of the group in the village. Today pastoralists live in North Africa, the Middle East, Europe, Asia and elsewhere. The cowboys who rode the range in the old West and drove the cattle to market were part of a pastoral culture.

Industrial Cultures

In the nineteenth century, responding to growing populations and an insatiable need for goods, several nations experienced an industrial revo-

Figure 2-12

Taking pigs to market in Peru. What kind of culture is shown here? Explain.

Analyzing a Culture

Anthropology can be practised in any number of settings including classrooms, social clubs, homes, sports arenas, restaurants or malls—any location, in fact, where culture can be observed.

Here's How

Anthropologists often use participant observation and data collection to conduct their studies, and they usually focus on the following categories.

Physical Environment:
What is the geography and climate?
How does the environment affect the culture?

Political and Legal System:
What are the political structures?
Who are the leaders?
How are laws made and enforced?

Economy:
What technology is used to provide goods and services?
Who participates in the economy?
How are goods and services exchanged?
What form of property exists and is considered important?

Family Life:
What is the structure and purpose of the family?
How does courtship and marriage take place?
How does child rearing and education take place?

Knowledge and Beliefs:
What scientific knowledge and technical skills exist?
What are the values of the culture?
What forms of religion are there?

Art:
What forms of art exist?
What is the purpose and importance of art?

Recreation and Leisure:
How is leisure time spent?
What games and sports exist?

Communication:
What gestures or other forms of non-verbal communication are used?
How much contact is considered acceptable?
How are language and writing used?

Material Goods:
What are the forms of food, shelter, clothes, tools, weapons, transportation, industry and art?

Practise It

1. Analyze one aspect of Canadian culture (or a subculture within it). Focus on just one of the categories above. Determine the method(s) you will use to gather information, and then conduct your study.

2. Report your findings to the class. Be sure to describe the method(s) you used as well as your findings.

lution. Science and technology had progressed to the point where non-human energy could be harnessed to power complex machines. Factories in Great Britain, Germany and the United States were built to house these machines and the workers who tended them.

Industrialism had an enormous impact on every aspect of life. Many people moved from small farms and cottage industries to cities where they found jobs in factories. This massive migration led to severe overcrowding and a whole host of social problems, while at the same time increasing

capitalism—a system in which individuals own property and the means to produce and distribute goods and services; people work and compete for the purpose of generating a profit

communism—a system in which the community owns property and the means to produce and distribute goods and services; people contribute according to their abilities and receive according to their needs

mass media—a means of communication (usually television, radio or newspapers) to a large number of people

overall wealth and the availability of consumer goods. Today, the industrialized world is growing; most of us are urban dwellers who work within the industrial system. Science and technology have continued to create innovations, extending our lives and improving our health.

But industrialism is a mixed blessing. While it has created vast wealth, it has also created greater inequalities, between individuals, groups and nations. New political and social ideas, such as capitalism and communism, have developed to determine how this wealth should be distributed. In addition, the massive consumption of natural resources and the waste products of the industrial system are now threatening our quality of life.

Communication-Based Cultures

By the mid-twentieth century, a new economic and technological era began, spurred by increasing reliance on electronically generated data. This phenomenon, sometimes referred to as the "information age," has also been described as the "second industrial revolution," the "post-industrial society" or the "electronic age." These remarkable changes have given rise to communication-based societies.

Communication-based societies have developed in two stages. The first stage was marked by the development of mass media that provided information to a broad audience. This stage affected the leisure and popular-culture aspects of societies, such as those in Canada, but had little impact on how most people earned a living. The second stage came with the development of computer technology. Computers and the Internet not only disseminate information more widely but also allow individuals to interact with the information. As a result, data, education and work are being transformed. More and more people are becoming involved in the information revolution, often working at home from computers. People are increasingly in touch with others electronically, both for work and for leisure.

Activities

Understand Ideas

1. Create a chart that shows how the economy of each of the six culture types has influenced each culture's ability to grow and change.

Think and Evaluate

2. In your own words, explain how studying other cultures can help us gain a better understanding of our own culture.

3. Brainstorm positive and negative changes to our culture resulting from the emergence of a communication-based society.

Research and Communicate

4. **a)** Watch the film from the National Film Board called *The Netsilik Eskimo*. Research the modern lifestyle of northern peoples, using the Skill Focus on page 37 as a guide. How has their culture changed from the lifestyle of previous generations? What problems are faced by young Inuit today?

   b) Write a short report of at least four paragraphs, outlining the results of your research.

Key Points

- Physical anthropology examines the biological nature of humanity, its origins and its variations.

- Cultural anthropology examines how cultures have developed and compares similarities and differences among them.

- Physical anthropologists study physical factors that they believe led to the development of human beings as a distinct species.

- Culture is the learned behaviour of human beings in response to their environment. It includes non-material elements such as thoughts, actions, rituals, customs, language and political structures, as well as material elements, such as clothing, tools, art forms and other items.

- We all belong to a culture, which we share with others, and which we learn from the moment we are born. Culture affects how we view the world and is shaped, in turn, by the environment. All cultures are logical ways of adapting to conditions.

- Types of cultures include those based on foraging, horticulture, agriculture, pastoralism, industry and communications.

Activities

Understanding Ideas

1. Can you isolate physical anthropology from cultural anthropology? In a paragraph, discuss why or why not.

2. Describe two theories of how physical and social factors may have triggered or encouraged the development of early humans. Which theory do you think is more accurate?

3. Create a chart to describe the research methods used to study each branch of cultural anthropology. Review Chapter 1 if necessary.

Think and Evaluate

4. How might anthropology contribute to other scientific disciplines? Provide specific examples to explain your answer.

5. **a)** Based on what you have learned in this chapter, describe the roles of nature (heredity) and nurture (learning) in anthropology.
   b) Which role do you think is more important? Give reasons to support your choice.

6. Anthropologist Jane Lancaster described sharing as "the rock upon which all human culture is built; it is what makes us human." Do you agree with this view? Why or why not?

Apply Your Learning

7. If Margaret Mead were alive today, what questions would you ask her about her goals, her work or her beliefs? Record at least five of these questions. Follow the guidelines on raising questions on page 24.

Research and Communicate

8. Prepare a research project on the life and work of one of the following anthropologists. Be sure to identify the person's branch of anthropology and to focus on his or her goals, interests, methods of research and final conclusions.
   - Franz Boas
   - Ruth Benedict
   - Margaret Mead

9. **a)** In magazines, journals or newspapers, find two articles about anthropological research. Summarize the main idea of each article and identify the branch of anthropology. How does each article address the nature-nurture debate?
   b) Present your summaries to the class.

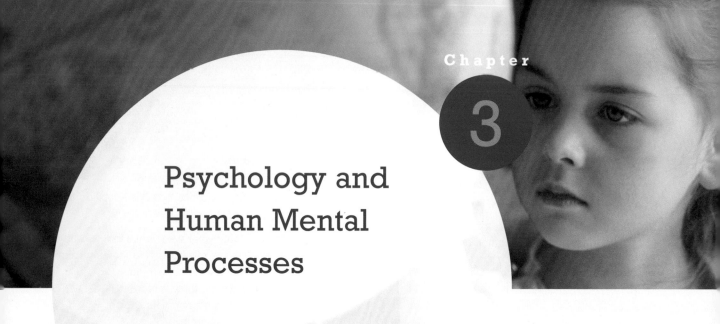

Psychology and Human Mental Processes

Key Terms

psychology

psychoanalysis

cognitive psychology

sensation

perception

cognition

conditioning

deductive reasoning

inductive reasoning

dialectical reasoning

Psychology, as a formal area of study, has existed since the late 1800s when people began to examine the human mind and human behaviour in a scientific manner. Today, psychology touches our lives in many ways. Psychologists study the way people work in an effort to help them improve their job performance. They study buying patterns and use what they have learned to help shape consumer habits. They provide counselling that helps people deal with life in a more effective manner. This chapter will introduce what psychologists know about human mental processes, including sensation, perception, learning, memory and thought. Start by testing your own perceptions. Look at the figures below.

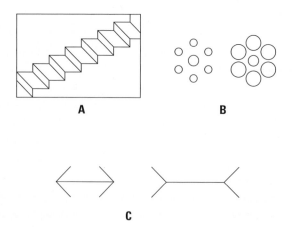

"A" is a reversible figure. Look at it until you can see the steps in two different ways. In "B," which inner circle is larger? In "C," which horizontal line is longer? Give your impressions and then measure. Suggest some reasons for what you see.

The Scope of Psychology

In some ways, everyone is a student of psychology. We all want to under-stand the behaviours of others as well as our own thoughts and behav-iours. This desire for understanding is the starting point for the study of psychology. **Psychology** can be defined as the scientific study of behav-iour and mental processes, and the factors that influence these processes.

Questions about human thought and behaviour have no doubt existed as long as human beings have been on Earth. However, while the ques-tions have remained the same, some of the early answers seem odd to us now. The ancient Greeks, for example, wondered why people had differ-ent personalities. They developed the idea that each person's body had four fluids, or "humours," which they called blood, phlegm, melancholy and choler. They believed that different combinations of these fluids caused different personality types.

Some early thinkers actually did develop important ideas about human thought and behaviour. Hippocrates (460–377 BCE), who has been called the father of modern medicine, was a careful observer of people. He noted that people with brain injuries acted differently from most people, so he concluded that the brain was the source of "our pleasures, joys, laughter, and jests as well as our sorrows, pains, griefs, and tears." The common belief at the time was that thinking took place in the heart. In the seventeenth century, John Locke (1643–1704) argued that the mind receives informa-tion from the senses, turns this infor-mation into complex ideas in the brain and then draws certain conclusions— an idea broadly accepted in modern psychology. However, it was not until the late nineteenth century that scien-tific studies of human thought and behaviour began, and modern psy-chology was born. Not every theory proposed since then can be taken as true without question, but standards of research and testing did become more rigorous as psychologists attempted to follow the scientific method.

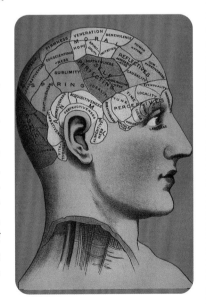

Branches of Psychology

Since the emergence of psychology as a distinct scientific discipline in the late nineteenth century, a number of approaches to studying the human mind have emerged. Today, a variety of opinions exist as to what psychol-ogy is and how psychologists should work.

Focus Questions

What is psychology?

Why do we study psychology?

What are the six major branches of psychology?

Which methods do psychologists use to counsel or conduct research?

phlegm—one of the fluids thought to cause sluggishness and apathy

choler—one of the fluids thought to cause anger and bad temper

Figure 3–1

The study of phrenology, which was in vogue at the beginning of the nineteenth century, was an early attempt to understand human behaviour. Phrenologists believed that human personality could be determined by bumps on the head. For example, thieves were supposed to have large bumps above the ears. We know today that there is no con-nection between the shape of the head and mental or person-ality characteristics.

William Wundt (1832–1920), the founder of **structuralism,** set up the first psychological laboratory in 1879 in Leipzig, Germany. He and his students tried to observe the inner workings of the mind by conducting experiments on sensation, perception and attention. Wundt and the structuralists asked people to practise introspection—to examine their thoughts—and describe everything that went through their minds. Wundt taught his students, who came from all over the world, to raise important questions and to use scientific methods in their research. These research results were published in scholarly journals. Although structuralism was a short-lived branch of psychology, it marked the arrival of psychology as a scientific discipline.

The American William James (1842–1910) took a different approach called **functionalism.** James was impressed with how people adapted their behaviour to the needs of their surroundings. He had read Charles Darwin's theory that human physical characteristics developed and adapted, enabling individuals to survive. James believed that mental characteristics had also developed to allow people to survive by solving problems. James and his colleagues began to look outside the laboratory to the world of people in everyday life. They studied the development of children, how learning and education could be improved, and how men and women behaved differently.

Sigmund Freud (1865–1939), perhaps the most famous psychologist, began his career as a medical doctor specializing in problems of the nervous system. He soon concluded, however, that many nervous problems were not physical in origin but stemmed from unconscious mental forces and conflicts. Freud and his followers developed new ideas about human motivation, child development, personality and abnormal behaviour. They practised an approach known as **psychoanalysis,** a process designed to uncover patients' unconscious thoughts by encouraging them to discuss their background, feelings and experiences with a trained psychologist. Today, psychoanalysis is not only a major branch of psychology but also part of our everyday thinking. Most non-psychologists are familiar with such psychoanalytic ideas as the subconscious, the ego, dream analysis and slips of the tongue (often called "Freudian slips").

At around the same time that Freud was developing his ideas, John Watson (1878–1958) was founding a new school of thought called **behaviourism.** His approach was very different from Freud's, however.

Connections

How is functionalism similar to the anthropologist's view of how cultures adapt? (See Chapter 2, pages 35–38.)

subconscious—the part of the mind that influences actions without one's full awareness

ego—the part of the mind that is most aware and deals with external reality

Figure 3–2

John Watson once claimed that given a dozen healthy infants and a controlled environment, he could train each of them to become anything he chose, from a doctor to a thief.

Figure 3–4

Canadian physician Wilder Penfield performed experiments in which he touched various parts of the exposed brain. The patient, who was conscious during the operation, would report such odd sensations as the smell of burned toast or a long-forgotten child-hood memory. Penfield was one of the first to discover that stimu-lating different parts of the brain triggers different sensations and memories.

Watson believed that in order to be scientific, psychology should only study what can be observed. Since the mind itself cannot be observed, behaviour was the only available source of data. Behaviourists began to study how individuals react to the environment. They took the view that all behavioural responses are the result of environmental stimuli.

Humanism developed in the 1950s, partly as a reaction against the dominance of behaviourism and psychoanalysis. Humanism emphasizes the unique qualities of human beings, especially their freedom and poten-tial for personal growth. Humanists say that people can take control of their lives. They are not dominated by their drives and emotions as the psychoanalysts insist, nor by the environment as the behaviourists would have it. Although these factors are important, say the humanists, human beings can make choices.

Cognitive psychology is the study of the mental processes involved in memory, learning and thinking. It has roots as far back as the late nine-teenth century when efforts were made to design intelligence tests. However, cognitive psychology really expanded in the 1950s and remains

stimuli (singular stimulus)— objects or events that produce a response from a person or other living thing. For example, when the phone rings (the stimulus), we usually answer it (the response).

Figure 3–5

Most psychologists choose one of these three areas. Which type of work in the field of psychology would you like to pursue? ▼

Types of work psychologists do	
Type	**Purpose**
Research psychology	To discover new knowledge in the field through research and study. Most research psychologists are affiliated with a university.
Applied psychology	To apply psychological knowledge to particular environments, such as schools or industry. Applied psychologists often work on site in factories, schools or other institutions.
Clinical psychology	To use psychology to help people define and deal with their problems. Psychoanalysts, counsellors and therapists are often clinical psychologists. They work in mental health clinics or in private practice.

a popular approach today. In recent decades, cognitive psychologists have focused on researching the brain and its processes. Increasingly sophisticated electronic monitoring of brain activity has allowed psychologists to pinpoint exactly what part of the brain is active when we talk, laugh, watch a movie or do anything else. Advances in computer technology and artificial intelligence (AI) have helped to motivate this type of research.

Psychological Research: Methods and Ethics

As discussed in Chapter 1, psychologists use a whole range of scientific methods: case studies, sample surveys, interviews, observation and experiments. In all methods of psychological research, but especially when conducting experiments with human subjects, ethical standards must be followed. To guide researchers, the American Psychological Association (APA) has provided a set of principles called the APA Code of Ethics:

- The investigator should inform participants of all features of the research that might influence their willingness to participate.

- There should be openness and honesty between investigator and participants. Reasons for concealment or deception should be given.

- Participants are free to back out at any time.

- The responsibilities of investigator and participants should be made clear from the beginning.

- The investigator should protect participants from physical and mental discomfort, harm and danger. Participants should be informed of any risk. All measures should be taken to minimize distress.

Connections

What position would cognitive psychologists take in the nature-nurture debate? (See Chapter 2, page 26.)

ethics—moral principles; rules of conduct

Activities

Understand Ideas

1. Define the primary concern or interest of psychology.

2. Create a timeline that shows the emergence of the six branches of psychology discussed in this section. On your timeline, record the main idea of each branch.

Think and Evaluate

3. **a)** Write five questions you would like to ask about mental processes or behaviour.

b) Review the research methods described in Chapter 1. For each of the questions you have written for Activity 3a, identify which research method would be most the appropriate. Give reasons for your choices.

Apply Your Learning

4. Review the three types of work psychologists do (see Figure 3–5). Select the area you think you would be most interested in pursuing and provide two reasons to explain your choice.

Sensation and Perception

Focus Questions

What is the difference between sensation and perception?

What functions does the mind perform during the process of perception?

What factors influence perception?

Figure 3–6

Process of sensation and perception

All branches of psychology are concerned with understanding human mental processes. These processes are complex, but we can make them easier to understand by dividing them into two stages. The first stage is **sensation,** the process that activates our sense receptors—sight, hearing, smell, taste and touch—and enables them to transmit signals to the brain. The second stage is **perception**—the process that allows us to select, organize and interpret sensory signals in the brain.

Input from our senses is essential for information to reach the brain. Helen Keller was prevented from acquiring information through sight and hearing, but not through touch. The following case study illustrates how important sensory input is to our ability to learn and relate to the world.

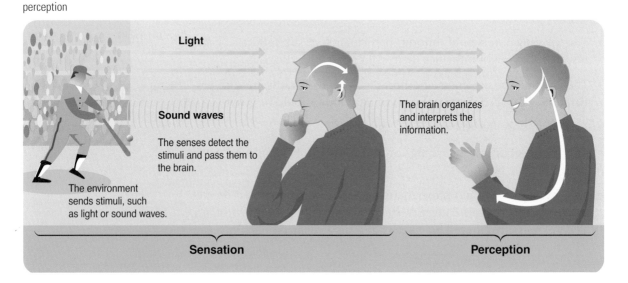

Light

Sound waves

The environment sends stimuli, such as light or sound waves.

The senses detect the stimuli and pass them to the brain.

The brain organizes and interprets the information.

Sensation

Perception

CASE STUDY

1. How did Helen Keller's disabilities affect her sensation and her perception?

2. How did she compensate for these problems?

From *The Story of My Life* by Helen Keller

Touch and a Strange New Sight

Helen Keller was born bright and healthy. By six months she was imitating words and short phrases. By her first birthday she was walking. Then, on a chilly February day, she contracted scarlet fever. Although she survived the illness, she was left blind and deaf.

For five years, Helen's parents tried to teach her. On her seventh birthday, they hired Anne Sullivan to teach her sign language. Anne tried to help her but became frustrated and discouraged. One day, Anne gave Helen a doll, which Helen threw on the floor. At that point Helen's life took a dramatic turn as she describes in the following passage:

I felt my teacher sweep the fragments to one side of the hearth, and I had a sense of satisfaction that the cause of my discomfort was removed. She brought me my hat, and I knew that I was going out into the warm sunshine.

Where Is Your Blind Spot?

The information we receive about the world is filtered through our senses: sight, hearing, smell, taste and touch. But are our senses as reliable as we think? For example, did you know that you have a blind spot in the centre of your eye? This is because there are no receptors to the optic nerve at the point where the retina (which triggers impulses through the optic nerve to the brain) attaches to the eyeball. Try this experiment.

Hold your book an arm's length away from your face. Close your left eye and fixate on the cat in the drawing below. Slowly move the book closer. You should be able to see the dog with your peripheral vision. When the book is about 20 to 25 centimetres away, the dog will disappear. That is because its image falls on the blind spot of your retina. The dog will reappear as you move the book closer or farther away.

This thought, if a wordless sensation may be called a thought, made me hop and skip with pleasure.

We walked down the path to the well-house, attracted by the fragrance of the honeysuckle with which it was covered. Someone was drawing water and my teacher placed my hand under the spout. As the cool stream gushed over one hand, she spelled into the other the word *water*, first slowly, then rapidly. I stood still, my whole attention fixed upon the motions of her fingers. Suddenly I felt a misty consciousness as of something forgotten—a thrill of returning thought; and somehow the mystery of language was revealed to me. I knew then that "w-a-t-e-r" meant the wonderful cool something that was flowing over my hand.

I left the well-house eager to learn. As we returned to the house every object seemed to quiver with life. That was because I saw everything with the strange new sight that had come to me.... It would have been difficult to find a happier child than I was as I lay in my crib at the close of that eventful day and lived over the joys it had brought me, and for the first time longed for a new day to come.

Figure 3–7 ▼

Helen Keller (right) worked on behalf of others like herself.

The moment Helen learned to connect the sensation of water with what her teacher was writing in her hand, her world changed. Eventually Helen Keller would graduate from college. As an adult she wrote books and gave speeches all across North America.

Powerful Processes

In many ways, our powers of sensation are amazing. To illustrate, psychologists have studied the absolute threshold for sensory awareness, that is, the smallest stimulus that we can detect 50 percent of the time. For example, we can

threshold—the limit below which a stimulus cannot be perceived or produce a response

- see a candle flame 50 kilometres away on a clear, dark night
- hear the ticking of a watch worn by someone standing 6 metres away in a quiet room
- taste sweetness in a solution in which one teaspoon of sugar has been dissolved in 7 litres of water
- smell a single drop of perfume diffused in the entire volume of a three-room apartment
- feel the wing of a bee fall upon our cheek from about one centimetre away

Our powers of perception are similarly impressive. A camera, for example, can only reproduce the images in front of the lens; a tape recorder can only record the sound waves travelling to it. In contrast, a human being makes instant and regular decisions about what to pay attention to and what it means. This ability is essential for survival and success. For instance, imagine you are driving along a road, listening to your favourite song on the radio. Suddenly a flash of colour appears in your peripheral vision. You immediately determine that a car is moving into your path. You touch the brakes, swerve and avoid an accident. No machine or computer can sense, perceive and react that quickly.

During the process of perception, the mind performs at least three functions: selecting, organizing and interpreting. Selecting sensation means paying attention to some things in the environment and not to others. For example, loud noises and bright colours are more likely to grab our attention; in a crowded and noisy room, we can pick out our own name from the myriad of other words spoken. Organizing sensation means shaping it into something we understand. The flash of colour in our peripheral vision is organized into a car moving into our path. In interpreting sensation, we decide what the sensation means. In this case, we decide that the car means danger and we should take immediate action.

Factors Influencing Perception

Have you ever raved to friends about a great film, only to have them rush out to see it and return disappointed? From the way they describe it, you wonder if you were watching the same film. How can people have such different perceptions of the same movie? The answer lies in the fact that perception is influenced by more than just the object being perceived. For example, your friend may have gone to the movie theatre on a night when the audience was particularly noisy or unresponsive. Or perhaps your

Figure 3–8

Each species is equipped with sensory powers that enable it to function in the world. When a human and a bee see a flower, they see different things. The human sees the image on the top. The bee, able to receive ultraviolet light better, sees the image on the bottom. The bee can see a "landing strip," which helps it land to gather nectar.

Reality or Illusion?

An illusion is an object or event that deceives us by giving a false impression. Look at the following perceptual illusions. In each case, consider what factor (the object of perception, the background or the perceiver) creates the illusion.

Figure 3–9

What makes these figures impossible? How do we try to make sense of them? ▼

Figure 3–10

Which of the two monsters looks bigger? Now measure them to determine their actual height. What does this exercise tell you about how we perceive things? ▼

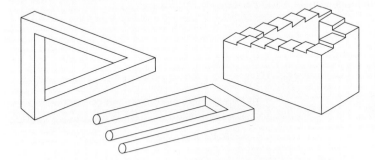

◄
Figure 3–12

Look at the picture and then turn it upside down. Notice how your knowledge of facial features misleads you. The eyes and mouth are right-side up on an upside-down face.

Figure 3–11 ▲

What do you see here, a young woman or an old woman?

friend watched the film at home on a VCR, and the special effects did not look nearly as impressive on the small screen. In addition, what we perceive has a lot to do with our own experiences and particular point of view. Your friend may have thought the main character was unsympathetic because he reminded her of a cousin she dislikes.

In other words, perception is influenced by three factors: the object itself, the background or surroundings, and the experiences and feelings of the person who is perceiving. None of us see the world in exactly the same way.

Connections

How does culture influence perception? (See Chapter 2, page 28.)

Sensation, Perception and Cognition

Sensation and perception are closely connected to learning. We rely on our senses to provide the raw materials the mind must work with. But learning involves more than just gathering sensations. We need to use that data to acquire knowledge. We also have to retain that knowledge in memory so we can apply it again to other situations.

Psychologists use the word **cognition** to describe how we acquire, store and use knowledge. In the following section we will look at how we acquire knowledge through learning. In later sections we will investigate how we store and retrieve information through memory, and how we use our knowledge through the process of thinking.

Activities

Understand Ideas

1. What is the difference between sensation and perception?

2. What three factors influence our perception?

Think and Evaluate

3. a) In what ways can human sensation and perception be compared with a video camera? In what ways are they different?
   b) In your own words, explain why human perception is unique and why it is so important.

Apply Your Learning

4. a) Imagine yourself walking through a haunted house. Describe the three factors that would influence your perception.

   b) Explain how sensation and perception are related to how you would experience your walk through the haunted house.

Research and Communicate

5. Choose an advertisement for a consumer product from television or in a magazine. Bring your example to class. Analyze the way the advertiser shapes viewer perceptions of the product. Consider how the advertiser presents the object itself as well as the product's surroundings. To what ideas or feelings—from the viewer's point of view—does the advertisement appeal?

6. Using the Internet, find other examples of visual illusions and bring them to class. Explain what the illusion is and analyze its source.

Focus Questions

What is learning?

What are the advantages and costs of our reliance on learning?

Learning

One of the results of organizing the information we collect from our senses is that we learn from our experience. Psychologists define learning as a change in knowledge or behaviour as a result of experience. While this definition may be different from your own concept of learning, its advantage is that it covers a wide range of various kinds of learning.

Most human thought and behaviour is the result of learning. A great deal of learning occurs during the first few years of life, although we continue to learn throughout our lives. Learning takes place in many different ways. We learn in school, of course, but we also learn in everyday encounters with life. For example, think of the difficult skills you learned before you started kindergarten: walking, talking, riding your bike, playing and getting along with others, to name just a few.

Other living species learn, too. Mammals such as dogs, cats and chimpanzees have a highly developed ability to learn from experience. Perhaps you have had a pet that could do tricks or knew how to get what it wanted by learning a new form of behaviour. Dogs can be trained to help people who are blind get around or to alert people with hearing impairments when the phone rings, a buzzer goes off, or someone knocks at the door.

Learning, however, is not the only influence on our behaviour. An important role is also played by innate drives and instinctive reactions—responses that members of a species are born with and that help them survive. Many species rely largely or completely on innate drives. For example, fish instinctively swim upstream to spawn; bees build hives and communicate messages without being taught. But drives and instincts do not allow individuals of a species to change their behaviour in order to deal with new conditions. The insect that buzzes against the light will continue to do so, despite the fact that it is in danger. The tortoise will insist on slowly crossing the busy road to get upstream.

Overall, the fact that humans rely more on learning than on instinctive responses is an advantage. We can change our thinking and behaviour to meet new situations and to succeed in a variety of conditions. Yet, this adaptability has a cost: compared to other species, our young must learn a great deal before they can look after themselves. For the first few years they depend on others—primarily parents—to protect, support and teach them. Happily, humans have also developed nurturing skills, forming close emotional bonds with their children.

Can an animal be trained to learn like a human being? The following case study describes one attempt to accomplish this feat.

Figure 3–13
Humans have learned to survive in different environments from under the surface of the sea to space. They also learn and adapt continuously. New technology can be a powerful force of change and learning.

instincts—inborn patterns of behaviour that are characteristic of a species

Hans Goes to School

At the beginning of the twentieth century, a German schoolteacher, Wilhelm von Osten, became obsessed with the idea that horses could be taught as much as people. He set out to test this hypothesis.

Von Osten spent four years teaching his horse, Clever Hans, in the same way German schools of the time taught children. He used repetition, flash cards and other devices. He began with simple problems and moved on to more complex ones. He rewarded Hans for correct answers with praise and carrots. Hans answered questions by shaking his head or stamping his hoof.

After four years, Hans could answer almost any question put to him in geography, history, science, literature, math or current events. Von Osten had total faith in the ability of his horse. Even when his trainer was absent, the horse could answer questions put by others. Von Osten never charged admission or gained in any way from Hans' abilities.

CASE STUDY

1. What did von Osten aim to prove?

2. Did the findings of Stumpf and Pfungst demonstrate that Hans had not learned anything? Explain.

3. What does this case tell us about learning? What does it tell us about proper scientific methods of conducting an investigation?

Figure 3–14

Wilhelm von Osten with his performing horse, Clever Hans. How did Clever Hans learn?

Connections

To what extent did Stumpf and Pfungst follow the steps in conducting an experiment? (See Chapter 1, page 9.)

A government scientific commission tested Hans and was convinced of his abilities. For example, Hans correctly tapped out numbers written on a board; he gave the correct time and date; he converted fractions to decimals. He responded correctly to questions in many fields of study.

Two psychologists, Carl Stumpf and Oskar Pfungst, were curious. They wondered about the conditions under which testing had taken place and tried their own experiments. They wanted to eliminate possible factors that might have interfered with the testing of Hans.

They soon found that when the tester, even von Osten, did not know the answer to a question, Hans' answers were wrong. They also found that when Hans wore blinders he could not answer correctly. Stumpf and Pfungst concluded that communication was taking place between the testers and the horse. They noted that Hans watched carefully when he was asked a question. They also noticed that the tester unconsciously leaned forward while waiting for the correct answer. When the correct number of taps was done, the tester tended to lean back. "Yes" and "no" answers were also unconsciously cued; a subtle nod by the tester would get the same response from the horse, while a back and forth head movement got a shake of the head from the horse.

Activities

Understand Ideas

1. From what two sources does all behaviour stem?

2. What are the advantages and disadvantages of learned and innate behaviour?

Apply Your Learning

3. Identify five to ten of the most important skills or lessons you have learned in your life so far. How did you learn these skills or lessons?

Kinds of Learning

We learn in many situations and in many different ways. Here we will look at two major types of learning that have been identified in psychology: conditioned learning and observational learning.

Conditioned Learning

Conditioning is defined as acquiring patterns of behaviour in the presence of an environmental stimulus. In other words, we learn to respond to a particular stimulus in a particular way. Behavioural psychologists believe that most human behaviour is the result of conditioned learning. Conditioning is one kind of learning we share with other species; Clever Hans learned through conditioning. Each one of us is conditioned to smile back when someone smiles at us, to respond when someone says good morning, or to stop for a red light at the intersection. There are two kinds of conditioning: classical and operant.

Classical Conditioning

Classical conditioning was discovered by Ivan Pavlov (1849–1936), a Russian physiologist who was studying digestion. His experiments involved measuring how much saliva dogs produced when they were given food. He noticed, however, that the dogs began to salivate before the food was in their mouths; the very sight of it caused them to drool. Then the dogs began to salivate simply at the sound of the experimenter approaching.

Pavlov set up an experiment to find out why these reactions occurred. He sounded a bell just before the food was brought into the room. After hearing the bell many times before they were fed, Pavlov's dogs began to salivate at the sound of the bell itself. The dogs had been conditioned to salivate in response to a new stimulus. He found that he could train his dogs to salivate at the sound of any number of bells, whistles and buzzers.

In general, classical conditioning involves learning to transfer a natural response from one stimulus to another. Before conditioning, the food automatically caused the dogs to salivate. Pavlov called the food the "unconditioned stimulus (US)" and the salivation the "unconditioned response (UR)." In other words,

US → UR

The bell is the "conditioned stimulus (CS)." During conditioning, the formula changed to

US + CS → UR

When the dogs began salivating in response to the bell alone, Pavlov called this a "conditioned response (CR)." The formula became

CS → CR

Focus Questions

What are the two major types of learning?

What is the difference between classical and operant conditioning?

Why is observational learning so important?

What four processes are crucial to observational learning?

unconditioned response—an automatic, unlearned reaction

conditioned response—a learned reaction

Do you find yourself getting hungry at the smells wafting from the kitchen? Do you look forward to spending pleasant times with your friends after school? Are you anxious at the thought of writing exams next week? Each of these reactions can be explained in terms of classical conditioning. Even our associations with different foods, colours, situations or people are often the result of classical conditioning. The following case study describes some early experiments with classical conditioning in humans.

CASE STUDY

1. Refer back to the APA Code of Ethics on page 45 to explain why the experiment with Albert would be considered unethical by today's standards.

2. Why did Peter lose his fear of the rat?

Learning to Fear

In 1920 behavioural psychologist John Watson performed an experiment. He showed Albert, an 11-month-old boy, a white rat. At first, the boy displayed no fear of the rat. But every time he approached it, the experimenter made a loud noise by rapping a steel bar. Soon, Albert began to cry and crawl away when he saw the rat. Classical conditioning caused him to associate the rat with an unpleasant situation and to feel fear. The conditioned stimulus, the rat, brought about a conditioned response, fear.

Another experiment was conducted by psychologist Mary Cover Jones who discovered how to use classical conditioning to reduce, or unlearn, fears in children. Three-year-old Peter had a fear of white rats. (You have to wonder where he acquired this fear.) Peter was put in a room with a caged rat but was also given his favourite dessert—ice cream. The next day, the cage was brought a little closer and more ice cream was offered. Eventually, Peter showed no fear of the rat at all.

Similar experiments have been done since to cure people of various fears, including fear of flying, heights and enclosed places. We also use classical conditioning regularly in our everyday lives. For example, you can

Unit 1: Social Sciences—Self and Others

learn to associate studying with a particular environment, such as a quiet corner of the library or a particular room in your house. Once you have made the association (and if the association is a positive one), you will likely find it easier to concentrate when you are in that environment.

Operant Conditioning

The behavioural psychologist B.F. Skinner wondered if Pavlov's ideas of stimulus and response could explain more complex human behaviour. Most behaviour, he noted, takes place voluntarily before being triggered by outside events. For example, you wave your hand to call a cab and it stops; a child asks for more juice and receives it; a driver slows down at a red light in order to avoid an accident. Classical conditioning did not explain these kinds of behaviour.

Skinner put a rat into a cage. The cage was rigged with a bar that, when pushed, allowed a pellet of food to fall into a dish. As the rat moved around the cage, it eventually pressed the bar and received a food pellet. The next time it pressed the bar, it got another pellet. Soon the rat was pushing the bar constantly. This is an example of operant conditioning.

Operant conditioning has had a powerful impact on how we look at learning in a number of areas. In training animals, for example, we recognize that a reward, or positive reinforcement, is crucial in bringing about desired behaviour. In raising children, parents often reinforce desired behaviour by smiling; they may also discourage undesirable behaviour by ignoring it. Those convicted of crimes or misdemeanours are subjected to punishment, or negative reinforcement, in the form of fines or incarceration. It is believed that these consequences will shape behaviour in desirable ways.

Behavioural psychologists suggest that rewards are more effective than punishments in changing behaviour. Punishments may stop undesirable behaviour for the moment, but are less successful in the long term. Once the threat of punishment is removed, the undesirable behaviour may return. Moreover, negative reinforcement does not indicate what behaviour is desired; it only teaches the subject what not to do. Positive reinforcement may have a more lasting impact.

positive reinforcement—an event, a situation or a condition that increases the likelihood that certain behaviour will recur

negative reinforcement—an event, a situation or a condition that decreases the likelihood that certain behaviour will recur

Figure 3–16

When coyotes in one area of the country began to attack sheep, local farmers were determined to hunt them down. However, one farmer tried another approach. He strewed the area with several sheep carcasses that contained a substance that made the coyotes sick. As a result, the coyotes began, once again, to feed on their natural prey. What kind of conditioning was used in this instance?

Try This!

With a straw held several centimetres from a partner's eye, blow a puff of wind gently at the same time as you tap the desk with your other hand. After several repetitions, put the straw in the usual position, but this time, while tapping the desk, do not blow into the straw when you put your mouth to it.

1. List your observations.

2. Explain these observations in terms of classical or operant conditioning.

Observational Learning

Conditioning explains only some kinds of learning. For example, how did you learn to play a musical instrument, drive a car, play a sport, make a presentation in class or behave in a socially acceptable manner? Behaviourists would say that much of what you learned was the result of shaping through conditioning. But you would never have been able to grasp the overall idea of how to perform a new task unless you had watched someone else do it. You learned by observing people who acted as models. The psychologist Albert Bandura identified four processes crucial to observational learning:

1. **Attention.** To learn through observation, you pay attention to the behaviour of others. To master a musical instrument, you listen carefully to those who play it well; to become a good basketball player, you watch others who play the game with skill and grace.

2. **Retention.** You store a mental representation of what you observe in your memory. You note how the person performed the task, what worked well and what results were produced by the behaviour.

3. **Reproduction.** You convert your stored memory into action. You may need to practise to do this well, whether it is playing a guitar or driving a car. You may have to return to the attention or retention process in order to clarify your mental representation.

4. **Motivation.** You must be motivated in order to practise the skill. You will have to believe that the skill is useful or important to you. Sometimes the motivation comes from outside, from an event or another person; sometimes you can develop your own motivation.

Observational learning is particularly important in children. Most of our early skills are learned through observation. Bandura devised many experiments to investigate how observational learning affects children,

Group Discussions

Group discussions are often a good way to start a social science investigation or to share results. In a discussion you have the opportunity to explain your own position, but you also need to listen to the ideas of others.

Here's How

1. Determine what the task is and how long you have to do it. Select the following:

- a group leader who will ensure that the discussion stays focused
- a secretary who will record ideas
- a reporter who will report on the discussion

2. Follow a few simple guidelines:

DO
- ask questions
- stay on topic
- listen to others and respond
- refer to facts
- summarize
- involve everybody

DON'T
- ignore others
- dominate the discussion
- repeat yourself
- insult other people
- sit without saying anything
- interrupt

3. Report back. After discussing the assigned topic, decide on the most appropriate way to make a report.

Practise It

Consider the behaviours or roles that people may play in a conversation shown in Figure 3–3. In a group, discuss how each behaviour would help or hinder a good discussion. Report back to the class.

Figure 3–3   Roles people play

Role	Sample comments
Supporter: praises and supports what others say	"That's a good point." "I agree." "That's helpful."
Organizer: starts the discussion; keeps on topic; encourages others to get the job done; summarizes ideas	"Let's not waste time." "Let's keep on topic."
Chatterbox: talks continuously; makes little or no contribution to the discussion	"And then I said…"
Peace-keeper: tries to resolve disagreements	"Let's see where you agree."
Questioner: asks for a clearer explanation and more information	"Can you give me an example?" "How do you know that?"
Provoker: tries to stir up discussion; ensures nothing is taken for granted	"Is there another way to look at this?" "Are we forgetting the problem at hand?"
Saboteur: tries to destroy the discussion	"This discussion is useless." "What a ridiculous idea."
Ideas-seeker: asks others to express their ideas and opinions	"How would you feel about that?" "I would like to hear Kim's point."
Show-off: tries to show how clever he or she is	"You ought to read [so-and-so] if you want to understand this."
Boss: acts like a know-it-all	"Your idea will never work."

particularly the effect of observed violence. The following case study describes one such experiment.

Imitating Violence

Bandura had a nursery school child draw a picture in one part of a room. An adult, in another part of the room, would approach an inflatable clown toy that pops back up when struck. The adult would punch, kick and sit on the clown, saying things like, "Kick him" and "Sock him in the nose."

The child was then taken to another room where there were several toys, including another clown. Bandura and his colleagues watched through hidden windows and noted the child's behaviour. They found that the children who had seen the adult acting aggressively tended to copy the behaviour. They beat up the clown, often using the same words as the adult did. Children who had not observed this violence were less likely to behave aggressively.

In later experiments, the adults were rewarded or scolded for acting aggressively toward the clown. Children who watched adults being rewarded became aggressive. Those who watched adults being scolded for aggression were less likely to show aggression than those who had seen no model at all.

Bandura's experiments have important implications for our society. The results imply that children who watch violent behaviour in their own homes, on television or in sports may be more likely to act aggressively. Recent research indicates that while television violence does not always cause viewers to act aggressively, it increases the likelihood of aggression in certain situations. When young children saw realistic violence, such as violence in a news clip, they tended to behave more aggressively than when they watched fantasy violence in a movie. Both groups were more aggressive than the group that did not view any violence. Other research shows that children who see violence modelled in their everyday lives by parents or friends are more likely to be affected by television violence.

CASE STUDY

1. Why did the children imitate aggressive behaviour toward the doll?

2. Sometimes adults were either rewarded or scolded for their behaviour. Why did these consequences affect the children's own behaviour?

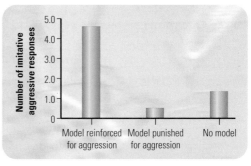

Figure 3–17
This graph shows how the number of responses was influenced by whether the children had observed a model and whether the model was rewarded or punished for aggressive behaviour.

Activities

Understand Ideas

1. In a brief paragraph, explain the difference between operant conditioning and classical conditioning.

2. What are the major elements of observational learning?

Think and Evaluate

3. Which form of learning—conditioned or observational—is more important when learning how to dance or play tennis? Give reasons for your choice.

Apply Your Learning

4. **a)** Devise a way to use classical conditioning to cure someone's fear of flying, fear of insects or fear of small spaces, such as elevators. Identify the conditioned and unconditioned stimuli and responses.

   b) How would you use operant conditioning to train a dog to fetch a ball, sit on command or come when called?

5. What knowledge or skills in your own life did you learn primarily through observation? Describe how each of the four elements applied to your learning process.

Research and Communicate

6. **a)** Using the Internet and your school resource centre, locate and read information about classical and operant conditioning.

   b) Complete a PMI chart (Plus, Minus, Interesting), showing pros, cons and interesting points for each of the two types of conditioning. Create three columns with the headings Plus, Minus, Interesting. Draw two wide rows with the headings Classical Conditioning and Operant Conditioning. These rows should have enough space for you to record a minimum of three points per column.

Focus Questions

What kinds of memory do we have?

What are the three levels of memory?

How can memory be improved?

Memory

Imagine what it would be like to have no memory at all. By the time you finished reading this sentence, you would have forgotten the beginning! We need memory to learn and to think. On the other hand, imagine what life would be like if every experience remained forever in your conscious awareness and you never forgot anything. You would probably not be able to focus on any one thing. We need to be able to remember and to forget selectively in order to function in life.

Most of us only think about memory when we have difficulty with it, for example, when we have just been introduced to someone and cannot remember his or her name. Why do we remember some things and not others? Can we improve our memory? Knowing how memory works can help to improve it.

What Is Memory?

Memory is the capacity to acquire, retain and recall knowledge and skills. What we often think of as memory—recalling specific knowledge—is actually just one of several kinds of memory. Remembering how to speak a language you have not spoken for a while, remembering the first day you attended school, and remembering where your locker is located all use different types of memory.

Researchers continue to find out more about how memory works and how different kinds of memory relate to each other. For example, psychologists at the University of Toronto studied a patient who suffered amnesia as a result of a motorcycle accident. Before the accident, he used to play chess. Today he knows that he can play chess, and he knows how to play, but he has no memory of ever having played the game before his

Figure 3–18

Some of the skills we learn become so automatic that we never forget them.

accident. The accident affected three types of memory in three different ways: His ability to remember events from the past (called episodic memory) is severely impaired; his knowledge of how the world works (semantic memory) is mildly impaired; and his memory of how to do things (procedural memory) is intact. Such studies of individuals with unique problems help us understand memory in general.

amnesia—a partial or total loss of memory

Levels of Memory

Psychologists have discovered that in addition to different kinds of memory, human beings have three levels of memory. Each level performs a distinct and necessary function.

Connections

Which research methods would psychologists use when studying how memory works? (See Chapter 1, pages 8–13.)

Sensory Memory

Sensory memory receives information from the environment through each of the senses: sight, hearing, smell, taste and touch. Sensory memory records information from these senses for only a few seconds. As you look around the room, for example, you may see a notice of an upcoming test. As your gaze passes, the image fades.

Sensory memory enables you to hold information long enough to record what is necessary from the environment. For example, it will allow you to remember the first part of this sentence while you read the last part, or remember your instructor's tone of voice at the beginning of a sentence as well as at the end. Sensory memory also allows you to select what you think should be retained from all the sensory information you are receiving: the feeling of the chair against your back, the sound of a noise in the hall, the taste of gum in your mouth, the sight of a squirrel in a tree, or the announcement of a pop quiz in the next few minutes.

Short-Term Memory

If the information catches your attention and you think it is important, it may be transferred to short-term memory. Short-term memory refers to what is going on in your conscious mind now as you consider this sentence and paragraph.

Short-term memory holds information for up to 15 or 20 seconds. If you continue to work with the information, it will stay longer. If not, it will either be discarded or stored in long-term memory. For example, if you are introduced to someone, you may pay attention to the name and store it in long-term memory; or you may fail to pay attention and then realize that the name is quickly gone.

Short-term memory can store about seven separate, unorganized items. Most of us can remember a telephone number long enough to move from the kitchen table to the phone. More than seven numbers starts to stress our short-term memory. However, we can work with more than seven items if we organize the information into groups. For example, the three-number area code of a phone number is one chunk of information, and

Figure 3–19

How good is your memory? What is on the other side of this coin?

the three-digit exchange is another, while the last four digits take up a third chunk of short-term memory.

Items are stored in short-term memory in several ways. The most common way to store information is by sound or as a mental picture. For instance, when you are learning a new language, you can memorize the vocabulary by listening to the way the words sound. Or, you can associate each word with an image of what the word means. Another way to store information is by associating it with personal meaning. Let's say you are learning a language because you are going on a trip to a country where the language is spoken. Knowing that these words will help you communicate will make it much easier to remember them.

Long-Term Memory

What do you remember best: the name of your friend or the image stamped on a Canadian nickel? One is important to you; the other is not. Yet, if you had to remember the image in order to spend the coin, you would soon become aware of it. Items that are important and have meaning to you are stored in long-term memory.

No one has reached the outer limits of long-term memory as a computer might when it reaches the end of its storage capacity. We can retain as much information as we want for as long as we want. However, we cannot always recall everything at will. All too often, a name will slip our mind, or a term may elude us on a science test. Is it possible to improve our ability to recall long-term memories? Yes it is. One way to do so is to

Figure 3–20

Ways to improve long-term memory. Many of these techniques can be applied more generally to improve the way we learn.

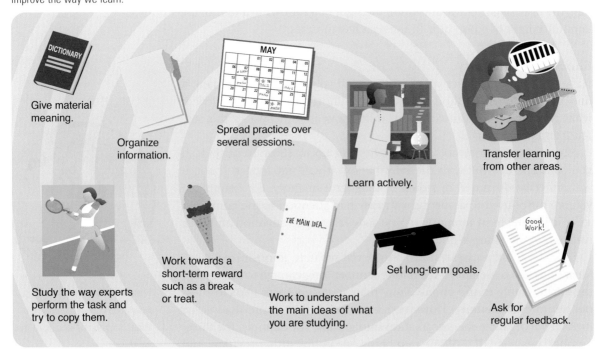

Give material meaning.

Organize information.

Spread practice over several sessions.

Learn actively.

Transfer learning from other areas.

Study the way experts perform the task and try to copy them.

Work towards a short-term reward such as a break or treat.

THE MAIN IDEA...

Work to understand the main ideas of what you are studying.

Set long-term goals.

Good Work!

Ask for regular feedback.

What Can You Remember?

1. **Test Your Sensory Memory:** Turn on a flashlight in a dark room. Swing your wrist around in a circular motion, shining the flashlight onto a distant wall. If you are fast enough, you will see a complete circle. Your visual sensory memory stores the beginning of the circle while you complete the end.

2. **Test Your Short-term Memory:** How many unrelated items can you store in short-term memory? Cover up the following numbers with a sheet of paper. Reveal the first row for five seconds, cover it up, then write these numbers on a sheet of paper. Repeat this process with each succeeding row. When completed, check your answers. When you make a mistake in two consecutive rows, you will know that the limit of your short-term memory is the number of items in the preceding row.

   76512
   830956
   7459271
   88325813
   447143563
   4765439679

3. **Test Your Long-term Memory:** Draw pictures from memory of the design on the reverse, non-monarch side of a one-, five-, ten- and twenty-five-cent piece. Check your drawings with the actual coins. How accurate were you? Why?

4. **a)** Look at the following letter combinations for 15 seconds. Put the book away. Think about something else for 30 seconds. Write down what you remember.

   sdh   gcv   trb   wsx   jbm   apf   vth

   b) Now do the same with the following letter combinations.

   boy   cat   toy   wax   job   axe   vat

   c) In which case did you remember most of the letters? Why? What methods did you use to help you remember?

store the memory effectively in the first place. As noted earlier, this means ascribing some personal meaning to the memory.

Another way of improving the effectiveness of long-term memories is to use efficient methods of retrieving them. Studies have shown that we can recall memories more easily under the same conditions we stored them. In other words, you are more likely to remember the information you learned in social studies class when you are in the classroom itself. A tour of your old elementary school may jog your memory of long-forgotten events, teachers and classmates.

Memories are easier to access if they are recalled regularly. A series of 15-minute study sessions will make it easier to retrieve information for an exam than a single, one-hour cramming session. It also helps if you can rest or sleep more often between study sessions instead of instantly moving on to another subject. New learning can interfere with memory retention.

Finally, it appears that long-term memories are easier to recall if they are organized and related to other information. For example, when you try to list the names of the Canadian provinces, you probably start at one end of the country and work your way over to the other side. If asked to list all the teachers you have had since kindergarten, you would most likely retrieve the information in chronological order.

Activities

Understand Ideas

1. Define three different types of memory and provide your own example for each.

2. In your own words, explain how short-term memory can hold more than seven items. Give an example other than the one given in the text.

Think and Evaluate

3. Compare and contrast short-term memory and long-term memory by providing two similarities and two differences.

Apply Your Learning

4. Draw a diagram, cartoon or other visual reminder to help you remember the three levels of memory.

5. List three ways the information you have just learned about memory can help you study more effectively.

Research and Communicate

6. a) Using the Internet and your school's resource centre, investigate two memory techniques. Consider the following list to help you get started: mnemonic, acronym, repetition, classification, visualization, word association.
   b) Describe the two memory techniques you chose in Activity 6a. In a paragraph, explain how you might use these techniques to help you study.

Focus Questions

How do we develop concepts?

What are the three major forms of reasoning?

Which strategies help us solve problems?

What are the four stages of the decision-making process?

Thinking and Using Knowledge

We have looked at how we acquire knowledge through sensation, perception and learning, and how we store and retrieve it through memory. In this section, we will continue our discussion of cognition by exploring how we use knowledge through thinking. Although cognitive psychologists have defined many kinds of thinking, we will examine four: developing concepts, reasoning, problem solving and decision making.

Developing Concepts

A concept is a category of objects, ideas or events that share characteristics. We use concepts when we group similar items together. For example, a baby learns that milk and juice both come in a glass, whereas food on a plate must be lifted with a spoon. These are very early concepts of the world. As we grow, we develop more sophisticated concepts.

Concepts allow us to connect objects, events and ideas that are similar and to distinguish those that are different. Without concepts, each item or

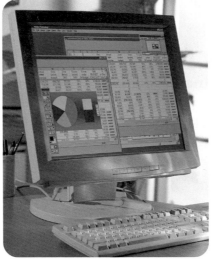

Figure 3–21
What concept would link all three of these items?

event would be unique. Thinking and generalizing would be impossible. By having the concept of "apple," you can infer that the apple you are about to eat will taste good. By having the concept of "kitten," you trust that the small cat you see will probably not attack you.

Concepts are often arranged in a hierarchical order. For example, a bicycle, a boat and an automobile can each be considered as a concept on its own, or grouped together under the concept of transportation. Mastering a topic often involves knowing how to conceptualize objects and events in that topic or area.

The concepts that we develop as we grow shape how we view the world. For example, as we saw in Chapter 2, the Inuit language has numerous ways to describe snow, allowing the Inuit to make distinctions that are important to their lives. How many variations do you know beyond slushy, crisp and melting? Now think of the number of words we have to describe automobiles (sportscar, sedan, truck, minivan, etc.). What does this tell you about the importance of the automobile in our culture?

hierarchical—ranked in order of importance or dominance

Reasoning

All reasoning involves using information to draw conclusions, but we use the information in a variety of ways. **Deductive reasoning** starts with a general principle and applies it to a specific situation. The classic example of deductive reasoning is the following:

Premise: All human beings are mortal.
Premise: I am a human being.
Conclusion: Therefore, I am mortal.

The first two statements are the premises—information we accept as true. The third statement is the conclusion we draw from this information. If the premises are correct, there is no doubt that the conclusion will be true.

Thinking Creatively

One of the most effective ways to think creatively is to brainstorm. Brainstorming allows you to think of a variety of solutions to a problem and offers a way for people working together to generate new ideas that might not occur to a person working alone. Brainstorming is used in business, in government policy making and in other situations where it is necessary to develop new ideas, new approaches and new solutions.

Here's How

Because spontaneous thinking is the key to creative brainstorming, the following guidelines are useful:

- If possible, work with a partner or small group.
- Do not reject any ideas until after the brainstorming session.
- Quantity is important. List as many ideas as possible.
- Use and expand the ideas of others.
- Don't hesitate to suggest ideas that, at the moment, may seem unlikely or "off the wall."
- Record all ideas.
- Set a 10-minute time limit.

Practise It

1. Work in a group to brainstorm a situation in which you might benefit from this kind of creative thinking. For example, you could assume that you have more homework for your Social Science class than you think you can possibly do.

2. Remain in your groups to brainstorm some possible solutions for the situation you have identified.

Inductive reasoning moves from the specific to the general, from observations to conclusions. For example:

Premise: I enjoyed the last book Margaret Atwood wrote.
Premise: This new book is by Margaret Atwood.
Conclusion: Therefore, I will enjoy this new book.

This type of reasoning is less airtight than deduction. There is no guarantee that we will enjoy the book, but only a strong likelihood that we will. However, many of the tough problems in our lives seem to depend on inductive reasoning.

dialectical—reaching a conclusion by combining opposing points of view, showing that different opinions can be compatible

Dialectical reasoning involves evaluating two opposing sides or points of view. This method is used when the solution is not clear cut, and opinions differ about what is true, what information is important or what actions should be taken. We use this type of reasoning when we listen to politicians from different political parties, or salespeople from different companies. Controversial social issues, especially, call for people to be able to view the problem from a number of angles, to recognize different opinions and to accept that there may be more than one answer or solution.

Some psychological research suggests that many people in our society do not reason dialectically and that television and other media tend to emphasize the quick answer or the sound bite, rather than carefully thought-out positions. In some cases, people assume that a correct answer always exists, obtainable through the senses or from authorities. In other cases, people recognize that absolute certainty may not be possible, but they do not know how to deal with such situations. A dialectical approach, on the other hand, acknowledges that while certainty may not always exist, some opinions may count more than others because they match the evidence available.

Problem Solving

Problem solving is the ability to deal with new situations for which there is no well-established response. You are problem solving when you figure out how to organize a term paper, solve a math problem, make your money last until the end of the week or choose the best route to your destination. Problem solving involves four steps, which can be learned and developed through practice: 1) defining the problem; 2) developing a strategy to resolve it; 3) carrying out the strategy; and 4) determining if the strategy is working. Several strategies can be used to solve problems, from trial and error to flashes of insight. Figure 3–22 lists some of these strategies and gives examples of each.

Decision Making

We make many decisions in life. Some are important such as what career to choose, and some are less important such as what to have for lunch. Decision making takes place whenever we have a choice of what to do.

Connections

How can the inquiry model be adapted to solve everyday problems? (See Chapter 1, pages 6–7.)

Figure 3–22

Think of a time recently when you used each of these strategies to solve a problem.

Problem-solving strategies

Strategy	Description	Example
Trial and Error	Trying different approaches until you find one that works	Figuring out how a new computer program works by pressing buttons
Hypothesis Testing	Testing a hypothesis and measuring its success	Applying what you know about other computer programs to determine how a new program works
Rule of Thumb	Using a general rule based on past experiences or acquired knowledge	A rule of thumb in answering multiple-choice questions is not to change your answer once you have made your choice
Insight	Having a new idea or suddenly gaining understanding; insight is often preceded by a period of time when the mind is mulling over the problem	Getting the point of a joke involves insight

When writing a paper, it is often helpful to leave your draft overnight; this "break" often leads to new insight into how to organize your work |

Applied psychologists have studied decision-making techniques to determine the most effective way to make decisions. They have identified four stages to the decision-making process:

1. **Determine alternatives.** Begin with a wide range of possibilities.

2. **Evaluate alternatives.** Ask the following questions: What information is available about each option? How will each option help me achieve my goals? What disadvantages does each option have for me or for others? Use a "pro and con" chart to help you make major decisions.

3. **Make a decision.** Choose the option that seems to provide the greatest advantages with the least costs.

4. **Act.** Act on the option you have chosen, knowing that you have done everything you could to make the best decision. Be prepared to deal with problems that may arise. Continue on the chosen course of action or make changes if necessary.

Activities

Understand Ideas

1. Define and contrast the three types of reasoning.

2. Explain four strategies for solving problems.

3. Make a flow chart or other diagram showing the steps in the decision-making process.

Think and Evaluate

4. Which problem-solving strategy best applies to each of the following problems?
   - organizing a term paper
   - solving a math problem
   - making your money last until the end of the week
   - choosing the best route to your destination

5. Suppose your Discman was stolen from your locker. You learn that it was stolen by the best player on your school's basketball team. This year's team has a good chance to compete for the provincial championship. If you report the theft, you know the player will be suspended from the team for the rest of the season.

   Use the four stages of the decision-making process to come to a final decision. Stage 1, determine alternatives, has been done for you. Finish the decision-making process by completing stages 2, 3 and 4.

1. Determine alternatives:
   a) Would you approach the player and threaten exposure if the Discman was not returned?
   b) Would you report the theft to the proper school authorities?
   c) Would you confront the player and demand the return of your Discman?
   d) Would you wait and report the theft after the season?
   e) Would you do something else? What would you do?

Apply Your Learning

6. Categorize each of the following as deductive, inductive or dialectical reasoning:
   a) Since all human beings live on Earth, and I am a human being, I must live on Earth.
   b) Most people who use the SQ3R method (Survey, Question, Read, Recite, Review) improve their reading comprehension. I will try the SQ3R method. I will probably do better on the upcoming test.
   c) I know that you believe in learning through observation. Personally, I think that repeating ideas improves learning. But I am coming to see the value of the arguments you make.

d) House cats are members of the feline group. This animal in my house is a cat. Therefore she is a feline.

7. Use the decision-making techniques outlined in this section to make a decision on an issue relevant to you. Be prepared to describe the process you used to make the decision, and the conclusion you reached. Here are some suggestions:
- what to do this evening
- which subject to spend more time studying
- whether to get a part-time job

- what charity to donate to
- which college or university to apply to

Research and Communicate

8. a) Use the four-step problem-solving process described on page 65 to solve a problem you have recently encountered. Be sure to include brainstorming to help you develop a strategy. Refer to the Skill Focus on page 64.

b) Write a report describing the process you followed in Activity 8a. Record your findings and the final outcome.

Sleep and Dreams

To this point, most of our discussion of psychology assumes we are aware and conscious of what we think and do. Yet, consciousness, the awareness of our sensations, perceptions and thoughts, occurs in varied states, including daydreams, sleep dreams, hypnotic and meditative states, hallucinations and visions. Not everyone experiences hallucinations or hypnosis, but we all experience sleep and dreams. In fact, sleep takes up almost a third of our lives, and when deprived of it, we feel terrible and our performance suffers. We obviously need sleep. But why?

Researchers are not sure why we sleep. Sleep may replenish chemicals used up during the waking period. It may also play a role in the growth process. During deep sleep, a growth hormone is released by the pituitary, a small gland at the base of the brain. As adults grow older, the pituitary gland releases less of this hormone and they spend less time in deep sleep.

Besides fatigue, the major effects of sleep deprivation are diminished immunity to disease, a slight hand tremor, irritability and inattention. When performing monotonous tasks such as long-distance driving, these effects can be devastating. On short, highly motivating tasks, sleep deprivation has little effect. But lack of sleep affects different people to varying degrees. A New York disc jockey named Peter Tripp stayed awake for 200 hours to raise money for a charity. After two days, he experienced visual illusions and lost the ability to perform even simple arithmetic. By the seventh day, he lost his sense of identity and had delusions of persecution. By the eighth day, he was hallucinating. On the other hand, Randy Gardner of San Diego stayed awake for 11 days without obvious effects. During his final night of sleeplessness, Gardner beat sleep researcher William Dement 100 straight times in a pinball game. Then he slept for 15 hours and woke up feeling fine.

Focus Questions

What stages do we go through while we sleep?

What is REM sleep?

How do scientists know that REM sleep is important?

How do cognitive psychologists explain the value of dreams?

hallucinations—false but convincing perceptions of objects or events experienced when fully awake

visions—images seen in a dream or in a trance, having some personal, spiritual or emotional significance

hypnosis—a condition of being in a sleeplike state, particularly susceptible to suggestions or able to recall forgotten memories

delusions—false beliefs

Stages of Sleep

electrodes—conductors that carry brainwaves (electrical currents from the brain) through wires to a recording instrument

By attaching electrodes to the scalp, researchers can record the brainwaves that tell the story of sleep life. Our brainwaves proceed through four stages every 90 minutes, repeating the pattern throughout the night. From light sleep (stage one), we sink into deeper and deeper sleep until we reach stage four. At this stage, we may be very difficult to rouse. Then we resurface through the stages until we return to stage one, when our brainwaves appear to be the same as when we are awake. It is during these periods of resurfacing that we have dreams.

Researchers can determine when subjects are dreaming by observing their eye movements. Their eyes move rapidly beneath the eyelids as if they were looking around. This is called "Rapid Eye Movement" or REM sleep. Scientists know that the REM stage is important; when they prevent people from experiencing this stage by waking them up regularly, the subjects become short-tempered and less able to concentrate. As the night wears on, the deep, stage-four sleep becomes briefer and then disappears, and the REM sleep period becomes longer. By morning, 20 to 25 percent of an average night's sleep is REM sleep.

Dreaming

Although we are more likely to remember or be awakened by our most emotional dreams, many dreams are ordinary. Usually we dream of events

Figure 3–23
Dream researchers can monitor the changes in our brainwaves as we move through the four stages of sleep. Here researchers watch over a volunteer who is sleeping in an experiment chamber with sensors connected to her head. With the volunteer is her pet cat.

related to daily life, such as an incident at school. Most dreams are not notably pleasant. People commonly have dreams about failing or experiencing misfortune, or being attacked, pursued or rejected.

What do dreams mean? Again, there are no sure answers. Sigmund Freud was the first modern psychologist to look at dreams seriously. He argued that a dream is like a safety valve that harmlessly discharges otherwise unacceptable feelings. According to Freud, dreams have hidden meanings and a language of their own, revealed through symbols, images and even puns. When interpreted, dreams usually express secret drives and wishes that would be threatening if expressed while we were awake. For example, Freud believed that dreams often have hidden sexual meanings, although most dreams are not obviously about sex. Many of Freud's critics, however, believe that dream interpretation leads down a blind alley. Some contend that even if dreams are symbolic, they can be interpreted almost any way one wishes. Others see dreams in terms of information processing. Cognitive psychologists, for example, suggest that dreams may simply be a way to sift, sort and fix a day's experiences in memory. They point out that following stressful experiences or intense learning, REM sleep tends to increase.

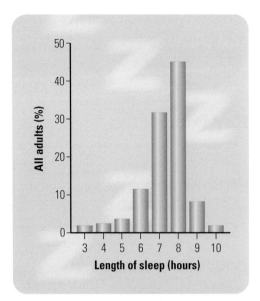

Figure 3–24

The idea that everyone needs eight hours of sleep is not true. Newborns spend at least two-thirds of the day asleep, the elderly about a quarter. This chart shows the results of a survey of nearly a million adults who were asked how many hours of sleep they felt they needed.

Activities

Understand Ideas

1. What two reasons do researchers give for why we sleep?

2. Provide two examples of what can happen to someone who is deprived of sleep.

3. Describe the four stages of sleep. When do we dream?

Think and Evaluate

4. "Dreams are a way to sift, sort and fix a day's experiences in memory." In a paragraph, agree or disagree with this statement. Provide three reasons to support your opinion.

Apply Your Learning

5. Keep track of your own sleep patterns over a five-day period. How many hours do you sleep on average? What symptoms have you noticed when you do not get enough sleep?

Research and Communicate

6. Conduct a survey to find out how sleep patterns among your classmates compare to those on the graph in Figure 3–24. Create a graph or some other visual representation to illustrate your findings. (See Skill Focus, page 11.)

Key Points

- Psychology is the study of human mental processes and behaviour.

- Humans learn in several ways, including through conditioning and through observation.

- Humans have a complex memory system made up of sensory, short-term and long-term memory.

- Four types of thinking are developing concepts, reasoning, problem solving and decision making.

- The mind is capable of different states of consciousness, including sleeping and dreaming.

Activities

Understand Ideas

1. Which theory of learning best describes how we learn each of the following behaviours?
   - pulling your hand away from a fire
   - speaking a language
   - caring for children
   - driving a car
   - playing a musical instrument
   - painting a picture

Think and Evaluate

2. In everyday life we hold many common sense ideas about human thought and behaviour. These views may or may not be supported by psychological research. Which of the following statements do you believe is supported by scientific research?
   - Seeing is believing. I can completely trust what I see with my own eyes.
   - The mind is like a camera; it records everything that comes to it through the senses.
   - Haley is a very emotional person. She inherited her emotional make-up from her father.
   - If you exercise your mind, you can improve your memory.
   - You can't teach an old dog new tricks.
   - I slept really well. I didn't dream at all.

Apply Your Learning

3. What is the main reinforcement we receive for each of the following behaviours?
   - answering questions in class
   - eating a tasty meal
   - seeing your friends
   - getting good grades in school
   - doing a job around the house

4. Identify what kind of thinking you would use:
   a) You are writing an essay comparing poverty in the Great Depression and poverty in Canada today. You decide on four categories for comparison.
   b) You have a test tomorrow, but you left your text at school. You phone your friend and suggest that you share a textbook and help each other study.
   c) You have to decide whether to take a summer course or to work for the summer. If you take the summer course, you can graduate one semester earlier. If you work for the summer, you will have more money for one semester. You decide to take the summer course and work part-time during the first semester.

Research and Communicate

5. a) Research the Multiple Intelligence theory put forward by Howard Gardner. Record the different kinds of intelligence he described.
   b) What is your best learning style? Explain your answer using Gardner's theory.
   c) In groups of five or six, share the results of your research. (See Skill Focus, page 43.)

Motivation and Emotion

The previous chapter investigated how we perceive, learn, remember and think. In this chapter, we will look at what psychology has to say about human behaviour—in particular, how our motivations, both conscious and unconscious, and our emotions affect the choices we make and the way we interact with others.

- Make and complete a chart similar to the one below.

- Work with a partner to compare charts. How do goals and reasons for wanting to accomplish them differ for the short term (today), the medium term (this year) and the long term (over your lifetime)?

- Share your conclusions with the class.

What do I want to do or accomplish?	Why?	Steps I am taking to achieve these goals
Today:		
1.		
2.		
3.		
This year:		
1.		
2.		
3.		
Over my lifetime:		
1.		
2.		
3.		

In This Chapter

- What motivates people to act as they do?

- How did Freud see the nature of the human mind?

- How does Maslow's Hierarchy of Needs explain human motivation?

- What role do emotions play in our lives and behaviour?

Key Terms

motivation

ego

unconscious mind

id

superego

defence mechanisms

cognitive component

physical component

behavioural component

companionate love

Motivation

Have you ever wondered why certain people do the things they do? Dian Fossey, for example, always wanted to study gorillas. She spent much of her life in the wild, defending gorillas against poachers. Sadly, Fossey was murdered by unknown assailants. Why did she choose gorillas as her focus of interest? And what drove her to be willing to risk her life for them? On a more mundane level, why do we get upset about certain things and not others? Why do some people have quick tempers, while others are more easygoing? What influence does heredity have on behaviour? **Motivation** is the study of why we do things—the causes of our behaviour.

Biological and Social Motivation

Motivation can be divided into two general categories: biological motivation, which refers to innate, physical needs such as hunger and thirst, and social motivation, which focuses on learned, psychological needs such as praise and success. In other words, some needs derive from nature, while others are driven by nurture. However, as with other "nature versus nurture" issues, psychologists continue to argue over the boundaries between these two categories.

To what extent are our motivations determined by nature, or our biological needs? While all psychologists agree that we are motivated by physical drives such as hunger, thirst and sex, they differ when determining the role biology plays in the origin of more complex behaviours. Sociobiologists study the genetic and evolutionary bases of behaviour in humans and other species. They argue that many behaviours are genetically programmed,

Figure 4–1

Dian Fossey with gorillas. What might have motivated Fossey? What motivates us to do the things we do?

Gathering and Recording Information

As you have seen, social scientists use a range of methods to gather information. In Chapter 1, you learned about case studies, experiments, surveys, interviews and observation. Literature review—looking at the studies of other researchers—is another social science method. This is also a method that students often use to research topics of interest.

Here's How

1. **Start with a question** or problem, as in any social science inquiry. Then develop a tentative answer or **hypothesis** that will help to focus your research.

2. Try several sources of information:
   - **Library:** Start with general reference works to get an overview of your topic. Then look for suitable books, magazine articles and newspaper articles.
   - **Computer searches:** You may find some information in the library on CD-ROM. You may also choose to use the Internet as a source, but use it only after you have found out as much as you can from other sources. Remember that information on the Internet is often badly organized and it is not always reliable. (See also Analyzing and Judging Information or Ideas, page 97.)

3. Ask yourself if the information you have found is **relevant.** Does it help to answer the question you are asking? If not, discard it, even if it is interesting.

4. **Take notes** of sources that will be useful. Follow these guidelines:
   - Make point-form notes in your own words. Read a whole passage first and then note down the main ideas and the key supporting details. Pay attention to the headings, subheadings and boldface terms. These are the keys to understanding the main ideas.
   - If you copy any passages from the source, use quotation marks to mark the work clearly as a quotation. Keep your quotations short. Remember to note the title of the book, the author, the publisher, the date of publication and the page number for each quotation. Using the ideas and words of others without giving proper credit is known as plagiarism and is considered highly dishonest.
   - Use reflective notes to clarify your understanding of your sources. Add comments such as "Key point," "Connects to...," "Needs clarification" or "What would happen if this changed?"

5. **Organize the information** you have gathered in a reasonable way. For example, you could consider the following categories: Nature of the problem, Cause of the problem, Ways to deal with the situation.

Practise It

1. Using sources in the library and/or on the Internet, gather information to write a profile of Dian Fossey. You may wish to use the following as your question for inquiry: What were Dian Fossey's major accomplishments?

2. Be sure to organize your information in appropriate categories. Consider the following questions: When and where was Dian Fossey born? What was her field of study? What were her aims and to what extent did she accomplish them? What were her most important contributions?

3. Submit your notes with your profile for either teacher or peer evaluation.

especially behaviours such as aggression and competition. They maintain that these behaviours evolved to help us survive in hostile environments.

Other psychologists, however, emphasize the social, or learned aspect of human behaviour. They point out that even with biological drives such as hunger, social motivations play a significant role. Under normal circumstances, the brain will regulate how much food we need to maintain a reasonable weight. However, social learning often overrides these biological cues and determines not only how much we eat, but how we eat and what we eat. The prevalence of both obesity and eating disorders in our culture indicates the importance of factors other than biological need in determining our eating habits. The sex drive, too, is highly influenced by social learning and experience. What is attractive to one person is not to another; what is considered desirable in one society is not in another.

Activities

Understand Ideas

1. What is motivation? Give an example from your own experience.

2. What is the difference between biological and social motivation?

Apply Your Learning

3. In what ways are each of the following activities biologically motivated, socially motivated or both? Explain your answers.

- playing hockey
- eating breakfast
- sleeping at night
- studying French
- blinking when an object approaches the eye
- drinking a cold glass of water on a hot day
- keeping regular hours
- getting together with friends
- showing respect for parents
- looking for a part-time job

Focus Questions

What was Freud's model of the mind?

According to Freud, what role does the unconscious mind play as a cause of human behaviour?

How does psychoanalysis help to understand motivation?

What did Jung, Adler and Horney believe about the causes of human behaviour?

Freud and Motivation

There are a number of ways to understand human motivation, or the causes of our behaviour. However, one name stands out above all the others who have studied this area: Sigmund Freud. Freud was born in Austria in 1856. As a teenager, he already showed signs of independence and brilliance. In 1873 Freud went to medical school in Vienna. After graduation he set up a private practice, specializing in disorders of the brain and the nervous system. However, he soon found that much of his medical training was of little help. People would come to see him with such problems as paralysis and numbness of the hand, but sometimes he could not find biological causes for these symptoms.

Freud became convinced that many of the physical problems his patients experienced were psychological in origin. At that time, most students of human behaviour believed that people were, in general, conscious of their motives. Freud claimed, in contrast, that people are unaware of many of their thoughts and motives because these thoughts and motives come from the "unconscious mind."

Freud's Theory of the Mind

Freud developed the theory that the human mind has three aspects, each of which influences the way we think, feel and act. These aspects are not physical parts of the mind, but rather different ways in which the mind works. He called these parts of the mind the ego, the id and the superego.

Figure 4–2
Sigmund Freud in his office

According to Freud, the **ego** is the conscious and rational part of the mind. Your conscious awareness of this printed page, of the chair you sit on and of the thoughts and memories of the moment, are experienced by the ego. The ego is the part of the mind where decisions are made, though such decisions may be influenced by the unconscious mind. The ego develops and changes as we live and experience different aspects of life.

The **unconscious mind,** said Freud, consists of the id and the superego. The **id** is composed of instincts that give rise to aggressive impulses and to biological drives that sustain and promote life, such as hunger and thirst. However, it operates at the unconscious level, below the level of awareness. The id seeks pleasure and avoids pain, sometimes in ways that are socially unacceptable or out of touch with reality. Freud believed that wishful thinking and dreams are indications of the id striving to fulfill its desires.

The **superego** is the part of the mind that acts as a conscience, telling us what we should and should not do. While much of the superego derives from the unconscious mind, it is also influenced by the values of our culture and the people with whom we live. For instance, parents are important agents in shaping the superego. They teach moral principles by punishing negative behaviour and rewarding positive behaviour. We avoid negative behaviour not only through fear of punishment and hope of reward, but also because we have learned to internalize ideas of right and wrong.

values—principles or standards considered worthwhile or desirable

According to Freud, when we are born, the mind is made up of only the id. As we grow and mature, we convert part of the id into the ego and the superego. The ego learns to deal with the drives of the id in ways that are socially acceptable and in line with past consequences. The ego operates according to the reality principle—that is, it must live according to the rules of society and the real world. It uses its rational abilities to manage and control the id by balancing desires against the restrictions of reality and the superego. However, conflict often erupts among the three aspects of the mind. The id may tell us to go ahead and enjoy, while the superego reminds us of what we "should" do. For example, when you are supposed to be studying, but the television in the next room beckons, you are experiencing a conflict between your id and your superego. The ego has to decide between the two.

internalize—incorporate into one's own set of values, attitudes and beliefs

> **Connections**
>
> In what ways does the superego reflect some of the non-material aspects of culture? (See Chapter 2, page 27.)

Figure 4–3

In Freud's concept of the mind only a small proportion of the total is above the surface, or conscious, level.

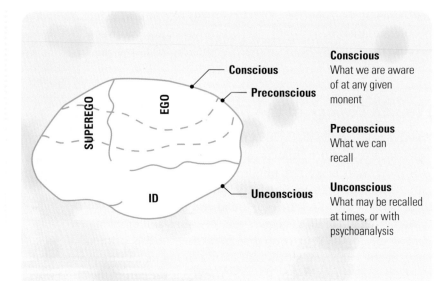

Conscious
What we are aware of at any given monent

Preconscious
What we can recall

Unconscious
What may be recalled at times, or with psychoanalysis

Figure 4–4

According to Freud's model, why would adults behave, generally, in a more restrained manner? ▼

Freud's model of the mind

	Id	Ego	Superego
What it does	Expresses sexual and aggressive instincts; follows the pleasure principle	Mediates between desires of the id and demands of the superego; follows the reality principle	Represents conscience and the rules of society
How conscious	Entirely unconscious	Partly conscious, partly unconscious	Partly conscious, mostly unconscious
When it develops	Present at birth	Emerges after birth, as child begins to learn through experience	Last system to develop
Example	"I'm so mad I could hit you" (felt unconsciously)	Might make a conscious choice ("Let's talk about this") or avoid the instinctive drive by denying it ("What, me angry? Never!")	"It is wrong to resort to physical violence."

Source: Adapted from Carol Wade and Carol Tavris, *Psychology, Sixth Edition.* Upper Saddle River: Prentice Hall (2000), p. 477.

psychoanalysis—a process whereby patients discuss their background, feelings and experiences with a trained psychologist

The Start of Psychoanalysis

Freud experimented with various ways of tapping into the unconscious mind as a way of understanding people's motives more clearly. He believed that early childhood experiences were a particularly important source of emotional problems and conflicts, even when patients did not fully understand or remember them. He tried hypnosis as a way of helping people to recall these experiences and come to terms with them.

Unit 1: Social Sciences—Self and Others

Gradually, Freud developed his technique of psychoanalysis, in which he used a variety of methods to help patients gain access to their unconscious thoughts. He used free association, for example, a process whereby patients responded to a word with the first thing that came to their minds. He also asked them to describe their dreams; then he would analyze the story of the dream in order to interpret the underlying meaning.

Freud believed that human beings have strong aggressive and sexual drives that come from the id. While we learn through the superego to control these drives, they do not disappear. They are rechannelled into behaviour or symptoms that seem unrelated. In order to rid ourselves of these symptoms, we first have to acknowledge the existence of these hidden urges. The following case study provides an example of Freud's treatment of such illnesses.

Miss Elizabeth

CASE STUDY

1. According to Freud, what caused Miss Elizabeth's pain?

2. How was Miss Elizabeth cured?

A young woman had suddenly become ill while standing at the death-bed of her sister, when she found herself unable to walk because of an excruciating pain which persisted in her legs....

The doctors said that with a wearing away of her sorrow for her dead sister the illness would pass. But a year had passed; she no longer mourned for her sister, and still she was sick.

Freud hypnotized her and asked, "Miss Elizabeth, please tell me what thought came into your mind at the moment when you first looked at your dead sister?"

The sick girl twisted in her sleep with a look of anguish. "A terrible thought, a horrifying thought," she murmured, "that I would like to marry my dead sister's husband!"

"And you fought off this thought?"

"Yes! Yes!...I put it out of my mind entirely. I have never dared to think of it since...."

Freud woke up the sick girl, who was twisting her hands and sobbing with anguish. "Do you remember what you told me?"

"Yes, I remember."

"Is there any thought," asked Freud, "which is too terrible to face? Are we not all human? Are we not all subject to temptation, sometime?"

The girl lifted her face...and a little hope showed in her eyes. "Do you mean I am not...utterly horrible, miserably weak?"

"Only those who run away from their troubles are weak....You ran away from your troubles by becoming ill. Rather than face the thought which came to you at your sister's bedside, you developed the pain in your legs. After that you no longer had to think of what troubled you; you had only to think of the pain.

"Being a cripple," he went on, "you were safe from falling in love with your brother-in-law, or he with you. You were safe from temptation. Your illness had a purpose; it avoided for you the temptation which you yourself were not brave enough to face!..."

"Do you mean that if I could face what horrified me, I would walk again?"

"Try," said Freud...."You have only to forgive yourself for what you thought. You have only to consider the temptation you had, reasonably and logically...."

Some months later, on hearing that Miss Elizabeth was to be present at a charity ball, Freud went with his wife. He saw the young woman who had come to him on crutches passing by to the strains of a Viennese waltz in the arms of a handsome young man whom she had chosen to marry! She no longer yearned for her brother-in-law!

From *Sigmund Freud* by Rachel Baker

---

defence mechanisms— unconscious mental processes used to protect the ego against anxiety, shame or other unacceptable feelings or thoughts

Freud pointed out that we often tend to deal with problems in the unconscious mind by using **defence mechanisms.** These processes allow the mind to hide or change a problem so that it does not bother us in a conscious way. For example, someone might repress an unpleasant experience, burying it in the unconscious. Although the person would not be conscious of the experience, it would still have an impact on his or her behaviour. Another person might regress to an earlier, less mature way of reacting in order to avoid dealing with a problem. He or she might resort to temper tantrums or sulking. Still another person might rationalize the problem by blaming it on an unrelated source or cause, rather than accepting responsibility. And someone else might go into denial, refusing to accept an unpleasant truth such as a serious illness or the loss of a friend.

In Freud's time, his theories were difficult for people to accept. Nineteenth-century people liked to think of themselves as rational individuals, totally aware of the mind and its workings. Also, they were not impressed with the idea that aggressive and sexual urges could be so important. Yet, eventually, Freud's theories gained wider acceptance. By the beginning and middle of the twentieth century, Freudian concepts and methods were not only accepted by psychologists, but were common in popular writings and media.

Further Developments in Psychoanalysis

Carl Jung (1875–1961) was an early colleague of Freud. He accepted many of Freud's ideas of the unconscious and its impact on mental health and illness. However, he questioned Freud's emphasis on sexual motivation and eventually broke away to develop his own views. Jung thought that while the unconscious mind did contain selfish and hostile drives, it also contained positive, spiritual forces.

Jung developed the idea that human behaviour was often motivated by opposite tendencies: good and evil, male and female, mother and father. For example, he called one pair of opposites "extroversion and introversion." The extroverted personality wants to be open to the things and the people in its environment, while the introverted personality is focused on itself and on meeting its own needs. Most of us have elements of both extroversion and introversion in our personalities. Jung felt that a balance of both tendencies is important.

Figure 4–5
Carl Jung

Jung believed, like Freud, in an unconscious mind, but he maintained that this part of the mind contained both personal experiences and common cultural experiences, which he called the "collective unconscious." The collective unconscious is expressed in a variety of images and symbols that are shared by all members of a culture, or even by all humans, and can be detected in myths or dreams. Possible examples would include archetypical figures found in the legends of many cultures, such as the hero, the nurturing mother, the wicked witch or the dangerous monster.

Alfred Adler (1870–1937) was also one of Freud's early colleagues. Like Jung, Adler argued with Freud over some aspects of his theories. Adler shared with Freud an interest in early childhood experiences and agreed that it was important to deal with one's aggressive and sexual impulses. But Adler felt that people's lives are governed by the need to overcome feelings of inferiority that are usually perceived by the conscious mind. In his book entitled *Problems of Neurosis*, he said, "The individual… feels his existence to be worthwhile just so far as he is useful to others and is overcoming feelings of inferiority." This idea was in opposition to Freud's belief in the importance of unconscious motives.

Karen Horney (1885–1952) accepted many of Freud's ideas regarding unconscious motives, but, like Jung and Adler, she also rejected a number of his theories, including his emphasis on sexual conflicts. She felt that conflicts develop as a result of feeling unsafe, unloved, or undervalued. She believed that individuals who experienced love and security as children would develop positive aspects of personality, while those who did not would create elaborate defence mechanisms to protect themselves.

Karen Horney also rejected Freud's negative concept of women, which she claimed reflected the values of the male-dominated society of which Freud was a product. In her book, *Feminine Psychology*, she wrote, "The view that women are infantile and emotional creatures, and as such, incapable of responsibility and independence is the work of the masculine tendency to lower women's self-respect." While Freud believed that most women felt physically inferior to men, Horney proposed that men felt threatened by women's ability to have children. She claimed that men compensated by focusing their energies on creative work. Women did not envy men's bodies, but rather the social power and privilege men possessed.

Figure 4–6

Cultural symbols such as this mandala from Tibet can be seen as an expression of the collective unconscious. They often represent universal harmony.

Figure 4–7

Karen Horney was one of the founders of humanist psychology.

Activities

Understand Ideas

1. Identify the three major aspects of the mind according to Freud, and explain the role each aspect plays in human behaviour.

2. In what ways did Jung, Adler and Horney agree with Freud? In what ways did they disagree with him?

Apply Your Learning

3. Review Figure 4–4. Give two or three other examples to illustrate the workings of the id, ego and superego.

4. Many people enjoy watching horror movies. What explanation do you think any two of the psychoanalytic psychologists might give for the attraction of such movies?

Research and Communicate

5. Conduct further research into the ideas of Freud, Jung, Adler and Horney. Take part in a panel discussion in which you and others discuss the following questions from the point of view of each of these people. (See Skill Focus, page 73; and Skill Focus, page 43.)
   - What are the major forces at work in the unconscious?
   - How does the unconscious mind influence our thoughts and behaviour?
   - What role do early childhood experiences play in individual motivations?
   - Are the motivations of men and women significantly different?

Focus Questions

How does Maslow's Hierarchy of Needs explain motivation?

What has been the major impact of Maslow's theory?

needs—physiological or psychological requirements for one's well-being; conditions for being motivated to take action

hierarchy—a ranking of people, items or ideas in order of dominance or priority

Maslow and Motivation

While Freud believed that the unconscious mind motivates us to act in certain ways, Abraham Maslow (1908–1970) took a different approach. He asked the questions, How do we decide which needs to fulfill first? and Do our motivations have any order of importance? For example, we know that there are times when hunger or thirst is often the most important motivator. As the nineteenth-century American social reformer Dorothea Dix once said: "Nobody wants to kiss when they are hungry."

A humanist psychologist, Maslow studied prominent people who lived fulfilling lives. He found that individuals such as Mahatma Gandhi and Mother Teresa, who devote themselves to important causes, show continuous personal growth throughout their lives. As a result of his research, Maslow developed a theory that human needs could be arranged in order, beginning with physiological needs, such as hunger, and progressing upward through needs such as love, achievement and understanding, to the final stage of self-fulfillment—a sense that one has achieved as much as one is capable of achieving.

Maslow believed that we need to meet each of the lower needs on the hierarchy before we can turn our attention to the next one. All people, he claimed, are motivated to fulfill their needs in this order, and they never stop striving to reach the next level. What's more, Maslow suggested, once we have met our needs at a certain level, we may go back to play at lower-need levels. For example, the person who has nurturing social relation-

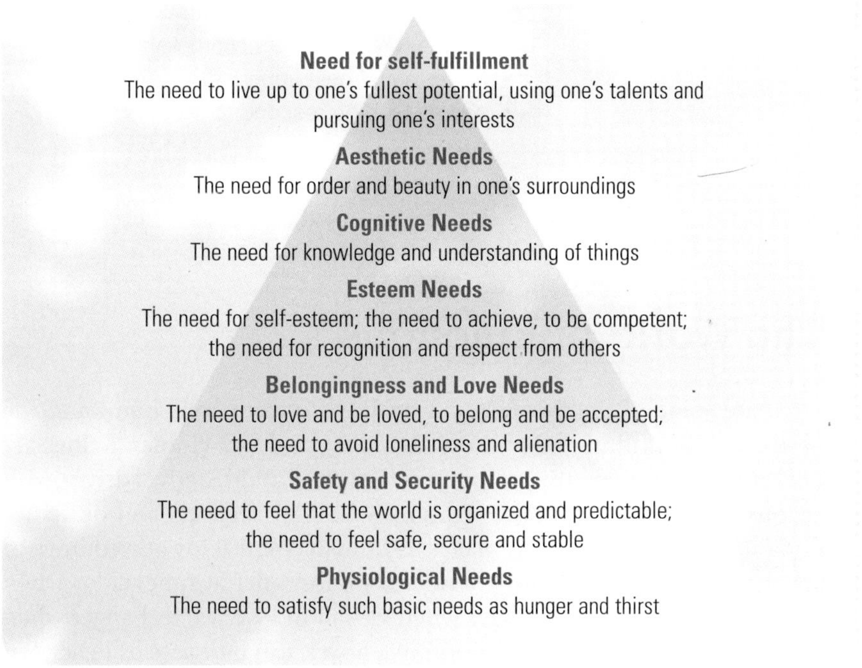

Figure 4–8

Maslow's Hierarchy of Needs

Need for self-fulfillment
The need to live up to one's fullest potential, using one's talents and pursuing one's interests

Aesthetic Needs
The need for order and beauty in one's surroundings

Cognitive Needs
The need for knowledge and understanding of things

Esteem Needs
The need for self-esteem; the need to achieve, to be competent; the need for recognition and respect from others

Belongingness and Love Needs
The need to love and be loved, to belong and be accepted; the need to avoid loneliness and alienation

Safety and Security Needs
The need to feel that the world is organized and predictable; the need to feel safe, secure and stable

Physiological Needs
The need to satisfy such basic needs as hunger and thirst

ships and a satisfying job may take safety risks by trying new activities such as whitewater rafting or wilderness camping.

Maslow's theory has had a major impact on psychology as well as other disciplines, such as the world of business where these motivational principles are used to increase employee productivity and job satisfaction. However, not everyone agrees that all people fulfill their needs in the order Maslow suggested. Some point out that individuals may place a higher priority on esteem needs than on love and belonging needs. Poverty or homelessness, for example, may not destroy a person's need for respect.

> **Connections**
>
> How might culture influence the order in which people fulfill their needs? (See Chapter 2, pages 26–28.)

Activities

Understand Ideas

1. Identify the stages in Maslow's model and provide an example of each.

2. In what ways does Maslow include both biological and social motivation?

Think and Evaluate

3. Maslow's theory does not explain the order in which most people fulfill their needs and approach life choices. Discuss this statement.

4. What might Freud think of Maslow's ideas of motivation? What might Maslow say about

Freud's ideas? Role-play a meeting between the two psychologists in which they discuss their theories of human motivation.

Apply Your Learning

5. a) Make a list of the things you would like to accomplish before you are 20, 30, and 40 years of age. For each age category, note why you want to accomplish these goals.

   b) Categorize each of these goals according to Maslow's hierarchy.

   c) Where are you currently located in the hierarchy? Provide some personal examples.

6. Not everyone agrees with Maslow's Hierarchy of Needs theory. Write a brief biographical profile on one of the following: Erik Erikson, Jean Piaget or B.F. Skinner. In your profile, be sure to include answers to the following questions:

- When and where was he born?
- What were his major accomplishments?
- What is his most important contribution?
- How would he respond to Maslow's theory?

Focus Questions

What are the components of emotion?

What factors shape our emotional make-up?

How do childhood experiences affect emotional development?

The World of Emotions

What are some of the factors apart from the unconscious mind and the need for self-fulfillment that motivate our behaviour? Human beings are not simply machines that respond to internal and external drives with actions or behaviours. We are creatures who have feelings, and our emotions are a large part of what makes us human. We feel joy at weddings or seeing loved ones after a long absence; we feel grief at funerals or when saying good-bye. We feel ecstasy when we fall in love; we feel anger when someone treats us rudely. Emotions, like drives, can motivate us to act. For these reasons, psychologists are very interested in understanding the role of emotions in our lives.

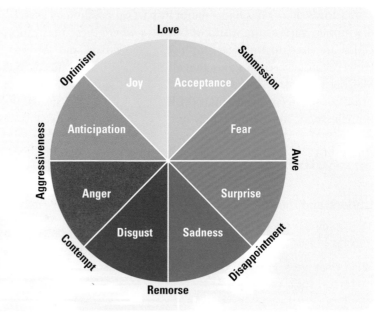

Figure 4–9

Mixing primary emotions. Some psychologists have isolated a small group of "pure" emotions called primary emotions, which sometimes combine to create other emotions. Robert Plutchik's model assumes that there are eight primary emotions, which are shown on the inside of the circle; those on the outside are examples of blended emotions. For instance, disappointment is shown as a mixture of sadness and surprise.

Psychologists say that emotions are made up of three major components. One is the **cognitive component**—the mental state, the conscious feeling of being happy, sad, angry or excited. The second is the **physical component**—the physical characteristics that accompany emotional reactions, such as tensed muscles, increased energy, a pounding heart and changes in body temperature. The third is the **behavioural component**—expressing the emotion through actions, withdrawal, body language or facial expressions.

Why do we feel emotions? One reason is that emotions are one of the factors that seem to motivate behaviour. We generally seek out experiences that are associated with positive feelings and avoid those that give us negative feelings. Also, emotions may be a survival strategy. In early times, human beings lived in dangerous and unpredictable environments. The best way to survive was to react quickly—to either attack or escape. This reaction is called "fight or flight." The experience of fear increases the production of adrenalin, a hormone that allows us to react quickly when danger is imminent. The facial expressions associated with anger are a signal to those close by to stay away or get ready to fight.

body language—physical gestures or postures that express thoughts and feelings

Our Emotional Make-up

Several factors shape who we are emotionally: heredity, learning and maturity. As you can see, both nature (in the form of heredity) and nurture (in the form of learning) play a part. There is much debate about which factor is most important or which comes first.

Heredity

We do inherit some of our emotional capacities, although to what extent is still open to debate. It is possible that all we are born with is a capacity for excitement, related to the fight or flight reaction. However, recent studies suggest that tendencies toward particular behavioural reactions may be inherited.

Cross-cultural research indicates that facial expressions, such as a smile, and physiological responses, such as an increased heart rate, are innate to some extent. When people in different cultures are shown various facial expressions, they usually agree on the emotion being expressed. These expressions seem to be the same even in children who are blind from birth and are unable to learn from watching others.

Learning

Our emotional make-up is largely determined by our learning experiences, especially those from our early years. Life experiences, and the examples set for us by others, provide models for us to follow in our emotional reactions to new situations. For example, research shows that men and women experience emotions with similar intensity. However, in Western society men and women are taught to express emotions in different ways. In one

Connections

What kinds of learning shape our emotional make-up? (See Chapter 3, pages 53–57.)

Reading Faces

Match each of the following faces with the emotion it displays. Then check your answers at the bottom of the page. What cues helped you decipher the facial expressions?

a) disgust   d) happiness

b) anger   e) sadness

c) fear   f) surprise

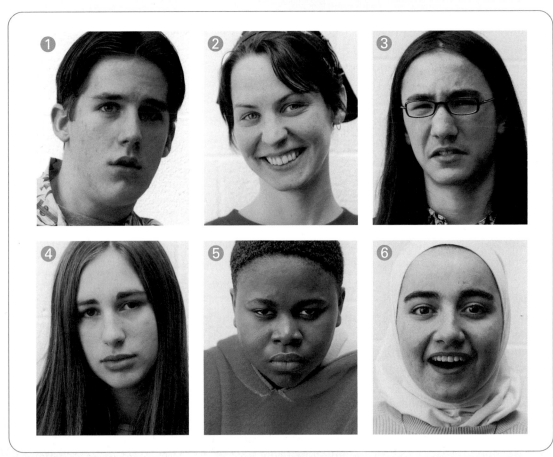

Answers

1. Fear 2. Happiness 3. Disgust 4. Sadness 5. Anger 6. Surprise

experiment, men and women were shown pictures of someone receiving a shock. The men actually had a stronger physical reaction (higher heart rate and more sweating) than the women did; yet, these same men rated themselves as experiencing lower stress than the women. Why? One explanation is that men in Western society are generally taught from an early age to suppress their emotions.

Maturity

Emotional feelings and reactions develop and change over a lifetime. An adolescent has a capacity for emotional reactions that children do not. Parents have feelings that come with having children. Older people have emotions unique to their own experiences. But what influences our emotional development to begin with? Studies such as the Harlow experiments indicate that no matter what stage of life we are in right now, events in early childhood have already had a profound effect on our emotional behaviour.

The Harlow Experiments

Psychologists Mary and Harry Harlow isolated rhesus monkeys in order to produce disease-free specimens. Their experiments revealed some unexpected side effects when the monkeys showed signs of emotional distress. Some stared into space or rocked back and forth for long periods. Others flew into rages when approached. Those who later became mothers ignored and sometimes attacked their young.

Realizing they had stumbled onto something important, the Harlows set up a series of experiments to investigate further. They raised a number of monkeys with surrogate mothers. Some surrogates were made of wire mesh with wooden heads; others were covered with soft cloth. The Harlows found that the monkeys spent much more time clinging to the "cloth mother" than to the "wire mother." This was true even when the wire mother had a bottle of milk attached. The monkeys would feed from the wire mother, then run to snuggle with the cloth mother.

In further experiments, the Harlows brought flashing lights, loud noises and mechanical "monsters" into the monkey cages to observe their reactions. They found that monkeys raised with the cloth mother would run to her, gain courage, then investigate and even attack the source of danger. Monkeys raised by a wire mother cringed fearfully in a corner. Even cloth monkeys, however, were a poor substitute for real mothers. Monkeys with real mothers learned how to play with other monkeys more quickly and showed mating and maternal behaviours that were more characteristic of monkeys in normal settings.

The Harlows and others have concluded that the early years are important in developing the ability to feel and express emotions. Later research has shown that human babies, too, need to be raised in a warm and loving environment in order to become mature and emotionally stable adults.

CASE STUDY

1. Why did the first group of isolated rhesus monkeys display unusual behaviour?

2. What conclusions can you draw from these experiments?

3. How can these conclusions be related to human behaviour?

Figure 4–10

A young monkey clings to its cloth surrogate mother.

Activities

Understand Ideas

1. What are the three components of emotion? Give examples for each.

2. What three factors affect emotional make-up?

Think and Evaluate

3. The Harlow experiment is interesting on its own, but it does not provide conclusive evidence to prove that early nurturing is important to human emotional development. List at least two questions raised by these experiments that would have to be addressed in order to reach this conclusion.

4. Do you think the Harlow experiment was ethical? Argue your view.

Apply Your Learning

5. List at least three emotions you have experienced that are not included in Plutchik's model of emotion (see the diagram in Figure 4–9).

Decide which of Plutchik's primary emotions might be mixed to produce these emotions.

6. How do you think your childhood experiences affected the way you express emotion? Discuss with your group.

Research and Communicate

7. With the sound turned off, watch part of a taped version of a television show or film. Identify the emotions being expressed by the various characters. Play back the same selection, this time with the sound on. How accurate was your assessment? To what extent does the dialogue add to, or change, your assessment of the emotions being expressed? What does this experiment tell you about body language?

8. Music often expresses emotion. Bring several selections of popular songs to class. Play them and have class members identify the emotions being expressed. Does everyone agree?

Focus Questions

What are the sources of love that most people experience?

What are the elements of different kinds of love?

Love

Love is among the most important of human emotions. We have already noted the effects of parental love on children's emotional development. Throughout our lives, most of us experience other forms of love as well: love from close friends, from family, from boyfriends or girlfriends, from spouses, or from our own children. Of these, none is so glamourized in Western society as romantic love.

Romantic love, as we know it, is a relatively modern idea. In the Middle Ages, romance was reserved for those outside of marriage and for the rich and aristocratic. In many societies, romantic love is not considered important or even desirable for marriage. Yet, in the West romantic love is portrayed in our myths, stories and media as essential for happiness in long-term relationships. But is it?

One theory divides love into two major forms: passionate and companionate. Passionate love is what we normally associate with romance and is characterized by the turmoil of intense emotions. For a time it becomes the focus of one's life. It leads to crushes, infatuations and love at first sight. Individuals in a passionate affair tend to idealize each other.

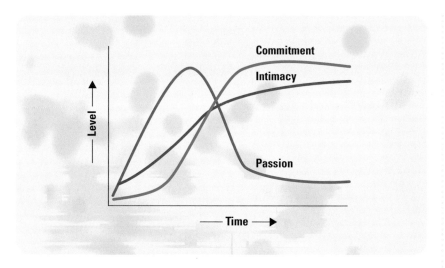

They feel lonely when they are apart and excited when they are together. However, a passionate love affair is sometimes short-lived; it may burn out or develop into companionate love.

Companionate love is calmer and more enduring than passionate love. It feels stable and reliable and is generally based on common interests and goals. Companionate love forms the basis for most long-term relationships. In "real life," many relationships may have elements of both kinds of love.

The cognitive psychologist Robert Sternberg has identified three major ingredients of love: passion (butterflies in the stomach, euphoria, excitement); intimacy (feeling free to talk about anything, being understanding and patient); and commitment (needing one another, being loyal). Over time, as passionate love gives way to companionate love, greater intimacy will tend to create stronger commitment.

Still other researchers have used John Alan Lee's Love Attitude Scales to define six distinct attitudes toward love: romantic, game-playing, companionate, possessive, pragmatic and altruistic:

- Romantic lovers emphasize physical beauty as they search for the ideal mate. They believe in true love, love at first sight and abiding passion.

- Game-playing lovers enjoy the chase more than the catch; they like to keep their partners a little uncertain.

- Companionate lovers take longer to develop a relationship. They value friendship, companionship and trust, and their relationships tend to last for a long time.

- Possessive lovers are very emotional; they often suffer from jealousy and worry.

- Pragmatic lovers want a practical and rational relationship based on mutual satisfaction. They seriously consider compatibility before committing to a relationship.

Connections

How might various branches of anthropology study the nature of love in different cultures? (See Chapter 2, pages 30–32.)

possessive—having or showing a desire to control and dominate

Figure 4-12

In some cultures, arranged marriages, such as this one between Canadian WWF wrestler Tiger Singh Ali and Harmeet Kier, are common. In many of these marriages, love grows even though the spouses did not know each other when they married.

- Altruistic lovers are gentle and caring without expecting a lot in return. They want to help their mates through good times and bad.

Most relationships combine several of these attitudes. Also, different cultures may emphasize different kinds of love.

Activities

Understand Ideas

1. Identify several characteristics of romantic and companionate love.

2. According to psychologist Robert Sternberg, what are the three ingredients of love?

3. Explain the six attitudes toward love as described by Lee's Love Attitude Scales.

Think and Evaluate

4. Agree or disagree with the following statement: It is more important to a long-term relationship to be companionate than to be passionate. Explain your answer in a paragraph using three specific reasons.

5. What ingredients can you add to Sternberg's three ingredients of love?

Apply Your Learning

6. How do you define love?

7. Which ingredient of love is most important to you?

Research and Communicate

8. Interview four people: one friend, two family members and one other adult. How do they define love? How important do they believe love is to a long-term relationship? Be prepared to share your findings with the class.

9. Find images of romantic love in songs, books, magazines, film or other media. What image do these sources portray? How does the media image of love differ from the interviews you conducted in Activity 8 above? How are they similar?

Key Points

- Human behaviour is driven by both biological and social factors.

- Sigmund Freud and his followers introduced the importance of the unconscious mind as a source of motivation.

- Freud divided the mind into three parts: the id, which unconsciously seeks pleasure and avoids pain; the superego, which seeks to enforce rules for acceptable behaviour in society; and the ego, which is influenced by both forces but must balance and regulate them at the conscious level.

- Maslow developed a hierarchy of needs that attempts to chart the progress of the individual toward self-fulfillment. He stated that we must satisfy our lower-level needs, such as food and security, before we can move on to higher-level needs.

- Human actions are often shaped by emotional reactions and feelings. Although emotions have a physical component, they are also learned.

Activities

Understanding Ideas

1. **a)** Identify two issues in this chapter that relate to the conflict between nature and nurture.
   b) Use this information to complete a three-column chart with these headings:
   Issue, Example suggesting influence of nature, Example suggesting influence of nurture.

Think and Evaluate

2. Work in a group to discuss and record your responses to the following questions: How do emotions affect behaviour? Can we control our emotions? Are our responses to emotions prede-termined by factors such as gender or cultural background? (See Skill Focus, page 43.)

Apply Your Learning

3. According to Maslow's hierarchy, identify which needs are likely being met in each of the following situations. More than one need may be met in each case.
   a) A group of friends meet at a restaurant.
   b) A teenager goes to an amusement park with friends.
   c) A soldier attacks an enemy under fire.
   d) A child runs home after a fight with a bully.
   e) A millionaire leaves everything to charity.
   f) A successful businesswoman enters politics at a salary lower than her previous earnings.
   g) A student volunteers at a food bank for several hours a week.
   h) A student spends every spare moment studying for final exams.

Research and Communicate

4. What needs and goals motivate people to act? Interview a number of people of different ages and walks of life. Ask them questions such as the following:
   - What are your most important values?
   - What things would you spend a great deal of time and money on?
   - What do you want out of life?
   Draw conclusions from your interviews. Suggest hypotheses for further research. (See Skill Focus, page 12.)

5. Keep a personal log of the range of emotions you experience over the course of a day. Every two hours (except when you are sleeping), jot down what you are doing and how you are feeling. After two days, review your log entries. How often do your emotions vary? Do the results surprise you at all?

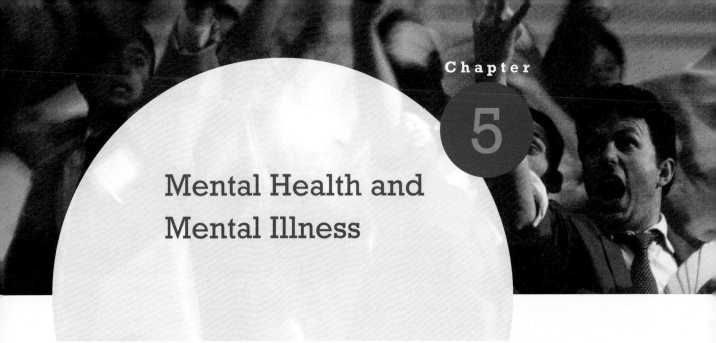

Mental Health and Mental Illness

Are mental health and mental illness entirely separate conditions at opposite ends of a see-saw, or do they blend and merge more gradually along a continuum of well-being? Distinctions between mental health and illness may not be as clear cut as we think. Although psychologists use their knowledge of mental processes, behaviour, emotions and motivation to help people who are having problems, human beings are complicated creatures, and it is not always easy to determine when they need psychological help. Psychologists often start with a focus not on mental illness, but on mental health. By determining the characteristics of mental "wellness," they are better able to assess the scale and complexity of psychological problems.

Mental wellness involves experiencing a wide range of emotions. Examine the "emotional temperature" thermometer below and discuss the following questions with your group:

- Have you felt all of these emotions in one day?

- Which emotion do you feel most frequently?

- How would you define the term "emotionally normal"? At what point do changes in mood or emotions become "emotional instability"?

- What causes the emotions of people to change?

- What role should society play in assisting people who frequently exhibit emotional instability?

- How would you advise someone who asked for your assistance because he or she was experiencing emotional instability?

Angry   **Annoyed**   **Coping/Satisfied Happy**   **Overjoyed**

Mental Health

Does **mental health** mean having no problems? No, but it does imply an ability to recognize the nature of these problems and to deal with most of them before they get out of hand. Although mental health is not related to intelligence or expertise, it does suggest the capacity to use the abilities we have in ways that allow us to function in a state of mental and emotional well-being. What are the characteristics of a healthy mind? Psychologists have suggested the following indicators of mental health:

- Mentally healthy people generally observe and understand what is going on around them.

- They judge their own reactions and capabilities realistically.

- They are aware of their own motives and feelings and can control their behaviour.

- They may sometimes act without thinking about consequences, but they can restrain their impulses when necessary.

- While they may not always behave as society expects, they do so deliberately and with a reason.

- They appreciate their own worth and feel accepted by others in their lives.

- They are capable of forming close and satisfying relationships with others and of being sensitive to others' needs as well as their own.

What if we do not always have all of these characteristics? Does it mean that we have a psychological or an emotional disorder? Not at all. There are times in all of our lives when stress or problems prevent us from functioning as well as we would like. This list is simply a guideline, a rough assessment of what it means to be mentally healthy.

Focus Questions
What is mental health?

What are the indicators of mental health?

Connections
How does our ability to fulfill our needs contribute to a state of mental and emotional well-being? (See Chapter 4, pages 80–81.)

Stress

Have you ever felt overwhelmed by the events in your life? If you have, then you are definitely familiar with stress. Mentally healthy individuals experience stress as a normal part of life. **Stress** is a physical and psychological response to circumstances in the environment that test our ability to cope. It can be a response to such varying situations as an upcoming test, a job interview, a graduation, a first date or a family argument.

Physical Responses to Stress

Much of our knowledge of stress comes from the work done by Canadian researcher Hans Selye (1907–1982). Selye identified and developed the

Focus Questions
What is stress?

How do we respond to stress, both physically and emotionally?

What causes stress?

How can we learn to cope with stress more effectively?

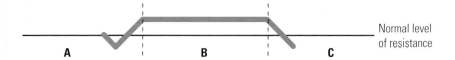

Figure 5–1

General Adaptation Syndrome. Stress is the body's physical and emotional reaction to painful events in the environment. Selye proposed that this reaction to prolonged stress progresses through three stages: alarm (**A**), resistance (**B**) and exhaustion (**C**).

Normal level of resistance

syndrome—a group of symptoms that consistently occur together

adrenalin—a hormone affecting circulation and muscular action, causing excitement and stimulation

idea of psychological stress. Born in Vienna, he spent his professional career at McGill University in Montreal. At McGill, Selye exposed laboratory animals to a variety of physical and psychological stimuli such as heat, cold, pain and restraint. Selye found that no matter what stimulus he applied, the animals exhibited similar physiological responses, which he called stress.

Selye developed a theory called the General Adaptation Syndrome to explain reactions to long-term stress. This syndrome consists of three stages: alarm, resistance and exhaustion. In the alarm stage, the organism recognizes the existence of a threat. The body reacts by producing hormones such as adrenalin to ready itself to fight or flee from the cause of the stress. If the stress persists, then the body enters the second stage—resistance. During this stage, physiological changes stabilize, or level off, as the organism becomes accustomed to the threat. Yet, hormone production and other physical responses remain high. While the body is better able to deal with the original source of the stress, it has much lower resistance to other stresses that come along. In the third stage, exhaustion, the body's resources are wearing down. The glands lower their supply of adrenalin, the body's immune system loses its ability to prevent disease, and physical illness—and sometimes death—may result. Because Selye's research led to recognizing the link between stress and physical illness, researchers continue to investigate this strong connection. (See Figure 5–1.)

Selye also developed the idea that not all stress is bad; in fact, some stress is necessary and actually feels good. This is "positive" stress, which Selye called "eustress." Examples include competing in an athletic event, falling in love or working hard on a project you enjoy. Instead of avoiding stress altogether, Selye claimed, people should search for eustress and deal more effectively with negative stress.

Figure 5–2

Studies show that some stress is actually good for you. This graph shows that too little stress is just as damaging as too much stress. In other words, feeling a little stressed before an exam is probably a good sign; but too much stress will be counterproductive.

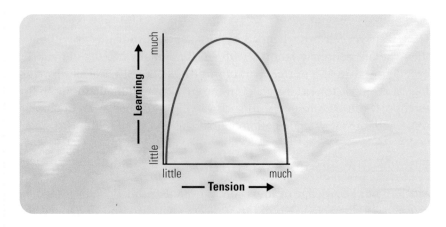

How Vulnerable Are You to Stress?

In your notebook, score each item from 1 (almost always) to 5 (never) according to how much of the time each statement applies to you.

1. I eat at least one hot, balanced meal a day.

2. I get seven or eight hours of sleep at least four nights a week.

3. I get and receive affection regularly.

4. I have at least one relative within 50 kilometres on whom I can rely.

5. I exercise to the point of perspiration at least three times a week.

6. I have an income adequate to my basic expenses.

7. I get strength from my religious beliefs.

8. I regularly attend club or social activities.

9. I have a network of friends and acquaintances.

10. I have one or more friends to confide in about personal matters.

11. I am in good health.

12. I am able to speak openly about my feelings when angry or worried.

13. I have regular conversations with the people I like about domestic problems (e.g., chores, money, daily life).

14. I do something for fun at least once a week.

15. I am able to organize my time effectively.

16. I drink fewer than three cups of coffee, tea or cola a day.

17. I take quiet time for myself during the day.

To get your total, add up your score for each item and subtract 17. Any number over 25 indicates vulnerability to stress. You are seriously vulnerable if your score is between 44 and 68, and extremely vulnerable if it is over 68.

If your score is over 25, make a list of steps you can take to cope with stress, based on the text on pages 95 and 96.

Causes of Stress

Stress can be caused by a number of factors: those that signal the loss of an important relationship, such as divorce; events that produce a sense of helplessness, such as a tragic accident; and factors that pose a long-term threat, such as a lingering illness or the loss of a job. Stress can also be caused by catastrophic events such as earthquakes, hurricanes and floods, or by life transitions, such as changing schools, getting married or starting a new job. Even a series of positive events can be extremely stressful.

Too many minor irritations and problems can also add up to major stress. Physical problems such as flu, headaches and backaches have been tied to the stress brought on by daily life. A major source of stress in most people's lives is having to decide between conflicting choices. Even if both choices are desirable, the act of choosing can produce anxiety and uncertainty. Although there may not be a satisfactory solution to some of the conflicts in everyday life, understanding the cause of the stress can help us cope.

> **Connections**
>
> Why would following a decision-making process help to alleviate stress? (See Chapter 3, pages 65–66.)

Figure 5–3
Do you think teenagers have more or less stress in their lives than adults?

The following case study looks at how shyness can be a source of stress for some young people.

CASE STUDY

1. According to the article, what can be done to overcome shyness?

2. Relate an experience in which you felt shy. Describe your physical response to the situation.

Stage Fright Every Day

Vanessa Venditello regrets missing out on her childhood. She was so shy that she couldn't even wear a bright yellow top for fear of standing out. Afraid to ask questions because she didn't want to be yelled at or have her classmates think she was stupid, Venditello kept her thoughts to herself. "I wanted to just hide and I thought that everybody was laughing at me," the 19-year-old recalls. "Whether it was true or not, that's the way I felt. Because of that, I was quiet and kept pretty much to myself. I hated it."

According to Katherina Manassis, a psychiatrist at Toronto's Sick Children's Hospital, the biggest misconception about shy people is that they are happy by themselves and do not want friends. "Shy people are terribly eager to have friends, but they're afraid that if they go into social situations, they'll be embarrassed, humiliated or laughed at," she says.

A child's learning environment plays a huge role in character development, says psychotherapist Karyn Gordon. "If your parents are shy and you use them as models, you can learn that's how you communicate." However, a person who was shy as a child can take small steps forward. Nineteen-year-old Mason Marchildon can now confidently voice his opinions and comfortably socialize with his peers. But he used to be shy and admits he still feels timid in unfamiliar situations. "I can't say I feel comfortable being introduced to or talking to someone whom I don't totally know," he says. Marchildon knows shyness is still a problem when it prevents him from speaking his mind. "I get into situations where I don't feel comfortable expressing fully what I feel."

There are ways to overcome shyness and everyone can learn to interact with others. Even if it makes your stomach turn inside out to contemplate doing so, Manassis advises shy people to face their fears to make them disappear. "Try and go into situations that involve other people," she advises, "and if that's hard, see if you can get a friend or family member to go with you."

Gordon says getting involved in extracurricular activities really helps. "It's painful at first because it's unfamiliar and outside of your comfort zone," she acknowledges, "but when you get involved in something, you feel a sense of belonging, which is really important in building up self-esteem."

Ultimately, it is up to shy people to take the initiative to change if they want to beat their insecurities. That first step is often the hardest, but shy people's anxieties often dissipate once they are actually interacting instead of just anticipating a frightening unknown. The realization that she had to make an effort to make friends motivated Venditello to conquer her shyness. "People aren't gonna come to you," she says. "You have to go to them. Don't be afraid of them and don't be afraid of what they're gonna think or what they're gonna say." Above all, she believes you should not allow shyness to limit you. "If you're determined to do something, don't think you should let anything stand in your way. Why not do what you want to do in your childhood, 'cause when you grow up, you can't ever be young again."

dissipate—lessen almost to the point of disappearing

From "Overcoming Pain of Shyness" by Christl Dabu

Coping with Stress

Stress researcher Richard Lazarus views stress as whatever is considered a threat to one's safety or well-being. In order to determine one's level of stress, he has developed a two-step process called **stress cognitive appraisal.** In the primary appraisal, the individual assesses the degree of threat that is present; during the secondary appraisal, the individual chooses a way to deal with this threat. Lazarus believes that the amount of stress people feel in a given situation will vary depending on the balance between these two factors. When harm and threat are high and resources to deal with these factors are low, they experience high stress. When harm and threat are low and resources are high, they experience moderate or low stress. This approach suggests that it is far more difficult to cope with stress caused by factors over which we have little control.

Some ways of handling stress are positive and lead to either solutions or healthy ways to live with stress. Others are negative because they fail to deal with the problem, or they lead to unhealthy reactions to stress. Kicking the dog, yelling at your sibling or simply running away may be tempting as short-term solutions, but they do little to relieve the problem. More effective techniques for coping with stress involve removing or altering the source of the stress, or changing your own mental or physical reactions to it. For example, if your stress is caused by a relationship, both you and your partner could get together to analyze what causes stress in the relationship and then discuss possible solutions. Of course, not all

Connections

Which problem-solving strategies would you find most useful in coping with stress? (See Chapter 3, page 65.)

Figure 5–4

Physical exercise, doing the things we love or just talking and confiding in others all help to alleviate stress during hard times. How do you cope with stress in your life?

Connections

How can the power of perception change your reactions to stress? (See Chapter 3, pages 46–49.)

relationships can be dealt with in this way. If no adequate solution can be found, you may have to consider ending the relationship.

Often small changes that make you feel more in control can make a big difference. In one study, it was found that nursing home residents experienced a great deal of stress because they felt that they were no longer in control of their lives and daily routine. When the conditions were rearranged so that the residents had some control over their daily lives, they became mentally happier and physically healthier.

Some stresses cannot be removed or changed. For instance, you may find that you do not have as much time as you need to study for the upcoming examinations—but you still have to write them. Or, you may have an unpleasant part-time job that you cannot leave because you need or want the money. But you can change your mental reactions to such stresses. You can put into perspective the importance of one test or one bad encounter on the job. You can learn to plan ahead and to manage your time more efficiently. You can seek support and advice from others you trust. These are positive approaches to circumstances that cause stress.

Stress reactions are physical as well as mental and emotional. Ways to change these physical reactions to stress will vary from one individual to another. One person may find that vigorous exercise is one way to let off steam; another may find that listening to music, talking to a friend or engaging in a hobby or sport is a way to ease tensions and, sometimes, find solutions.

Skill
F●CUS

Analyzing and Judging Information or Ideas

Whenever you listen to someone speak or whenever you read some material, it is important to analyze and judge the information or ideas presented.

Here's How

1. Analyze the information in the following ways:
- Identify the major point being made. In most social science readings or essays, the major point is in a thesis statement at the beginning of the paper or speech.
- Determine the main parts of the argument presented. In other words, what are the most important subtopics in the argument?
- Locate the evidence used to support each part of the argument.
- Identify the conclusion reached.

2. Judge the information in the following ways:
- Are all the details relevant to the main point?
- Is the evidence factual? Is it based on observation and other data, or is it based on hearsay and personal opinion?
- Is the evidence reliable? Is the source of the information so credible that the statement can be accepted as truth?

Practise It

1. Review the sections of this chapter on Causes of Stress and Coping with Stress. Analyze the information according to the guidelines above. Take point-form notes for each of the steps in the guideline.

2. Discuss your analysis with a partner or in a small group.

Activities

Understand Ideas

1. According to Selye, what are the stages of long-term stress? Provide an example for each stage of stress.

2. How can stress be defined as positive? Provide an example from your own experience.

3. Refer to a situation (either real or imagined) to explain Lazarus' two-step stress cognitive appraisal.

Think and Evaluate

4. How is it possible for a situation to cause negative stress in one person and eustress in another? Provide an example to illustrate your reasons.

5. Review the case study entitled Stage Fright Every Day. Do you think that shyness is the result of nature or nurture? Explain your answer.

6. In groups of two or three, brainstorm effective ways to deal with stress. Share your strategies with the class. (See Skill Focus, page 64.)

Apply Your Learning

7. a) Identify at least five factors or conditions in your life that cause you stress and rank them in order from most to least stressful.
b) How do you deal with each of these stress factors? How effective are these methods?
c) Review the section on Coping with Stress (pages 95–96). Which of these suggestions could you apply to your own life?

Chapter 5: Mental Health and Mental Illness

8. a) Survey students in your school about the factors that cause stress in their lives.

   b) Draw a conclusion as to the most widespread causes of stress among your respondents.

9. Survey your parents or others of their generation. What are their most common causes of stress?

10. a) How are alcohol or drugs used as a way to deal with stress?

   b) Find four newspaper articles, two on alcohol use and two on drug use. Referring to your articles, write a detailed response to the following question: Why is the use of alcohol or drugs an ineffective way of coping with stress? (See Skill Focus, page 97.)

Focus Questions

What is mental illness?

What causes mental illness?

How have views of mental illness changed over the years?

genetic predisposition— an inherited tendency or susceptibility

interpersonal maladjustment —inability to cope with whatever behaviour is required to form and maintain a relationship with another

antisocial—contrary to established social practice; hostile or disruptive

What Is Mental Illness?

As we have seen, too much stress, or stress that is mishandled, can lead to a breakdown in physical health. Mental health can also be a casualty to excessive negative stress. This is why psychologists pay close attention to signs of **mental illness**—a disorderly functioning of the mind. Of course, not all mental illness is caused by stress. Some illnesses are caused by psychological factors such as early childhood experiences, or biological factors such as brain function, disease or genetic predisposition.

Psychologists sometimes refer to mental illness as abnormal behaviour—behaviour that is out of the ordinary and does not conform to the behaviour of most people. But what is considered "normal" human behaviour varies widely, from person to person and from group to group. In fact, there are times when it is healthier not to conform to the society you live in. As the Indian philosopher Krishnamurti said: "It's no measure of health to be well adjusted to a profoundly sick society." Even so, most psychologists would agree that some people do suffer from emotional or mental disorders that require treatment. How do we as a society decide which behaviours constitute mental illness? How do we distinguish between illness and originality or between illness and non-conformity?

Some psychologists define behaviour as "abnormal" if it is characterized by one or more of the following: irrationality, personal suffering or interpersonal maladjustment. In Canada, several criteria are used to make this judgment. Two criteria are persistent personal unhappiness and the inability to function in society; another is antisocial behaviour that harms other people. In fact, individuals can be kept in custody if they pose a threat to themselves or to others.

Changing Views of Mental Illness

Ideas of mental illness and how to deal with it have changed over the centuries. In the Middle Ages, for example, it was widely believed that abnormal behaviour was caused by evil spirits in the body. Exorcism was used as a religious ceremony to cast out suspected evil spirits. Other methods included praying, fasting and drinking foul substances that could cause

A skull found in Peru shows a hole chipped through the cranium to allow evil spirits to escape.

In Europe during the Middle Ages, many people who acted differently from those around them were thought to be witches and were burned at the stake.

Figure 5–5

Treatments for mental illness have varied through time and have often been unsympathetic. Do you think that people today are more accepting of behaviour that differs from their own?

vomiting. People who continued to behave in ways considered deviant (different from what was considereed normal) were accused of being witches or warlocks (male witches) who had made a pact with Satan. Thousands of "witches" were burned at the stake in Europe and in the United States.

By the eighteenth century, those who behaved abnormally were confined to asylums, literally "places of refuge." In reality, however, asylums were terrible places where unfortunate victims were kept in chains, and nothing was done to help them with their disorders. It was not until 1793 that the modern era of treatment began: a physician named Philippe Pinel became director of the Bicetre Hospital in Paris. Dr. Pinel removed the chains and allowed patients to move about the hospital grounds. Rooms were made more comfortable and violent methods of treating people were abandoned.

For much of the nineteenth and twentieth centuries, confining people in asylums remained the primary treatment for serious disorders such as schizophrenia. For other problems, such as anxiety and mood disorders, psychoanalysis and other forms of psychotherapy were common. By the late twentieth century, new medical drugs became available to treat a number of disorders. These treatments have improved significantly over time to the point where many people have been released from institutions and are able to lead productive lives. However, removing people who are mentally ill from institutions has often left them without community support. Add to this the continuing stigma that surrounds mental illness in North American society, and it is no wonder that some mentally ill individuals end up homeless or living marginal lives.

psychotherapy—treatment for mental illness in which the patient talks through the problem with a trained therapist

stigma—a sign of disgrace or discredit

Activities

Understand Ideas

1. a) What are the characteristics of abnormal behaviour?
   b) Why is abnormal behaviour, in itself, not enough to indicate mental health or illness?

2. What important developments changed how mental illness was viewed and treated?

Think and Evaluate

3. Why were Philippe Pinel's reforms considered the beginning of the modern era regarding the treatment of mental illness?

Apply Ideas

4. In a group of three or four students, brainstorm examples of behaviours that are not considered "normal" by society, yet may not be an indication of mental illness. Explain your choice of examples.

Research and Communicate

5. a) Research the life and work of Philippe Pinel and write a brief profile of his views and major accomplishments.
   b) Review the section on conducting interviews in Chapter 1, pages 11–12. Prepare a list of questions as though you were preparing to interview Philippe Pinel.
   c) With a partner, pick the role of either the interviewer or Pinel, and role-play an interview about Pinel's philosophy and reforms.

Focus Questions

How prevalent is mental illness in Canada?

What are the major types of anxiety?

What will cure a phobia?

What causes depression?

What is bipolar affective disorder?

What are the symptoms of schizophrenia?

Why are psychopaths potentially dangerous?

How can you identify substance dependence?

Categories of Mental Illness

About one in five Canadians suffer from mental illness at some point in their lives. Harvard University researchers have estimated that depression alone will disable more working people in the world than AIDS, cancer and heart disease combined. Note the following facts about mental illness in Canada:

- **16%** of health expenditures in Canada are for psychiatric disorders.

- **40%** of patients' visits to family doctors are related to emotional, not physical, problems.

- Almost **3 million** Canadians have serious depression at a given time, but only about one third of these people will seek treatment for it.

- **80%** of suicides are carried out by people with depression.

- About **2.4%** of teenage boys and **7%** of teenage girls suffer from depression; teenage girls are **five times** more likely to suffer symptoms of serious depression than preteen girls.

- **79%** of psychiatric diagnoses are for anxiety and depression.

- Approximately **10%** to **25%** of North Americans suffer from anxiety disorders.

- About **300 000** Canadians, or **1%** of the population suffer from schizophrenia; another **1%** are bipolar. Both illnesses commonly begin in late teens to early 20s.

bipolar—demonstrating two extreme and opposite forms of behaviour

- Of those diagnosed with schizophrenia, **50%** will recover completely or improve moderately over 10 years.

Mental illnesses used to be categorized in two main groups: neurotic disorders, which tended to be less serious, and psychotic disorders, which included the more serious conditions, such as schizophrenia. In 1980, the American Psychological Association changed its classifications, doing away with the neurosis/psychosis distinction in favour of numerous categories based on similar symptoms. Among the most important classifications now used in the *Diagnostic and Statistical Manual (DSM III R)* are anxiety disorders, mood disorders, schizophrenic disorders, personality disorders and substance-related disorders.

Anxiety Disorders

As we have already seen, anxiety arising from stress is part of everyday life. However, when anxiety becomes severe or prolonged, it can cause a variety of disorders. Among the most common are generalized anxiety disorder, phobias and obsessive-compulsive disorders.

Generalized Anxiety Disorder

Usually anxiety has an observable cause, such as an upcoming exam or a crumpled fender on the family car. **Generalized anxiety disorder,** however, can occur without any obvious reason. One of the first to diagnose and treat anxiety disorder was Sigmund Freud. He said that it is important for people with such reactions to understand and deal with their repressed conflict or anxiety. When they do, the physical symptoms will likely disappear.

While most people suffering from generalized anxiety disorder understand the nature of their problem, they may not be able to identify the underlying causes. They often have trouble coping under certain circumstances, displaying unusual fear and trying to escape the situation. People with generalized anxiety fear that dreadful things will happen—these fears seem to appear for no apparent reason and may become so severe that sufferers feel overwhelmed and cannot function. Individuals may experience anxiety attacks with a variety of physical symptoms, including accelerated heartbeat, faintness, numbness, chills or flushed skin.

Phobias

A **phobia** is a form of anxiety that involves an intense, irrational fear of certain objects or situations. Such fears are out of proportion to the dangers involved. Many of us have fears of one thing or another: snakes, heights, or enclosed spaces, for example. However, these fears are classified as phobias only when they directly interfere with our lives.

Connections

How might conflict between the superego and the id contribute to generalized anxiety disorder? (See Chapter 4, pages 75–76.)

repressed—excluded from the conscious mind

Figure 5–6

Fear of spiders is one of the more common, mild phobias that affect people. Do you think such fears are based on unresolved conflicts, or on actual negative experiences?

Figure 5–7

Phobias develop due to "unreasonable" fears—fears that have no basis in reality but feel very real to the sufferer.

Types of phobias

Phobia name	Unreasonable fear of	Phobia name	Unreasonable fear of
acrophobia	high places	hydrophobia	water
agoraphobia	open places	lalophobia	public speaking
algophobia	pain	phobophobia	fear
astraphobia	thunder or lightning	xenophobia	strangers
claustrophobia	enclosed spaces	zoophobia	animals

Freud believed that a phobia is the mind's defence against anxiety even though the particular object or situation that causes fear bears no relationship to the source of the unconscious anxiety. Conquering such phobias involves finding and dealing with the real cause of the anxiety. On the other hand, Skinner and learning theorists maintain that phobias often result from negative experiences. For example, a fear of flying may be caused by either experiencing a near air disaster or simply imagining it. Learning theorists believe that such phobias can be treated by conditioning techniques that associate pleasant experiences with the feared object or situation.

Obsessive-Compulsive Disorder

An **obsession-compulsive disorder** is also a form of anxiety. An obsession is a persistent, unwanted thought. The person may know that the recurring thought is unreasonable but still cannot get rid of it. Examples of obsessions include an unreasonable fear of failure or thoughts of food.

Figure 5–8

Anorexia and bulimia are forms of an obsessive-compulsive eating disorder. To what extent are societal values to blame for this obsession with being thin?

An obsession may be followed by a compulsion— the tendency to perform an act repeatedly in order to relieve the anxiety. In one instance, a bank teller became obsessed with the fear of making mistakes while counting money, so he resorted to counting the money over and over.

Many people have minor obsessions and compulsions. How many times, upon leaving the house, have you had the nagging feeling that you have forgotten to lock the door or turn off the computer? How would you know if this repeated feeling or thought is an obsession? This thought would lead to obsessive-compulsive behaviour only if you continually returned to check and never left the house.

In some cases, obsessive compulsive behaviour can cause serious, even life-threatening problems, as the following "Society Matters" feature shows.

How Can Dieting Be Fatal?

Eating disorders such as anorexia nervosa and bulimia share characteristics with other obsessive-compulsive disorders. People with eating disorders are obsessed with their body image. Bulimics binge-eat (eat large amounts), then purge themselves by vomiting or abusing laxatives or diuretics. Anorexics reduce their food intake, often to the point of starvation, yet may still believe they are overweight. Sometimes they exercise compulsively in an effort to burn calories.

Eating disorders can be very serious. Anorexia can lead to cardiac arrest and other medical conditions, or even death from starvation. Bulimics who abuse laxatives, diuretics and other drugs are at risk as well. Fortunately, many victims of eating disorders can be treated successfully through a combination of therapy and medications.

Who Suffers from These Disorders?

The vast majority of sufferers are adolescent or young adult women. Men and older women also contract the disorder, but much less frequently.

What Causes Eating Disorders?

Eating disorders seem to arise as a way of dealing with anxiety. They stem from a range of societal, personal and family factors, but experts agree that these illnesses are often triggered by concerns about body image. This explains the high incidence of anorexia and bulimia among young females, who are more likely than other groups to be concerned about their body image. The National Eating Disorder Information Centre offers the following advice:

Many women in our culture are pressured to conform to an unrealistically thin body size—an image that is idealized in our mass media. This pressure results in women often restricting food intake or over-exercising in order to shape their bodies into what is held up as the "ideal." Getting caught in a cycle of dieting can lead to binge eating, loss of self-esteem, more dieting/binge eating and a sense of being out of control. The development of a full-blown eating disorder such as anorexia or bulimia often stems from this cycle.

Certain personality traits have been linked with eating disorders. Anorexics tend to be perfectionists. They often do well in school and are athletic and well behaved. However, their willingness to please others leaves them without resources to deal with the typical problems of adolescence and young adulthood. By controlling their weight, anorexics hope to gain approval from others, as well as control over one part of their lives. Bulimics tend to be impulsive and may engage in risky behaviour. They overeat in order to relieve feelings of anxiety, then purge themselves to relieve the resulting guilt and depression.

The fact that eating disorders often run in families has led some to conclude that there may be a genetic component to the illness. However, others have suggested that behavioural and environmental factors could account for this trend in families where there is too much emphasis on weight and physical attractiveness.

What Do You Think?

1. Do the media encourage eating disorders? If so, how?

2. What do you think could be done to counteract some of the unrealistic expectations that are placed on young women to be thin?

CASE STUDY

1. What is this disorder?

2. What is the difference
   between someone
   who is neat and
   someone who has
   a disorder?

From *The Quiet Furies* by E. McNeil

Diagnosing a Disorder

I can't get to sleep unless I am sure everything in the house is in its proper place so that when I get up in the morning the house is organized. I work like mad to set everything straight before I go to bed, but, when I get up in the morning, I can think of a thousand things that I ought to do. I know some of the things are ridiculous, but I feel better if I get them done, and I can't stand to know something needs doing and I haven't done it. I never told anybody but once I found just one dirty shirt and washed, dried and ironed it that day. I couldn't bear to leave it undone. It would have bothered me all day just thinking about that one dirty shirt in the laundry basket.

Mood Disorders

Mood changes affect us all at various times. Mood disorders, however, are not the kind of everyday moods that we all experience—they are long lasting and severe. Two important mood disorders that require treatment are major depression and bipolar affective disorder.

Someone with **major depression** is deeply unhappy and finds little pleasure in life. This state is often accompanied by anxiety, sleep problems, changes in appetite and, sometimes, suicide attempts. Some people experience major depression only once, get treatment and never have a recurrence. For others, however, such depression can recur several times. It is important that friends and family encourage the sufferer to seek help.

People with **bipolar affective disorder** experience extreme mood changes far beyond the range considered normal. These moods are both manic and depressive. The manic stage is marked by confused and aggressive behaviour, often accompanied by exaggerated gaiety, unlimited energy and difficulty sleeping. For example, in one case, a dentist installed 20 chairs to handle non-existent patients. Manic stages are usually followed by depression, characterized by extreme fatigue, sadness and a sense of futility. In this state, the individual may become extremely withdrawn.

At one time, people who suffered from depression felt stigmatized, or disgraced, by their disorder. However, in recent years, several prominent figures have disclosed their difficulties with depression in an effort to make people aware of how widespread the problem is and to help them understand that effective treatments are available.

Figure 5–9

Comedic actor Jim Carrey has struggled with depression, despite his successful movie career.

Activities

Understand Ideas

1. Create a chart to compare how Freud and Skinner would a) explain the origin of phobias and b) treat phobias.

2. Explain what is meant by anxiety disorder and provide three examples.

3. Identify the characteristics of phobias and obsessive-compulsive disorders. Provide an example of each type of disorder.

4. How are mood disorders different from the wide range of moods that everyone experiences during the day or throughout the week?

Think and Evaluate

5. Review the facts about mental illness in Canada (see pages 100–101). What conclusions can you draw from this data?

6. Why are eating disorders a form of obsessive-compulsive behaviour?

7. What is the difference between major depression and bipolar affective disorder?

Apply Your Learning

8. Review the inquiry model discussed in Chapter 1 (see page 6). How can you use this model to diagnose a mental disorder? Use the example of abnormal behaviour described in the case study on page 104 to show how following the steps in the inquiry process can lead you to a diagnosis.

Schizophrenic Disorders

Overall, **schizophrenia** is marked by distortion of reality, social withdrawal and disturbances of thought, perception, motor activity and emotions. There are several forms of schizophrenia. Some schizophrenics withdraw completely; they lose interest in the world and become totally apathetic. Catatonic schizophrenics become rigid and mute, holding one position for hours without moving. For others, the disease is often characterized by disordered speech and thought, or hallucinations and delusions, sometimes of a bizarre nature. For instance, one patient believed that someone was shooting harmful rays through the walls of the house.

Psychologists continue to study this devastating disease, searching for a cause and a cure. Recent research suggests a genetic component for schizophrenia. Such progress provides hope that, in the future, the genetic disorder can be treated. In the meantime, drug therapy has made great strides in helping many schizophrenics lead productive lives.

apathetic—having or showing no interest or emotion

delusions—false beliefs, often of one's importance or of being persecuted

Personality Disorders

Personality disorders affect people's ability to function in society, making it difficult for sufferers to relate to others or to hold a job. These individuals are often loners, and are highly suspicious and mistrustful of others in almost all situations. They may lie, break laws, or feel they are being persecuted; they also view their own behaviour as perfectly normal.

Figure 5-10

Most people learn in childhood that good behaviour leads to acceptance. Psychopaths, in contrast, behave antisocially.

CASE STUDY

1. What symptoms suggest that Roberta has a personality disorder?

2. What connection, if any, is there between Roberta's upbringing and her behaviour?

From *The Mask of Insanity* by H. Checkley

One of the most disturbing personality disorders is the psychopathic personality. Psychopaths show a total disregard for the rights and well-being of others. They feel no remorse or guilt after causing someone harm or after committing immoral or criminal acts. They also find it difficult to form lasting relationships and have little or no insight into their own behaviour. When they fail to succeed in life or to form any meaningful relationships, they often blame others and the world in general.

What causes this disorder? It used to be thought that psychopathic personalities were the result of nurture—a childhood lacking in love and acceptance, coupled with emotional, physical or sexual abuse. While most children grow up learning that good behaviour leads to acceptance and bad behaviour results in temporary rejection, the child with psychopathic tendencies learns that there is nothing to lose by behaving antisocially. Recently, however, such explanations are being questioned. It is thought that nature, or biological factors such as disturbances in brain function, may also play a role. Consider the following case:

Roberta

"I can't understand the girl, no matter how hard I try," said the father, shaking his head in genuine perplexity. "It's not that she seems bad or that she means to do wrong. She can lie with the straightest face, and after she's found in the most outlandish lies she still seems perfectly easy in her own mind." He had related how Roberta, at the age of 10, stole her aunt's silver hairbrush, and how she repeatedly made off with small articles from the dime store, the drug store, and from her own home.

Neither the father nor the mother seemed a severe parent. Also, there was nothing to suggest that this girl had been spoiled. The parents had, so far as could be determined, consistently let her find that lying and stealing and truancy brought censure and punishment. As she grew into her teens she began to buy dresses, cosmetics, candy, perfume and other articles, charging them to her father. He had no warning that these bills would come. For many of these things she had little or no use; some of them she distributed among her acquaintances. As a matter of fact, the father, previously in comfortable circumstances, had at one time been forced to the verge of bankruptcy.

In school Roberta's work was mediocre. She studied little and her truancy was spectacular and persistent. She seemed to learn easily when she made any effort at all. "I wouldn't exactly say she's like a hypocrite," her father said. "When she's caught and confronted with her lies and other misbehaviour she doesn't seem to appreciate the inconsistency of her position. Her conscience seems still untouched..."

Having failed in many classes and her truancy becoming intolerable to the school, Roberta was expelled from the local high school. Employed in her father's business as a bookkeeper, she used her skill at figures and a good deal of ingenuity to make off with considerable sums.

How to Identify Substance Dependence

How can someone tell whether he or she is dependent on a substance? Psychologists use questions similar to the ones below. Anyone who answers "yes" to three or more of the following questions should consider talking to a substance-abuse counsellor.

- Do you take more of the substance over a longer period of time than you intended?

- Do you recognize that you use too much of the substance and try to control your consumption but fail?

- Do you spend a lot of time obtaining, using and recovering from the effects of the substance?

- Does use of the substance interfere with your ability to work, study or meet family obligations?

- Are important social, job and recreational activities less important than use of the substance?

- Are you experiencing major problems because of the substance but are still using it?

- Have you developed tolerance to the substance and are taking more to achieve the same feeling?

- Do you experience withdrawal symptoms when you stop, or reduce, substance use?

- Do you continue to take the substance in order to avoid the pains of withdrawal?

Substance-Related Disorders

Substance-related disorders refer to the harmful use of substances such as alcohol, tobacco or drugs, leading to significant impairment or distress. These disorders are usually classified as substance "abuse" or substance "dependence," depending on the problems involved. Substance abuse is diagnosed when individuals repeatedly use substances in dangerous or illegal situations, or when use interferes with their ability to function at work, at school or at home. Substance dependence is diagnosed when users become physically and mentally addicted, requiring increasing amounts of the substance to achieve the desired effect. These individuals also find that they cannot cut down on the amount and will do anything to obtain the substance, experiencing severe withdrawal symptoms if the substance is not available.

The consequences of substance dependence vary. Alcohol abuse, for example, can lead to car accidents and serious personal problems in families and at work. Long-term alcoholism also has a deadly impact on the major organs, such as the liver and the brain. Tobacco use is strongly related to cancer and emphysema. Drug use can cause hallucinations, paranoia, memory loss and a host of other psychological and physical disorders.

If consequences are so serious, why do people become dependent on these substances? Psychologists have identified a number of conditions

withdrawal—the process of discontinuing an addictive substance, often accompanied by uncomfortable, painful and sometimes life-threatening physical and psychological reactions

emphysema—enlargement of the air sacs in the lungs, causing breathlessness

paranoia—a mental illness characterized by unwarranted feelings of persecution and jealousy

that contribute to addiction. Some people appear to be particularly vulnerable—that is, they are biologically more likely than others to become addicted. Others come to rely on a substance as a way of coping with problems, dealing with anger or fear, or relieving pain. Dependence can also be encouraged by a close association with peers who drink heavily and use drugs.

Getting Help

Focus Questions

What resources are available for getting help?

- Why is a combination of treatment options often recommended?

Occasionally, everyone needs help with personal problems. In many cases, we turn to a friend or family member for a sympathetic ear, a new way to look at the problem or, perhaps, a solution. There are times, however, when problems appear too complex to be resolved with the help of an understanding friend. At such times, it is important to realize that there are many places to go for professional help and advice. School guidance counsellors, clergy, stress counsellors, doctors, addiction therapists and psychologists are all trained to help with problems that seem too big to handle alone.

For many of the mental illnesses discussed in this section, a single approach may not be sufficient, and what works for one person may not be effective for another. Various responses are often required, combining several approaches such as psychotherapy, behaviour therapy, support groups, medication and, sometimes, hospitalization. The following chart summarizes some of the options available for treating different psychological problems and disorders.

behaviour therapy—the treatment of inappropriate or distressing behaviour patterns through the use of basic learning principles

Figure 5–11
A variety of techniques have been developed to help people better understand their psychological problems. Psychologists try to use one or more of these techniques to treat the individual patient and problem.

Treatment options for mental disorders

Disorders	Treatments
Anxiety	Psychotherapy Behaviour therapy Anti-anxiety drugs
Mood disorders	Counselling Psychotherapy Anti-depressant drugs
Personality disorders	Drugs Hospitalization
Schizophrenia	Drugs Psychotherapy Hospitalization
Substance abuse or dependence	Counselling Behaviour therapy Self-help groups (e.g., Alcoholics Anonymous)

Activities

Understand Ideas

1. a) Describe the symptoms of different types of schizophrenia.

b) Recent research is focusing on determining the cause of schizophrenia. Which side of the nature-nurture debate does this research support? Explain your answer.

2. a) What are the symptoms of the psychopathic personality?

b) What possible causes, if any, have been identified?

3. Under what conditions is substance use considered to be a dependency?

Think and Evaluate

4. Review the case study on page 106. How serious do you think Roberta's personality disorder is? Do you believe that her symptoms could pose a threat to others? Why or why not?

5. a) Among the reasons given for substance abuse, which reason do you think is most compelling? Why?

b) Could all of these reasons apply to one person? Explain why or why not.

Apply Your Learning

6. What psychological disorders seem to apply to each of the following cases?

- Sergei was recently very depressed. Now he feels on top of the world. He has a plan for putting his high school on nationwide television.
- When Jasmine wakes up in the morning, she feels so panicky that she can feel her heart racing and her palms sweating.

- Alfredo is too young to drink so he pays older students to buy him a case of beer whenever he can afford one. He has spent all of the money he made from his part-time job in this way. Recently he lost his job because he was making too many mistakes.
- Pierre cheats on his exams and never feels guilty. Stealing money from his mother's purse is beginning to feel like a game; next time he'll blame it on his sister.
- Matthew always feels frightened in a crowd, but he doesn't know why. He avoids crowds whenever he can; if he finds himself surrounded by too many people, he panics and leaves as quickly as possible.
- Rajinder sometimes hears soft voices and isn't sure if they are real or not. Once she saw the kitchen table run away on its legs.
- Kathryn owned a restaurant. She bought all of her supplies on credit and never bothered to pay her bills. When the bills began to add up, Kathryn declared bankruptcy. She moved to another town and bought a house with the money she had saved. She doesn't feel guilty about the people she cheated, and if she wants to, she will do it again.

Research and Communicate

7. a) Research one type of substance-related disorder. Is this disorder an abuse or a dependence? Explain your answer.

b) In a written report, evaluate the negative effects of this disorder in terms of emotional, social and physical well-being. Be sure to describe the research methods you used. (See Skill Focus, page 73; and Skill Focus, page 97.)

Key Points

- Mental health is not always the same thing as conforming to society expectations. Sometimes, it is healthier to go against the behaviour of the majority.

- Stress is a natural human response to both positive and negative events or situations.

- Handling stress involves altering one's response to it, rather than eliminating it altogether.

- Mental illness is defined as behaviour that causes the individual pain, interferes with normal functioning or is a danger to others.

- The most common categories of mental illness are anxiety disorders, mood disorders, schizophrenia, personality disorders and substance-related disorders.

Activities

Understand Ideas

1. **a)** Create a timeline that illustrates the history of how mental illness has been viewed and treated. Be sure to include dates, names and details on your timeline.
   b) What is your prediction regarding the direction of treatment in the future?

2. What role does the nature-nurture debate play in the diagnosis and treatment of the disorders discussed in this chapter? Provide examples to illustrate your points.

Think and Evaluate

3. Create a chart to analyze the following reactions to stress. Indicate positive and negative aspects of each.
   - ignore the problem
   - leave the situation
   - exercise

- talk to a trusted friend
- use alcohol or drugs
- spend time at a hobby
- eat
- react with anger or violence
- make a conscious effort to relax
- understand your strengths and limitations
- organize and plan your life
- get enough sleep and rest
- take one thing at a time

4. What is the difference between an annoying habit and an obsessive-compulsive act?

5. **a)** Identify at least one of your fears. Is this fear "just a fear," or is it a phobia?
   b) What strategies or solutions could you try to help you deal with this fear or phobia?

Apply Your Learning

6. What was your score on the questionnaire, How Vulnerable Are You to Stress (page 93)? If your score was below 25, describe what you do to manage your stress so effectively. If your score was above 25, explain the causes of your stress and how you might reduce your vulnerability to stress in the future. Use your chart from Activity 3 as a guide.

Research and Communicate

7. Select one psychological disorder that interests you the most. Prepare a research report describing the symptoms, causes and treatment options for this disorder. How have your findings influenced your views regarding the nature-nurture debate? (See Skill Focus, page 97.)

8. Arrange for one of the following to visit your class: a therapist, a psychologist or a representative of Alcoholics Anonymous or Narcotics Anonymous. Prepare questions ahead of time to find out more about getting help for mental disorders. (See Skill Focus, page 24.)

Sociology, Socialization and Personality

As members of society, we are always interacting with the world around us. Throughout our lives we learn from others, developing as individuals and as part of a group. Start thinking about your own social development. How did you acquire the knowledge and the skills listed below? Were you taught by one particular person or by several? Were you taught in a formal way, through lessons, or in a less structured manner? Record your point-form answers in your notebook or on a sheet of paper.

- how to talk
- how to co-operate in games
- knowledge of current affairs
- how to read and write
- table manners and etiquette
- how to earn a living
- how to enjoy leisure time
- how to relate to a future mate

Discuss your responses as a class. What can you conclude about how we learn to function in society?

In This Chapter

- What are sociology and social psychology?
- How do societies shape the personal and social development of children?
- How does socialization occur?
- What is personality?
- How does personality development continue over a lifetime?
- How can we assess personality traits?

Key Terms

sociology

social psychology

socialization

isolates

agents of socialization

gender

personality

sense of self

cognitive development

social—living together in organized communities

Figure 6–1
The French sociologist Emile Durkheim maintained that people are a product of their social environment and that behaviour cannot be understood completely in terms of individual biological characteristics.

cult—a religious organization that tends to worship its leader and remains outside the cultural traditions of society

ritual—involving acts required in religious observance

social classes—groups of people who are ranked according to certain economic, social or cultural characteristics

The Scope of Sociology

There are two social sciences that focus on human behaviour in a broad, social context. **Sociology,** as we learned in Chapter 1, is the scientific study of people in groups—the relationships between people and the social structures they develop. **Social psychology,** on the other hand, is the study of individuals within their social and cultural setting. The social psychologist examines how society influences human mental processes and how it contributes to the development of individual behaviours and personalities. In this chapter, we will look at how sociology and social psychology account for the way humans develop as social beings.

The goal of sociology is to understand and explain patterns of social behaviour—how people interact. Why, for example, would someone give presents on certain occasions, shake hands with new acquaintances or give up a seat to an elderly man on a bus? Sociologists study small groups such as two people meeting on a street corner, or larger groups such as families, communities or nations. They also examine social issues such as aging, poverty, crime and mental illness.

Approaches to Sociology

As with other social sciences, sociology can be approached from different points of view. **Structural functionalism** takes the view that various segments of a society serve a purpose for the society as a whole. Like the organs of the body, each segment has necessary work to do. For example, the family has the task of raising children and providing emotional bonds; the school has the function of teaching children important knowledge and skills. Structural functionalists believe that social problems are temporary, like an illness that can be cured, and that the functions of social groups and institutions will improve over time.

One important figure who based his work on this approach was Emile Durkheim (1858–1917), an early French sociologist who is considered to be one of the founders of modern sociology. Durkheim believed that individuals identify with society as a whole and see themselves as part of the larger picture. For example, when studying the nature of suicide, he argued that strong social ties tend to reduce the likelihood of suicide. On the other hand, excessive social ties, especially to cults with distorted values, can sometimes lead to ritual or mass suicides.

Conflict theory expresses the view that power, not function, holds a society together. Society is seen as groups of people acting in competition. This competition, or conflict, may erupt to bring about change, which sometimes leads to progress or improvement. In conflict theory, one important area of research is the study of social classes and their problems and demands. Karl Marx (1818–1883), the leading conflict sociologist of the nineteenth century, studied class conflicts throughout history. Due to his influence, conflict theory continues to be a major approach to analyzing society.

Symbolic interactionism focuses on how individuals learn about their culture—how they subjectively interpret, then act upon, their social worlds. In this view, people are internally motivated by what they have learned, not externally motivated by social or economic conditions, as the conflict theorists maintain. The early German sociologist Max Weber (1864–1920) believed that sociologists must put themselves in the place of the people they are studying in order to understand how they think and why they act as they do.

Feminist sociology focuses on women and gender inequality in society. This view of sociology emphasizes a better understanding of the social roles of men and women in different cultures. It strives to raise awareness and to bring about change, both socially and politically. Feminist sociology has brought to our attention important concerns such as discrimination, spousal violence, date rape and stalking. This point of view accepts a cross-disciplinary approach that draws on knowledge from many fields such as history, economics, psychology and anthropology. Dorothy Smith, for example, is a well-known Canadian sociologist whose work is rooted in the actual experiences of women.

> **subjectively interpret**—explain meaning based on personal experience or views

> **stalking**—following and harassing with obsessive, unwanted attention

Sociological Research and Ethics

Sociologists follow the inquiry model and use all of the research methods outlined in Chapter 1, depending on the nature of their inquiry. When deciding which method is most appropriate, they consider the following questions:

- Who can provide the information? How many people will that involve?

- What kind of information is needed—detailed information about a situation or answers to specific questions? Are there relationships or variables between things or ideas that need to be determined?

- How much certainty or reliability is needed? For example, is statistical or descriptive information needed?

- How much research time is required? Does the study require observation over time to note change, or will one set of observations be enough?

- Is one case sufficient or is it better to sample a variety of situations?

Like other social scientists, sociologists work with people. As we discovered in Chapter 3, the American Psychological Association provides a Code of Ethics as a guide for research purposes. Similarly, the American Sociological Association (ASA) has also issued a Code of Ethics for sociologists to follow:

"So, you're a *real* gorilla, are you? Well, guess you wouldn't mind munchin' down a few beetle grubs, would you? ... In fact, we wanna see you chug 'em!"

Figure 6–2

Which research method is being used here? Do you think it is appropriate? Can you suggest other research methods that might work just as well?

Connections

What are the similarities between the ASA Code of Ethics and the APA Code of Ethics? (See Chapter 3, page 45.)

- Researchers should be objective and honest.

- Researchers should respect the privacy and dignity of their subjects.

- Research subjects must be protected from personal harm.

- Researchers should respect the confidentiality of the subject.

- Researchers should disclose sources of financial support.

- Researchers should not misuse their role as researcher.

In addition, federal legislation requires researchers to obtain informed consent in order to use their subjects' thoughts, feelings or actions in a research project. Subjects should know the purpose of the study and the consequences that might affect their consent. With these ethical considerations in mind, examine the following case study.

CASE STUDY

1. What was the purpose of Whyte's research?

2. Why did Whyte use an "informant"?

3. Was this research ethical?

informant—a confidential source of information

stereotypes—perceptions based on preconceived, standardized ideas

Street Corner Research

In the late 1930s, William Foote Whyte became curious about the lives of young men who lived in a poor district of Boston. He tried approaching them directly and striking up a conversation but found that they were immediately suspicious of him. He befriended "Doc," a young man in the neighbourhood, and explained his problem. Doc decided to help him by gradually easing him into a circle of young men who hung around the local pool hall. Doc gave Whyte tips on how to approach the men, on what to say and what not to say. Doc was Whyte's "key informant."

Whyte's research resulted in a classic work, *Street Corner Society*. It dispelled many stereotypes that Bostonians had of these young men. Whyte found that the members of this community were often hard-working immigrants of the first and second generation. Many achieved considerable success and sent their children to college. Whyte himself married one of the young women from that neighbourhood.

Activities

Understand Ideas

1. What is the difference between sociology and social psychology?

2. Following the guidelines in the Skill Focus on page 115, write a paragraph identifying the four approaches to sociology. In your paragraph, briefly note the characteristics of each.

Think and Evaluate

3. Which approach to sociology would be most concerned with each of the following issues? Provide reasons for your choice.
   - What major goals should schools have?
   - Why do we need nursery schools?
   - How can we provide a better standard of living for the working poor?

Writing a Paragraph

A paragraph is a cluster of sentences that have a reason for being together. While a sentence expresses a single idea, a paragraph expands on the idea to illustrate, develop or prove it. The ability to write a good paragraph is essential for doing any extended writing, such as a letter, essay or research report.

Here's How

1. Plan your paragraph as you would any other writing task.

2. State the main idea of your paragraph in the opening sentence, which is known as the topic sentence.

3. Provide details in the remainder of the paragraph to support the main idea. You could write several sentences that include arguments, explanations, facts, statistics or examples that clearly relate to what you are trying to show.

4. Write a concluding sentence that sums up your ideas.

Practise It

Arrange the following sentences into a proper paragraph, following the guidelines above.

- Why has the divorce rate changed? What factors govern individual and group behaviour? These are the kinds of questions that researchers from both social sciences ask.
- Both sociologists and social psychologists seek to understand what happens in societies and why it happens.
- Although their research may involve the same topics, the subject is looked at from slightly different points of view.
- Why, for example, do people offer a toast at the beginning of a meal, shake hands with new acquaintances or teach children to say "please" and "thank you"?

- How do people view their work and their workplace?
- Why do women continue to make less money than men for equal work?

4. Which sociological approach do you believe is the most appropriate for examining society in the twenty-first century? Make specific reference to the four views described in the text.

Apply Your Learning

5. **a)** Review and list the steps of the inquiry model and the research methods described in Chapter 1.

   b) Decide which method of gathering data would be most appropriate for each of the following sociological questions:
   - How do nursery-school teachers plan the day for small children?

- What views do most parents have of how to raise children?
- What challenges in life are most important at different ages?
- What personality traits are most admired? For example, what traits do people admire in a public figure? What traits do they want to see in a friend?

6. **a)** Using the ASA's Code of Ethics, examine the case study entitled Street Corner Research. Was Whyte's research ethical? Write a paragraph explaining your views, making specific reference to the Code of Ethics.

   b) As a class, debate this statement: It is practically impossible for the ASA to enforce its Code of Ethics.

What Is Socialization?

All human beings grow up in a social environment. Through social contact, individuals learn to think and act in certain ways. Sociologists call this type of learning **socialization.** Socialization allows new members to learn the accepted ways of behaving within a specific culture.

Sociology and the Nature-Nurture Debate

In sociology, as in anthropology and psychology, there is a debate as to how much of an individual's development and behaviour are products of nature (heredity) or nurture (socialization and environment). Some social scientists maintain that much evidence can be found in the study of identical twins to support the view that human development relies heavily on nature. The Minnesota Center for Adoption and Twin Research studies twins who have been raised apart. If nurture is more influential than nature, then these twins should be significantly different in personal traits, behaviours and abilities. What does the case study below suggest?

Figure 6–3

Identical twins Henrik (left) and Daniel Sedin from Sweden were among first picks in an NHL entry draft. Is it possible to tell whether their talent in hockey comes from nature or nurture?

CASE STUDY

1. In spite of separation, what similarities were shared by each set of twins?

2. Based on this study, what conclusions can you draw about nature versus nurture?

The Eerie World of Reunited Twins

Jerry Levey was uncomfortable. The New Jersey volunteer fire captain was ending a weekend at a local firefighters' convention. From across the room, however, a conventioneer was staring at him curiously. Finally the man approached him. "He told me his name was Jim Tedesco," Levey recalls, "and then he asked me if I had a twin brother." Levey assured him he did not, but Tedesco persisted. There was a man in Paramus, he explained—another fire captain, it so happened, who could be Levey's double. Levey laughed it off. If he had a twin he'd certainly know it.

Tedesco wasn't swayed. Later he phoned Levey with more information: his Paramus friend was born on April 15, 1954. Was there anything special about that date? "I nearly dropped the phone," Levey recalls. "That's my birthday." Tedesco arranged for the two men to meet. When his mysterious friend entered Levey's firehouse, Levey went silent with wonder. "I was looking in the mirror," he says. "We had the same mustache, same sideburns, even the same glasses." For a long moment the Paramus twin stared back at him. Suddenly the fire chiefs whooped in concert.

Each man already knew his biological parents had put him up for adoption, but neither had ever suspected that a sibling had been given up at the same time. The brothers discovered that they had more than looks and work in common. Both were bachelors, compulsive flirts and raucously good-humoured. "We kept making the same remarks at the same time and using the same gestures," says Jerry. "It was spooky."

raucously—loudly; in a rowdy way

Also fascinating were Daphne and Barbara, a bubbly pair of Finnish twins. Despite growing up in opposite socioeconomic circumstances, they were both penny-pinchers. And both were stingy not just with their money, but also with their opinions, refusing to take stands on even the most innocuous issues. Both had suffered miscarriages during their first marriage but went on to have three healthy children. The women also shared a fear of heights. Shortly after meeting for the first time, they began finishing each other's sentences and answering questions in unison.

innocuous—harmless

The Minnesota study is yielding a wealth of data on the heritability of characteristics for the population at large. Researchers suggest that such problems as antisocial leanings, depression and alcoholism might involve genes.

From "The Eerie World of Reunited Twins" by Clare Mead Rosen

As these studies show, separated twins who are genetically identical display many remarkable similarities that go far beyond physical traits. However, they also show differences in areas such as attitudes and values. These differences provide support for the importance of environment and socialization in addition to inherited characteristics. Further evidence regarding the impact of social learning on individual development can be found by looking at what happens when socialization does not occur. Examples include children who have lived the first years of their lives locked in basements or attics with little human contact. These children, called **isolates,** have been physically, socially and emotionally deprived. Researchers have found that they have severe developmental problems.

deprived—neglected; denied basic care

Isolated Children

Anna: Soon after birth, Anna was taken to a children's home and was looked after by a nurse. Everyone who cared for her then said that she seemed quite normal. Before her first birthday, however, she was returned to her mother's home where she was kept locked in a room with little human contact for five years. Anna spent her time slouched over in a

1. In what ways were Anna and Genie deprived?

2. What were the results of this deprivation?

broken chair. She was fed only milk. No one bothered to train her in any way, to bathe or hold her. Shortly before Anna's sixth birthday, she was found and taken to a group home.

atrophied—wasted away through lack of nourishment or lack of use

Anna had been still for so long that her muscles had atrophied. Her feet fell forward so that her legs and feet were in a straight line. She neither smiled nor cried but made only a slight sucking sound. Occasionally she frowned for no apparent reason. She responded so little to her surroundings that, at first, researchers thought she was unable to hear and see.

Over a period of about five years, Anna learned to walk well and to dress herself. She could not fasten buttons and never managed a knife and fork. She learned to talk at the level of a two-year-old. No one knows how far she would have progressed because she died of a blood disease when she was 10 years old.

Genie: Genie was found in California during the early 1970s at the age of 14. She had been tied to a chair, beaten and never spoken to for almost seven years. From the time Genie was found, people tried to teach her to communicate. She learned to put words together in ways similar to a young child. For example, she might say "Another house have dog." But she never became fluent and could not use proper grammar or make complex sentences.

Fortunately, such cases are rare, but they do teach us what can happen when a child is isolated and deprived of opportunities for normal growth. We can see that adequate socialization at a young age is essential for full development—physically, emotionally, psychologically and socially.

Activities

Think and Evaluate

1. Referring to The Eerie World of Reunited Twins (page 116), use the questions below to analyze information on twin research:
   a) What evidence is there that identical twins share certain inherited personality traits?
   b) What evidence is there that identical twins do not share certain inherited personality traits?
   c) How was this evidence collected?
   d) What further evidence would you like that the case study did not provide?
   e) How does the study of identical twins contribute to our understanding of the nature-nurture debate?

2. Referring to the case study above, Isolated Children, use the following questions to analyze information on isolates:

   a) Identify at least three components necessary for normal development.
   b) What evidence is there that human contact and socialization are essential for normal development?
   c) How does the study of isolated children contribute to our understanding of the nature-nurture debate?

Apply Your Learning

3. a) Write a list of five characteristics or abilities you believe you possess.
   b) Decide which of these characteristics or abilities you share with other members of your family.
   c) What conclusions can you draw? Share your findings with a partner.

Agents of Socialization

Focus Questions

What the are the main agents of socialization?

What are the causes and effects of child abuse?

How does gender affect socialization?

How do agents interact in the process of socialization?

Socialization takes place through interaction with others. The types of social contacts or influences we experience are called **agents of socialization.** At various stages of life different agents will exert their influence in varying degrees. In the first few years, the family will be the chief agent of socialization, while peers will have less importance. During adolescence, peer groups, school, culture and media will play increasing roles as socializing agents. Later in life, clubs, social or political groups, religious institutions and workplaces become other agents of socialization. Organizations such as the Children's Aid Society, women's shelters, and family and cultural centres also play a role. Of course, it is possible that all of these agents will pull an individual in different directions. For example, school curriculum, peer influence and parental ideas may conflict. In complex societies that offer divergent priorities and values, people must eventually choose from many opposing options.

The Family

The first and most significant socializing agent is usually the family. This is known as the primary agent of socialization. Strong emotional relationships within this small group of people have an enormous impact on the developing infant. Family members are highly motivated to encourage the infant to progress to his or her fullest potential. As we saw in the case study on isolated children, these relationships are important to the child's development. Love, concern and attention in the early years can affect a child's entire life.

The family socializes children in both intentional and unintentional ways. Children learn to think, talk, walk, play and feed themselves under the watchful eyes of parents and siblings. They usually learn basic values by being told what is right or wrong. Family members encourage or scold children in a conscious effort to shape behaviour. But children also learn

Adam @ home

Figure 6–4

Families socialize children in intentional and unintentional ways.

unintentionally. They observe how family members react to situations and to each other. From viewing those around them, they pick up ideas about themselves and others and about basic values, attitudes and expectations. Sometimes, to the embarrassment of the parents, the actions and words of young children reveal that they have actually learned things that were not intended. As we saw in Chapter 3, observational learning is very powerful—every action taken and every word spoken in the presence of a child provides an example or role model for future behaviour.

Child Abuse

The family is not always an effective socializing agent. Although most parents raise their children with care, patience and love, some are unprepared or unwilling to take on the task of parenthood and may neglect or abuse their children. Neglect is the failure to provide the physical or emotional necessities of life, as in the case of isolates described in the previous section. Abuse takes several forms. Physical abuse involves assault or inflicting physical harm; emotional abuse may include repeatedly criticizing the child or subjecting the child to an unhappy or disturbing environment. Sexual abuse occurs when an adult, sibling or peer touches a child sexually or inappropriately.

Neglect and abuse have become significant problems in our society and can have serious immediate and long-term effects. Each year more children die of beatings at the hands of their parents than as a result of any major childhood disease. What kinds of people batter their children? Contrary to popular opinion, child abusers come from all socioeconomic backgrounds. Most abusers are not otherwise abnormal—only a very small number are mentally ill; however, they often have serious emotional and social problems.

What causes people to abuse their children? Frustrated by their jobs or by not being able to find work, parents sometimes lash out. Some parents, cooped up day after day with their children, may become emotionally worn down, unable to control their tempers. Although all parents feel frustration and anger at times, the minority who cannot control their emotions become abusers. Often abusive parents were abused themselves as children. In some cases, child beating can be traced back more than three generations. This recurring pattern of abuse is known as the "cycle of violence." Abusive parents may unconsciously repeat experiences from their own upbringing, or they may actually believe that this is the right way to raise children because it was how they were raised. Other battering parents have unrealistic ideas of what their children should be able to do, interpreting a child's inability to do something as a sign of deliberate disobedience. Some babies have been beaten for wetting the bed.

How can we deal with child abuse, especially when it occurs so often in the privacy of a home? Health-care workers and teachers who suspect a child is being abused are required by law to report their suspicions. Depending on the type of abuse and the willingness of the parent to

Connections

How do Albert Bandura's studies on imitating violent behaviour add to our understanding of the "cycle of violence"? (See Chapter 3, pages 56–57.)

accept counselling, the child may be removed from the home and placed with a foster family, temporarily or permanently. With professional help, child-batterers who want to change can learn to alter their behaviour.

The Peer Group

By the age of two or three, children come into contact with their peers—others of the same age. Now they are exposed to a new world of personality types, behaviours and attitudes. The peer group begins to act as an agent of socialization in the backyard sandbox with neighbourhood friends, but it later expands in kindergarten and primary school. From these early contacts, children begin to gain an awareness of how they appear to other people. What parents may have accepted as "cute" or even unpleasant behaviour, the peer group is less likely to put up with. These new expectations place pressure on young children to conform to the peer group; children who do not conform are often ignored, or they frequently quarrel with their friends and classmates.

During adolescence, peer-group influence grows in importance. Sociologist David Reisman and anthropologist Margaret Mead suggested that in a rapidly changing society such as ours, children tend to learn more from their peers. In societies where change is slower, however, children are more likely to accept the wisdom passed on by an older generation. For example, think of computer technology. Often young people have more knowledge and skills than the previous generation. On the other hand, children continue to learn basic values from people of all ages, especially those with more life skills and experience.

Of course, as adults we tend to actively choose our peer groups since we are no longer restricted by chance or location. We join groups with people who have similar interests and work in areas with like-minded people. The influence of peers continues throughout life.

Figure 6–5

How will peers act as an agent of socialization at each of these stages of life?

Who Is Responsible for Socializing Children?

Traditionally, the family has been the primary agent of socialization for children. But in today's fast-paced world of marriage break-down, financial pressures and modern life, families appear to be less able to successfully perform this function.

Forget why Johnnie can't read. The new crisis facing Ontario's schools is that Johnnie can't behave. In grade schools across the province, behaviour has spun out of control. Rookie teachers stand stunned as eight-year-olds swear in their faces, throw desks, kick books and stab each other with pens.

In a month when knives and guns have been brandished in some Ontario schools, teachers say the root of such violence is showing up more and more among young children—yet the teachers feel frighteningly ill-trained to handle it. A growing number of teachers and principals say they spend up to 40 percent of their day simply breaking up fights, calming kids down and trying to restore enough order to get on with the class.

But their behaviour is a symptom of a deeper crisis, teachers warn. These children are not evil; they are troubled. They are, say experts, prisoners of war—the war within modern marriage, the war families wage against mounting financial pressure, the war seen in the violence of television, the war of the rush of modern life. Some are emotionally disturbed, yet face as long as a one-year wait for psychiatric treatment in Ontario's overbooked mental health centres. But while they wait for professional help, they must stay in school because of their ages. Other kids don't even make the waiting lists because their parents won't admit they need help.

But the majority, teachers feel, simply lack the social skills to act properly with other people. Either such skills are not used at home, or some other trauma is upsetting the child, from poverty to violence, from sexual abuse to divorce, from a parent being fired to a parent sent to jail, from poor parents too tired to spend time with their kids to rich parents too tired to spend time with their kids.

One principal agrees that some of the behaviour problems are caused by children whose greatest need is for more care and attention, not cash. "It's been said that workaholism is the toughest addiction on kids. When the workaholic is around, it's usually quite magical, because they're over-achievers and try hard to be good parents—but because they're workaholics, they're often not around and the kid is left hanging," he says. "What's amazing is, the public has not connected what's going on at home with school performance. If violence happens in a family once a week, the family's on eggshells the rest of the time—and what happens to that kid's learning? Or you try to teach the children of an alcoholic, and they may be too flaky to calm down."

From "Bad Behaviour Creating Crisis in Schools" by Louise Brown

What Do You Think?

1. According to this article, how are families failing in their role of socializing children?

2. Do you think that other agents of socialization such as schools, family centres and Children's Aid Societies should pick up the slack?

3. Do you agree that families today are not successful in socializing their children?

The School

The school enters a child's life as an agent of socialization around the age of four or five and remains an important influence for the next 12 to 20 years. Its stated social goal is to socialize children in the knowledge, skills and attitudes necessary to help them function as adults in society. Before industrialization, children learned most of what they needed to know from family and peers. By the early twentieth century, most children were going to grade school to learn the three "R"s of reading, writing and arithmetic, but not much more. Today, formal education can extend well into adulthood; many people go back to school to continue their education, to learn essential job skills or to train for a new profession.

The formal curriculum of schools teaches the technical and cultural heritage of society and helps prepare students for careers. The informal, or "hidden," curriculum teaches attitudes and habits such as organization, reliability, promptness, co-operation and respect for authority. The school also provides a place where students meet and mingle with their peers in age-graded situations, offering opportunities for peer socialization.

Culture

Each human being grows up in a unique environment; therefore, to some extent, socialization on an individual basis will differ. But in a broader context, socialization will also vary between one culture and another.

Does Culture Influence Socialization?

Why do some adolescents turn to alcoholism, drug use and crime while others do not? The difference may be in how they are socialized. According to psychologist Bruno Bettelheim, children learn best from the example of their parents.

Swedish researchers compared the home life of law-abiding and delinquent teenagers. They found the major difference was the emotional atmosphere. Teenagers who behaved well tended to have parents who lived according to their stated values and encouraged their children to do the same. The parents of problem teenagers had conflicting values or were inconsistent in putting their values into practice. They often tried to make their children live by rules they themselves did not follow.

In another study, researchers compared Japanese and American child rearing and saw important differences. When American children ran around in supermarkets, their parents usually told them to stop, or said: "I told you not to do that!" Japanese parents usually did not tell their children what to do. Instead they asked them: "How do you think the storekeeper feels when you run around like this?" Bruno Bettelheim uses this example to illustrate how Japanese parents encouraged their children to think for themselves and to act accordingly. Such parenting, he says,

Figure 6–6

In some parts of the world it is usual for siblings to play an important role in rearing children while parents are at work. What difference do you think this might make to the socialization of children?

CASE STUDY

1. According to Bettelheim, how do children learn best?

2. In this case study, what are the cultural differences between American and Japanese parenting?

3. What does Bettelheim believe about successful parents?

enhances a child's self-respect, while to be ordered to do something diminishes self-respect. Bettleheim concludes that successful parents show their children how deeply they are loved and let their children know when they are disappointed in them, without being critical or punitive.

Sex and Gender

One important aspect of culture is the perception of gender roles. Sociologists distinguish between the terms *sex* and *gender*. The sex of an individual, whether biologically male or female, is determined at conception. Gender, on the other hand, is learned from birth and throughout life. **Gender** includes the social roles and psychological characteristics that a society recognizes as appropriate for a man or a woman; these attributes are the result of socialization rather than biology. During various stages of a person's life, other agents of socialization reinforce the cultural definitions of what is "feminine" and what is "masculine."

Gender socialization begins early. One study asked parents to describe their babies, who were only 24 hours old. Parents described baby girls as softer, finer featured, less alert, weaker and more delicate. They described baby boys as firmer, larger featured, better coordinated, more alert, stronger and hardier. None of the psychologists or medical personnel could see any of these differences between the boys and the girls.

As children grow, parents and family life continue to be important in gender socialization. For example, in a study of assigned household tasks, a clear division of labour was found. The boys were usually asked to mow the lawn, shovel snow, take out the garbage and do yard work. Girls were expected to clean the house, wash dishes, cook and babysit.

Research indicates that teachers, too, interact differently with boys and girls. The differences result in greater feelings of control among boys and more feelings of helplessness among girls. Boys often have higher expectations of success at the beginning of a school year, even when the girls performed better the year before. Girls and boys gradually begin to select

Connections

What did anthropologist Margaret Mead discover about gender socialization? (See Chapter 2, pages 26–27.)

Figure 6–7

Although most girls and boys continue to be socialized in traditional ways, many more women in modern society are fulfilling roles previously thought to be appropriate only for men.

Organizing Ideas with Concept Maps

Concept maps are diagrams that can assist you in identifying ideas and detecting relationships among them. Psychologists maintain that because concept maps are so visual, they tap into the way the mind actually represents ideas. For these reasons, they are useful tools that can help you understand a topic, review for a test or organize your ideas for a paper or presentation.

Here's How

1. Write the topic or major idea in the centre of a page. Circle it.

2. Ask yourself what other ideas come to mind that are related to the topic. Write each of these ideas around the main topic. Circle them and connect them with lines to the central idea.

3. You may want to write a brief explanation on these lines explaining the connection between the related ideas and the main topic.

4. Examine the related ideas to see if any independent relationships exist among them. If

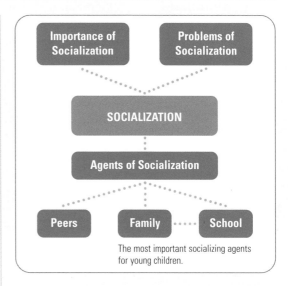

The most important socializing agents for young children.

there are any relationships, draw a line between those ideas.

Practise It

Using the model above, make your own concept map of socialization. Add other ideas and brief details for each of the ideas shown in the model.

subjects on the basis of gender role, encouraged by teachers and other authority figures in the school. A traditional curriculum will often reinforce this tendency, with boys taking woodworking and auto mechanics and girls taking classes in nutrition and sewing. These and other socialization practices result in the streaming of males and females into traditional careers.

An interview study of 150 Canadian teenagers found that girls were likely to choose traditional feminine occupations and to be less confident in their chances of success. The girls also saw women as primarily responsible for home and child care, and tended to choose work that would fit in with these duties. However, as society changes, gender socialization changes as well. In recent years, increasing numbers of women have joined the workforce in roles previously considered suitable for men. Sometimes, however, attitudes and socialization are slow to accept new conditions.

The Media

In our society, mass media shape behaviour and attitudes. Through television, radio, newspapers, magazines, CD-ROMs and the Internet, young people are bombarded with images of how to think and behave. Since communication has a wide impact on most members of a society, it is a powerful agent of socialization. Moreover, the media often present information as absolute and unquestionable, especially in matters of values, taste and culture. Such messages are difficult to view critically. Although some images of acceptable lifestyles represent stereotypes, they can still have the power to shape the opinions of a receptive audience.

Activities

Understand Ideas

1. **a)** Identify as many agents of socialization as you can.
   b) Return to the list of skills and knowledge on the first page of this chapter. Which agent of socialization was most influential in each case?

2. Make a concept map to organize the information on child abuse (see pages 120–121). Include the following topics: Nature of the Problem, Causes, Consequences and Dealing with the Problem.

Think and Evaluate

3. Identify the types of socialization causing problems for Shenaz, Paul and Lynette. How would you deal with each of these situations? Give reasons for your course of action.
   - Shenaz is at pre-school. She doesn't like it when people get on the adventure playground in front of her. Yesterday, she bit the child climbing up the ladder ahead of her.
   - Last year, 17-year-old Paul and his girlfriend had a baby. Paul takes care of the baby when he is not at school or working part-time. He gets frustrated when the baby cries. Last week, he spanked the baby for having a wet diaper.
   - Lynette is 16 years old. She is the eldest in her family. Last year, her parents divorced. She, her mother and two brothers moved to low-income housing. Lynette is doing well in school, but she wants to quit and get a job to make things easier for her brothers and mother. Her mother is encouraging her to finish her education.

4. Do you think Japanese methods of discipline are more effective than North American methods? Make specific references to Bettelheim's example in the case study on pages 123–124.

Research and Communicate

5. **a)** Review the guidelines in Chapter 1 for Conducting Observation Research (page 13) and Analyzing Data (pages 14–16).
   b) Prepare a checklist to help you observe several television shows. Complete a content analysis of how children are treated on shows such as situation comedies or children's programs. Do you see gender stereotyping? Draw conclusions from your observations.

6. **a)** Review two other sets of guidelines in Chapter 1: Conducting an Interview (page 12) and Conducting a Sample Survey (page 11).
   b) Conduct an interview or distribute a questionnaire to determine which of the following strategies parents use to discipline children. What reasons do parents give for choosing one method over another?
   - explaining
   - physical punishment
   - ignoring behaviour
   - smiles
   - verbal anger
   - withdrawing privileges
   - frowns
   - rewards
   - some other method

c) What discipline strategies would you use to encourage positive socialization in your children?

7. a) Review the Skill Focus in Chapter 4 entitled Gathering and Recording Information (page 73). Now consult your concept map in Activity 2.

b) Research the literature for articles that contain examples of child abuse. Summarize the facts of each case. What course of action would you recommend in each situation: counselling the parent, removing the child from the home, or imprisoning the abuser? Defend your point of view in a written paper. Be sure to follow the guidelines you reviewed in Activity 7a.

Personality

Focus Questions

How is personality defined?

Which factors affect personality development?

What are Piaget's stages of cognitive development?

What are Erikson's psychosocial stages?

What is a healthy personality?

How do you assess your own personality?

Socialization is one of the factors that sociologists identify as contributing to **personality**—a usual way of thinking, feeling and acting that is unique to an individual. It is natural to be curious about what makes each person unique. Every day we meet many people, all with their own set of personality traits or characteristics. But social scientists, both sociologists and psychologists, go further in examining personality. They search for answers to the following questions: How are personalities formed? What kinds of personalities are there?

How Does Personality Develop?

The nature-nurture debate has influenced our understanding of how personality is formed. For example, you may wonder whether some of your personality traits are inherited. Perhaps you have a sensitive nature just like your father or a keen sense of adventure just like your grandmother. Although newborn babies do show varying reactions to situations, they are not born with their personalities already formed. The way babies are treated and the personalities of the people surrounding them shape their development. For instance, a baby who is more active and appears to demand attention may actually get more attention than a quieter baby. On the other hand, children of outgoing parents will have more social experiences than children of reserved parents and may develop accordingly.

Cultural attitudes will also influence personality development, encouraging some personality traits and discouraging others. Traditionally, for example, many Western cultures encouraged males to be more active and females to be more passive. As you saw in Chapter 2, anthropologist Margaret Mead found societies where the opposite was true. Today, men and women are both encouraged to express a wider range of personality traits.

Some people believe that the order of an individual's birth within a family may play a role in personality development. The first-born child is

Figure 6–8

It has become much more common in Western cultures for fathers to take on nurturing and home-making roles, while more women work outside the home. What differences will this role reversal make to the socialization of children?

usually considered "special" because he or she is first. Parents are able to give their full attention to raising this child until the next one is born. Those who agree with this theory maintain that being first allows the oldest siblings to experience a richer environment than younger siblings and leads to their ability to be more social and affectionate. First-born children tend to be higher achievers than their younger siblings. Youngest children are also given special attention by parents and older siblings. A childhood spent socializing with others allows later-born children to become more outgoing than first-born children. Middle children, in contrast, possess no special role within the family and are not singled out for any special treatment. As a result, some may have lower self-esteem.

Some theories about the development of personality are closely linked to theories of child development. Through a variety of processes including socialization, children learn to define themselves and those around them. Various psychologists have proposed different models of child development that contribute to the growth of personality and a **sense of self**—an awareness of what it is that makes each of us unique.

Sigmund Freud and Personality Development

As you saw in Chapter 4, Sigmund Freud believed that the main force behind personality development was the unconscious mind. It is through the process of socialization, however, that the ego and superego develop in order to control the basic drives and instincts of the id. Through interacting with others, especially family members, the child develops a balanced personality that satisfies needs and wants, judges and acts on what is right and makes decisions appropriate to both the self and the society.

Jean Piaget and Cognitive Development

Jean Piaget (1896–1980) was interested in how children develop the ability to learn. Piaget showed that **cognitive development**—how people learn and use knowledge—is influenced by both social and psychological factors. He maintained that there are definite stages of mental development that change with the age of the child. However, these stages are influenced by the social experiences of the child, which is why socialization is so important to mental development. Piaget identified four stages in the cognitive development of children:

1. **Sensorimotor stage:** occurs between birth and age two. Babies look, touch, taste and listen. They know the world, not through thought, but only by direct experience.

2. **Pre-operational stage:** occurs between age two and seven. Children can experience the world mentally by using forms of communication, such as speech and print. They can think about things they are not immediately experiencing. However, they continue to view the world from their own point of view and cannot see things from the point of view of others.

Connections

What type of learning would be most important in each of Piaget's stages of cognitive development? (See Chapter 3, pages 53–57.)

Figure 6–9
These photographs illustrate Piaget's four stages of development. Identify each stage.

3. **Concrete operational stage:** develops between the ages of seven and eleven. These children can do complex operations, such as arithmetic and measurements, as long as the physical objects are present. They learn to think in terms of cause and effect, and they can see things from the point of view of others.

4. **Formal operational stage:** begins to develop in adolescence. Adolescents can think abstractly—that is, manipulate ideas without physical objects being present. At this stage, they use logic to see what evidence is available to support different ideas. They can also imagine alternatives to reality—other possibilities in life.

In recent years, other researchers have claimed that Piaget's stages are not as rigid as he thought and can be achieved earlier through socialization at home and at school. Nevertheless, it was Piaget who introduced the idea that personality develops over time and that children can shape their own social world as they grow.

Charles Horton Cooley and the Looking-Glass Self
Sociologist Charles Horton Cooley (1864–1929) believed that our sense of self or identity is developed during a process very close to socialization.

He maintained that our sense of self was derived from others, a theory he explained by using the image of a looking glass. The reactions of others, he said, are like mirrors that show us who we are. We look to others to see the reflection of our psychological selves as we look in mirrors to see the reflection of our physical selves. First, we imagine how important people in our lives view us; then we react to this perception with feelings such as pride or embarrassment. As a result, we develop a set of beliefs about ourselves: we say we are smart, funny or clumsy. At first, our parents serve as the looking glass. With time, our circle of interaction expands, and other people also serve as mirrors, building and organizing our self-concept.

self-concept—self-awareness and self-image

George Herbert Mead and Role Taking

Like Cooley, George Herbert Mead (1863–1931) maintained that the self develops through social interaction with others. Mead described this process as three stages of role taking. In stage 1, the preparatory stage, children imitate the behaviour of people around them, such as parents or older brothers and sisters. In stage 2, the play stage, children act out the roles of adults, such as a doctor or teacher. Through this play, children begin to understand the responsibilities of others. In stage 3, the game stage, children play group games and discover the rules and roles within a team. They learn the expectations of the game and, over time, come to understand that there are expectations, rules and responsibilities for every role within society.

Erik Erikson and Lifelong Development

The development of the self does not end with childhood or adolescence; it is a lifelong process. According to developmental psychologist Erik Erikson, human psychological and personality growth do not end with physical maturity but continue throughout life. Erikson explains that in life there are several stages, which he calls "psychosocial stages" to indicate that they involve the interaction of the individual and the society. This interaction changes at each stage, involving different kinds of tasks or challenges, different types of significant social relationships and various possible outcomes. Success in meeting the major task at each given stage, says Erikson, allows the individual to proceed to the next one. Failure to meet the challenge in a positive way can prevent the individual from moving to the next stage. Erikson states that resolving the challenges at each stage leads to healthy personality development. (See Figure 6–10.)

psychosocial—both psychological and social

Personality Types and Traits

Because the mystery of personality has always fascinated us, it is one of the most studied of human qualities. As far back as the second century, the Greek physician Galen believed that people could be divided into four main personality types: melancholic (depressed, spiritless); choleric (irritable, violent); phlegmatic (calm, lazy); and sanguine (optimistic, cheerful, loving). Modern psychologist Hans Eysenck built on Galen's ideas by

Erikson's stages of development

Stage	Age	Challenge
Infancy and childhood	0 to 11 years	In the early years, relationships are usually with parents, family and nearby friends. The focus of these early years is to develop emotionally, socially, intellectually and physically so as to take one's place as an adult in society.
Adolescence	11 to 18	During this period, the young person strives to develop the concept of personal identity. Although this process may be painful and upsetting at times, it is necessary. Adolescents who develop a good self-image feel purposeful and competent. Those with a negative self-image feel unworthy and incompetent.
Early adulthood	18 to 25	At this stage, two concerns are most important: learning to form close, lasting relationships and commitment to a career choice. Both of these areas demand adjustment. People who achieve these goals can enjoy a close relationship and a satisfying career.
Middle adulthood	25 to 50	At this time, individuals develop a sense of being productive and accomplishing something worthwhile. Feelings of satisfaction may result from helping their children become adults or from making a social contribution. Feelings of regret may come from realizing that earlier goals have not been achieved. Later in this period, some people restructure their lives, sometimes branching out into new areas of endeavour.
Late adulthood	50 and over	In some societies, such as traditional China, this is a time for power and prestige. Elders are revered; their wisdom is respected. In industrial societies, the early years of this stage may bring power and prestige as people reach the top of their occupational ladders. In later years, people are often forced to retire. Although this stage can be a time of financial hardship and loneliness, many seniors live active and productive lives, pursuing projects they had no time for when they were younger.

Figure 6–10 ▲

Why did Erikson call these stages of development "psychosocial"?

medicine wheel—a circle of stones with additional stones positioned like the spokes of a wheel; used as a site for rituals and meditation

adding the dimensions of extroverted/introverted and stable/unstable. He used the diagram in Figure 6–11 on page 132 as a way to define personality traits. The medicine wheel of some Aboriginal traditions also divides humans into four aspects: emotional, mental, spiritual and physical.

This interest in personality continues even today as several recent models attempt to classify traits by describing various combinations of four or sometimes six personality types. Sociologists and psychologists all agree that in spite of quadrants and categories, individuals vary endlessly in the personality traits they possess. But humanist psychologist Carl Rogers took a slightly different approach by identifying the characteristics of what he called a healthy personality. Rogers found that people with healthy personalities tend to like themselves and make decisions based on what is right for them. In their relationships, they listen to others and try to understand and accept them. They trust their own experiences and are willing to accept both the good and bad aspects of their own personality. Healthy people are more concerned with self-evaluation than with how others judge them. They recognize that growth is a painful but necessary process because it allows them to express their own individual uniqueness.

Figure 6–11 ▷

List the characteristics you believe apply to yourself. In which quadrant do most of them fall? Now list the characteristics you think apply to a partner, someone you know reasonably well. Compare notes with your partner. How much does your perception of your own personality agree with your partner's? What conclusions can you draw?

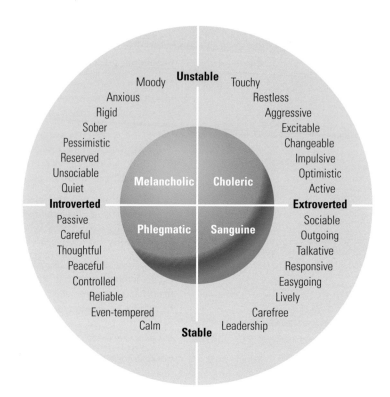

The psychologist Abraham Maslow identified personality traits of those he considered self-actualized—people who successfully meet their needs and fulfill their potential. These individuals

- see things as they are, not as they wish them to be
- accept themselves for what they are, even though they may have some regrets
- think and behave independently, although they are willing to conform in small matters
- have a task or mission in life rather than focus primarily on themselves
- stick with what they think is right rather than be swayed by others
- react with emotion to important life experiences
- have concern for and a sense of kinship with other human beings
- experience deep emotional ties with other people
- accept differences among people
- live according to definite moral or ethical standards
- have a sense of humour that is not unkind to others
- can see some of the faults or limitations of their own culture

Connections

What are the similarities between the indicators of mental health and what Maslow identified as the personality traits of self-actualized people? (See Chapter 5, page 91.)

Assess Your Own Personality

Carl Jung first developed the idea that personalities tend to be either extroverted or introverted. Jung defined extroverts as more interested in the world around them and in other people. He described introverts as more preoccupied with their own thoughts and feelings. Of course, the world needs all kinds of people—those who are extroverts, introverts or a combination of the two. Understanding our own personality traits gives us greater insight into ourselves, our relationships and the type of work and play we prefer.

Most people have a combination of these characteristics. How strong is each characteristic in your own personality? The following personality assessment will help you find out. Write the letter you choose for each answer in your notebook.

1. In group conversations
   a) I often take the lead.
   b) I would rather listen than talk.

2. Would you most like to spend an evening
   a) at a loud party with good company?
   b) at home reading or listening to music?

3. Others usually see me as
   a) active and lively.
   b) quiet and restrained.

4. Spending time by yourself is something you
   a) try to avoid.
   b) find enjoyable and refreshing.

5. When you make a phone call do you
   a) dial and say whatever comes to mind?
   b) rehearse what you will say?

6. At the end of a day dealing with lots of people, do you
   a) feel energized?
   b) need some quiet time?

7. When the phone rings at home, do you
   a) always answer it?
   b) sometimes don't answer if you don't feel like talking?

8. Do you come up with your best ideas
   a) in a group with other people?
   b) on your own?

9. I like to have
   a) many casual friends.
   b) a few close friends.

10. I would rather
   a) sell things to people.
   b) write a book.

11. Most of the time I would rather
   a) do things rather than talk about them.
   b) talk about ideas.

12. When in a crowd
   a) I feel energized.
   b) I would like to get away.

13. Most of the time
   a) I want to be the centre of attention.
   b) I enjoy working behind the scenes.

Total your **a**'s and **b**'s. Ten or more "**a**" responses mean that you tend to be an extrovert: You are happiest when you are with other people and you draw energy from being around them. Ten or more "**b**" responses mean that you tend to be an introvert: You are more comfortable when you are not in social situations and you feel that other people draw energy from you. If you scored about the same number of **a**'s and **b**'s, you probably experience a combination of both tendencies and feel comfortable when you are with people and when you are alone.

Does this self-test agree with your own self-assessment? Share your results with at least two other people. Do the results match how others see you? How valid do you think such self-tests may be?

Activities

Understand Ideas

1. Design a chart to summarize the ideas of Freud, Piaget, Cooley and Mead. In your chart, identify which ideas support the view that nature plays a role in child development and which support the view that nurture plays a role. Use the following headings: Psychologist, Key Ideas, Nature, Nurture.

2. Compare and contrast the way Galen and Eysenck analyzed personality.

3. How is Rogers' view of personality different from Cooley's?

4. **a)** Create a concept map illustrating Rogers' description of a healthy personality.
   b) What similarities do you notice between Rogers' and Maslow's views of healthy or self-actualized personalities? How do these views compare with Erikson's concept of a healthy personality?

Think and Evaluate

5. **a)** Draw a timeline illustrating Erikson's stages of development.
   b) What stages would you add, alter or delete? Make at least one change and explain your reasons.

6. What is your opinion of Cooley's looking-glass self? Support your answer by discussing what you see as the theory's strengths and weaknesses.

Apply Your Learning

7. According to Erikson, what psychosocial stage does each of the following statements describe?
   - On the celebration of her 93rd birthday, a woman makes a speech reviewing her long and successful life.
   - A university student is traumatized by the break-up of his first serious relationship.
   - A secondary student goes to the guidance office to sign up for the co-op program.
   - A baby crawls confidently across the floor to her father.
   - An elementary student wins an honourable mention at the science fair.

8. **a)** Evaluate your own personality using Rogers' or Maslow's criteria.
   b) In a paragraph, summarize your personality based on these criteria. Be sure to follow the guidelines for writing a paragraph in the Skill Focus on page 115.
   c) Compare this result to the conclusion you reached using Jung's method of self-assessment.

Research and Communicate

9. To what extent are Erikson's ideas valid for people in your community? Interview several people representing different age groups to determine their major problems, goals and concerns. Based on these interviews, how valid are Erikson's psychosocial stages?

10. Plan a visit to a day-care centre or a family with young children. Plan your observation strategy in advance. Report on how teachers or parents treat, socialize and teach these children and how they adapt activities to suit their various stages of development.

11. Develop a game or toy for a particular stage in Piaget's process of cognitive development. Give your rationale for why the game or toy is appropriate for this stage.

Key Points

- Sociology is the study of the relationships between people and the social structures they develop; social psychology examines how individual behaviours and personalities develop within a society or cultural setting.

- Socialization is the process whereby individuals learn certain behaviour patterns, skills, values and beliefs that are expected by a society.

- Most social scientists believe that both nature and nurture play a part in an individual's development.

- The damaging effects of social isolation prove the importance of social experience to normal human development.

- The main agents of socialization include family, peer groups, school, culture and mass media.

- Erik Erikson identified challenges that individuals characteristically face at each stage of life from childhood to old age.

- Socialization and other processes of self-development allow an individual to develop a personality—a pattern of feeling, thinking and acting that is unique to that individual.

Activities

Understand Ideas

1. Develop a concept map to illustrate the factors that contribute to personality development and what effect each factor might have.

2. Does Erik Erikson see development as something that happens to people or something that people make happen? Explain your answer.

Think and Evaluate

3. **a)** Identify three forces that you believe have shaped your gender.

b) What do you think is the most important influence in gender socialization? Give two reasons to support your answer.

4. Do you agree with the theory that birth order contributes to personality development? Why or why not? Does this theory correspond to your own experience regarding you and your siblings, or your parents and their siblings?

Apply Your Learning

5. Which do you think has had a greater role in your personal development, nature or nurture? Consider the impact of inherited characteristics, socialization and personality development. Write a short essay expressing your view. Be sure to supply specific examples to support your argument.

Research and Communicate

6. Develop a sample-survey questionnaire to determine which of the following behaviours parents value most in their children, and what methods they use to encourage their children to learn these behaviours. Present a brief report of your findings. (See Skill Focus, page 11.)
   - independence
   - obedience
   - conformity
   - responsibility
   - aggressiveness
   - willingness to co-operate
   - leadership
   - sociability
   - creativity
   - competitiveness
   - caring
   - high moral standards

Unit 1: Build Your Research and Inquiry Skills

1. Study a Cultural Scene

Issues
- How do people behave within a specific cultural scene?
- What meaning does the cultural scene have for the participants?

Inquiry and Analysis
- Choose a cultural scene of interest. This scene can be any situation that has more than one person. For example, you might choose a sports event at your school, dinnertime with your family, or a gathering of your friends at a coffee shop.
- Plan how you will use participant observation to gather data.
- Take part in the cultural scene—observe, talk with the participants, take notes.
- Organize your notes under the following headings: observed behaviour; why the behaviour may be important for the participants; any material culture that may be significant.
- Record your observations in an organized way.
- Draw conclusions about the scene and its meaning for the participants.

SKILL REVIEW: **Conducting Observation Research, page 13.**

Communication
- In small groups, share your findings.
- As a class, discuss the methods you used and summarize your findings.

SKILL REVIEW: **Group Discussions, page 43.**

2. The Best Way to Learn

Issues
- What are some effective ways to learn?
- Do these ways differ according to the subject or activity?

- How can we improve our own learning?

Inquiry and Analysis
- Interview several people who either learn or teach a number of different activities. Talk to at least two people who teach and three people who learn.
- Prepare an interview sheet beforehand. Include questions that ask what is being learned or taught, what are successful and not so successful ways to learn or to teach in that field, how successful learning is measured and what we can know about other areas of learning based on this research.
- Set up and carry out your interviews.

SKILL REVIEW: **Conducting an Interview, page 12.**

Communication
- Share your research with a small group. Draw general conclusions about learning from the interviews conducted by people in this group.
- Write several paragraphs that answer the following question: What are some of the different ways to learn effectively?

SKILL REVIEW: **Writing a Paragraph, page 115.**

3. Our Emotional Nature

Issues
- Why do some people appear to be more emotional than others?
- What factors influence our emotions?

Inquiry and Analysis
- In groups of four or five, brainstorm about the source of emotions. What factors influence your emotions? To what degree are your emotional reactions the result of nature or nurture? Record your responses on a flipchart or blackboard.

SKILL REVIEW: **Thinking Creatively, page 64.**

Communication
- Review your group's responses. Choose ideas that apply to your own emotional make-up.
- Write a paragraph stating your hypothesis about the role of nature and nurture in your emotional responses.

SKILL REVIEW: **Writing a Paragraph, page 115.**

4. Stress in the Modern World

Issues
- What factors tend to produce stress?
- What impact does stress have on teenagers?
- What methods are most useful in dealing with these factors?

Inquiry and Analysis
- Prepare a sample survey to find out which factors are most likely to produce stress among your classmates. Consider factors such as school work, family relationships, peer relationships and part-time work.
- Ask what impact stress has. Ask about results such as sleeplessness, poor performance at school and arguments with family or friends.
- Find out which methods are most commonly used to deal with stress.

SKILL REVIEW: **Conducting a Sample Survey, page 11.**

Communication
- Present your findings in the form of a concept map entitled "Stress in the Modern World."

SKILL REVIEW: **Organizing Ideas with Concept Maps, page 125.**

5. Mental Illness and Therapies

Issues
- How are mental illnesses categorized?
- What treatments and therapies are available for various types of mental illness?

Inquiry and Analysis
- Review the information on mental disorders.
- Using the library and Internet, research what kinds of treatments are currently available for treating these disorders.

SKILL REVIEW: **Gathering and Recording Information, page 73.**

Communicate
- Record the information you have gathered in the form of a chart with these headings: Category of disorder, Specific disorder, Treatments.

6. Socialization of Children

Issues
- Should children be punished for misbehaving? Or should other forms of teaching acceptable behaviour be used?

Inquiry and Analysis
- Review the section on conditioning (page 55) to explain why some theorists believe children should be rewarded when they behave or punished when they misbehave, so that they can learn acceptable behaviour.
- Review the section on socialization (page 119) to explain why some theorists believe that children are more likely to learn appropriate behaviour through a process of modelling (or following the behaviour of others they admire).
- Decide on your own view.

SKILL REVIEW: **Analyzing and Judging Information or Ideas, page 97.**

Communication
- Discuss your views with the class.
- If possible, invite a child psychologist to speak to the class on this issue. Be sure to prepare your questions in advance.

SKILL REVIEW: **Raising Questions, page 24.**

Unit 1: Demonstrate Your Learning

Task 1–1: What Does It Mean to Be Human?

Background Information

From earliest times, philosophers, artists and poets have tried to determine and define what it means to be human. In recent times, social scientists have also added their voices to the search. Each of these disciplines—anthropology, psychology and sociology—searches for the answers in its own manner and from its own point of view. Each asks different questions, observes in different ways and develops its own opinion of what it means to be human.

Anthropologists, as we have seen, look at the cultural and physical nature of humans. We have seen how Jane Goodall and other physical anthropologists have made comparisons with various species in order to help answer this question. Psychologists consider the thoughts and behaviours of individuals. Freud, Jung, Piaget and others have struggled to penetrate the human mind and the sources of human behaviour. Sociologists study social interactions, groups and the social structures that people create. They examine human behaviour in its social context in order to identify the social forces that shape us.

We can use the research and the findings of these and other social scientists in order to develop our own personal concept of what it means to be human. This quest is the purpose of the following performance task.

Your Task

In this task you will

- identify and describe what you think are the five most important characteristics of human beings
- show that you are familiar with some of the major ideas of anthropology, psychology and sociology
- **either** write a position paper that states your point of view and defends the characteristics you have chosen **or** prepare a collage that shows your views of what it means to be human

Review What You Know

1. Review the following terms from this unit, making sure you understand what they mean:
- anthropology (page 5)
- psychology (page 5)
- sociology (page 6)
- human physical traits (page 23)
- culture (page 26)
- perception (page 46)
- learning (page 50)
- mind (page 75)
- emotion (page 82)
- socialization (page 116)
- personality (page 127)

Think and Inquire

2. From the ideas you have reviewed, list 10 characteristics that you think make us distinctive as human beings.
3. Identify which of these characteristics are unique to humans and which are shared with other animals.
4. Choose the five characteristics that you think are the most important aspects of being human.
5. For each of the five characteristics you have chosen, explain why you believe it makes us distinctive as human beings.

Communicate Your Ideas

6. Choose one of the following:

- Explain your ideas in a position paper of about 750 words, in which you identify the five characteristics you believe are most important to being human, and defend the choices you have made.

- Make a collage to present the five characteristics that you have chosen. You might consider using an image of a human being, surrounded by visual representations of the characteristics. Attach a brief written description of the characteristics to your collage, explaining why you believe they are the most important to being human.

SKILL REVIEW: **Writing a Position Paper, page 323.**

Apply Your Skills

7. In completing this task, you will demonstrate the following skills:

- reviewing ideas
- organizing ideas
- analyzing ideas
- judging ideas
- applying ideas
- drawing conclusions
- writing a position paper or preparing a collage

Criteria for Assessment

Position Paper

Introduction
- states the issue or question clearly and accurately
- states position or point of view clearly

Body
- draws on appropriate information from the text
- states main arguments clearly
- supports arguments with evidence
- writes arguments in a logical and convincing way
- organizes arguments in an effective manner

Conclusion
- sums up main arguments
- restates the general position

Language and Conventions
- grammar is correct
- spelling is correct
- cover page includes title, student's name, course, teacher's name, date

Collage
- draws on appropriate information from the text
- identifies human characteristics clearly
- displays appropriate visuals
- provides neatly written captions and headings
- provides a clear written description, explaining why chosen characteristics are the most important in determining what it means to be human

Unit 1: Demonstrate Your Learning

Task 1–2: Nature or Nurture?

Background Information

You may have noticed that some traits are more common among people who are related. A child's interest in the arts or in science, for example, may lead to the comment "She is just like her father." Sometimes the personality, or appearance, of a young child reminds family members of a parent or a grandparent. We jump to the conclusion that heredity is the origin of the child's traits.

Yet we recognize that many human characteristics depend largely on the young person's experiences and environment. Personality and its expression are shaped by culture and social surroundings. Interest in science or art, for example, may not develop if it is not part of the child's experience.

Do you believe that you are the person you are mainly because of genetic inheritance or because of your environment? This question, which anthropologists, psychologists and sociologists have been wrestling with for years, has been called the nature-nurture debate, as if only one of the causative factors was possible. Yet, it is clear that both biology and experience or learning have a powerful influence.

Your Task

In this task you will

- examine the following questions:
  - In what ways are we shaped by biological or hereditary forces (by nature)?
  - To what degree are we shaped by experience and learning (by nurture)?
  - To what extent do we have choices that we can exercise through decision making and problem solving, regardless of either nature or nurture?
- record your findings in the form of a large organizer
- **either** present your information as an essay **or** hold a class debate on the nature-nurture issue

Review What You Know

1. Review the following terms from this unit, making sure you understand what each one means:
- nature (page 26)
- nurture (page 26)
- perception (page 46)
- learning (page 50)
- emotions (page 82)
- mental health (page 91)
- personality (page 127)

Nature or Nurture?

Human Characteristics	Influence of Nature	Influence of Nurture	Discussion and Conclusions
Perception			
Learning			
Emotions			
Personality			
Mental Health			
Interests and Abilities			

Think and Inquire

2. In consultation with your teacher, determine how many of the following characteristics you will explore: perception, learning, emotions, personality, mental health, interests and abilities.

3. Using the text, take notes for each of the characteristics you have chosen.

4. Organize your ideas in a chart similar to the one opposite. For each characteristic, decide on the influence of nature and/or nurture.

5. Draw a conclusion about the influence of nature and nurture on human beings. Indicate why your conclusion must be limited to the evidence.

SKILL REVIEW: **Gathering and Recording Information, page 73; Analyzing and Judging Information or Ideas, page 97.**

Communicate Your Ideas

6. In consultation with your teacher, decide whether your final product will be an essay or a debate.

7. If you are writing an essay, be sure to answer the three questions identified in "Your Task."

8. If you are holding a debate, use the following topic: "Be it resolved that nurture has a greater impact than nature in shaping human behaviour."

SKILL REVIEW: **Writing an Essay, page 248; Debating, page 302.**

Apply Your Skills

9. In completing this task, you will demonstrate the following skills:
   - reviewing concepts
   - organizing ideas
   - applying ideas
   - interviewing
   - observing
   - creating and using a sample survey
   - using an organizer
   - writing an essay

Criteria for Assessment

Essay

Introduction
   - states the issue or question
   - states position and hypothesis
   - summarizes the method of research

Content
   - deals with all categories identified in organizer
   - supports hypothesis with evidence
   - presents arguments in an organized and persuasive manner
   - organizes paragraphs effectively

Conclusion
   - provides a summary of the analysis
   - states the general conclusion

Language and Conventions
   - grammar is correct
   - spelling is correct
   - references are accurate
   - appearance and format follow conventions

Debate

Understanding
   - shows understanding of the main points in the nature/nurture debate

Planning
   - shows preparation in strategy and presentation

Clarity
   - organizes speeches and rebuttals to make each point clearly

Proof
   - links evidence and examples to each argument

Persuasiveness
   - expresses ideas clearly, effectively and with enthusiasm

Rebuttal
   - rebuts opposing ideas convincingly

Unit

2

Social Groups and Organization

Unit Overview

nit 1 introduced the approaches of anthropology, psychology and sociology. Applying these three social sciences, you investigated a number of issues about human beings and their thoughts, behaviours and feelings. A central question in Unit 1 was, How can anthropology, psychology and sociology help us understand ourselves as individual human beings and as members of society?

In Unit 2, you will continue to develop your understanding of individual behaviour within a social setting by focusing on how human beings think and act within social groups and in different types of organizations. The three social sciences will help you in this investigation.

Anthropology, Psychology and Sociology in This Unit

Through the eyes of the anthropologist you will see that people all over the world form groups for different reasons. Some groups, such as the family, appear in every culture, although the specific structure of the group will vary. Other groups, such as complex organizations, only appear in some societies to fulfill certain functions. You will also discover how and why groups and organizations in almost all cultures change over time.

The psychological approach will show how people think and behave in group situations. What impact do the groups you belong to have on your thoughts and behaviour? How do individuals affect the thoughts and behaviours of other members in the group? Psychology offers us the opportunity to learn what social groups mean to us, how we perceive differences among us and how groups affect us, both positively and negatively.

Because sociologists study the interactions of people in society and the social structures they create, this approach will examine the social groups and organizations people develop. What groups do you belong to? Why do you belong to these groups? What kind of society do you live in? What happens when cultural differences in a society lead to prejudice and discrimination? Canadian society, in particular, will be the focus of our discussion.

Unit Expectations

- What are the characteristics of different types of groups in Canadian society as identified by anthropology, psychology and sociology?

- What is the psychological impact of group cohesion and conflict on individuals, groups and communities?

- What are the characteristics, advantages and disadvantages of formal organizations?

Chapter Topics

Chapter 7: The Family: A Primary Group

Chapter 8: Groups, Cliques and Social Behaviour

Chapter 9: Formal Organizations

Chapter 10: Crowds, Mass Behaviour and Social Movements

Chapter 11: Culture and Discrimination

Research, Inquiry and Communication Skills

Using Statistics

Making and Reading Graphs

Writing a Response Paper

Writing a Social Science Report

Making Comparisons

Understanding Value Statements

Identifying Bias

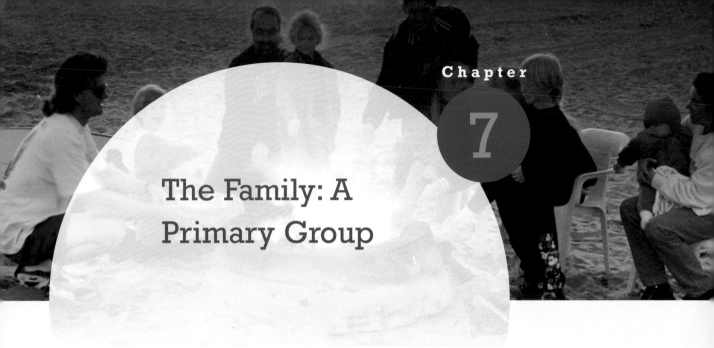

The Family: A Primary Group

Key Terms

nuclear family

extended family

blended or reconstituted family

single-parent family

common-law family

arranged marriages

free-choice marriages

shared roles

conventional roles

dual-career roles

spousal abuse

The family is found in some form in every known society. Families share close emotional ties, raise children and care for individuals as an economic unit. Each one of us is a member of a family, yet not all families are exactly alike.

When you think of a family, what descriptions come to mind? Think of families you know. Think of families on TV or in books. What characteristics are common to all families? What characteristics are different?

Work with a group to review the list below. Which of the groupings would you consider to be a family? Give reasons for your choices. Choose one member of the group to take point-form notes of these reasons. Then, using these notes, write a list of the characteristics that define a family. Return to your list once you have finished this chapter. Revise your list in light of what you have learned.

- a group of biologically unrelated people who share an apartment

- a father, mother and children

- several young adults, brothers and sisters who reside together

- a married couple

- a mother or father and children

- a same-sex couple, with or without children

- three generations in one household: grandparents, parents and children

- a group of biologically related people living in one house, such as a father, child and an uncle

Families: Forms and Functions

The family is an essential social group in every known society, even though its structure and functions may vary. One definition of a family is "two or more people related by blood, adoption or marriage who live together." This definition is very broad and covers various types of families that sociologists have described. All of the following types exist in Canada.

- **nuclear family:** one or two parents and unmarried children living together

- **extended family:** relatives in addition to parents and unmarried children living together

- **blended or reconstituted family:** parents with children from one or more previous marriages or unions

- **childless family:** a couple

- **single-parent family:** a parent—either mother or father—with one or more children

- **common-law family:** unmarried couple with or without children

It is likely that your family falls into one of these categories. Whatever their structure, most families fill a variety of functions. Families care for members by feeding and clothing them and providing them with other necessities of life. Families help socialize children by teaching them how to interact with others and behave in a socially acceptable way. Families also provide their members with affection, motivation and a sense of identity.

Families Across Time and Place

The shape of families and the needs they meet change over time, depending on circumstances such as geography and the economy. Anthropologists have identified several stages in human economic systems that have led to changes in family structures.

Hunting and gathering societies have existed for the greatest part of human history. The Inuit and Cree of northern Canada were once hunter-gatherers. Today some remnants of hunter-gatherers continue in remote parts of central Africa and South America.

This form of family usually consists of about 10 to 12 people, including parents, grandparents, children and unattached relatives. Both men and women are important to survival as, typically, men hunt while women gather plants, berries and roots. In hunting and gathering societies, families meet most human needs.

Agricultural societies developed about 5000 years ago when people domesticated animals and planted crops. Anthropologists believe that, at

Focus Questions

What is a family?

What are the functions of a family?

How have families changed over time?

Connections

How does the family act as an agent of socialization? (See Chapter 6, pages 119–121.)

Figure 7–1

Work, both inside and outside the home, changes family structure through time and in different places. What type of society is shown here?

Connections

Which of Maslow's hierarchy of needs do families help to fulfill? (See Chapter 4, page 81.)

this stage of development, the roles of men and women became more rigid. Men controlled the agricultural work and community responsibilities while women were responsible for work in the home. The family in agricultural societies met most human needs.

Industrial societies emerged more than 200 years ago with the coming of the Industrial Revolution. Men and women moved from the countryside to the city to find work. Economic survival depended upon working for someone else in factories or other organizations. Gender divisions increased as men took the best, well-paying jobs, and women usually worked at unskilled jobs until they had to stay at home with the children. While a large extended family was an economic benefit in earlier societies, the smaller, nuclear family was more mobile and better able to move to find work in industrial societies. As a result, the nuclear family became the dominant family type.

In the **post-industrial society** of the late 1950s and the 1960s, many married women began working outside the home. Many worked to help support the family, but the feminist movement of the 1960s also had a powerful impact. Women found that working outside the home could be psychologically satisfying as well.

Changing Family Patterns in Canada

Families in Canada have experienced many of the changes described above. In the 1940s and the 1950s, most families in Canada, as in other industrial nations, were nuclear. By the 1970s and 1980s about 51 percent of married women worked outside the home. The percentage of single-parent families increased by 11 percent as divorce and single parenthood became more common. In 1996, 12 percent of Canadian adults were female single parents, and 2.5 percent were male single parents. Figures 7–2 and 7–3 show some of the other changes that were occurring in Canada during this period.

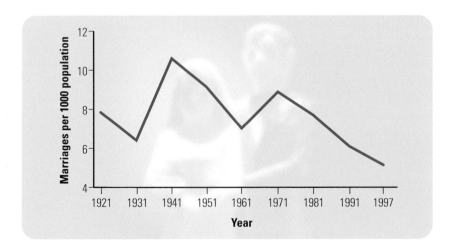

Figure 7–2
Marriage rates in Canada, 1921–1997

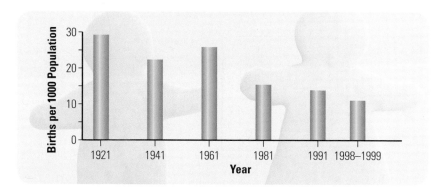

Figure 7–3
Birth rates in Canada, 1921–1999. What initial conclusions might you draw about the future of the family based on the information in these two graphs?

Using Statistics

Statistics is the science of collecting and analyzing data, especially in the form of numbers. Statistics allow social scientists to present many facts or examples in a simple way.

In this country, many of our statistics come from Statistics Canada, a government agency that collects important data about Canadians. The government conducts a full census, or official count of the population in various categories, every 10 years, in the year after the start of the decade (e.g., 1991, 2001, etc.). It also conducts a "mini-census," to gather statistics in selected areas, five years after the full census (e.g., 1996, 2006, etc.). You can see in Figure 7–4 that the data comes from these census years.

It's important to know how to analyze statistics and how to use them.

Family structure in Canada, 1971–1996

	Husband-Wife Families[1]			Single-Parent Families			Total	Total Number of Families
	Married	Common-Law	Total	Male Head	Female Head	Total		
				%				000s
1971	—	—	90.5	2.0	7.4	9.4	100.0	5053.2
1976	—	—	90.2	1.7	8.1	9.8	100.0	5727.9
1981	83.1	5.6	88.7	2.0	9.3	11.3	100.0	6325.0
1986	80.1	7.2	87.3	2.3	10.4	12.7	100.0	6735.0
1991	77.2	9.9	87.0	2.3	10.7	13.0	100.0	7356.2
1996	73.7	11.7	85.4	2.5	12.1	14.6	100.0	7837.8

[1] Prior to 1981, common-law families were included in the same category as married-couple families.

Source: Statistics Canada, Census, 1991. Statistics Canada, 1996.

Figure 7–4 ▲

Family structure is one of the categories in which Statistics Canada collects data every five years.

DILBERT reprinted by permission of United Feature Syndicate, Inc.

Figure 7–5

Statistics might sound impressive, but we need to treat them with care. Review the use of medians in Chapter 1. Why is the use of percentages in this case meaningless?

Here's How

When **analyzing** statistics, ask yourself the following questions:

- Is the source reliable?

- Do the figures apply to the relevant time period? Do they apply over a long enough period to be meaningful? Are they recent?

- If the statistics were drawn from a sample, was it large enough to be representative? For example, a survey of one class might show that 100 percent of students come from two-parent families. This would not mean that all, or even most, students in the school come from two-parent families.

When **using** statistics, follow these guidelines:

- Be sure to use only the statistics that you need to make your point, especially if you have gathered the data yourself. Sort your data into a few categories that are pertinent to your purpose.

- Where possible, convert raw data into percentages. It is often easier to evaluate data when we know what percentage it represents.

Practise It

1. Review Figure 7–4. What is the source of information? How reliable is this source likely to be?

2. Describe the changes that have taken place in **a)** husband-wife families, and **b)** single-parent families between 1971 and 1996. Can this data be used to describe a trend (a general direction over time)? Explain.

3. What predictions could you make about future trends based on this data? How certain could you be? What information would you need to be certain?

Activities

Understand Ideas

1. **a)** Make a list of important needs that are met by being part of a family.
   b) Arrange the list of needs in order of priority.
2. Summarize factors that have influenced the structure of families.

Think and Evaluate

3. **a)** What social institutions, other than the family, help meet each of the following needs?
   - caring for the aged
   - caring for the sick
   - companionship
   - entertainment
   - providing a sense of purpose
   - raising children
   - teaching values
   - training and educating the young
   - transmitting religious beliefs

   b) Does the existence of these institutions mean there is less need for families to fill these roles? Explain your view.

Stages of Family Life

Most people will be part of two families in their lives: the family of origin into which they were born, and the family that they may choose to form as adults. In both of these families, they will move through different stages. The typical family life cycle is as follows:

Stage 1: Single young adults move out of the parental home, but may come back for food or to do laundry.
Stage 2: Singles eventually marry. At first, both partners often work outside the home.
Stage 3: The young couple starts a family. One parent may stay at home, but often both parents continue to work.
Stage 4: The children become teenagers. Parents are usually 40 or older with established professional and personal lives. Teenagers often bring challenges to family life as they start to establish their independence and to follow their own schedules.
Stage 5: The teenagers grow into young adults and move away to school or into their own home.
Stage 6: Parents now reach middle age. They may retire and seek new challenges in work or leisure.
Stage 7: Retired couples may move to a smaller home, spend their time in new interests and pursuits such as travel, and often enjoy spending time with their children and grandchildren.

Focus Questions

What is the cycle of family life?

What is an arranged marriage?

What is a free-choice marriage?

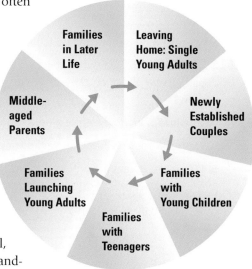

Figure 7–6
Family life cycle. Where does your family fit into this cycle?

Note that different types of families will follow different cycles. For example, for single-parent families, reconstituted families and other forms of the family, the cycle will be different.

While most Canadians do get married and form new families, in recent years, many seem to be putting it off a little. Between 1970 and 1991 the average age for men marrying for the first time climbed from 25 years of age to 30. The average age for women during that same period rose from 23 to 28 years. In 1996, 73.8 percent of Canadian adults were married, and 11.7 percent were common-law couples.

Types of Marriages

New families are formed in different ways. Two of the most common ways begin with an arranged marriage or a "free-choice" marriage. These two kinds of marriages are not opposite ways of choosing a partner. Most arranged marriages take the concerns of the individuals into account to some degree while most free-choice marriages are influenced by parents, family and wider society.

Connections

Why does the type of marriage define a couple's concept of love? (See Chapter 4, pages 86–88).

The True Love Opinionnaire

Read each of the following statements. Using a sheet of paper or your notebook, write **A** if you agree, **D** if you disagree. Think about the reasons for your answer, and record them if you like.

1. If you really care for someone, there is nothing wrong with doing whatever you have to do, even lying, to get the person to love you.

2. If you are really in love, the longer you and your partner are together, the stronger your love grows.

3. True love is worth dying for if necessary.

4. True lovers should never flirt with other people.

5. Lovers are always happy.

6. It is never right to scheme just to get someone you like to go out with you.

7. It is unwise to go against parental wishes in choosing a marriage partner.

8. True lovers should spend as much time together as possible.

9. "Love at first sight" is enough to justify getting married immediately.

10. If you are really in love, physical appearance does not matter.

11. Love never happens suddenly. It always needs time to grow.

12. It is never right to go out with someone just because she or he is popular.

13. Physical attraction must always come before true love.

14. If you are really in love, family connections or social standing is not important.

Arranged marriages have been the norm in many societies for centuries. Such marriages are considered as a union between two families, not between two individuals. These marriages often reflect the religious, social or cultural concerns of the families. Supporters of arranged marriages say these marriages have a better chance of success and that partners learn to love each other over time. Other supporters say that marriage is too important to leave to the whims of young people. Which of these aspects are evident in the following article?

CASE STUDY

1. Before reading, list three things you think you know about arranged marriages.

2. After reading, add facts you have learned to your list. Has your view of arranged marriages changed?

An Arranged Marriage

In a few short weeks, Lakshmi Rao will marry the man of her dreams. She's only seen him twice, and never dated him—or anyone else for that matter. But all she feels is excitement for the slim man with the moustache she last saw in April. "I just fell in love with him on first sight. He's very patient, listens to everything I say and I just blather on," she says with a laugh. "On Valentine's Day he sent me a tape of love songs."

Rao's marriage, similar to those of most of her East Indian friends in Edmonton, is arranged. Traditionally, these unions are more than anything a marriage of families. With the event planned by parents, the bride and groom have little say and don't meet until the wedding day. Love doesn't always enter the equation.

But Rao's arranged marriage has a modern flavour: she met her fiancé and likes him. "My parents said if I ever found anyone (to marry), they'd agree to it, but I'm just a very shy person. I told my parents to just go ahead and find someone," says Rao, 25. Reactions among her non-Indian friends range from envy to horror. "One female friend thought it would make everything a lot easier. But some didn't like the idea; they thought it was weird...."

Her father began the search. Tall, Hindu, vegetarian and educated with a love of children and travel—Rao handed her father the list of attributes she sought.

Through family friends they learned of a young Hindu man named Satya living in New Jersey. He grew up in India and did his Ph.D. in pharmacology at the University of Alberta. Rao sent him a photo. He sent one back and they talked on the phone. Then he called to announce his visit to Edmonton. "I was excited but scared. It's like a blind date. I didn't know what to expect," Rao says, fingering her thick braid.

Luckily, she liked the soft-spoken, friendly man her father brought home from the airport. "He was very jolly and that eased the tension. I felt like I wasn't being judged. I liked him on the spot." They spent the weekend together, discussing tennis, long walks in the park, careers, marriage, children, even furniture shopping. He returned to New Jersey and a few weeks later, asked for her hand.

From "Parents Picked Him but Lakshmi Loves the Guy" by Morina Jimenez

Figure 7–7

Wedding customs vary from one culture to another. What can you learn about some customs from these photographs?

Orthodox Jewish wedding

Henna decorations, Hindu wedding, India

Traditional Aboriginal wedding

Wedding gift of money, Pakistan

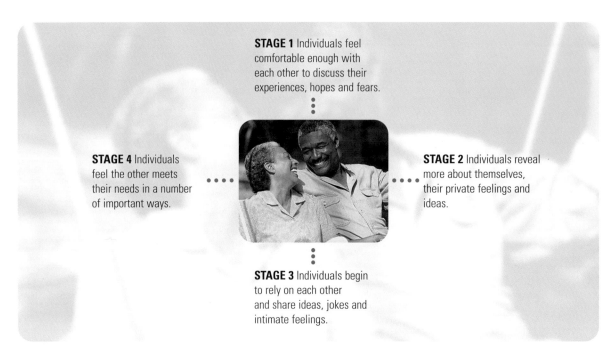

STAGE 1 Individuals feel comfortable enough with each other to discuss their experiences, hopes and fears.

STAGE 4 Individuals feel the other meets their needs in a number of important ways.

STAGE 2 Individuals reveal more about themselves, their private feelings and ideas.

STAGE 3 Individuals begin to rely on each other and share ideas, jokes and intimate feelings.

Figure 7–8
The Wheel of Love

Free-choice marriages are often based on romantic love with the belief that personal and emotional compatibility and love are more important than family concerns. One sociologist, Ira Reiss, has identified what he calls the "Wheel of Love" as shown in Figure 7–8. Even with free-choice marriages, however, social interests continue to influence the choice of partners. In fact, individuals tend to choose partners similar to themselves in a number of ways. Marriage partners tend to live in the same geographic area and to come from similar social and cultural groups. People often marry others who are similar in intelligence, education, physical appearance, age, religious and ethnic background, and personal habits.

Is free choice a good way to choose a life partner? Many people believe it is the only way—that individuals need to find and fall in love with their partners. Others argue that young people are fooled by fleeting romantic feelings, that romantic love is not a good basis for the many experiences and stresses of life. Critics point to high divorce rates as evidence that free choice does not work.

CASE STUDY

1. What expectations and pressures influenced this couple's choice?

2. Do you identify more with Tom or Dawn? Explain.

Falling in Love

Many children are raised with the fairy-tale fantasy that one day they will meet a perfect partner—the prince or princess of their dreams—and be swept away to marry and live happily ever after. Sociologists have interviewed married people to understand what really happens. Here is one example.

Question: How did you decide that this was the person you wanted to marry?

A 29-year-old mother of three, married 11 years, recalls:

We met at a party and talked all evening. We continued to see each other often and became closer as time went on. I always knew that I wanted to marry someone different from my father, someone warm and outgoing—someone who would treat me as an equal partner. Tom was wonderful, and my family and friends all liked him. In many ways, he was everything I could wish for, but sometimes I felt that something was missing. In movies and books, it's always love at first sight—passion, romance and perfect harmony! I think I was in love with Tom, but was I feeling the way I was supposed to feel? Anyway, we got married and had three beautiful children. I'm very happy, but if I had it to do over again, I wouldn't have gotten married so young. Choosing a life partner is an awesome responsibility.

Her 30-year-old husband tells the story from his point of view:

As soon as I saw Dawn, I fell in love with her. She was the girl of my dreams—beautiful, smart and full of energy. We discussed everything under the sun, and there was a special "chemistry" between us. We talked about getting married, but we really wanted to wait until we finished university. But we hit a snag—because we chose to go to school out of town, my parents gave me an ultimatum. We could go away together only if we got married; so we did. I'm not sorry, but things were a little tough at first. It might have been better to wait.

Activities

Understand Ideas

1. Draw a symbol for each of the seven sections of the family life cycle.

2. Make a Venn diagram similar to the one below. List the characteristics of arranged and free-choice marriages in the appropriate circles. Place common characteristics in the overlapping section.

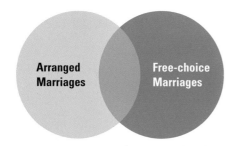

Think and Evaluate

3. How does your view of love, as revealed by the Love Opinionnaire, differ from those described in the case studies?

4. a) Do a PMI (Plus, Minus, Interesting) chart on arranged marriages.

b) Now do a similar PMI on free-choice marriages.

c) Be prepared to share your ideas with the class.

5. What kinds of differences between partners are likely to make for a happier marriage? Give reasons for your view.

Research and Communicate

6. Develop a short questionnaire measuring what young people expect from their future marriage. Try out the questionnaire on at least five people and tabulate the results. (See Skill Focus, page 11.)

Roles in the Family

As you learned in Chapter 6, a social role can be defined as the attitudes, behaviour, responsibilities and rights that accompany a social position in society. Each one of us plays many roles in our lives: friend, son, daughter, parent, employee, student and others. The roles played by family members have undergone many changes in the last few decades.

The change in labour force participation (see Figure 7–9) is one of the factors that has affected the family and marriage roles. In some marriages, partners take **conventional roles.** This division of roles is based on the belief that men and women have separate areas of activity. One partner, usually the woman, takes primary responsibility for the home and child rearing. The other partner, usually the man, works outside the home. When the woman works outside the home, it may be part-time work. This role division is becoming less common as more women remain in the labour force after beginning a family.

Increasingly, partners in a marriage have **shared roles,** where both partners work outside the home and assume household responsibilities. However, in this form, employed women still take primary responsibility for housework, spending on average 20 to 37 hours a week on it. By comparison, men spend on average 10 to 15 hours on housework.

When both spouses have permanent careers for which they are specially trained, they have **dual-career roles.** Sharing of household tasks is often more equal. Family income is likely high, so the couple can afford to buy services, such as housecleaning and child care. Satisfactions are high in this kind of family, but so are the stresses that come with two careers.

conventional—based on established practices or acceptable standards; traditional

spouse—a husband or wife, married or common-law

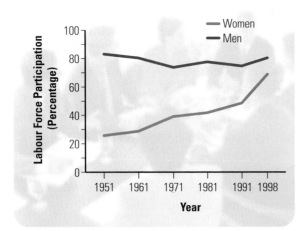

Figure 7–9
Labour force participation by gender in Canada, 1951–1998

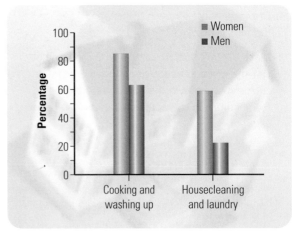

Figure 7–10
Percentage of women and men performing selected household chores, 1998. What does this bar graph show about the participation of men and women in household chores? What explanation would you provide for this?·

Zits

Figure 7–11

What roles do teens play in the family? Why are the teenage years sometimes challenging for families?

Skill F•CUS

Making and Reading Graphs

Graphs present statistical information in a clear and dramatic way. **Line and bar graphs** allow the reader to recognize trends instantly. **Pie graphs** can be used to show proportion very clearly.

Here's How

- In making or reading a line or bar graph, start with the axes: the vertical and the horizontal. The vertical axis often gives information about changes in events. The horizontal axis often gives information about the time period. (See Figures 7–9 and 7–10.)

- In making or reading a pie graph, it's important to understand that the whole pie represents the total of what is being considered. The pie is then cut according to the percentage or proportion belonging to each part. For example, from Figure 7–4, you could draw the pie graph shown in Figure 7–12.

Practise It

1. Return to Figure 7–4. Draw the following. You may wish to use a computer program to prepare your graphs.
   a) a line graph showing the data on husband-wife families
   b) a bar graph showing the data on single-parent families
   c) a pie chart showing the categories of husband-wife and single-parent families within the divisions shown in the pie chart in Figure 7–12

2. **a)** What criteria would you use to assess a graph? List at least three criteria.
   b) Using these criteria, assess the graphs you have drawn. Which graph is the best? Give at least three reasons for your choice.

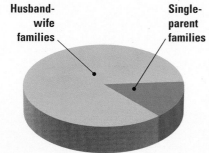

Husband-wife families

Single-parent families

Figure 7–12
Proportion of husband-wife families to single-parent families in Canada, 1996

Single-Parent Families

Single-parent families make up approximately 14 percent of all families in Canada. Most single-parent families (58 percent) result from separation or divorce; some (28 percent) from the death of a spouse. Some single parents (14 percent) never married. In most cases (82 percent), single-parent families are headed by women.

Single parenthood has increased in recent decades. One reason for this increase is the greater willingness of unmarried women to raise their children alone. Another reason is the increased rate of divorce in Canadian society since the 1970s. In most cases of divorce, mothers are awarded custody of children.

Single parents assume a wide range of roles and responsibilities. Usually they provide for the family economically, as well as look after household tasks and raise children. The degree of role overload will depend upon the support the single parent gets from family and from the other parent. In surveys, single parents indicate their greatest problem is having total responsibility for child care.

Many single parents also face financial problems. More than half of single-parent families in 1990 had incomes below the poverty line. These families spent 20 percent more of their income on food, shelter and clothing than the average family. Single-parent families comprise almost half (47 percent) of all low-income families in Canada.

When the single parent is a woman, it is possible that having a child has interfered with her education and therefore her ability to get a job that

poverty line—income below which people are considered poor

Figure 7–13

What are the most significant problems faced by single parents?

Problems single parents have raising children

Problems	Number	% of Sample[1]
No problems	54	16
Lack of a father/mother role model	102	30
Discipline problems	109	33
Tired of having all responsibility for child care	123	37
Difficulty arranging child care for social outings	72	21
Difficulty arranging child care when child is ill	82	24
Lack of time	15	4
Emotional stress	17	5
Financial constraints	37	11
Inadequate child care	9	3
Other	15	4

[1]Percentages total more than 100 because respondents gave up to 3 responses.

Source: City of Calgary, Social Services Department, 1985.

Unit 2: Social Groups and Organization

Are Single Parents Treated Fairly?

Even though the number of single parents is rising in Canada, these parents often find that there is little understanding for the problems they face. This letter was submitted to *Modern Woman Magazine* by a single mother.

Dear critical strangers,

Something happened recently in the vegetable market parking lot that really upset me. Maybe I'd been having one of those days and didn't realize it at the time. Maybe it was one look too many.

I'd been shopping with my six-year-old daughter. We always have a good time at the market choosing among so many fresh things. She loves to pick just the right apple and the perfect bunch of bananas. I'd spent what little cash I had, and had only enough left over to fill up The Beast—my 17-year-old car that's a little rusty, a little blue, and features a display of duct tape. (We don't use that door.) You've heard the term "belching smoke." Well, The Beast, when started, just belches. It is very noisy and it smells very, very bad. Despite all that, I turn the ignition key and pretend I'm oblivious to the distraction that my car causes. I wait patiently until she decides that it's okay to start going, signalled by just the right rev and rattle.

The driver of the car next to me got into his car and left his passenger standing at her door. She eyed my car back to front, wrinkled her nose, looked at me and sneered. I let that one go. She did it again, and that was it. I rolled down my window and with as much attitude as I could muster, said, "I know it stinks, but with a deadbeat dad, this is the best I can do." Her reply was, "Well, I guess it gets you from A to B." "No," I said, "as a matter of fact it doesn't do that very well either." She was getting a bit nervous by now, clawing at the door hand and yelling at her companion to let her in. I didn't have anything else to say anyway and rolled up my window.

What upset me the most was how she looked at me as if I was less than her. I work, feed, clothe and house two children by myself. I usually just get verbal abuse if I dare ask for any support. Do people think I choose to drive this old car, that I choose to buy vegetables and meat from the last-day-for-sale section? Would anyone actually choose this?

I am not less because I am a single mother. More often than not I am more. I have to be. Like those mornings when I have to drag myself out of bed. Those afternoons at work thinking about the chores I have to do when I get home. Those nights I lie awake worrying about paying the rent.

Things will get better eventually; my children and I will get by. Not with the best, the most expensive or the newest of anything, but we'll get there. A cash handout won't help, nor do I want one. What will make the road easier is the occasional show of support, even just a smile. I would like that at least from a woman, a mother. I would like to have faith in my own gender.

Later, my daughter in her innocence asked me if I know that woman. I laughed and said, "No, not really." But I do. I see her at little league games, school meetings and the company picnic. I see her everywhere....

What Do You Think?

1. According to this article, how do most people treat single parents?

2. According to the letter, what other difficulties are faced by single parents?

3. What is your view of single parents? Does this letter change your view? Discuss your opinion.

pays well. Moreover, if she works outside the home, she must find child care, which is costly. One Edmonton study showed that, at minimum wage, a single mother with two children would have to work 91 hours a week to earn a poverty-line income. One Canadian study found that in the first year of divorce, women's family income dropped by 40 percent, while men's incomes increased slightly. The financial difficulty increases for women whose ex-husbands fail to pay court-ordered support payment for their children.

Activities

Understand Ideas

1. In the post-industrial society, many married women began working outside the home. How has this affected family members' roles inside the home? Present your ideas in the form of a web diagram.

Think and Evaluate

2. Identify and explain two benefits for the family when women work outside the home. Identify and explain two drawbacks for the family when women work outside the home.

3. John is a 12-year-old boy whose mother is a single parent. The mother has just found a job, so John takes care of himself after school. In what ways do you think John will have to adjust to this change?

Research and Communicate

4. Work in pairs to investigate what services your community has to assist single-parent families. Make a T-chart to organize the information. Label the left side of your chart "Source of information" and the right side "Services identified."

5. Conduct a survey to find out what kinds of marriage roles are most common in families you know, and what kind of family is considered most desirable. Discuss your findings with the class. Describe the information you gathered and provide your personal opinion on marriage roles.

Focus Questions

What is spousal abuse?

How can we deal with spousal abuse?

abuse—improper or harmful treatment resulting in physical or emotional injury

domination—control

Family Problems: Spousal Abuse

Families, like all social groups, sometimes experience problems. While the family is often a source of support, comfort and affection, it can also be a source of violence against spouses, children and the elderly. It is estimated that 29 percent of Canadian women have, at some time, suffered abuse from their partners. In some cases, the man in the relationship is abused, but abuse that results in injury is overwhelmingly against women.

Why do individuals turn against a partner? There is no way to identify abusers by their background. They can be rich or poor, live in rural or urban settings and come from any ethnic and religious group. However, men who abuse their partners tend to come from a family with a history of violence. They often believe that they have the right to dominate their spouses. Sometimes such attitudes are supported by other males in their particular group of acquaintances. When their domination is threatened, these men experience stress and they react to re-establish control.

How Can You Identify Abuse?

How is **spousal abuse** defined? The Strauss Conflict Tactics Scale (1979) is one measure. It asks participants about their responses to family disputes. Which of the responses would you classify as examples of abuse or violence?

Participants are asked which of the following they have done during a dispute in the previous year:

1. discussed the issue calmly
2. got information to back up your side of things
3. brought in or tried to bring in someone to help settle things
4. insulted or swore at the other
5. sulked and/or refused to talk about a problem
6. stomped out of the room or house
7. cried
8. did or said something to spite the other
9. threatened to hit or throw something at the other

10. threw, smashed, hit or kicked something
11. threw something at the other
12. pushed, grabbed or shoved the other
13. slapped the other
14. kicked, bit, or hit the other with a fist
15. hit or tried to hit the other with something
16. beat up the other
17. threatened the other with a knife or gun
18. used a knife or gun on the other

Now compare your answers with the Conflict Tactics Scale classification shown below. Does the classification surprise you in any way? Would you disagree with any items in the classification? Discuss your opinions with the class.

Answers

The scale classifies items 4 to 6 as examples of **verbal violence** and items 9 to 18 as **physical violence.**

Feminist theorists maintain that dominant social attitudes support male power. Boys, more than girls, are taught to be tough and to hit. Patriarchal attitudes, which support male domination within the family, can endorse the use of power of one partner against the other. In egalitarian marriages, where power is shared, there is less chance of spousal abuse. Where either husband or wife dominate to an extreme, there is greater chance of one partner being abused.

Why do many abused women refuse to leave their partners? A psychological pattern described as **battered woman syndrome** is one explanation. Abused spouses become, understandably, anxious and fearful: they develop emotional disorders and a pattern of learned helplessness. This syndrome has been an accepted legal defence used by women who have killed their abusive partners after years of suffering abuse.

Another factor to consider is the lack of alternatives open to victims of abuse. In many cases, women are economically unable to leave and

patriarchal—male is seen as the head of the family or organization

egalitarian—with equal rights

learned helplessness—a lack of self-confidence caused by being told repeatedly that one is unable to help oneself

Connections

What are the similarities between spousal abuse and child abuse? (See Chapter 6, pages 120–121.)

support themselves and their children. They may have nowhere to go at a time when shelters are short of space. An abused woman may also fear her spouse's reaction to her attempt to leave.

Dealing with Spousal Abuse

Public attitudes toward spousal abuse are slowly changing. The belief that what happens in the home is private and nobody else's business has worked against the abused spouse in the past. At one time, police and the courts did not take such abuse as seriously as they should have. Now they are more likely to lay charges in spousal abuse cases.

But some observers argue that more changes are needed. They say that support organizations need to be better equipped to offer help, and there should be more shelters for victims of abuse and their children. They also argue that legal responses should be strengthened. In 1993 "stalker" legislation was introduced that made it illegal for abusers to approach their victims, but these laws are not always enforced consistently.

Education is also important in dealing with the issue of abuse. Young people need to be aware of the problem, its roots and its consequences. They also need to understand the signs of violence. Recent studies of courtship have indicated significant violence among dating and engaged couples. Violence is clearly problematic, yet in one study, 37 percent of victims and 31 percent of aggressors interpreted violence as the natural result of love. "He wouldn't hit me if he didn't love me" is often heard. Teens should understand that violence is never a solution to interpersonal problems. Moreover, if violence is used once, there is a good chance it will be used again.

Family Breakdown and Divorce

Focus Questions

What is divorce?

How common is divorce in Canada?

What impact does divorce have?

adultery—a voluntary sexual relationship between a married person and someone who is not his or her spouse

Although marriage has traditionally been seen as a lifelong commitment, a growing number of marriages end in divorce. Until the 1960s, the Canadian divorce rate was, by today's standards, extremely low. It was legally difficult to get a divorce, since adultery and desertion were the primary grounds. Social attitudes were against divorce and it was viewed as something that occurred only in extreme situations. Unhappy couples were often counselled to "make the best" of the situation. In addition, most women could not afford to leave the economic security of the family, since they were usually untrained for work outside the home.

The 1968 Divorce Act, however, widened the grounds for divorce to include physical or mental cruelty. No-fault grounds included permanent marriage breakdown such as imprisonment or desertion for five years, alcohol or drug addiction and separation for three years. In 1985, amendments to the Act included living separately for just one year as grounds for divorce. These changes resulted in an immediate growth in the divorce rate. Since 1987, however, the number of couples getting a divorce has levelled off and even dropped somewhat.

Impact of Divorce

Family breakup and divorce have a strong emotional impact on everyone involved, both partners and children. During and after separation, individuals suffer from the loss of important relationships, whether they were satisfactory or

not. It takes time for an individual to adjust to the loss. Yet people who are leaving an unsatisfactory marriage usually believe divorce will bring more benefits than disadvantages.

When children are involved, the emotional stress may last longer. Many Canadian children have learned to deal with the effects of divorce. Few children want their parents to divorce and many cling to the fantasy that their parents will reunite. Younger children experience greater short-term impact. However, very young children who do not remember pre-divorce life adjust better in the long run. In the initial period after the divorce, boys can have a more difficult time adjusting. They often miss their father and may have more conflicts with their mother. In the long run, however, girls may be reluctant to form close relationships because they fear being betrayed.

Often the level of parent conflict before and after separation plays a role in a child's response. When a child recognizes that married life for the parents was filled with conflict, he or she may have an easier time adjusting to the separation. Moreover, when partners co-operate after separation, it is easier for the children. Continued contact with other family members is also important in adjustment. The following study reveals that many different factors are at play when evaluating the impact of divorce.

Devastation of Divorce Disputed

A major study of more than 20 000 children disputes the long-held belief that divorce triggers long-term problems in many children. The study suggests that many of the problems arise during the period before the divorce occurs, when the children are growing up in a sharply dysfunctional family.

The international research team, headed by sociologist Andrew Cherlin of Johns Hopkins University, concludes parents should not stay together for the sake of the children when severe problems exist within marriage. They also recommend that new efforts be made to provide emotional support to children in such dysfunctional families.

Figure 7–14

In what circumstances might a child benefit from the divorce of his or her parents?

Figure 7–15

What factors explain changes in divorce rate?

Divorce rates in Canada, 1921–1997	
Year	Divorces per 100 000 Population
1921	6.4
1941	21.4
1961	36.0
1981	278.0
1991	280.0
1997	224.7

Source: Statistics Canada, *Marriage and Divorces*, 1997.

CASE STUDY

1. When might divorce benefit children?

2. Is divorce a single event or a longer-term process?

3. When do children suffer most as a result of divorce?

"Our study suggests that divorce isn't an event that occurs one day when a judge raps a gavel," Cherlin said, "but a process that begins long before then and extends long afterward."

Clinical psychologist Robert Emery of the University of Virginia cautioned that the new study does not mean that there are no ill effects of divorce and that divorce isn't difficult. It does mean that we have to be careful about attributing behaviour difficulties in children to the event of a divorce rather than to other aspects of family relations.

"Children in intact marriages that have long-standing intense conflict are worse off than other kids," Cherlin said. "At the extreme, among families racked by intense conflict, violence and substance abuse, many children would be better off if their parents split up. But in the average divorce, where one parent is merely bored or unfulfilled, I'm not at all convinced that children are better off if parents divorce."

Activities

Understand Ideas

1. Create a chart to summarize information from this section. Use the following headings: Definition of Abuse, Causes of Abuse and Dealing with Abuse.

2. Make a list of the legal, social and personal factors that have made divorce easier in recent times. Write a paragraph to summarize these factors.

3. What are some of the effects of divorce upon family members?

Think and Evaluate

4. Give your opinion on one of the following, stating your reasons:
   a) Should divorce be harder to obtain?
   b) Should couples who are thinking about divorce be required to undergo counselling first?

Research and Communicate

5. **a)** Investigate what can be done in your community to help a person who is being abused. Find five different ways to help someone with this problem.
   b) Create a class bulletin board that shows the challenges as well as the sources of assistance in cases of abuse.

6. Assume the role of a newspaper advice columnist. Write a reply to someone who has asked what to do about violence in his or her relationship. Begin your response with "If I were Ann Landers, I would suggest you...." Provide at least three reasons why your suggestions should be followed.

Key Points

- The family is an important social group in nearly every society.

- Families fulfill many important needs: to give and receive affection, to raise children and to provide economic and psychological support.

- In some societies, the family is the only social group, and it fulfills most, if not all, human needs. In societies such as our own, the family is one of a number of social groups and it specializes in certain areas.

- The family adapts to new social conditions and needs. Since our society is changing rapidly, it is not surprising that new forms of the family and new family patterns have emerged.

- At present, there are a number of types of families including nuclear, extended, single-parent and other forms.

- In the process of change, stresses and strains are bound to occur.

- Some families also have problems. Abuse and divorce are two of the most serious. Steps can be taken, however, to deal with both of these problems.

Activities

Understand Ideas

1. Use diagrams to show the structure of each of the following: a nuclear family; an extended family; a blended or reconstituted family; a single-parent family. (See Skill Focus, page 125.)

2. Create a sequence chart that identifies the four stages of family structures. For each stage of development, record the time period (e.g., past or present), gender roles and location of work.

Think and Evaluate

3. a) Is the family life cycle shown in Figure 7–6 applicable to all families? Explain.
   b) Would you like to follow this family life cycle? Give reasons for your view.

Apply Your Learning

4. Find a photograph of your family or a family you know well. Identify who is in the picture. Then identify and explain the familial role of each person in the picture.

Research and Communicate

5. Do you think single-parent households can do as good a job raising children as two-parent households? Write a four-paragraph comparison essay to answer the question. (See Skill Focus, page 115.)

   - Paragraph 1: Introduction. State your opinion; write summary sentences that hint at your conclusion.
   - Paragraph 2: Describe and evaluate single-parent households.
   - Paragraph 3: Describe and evaluate two-parent households.
   - Paragraph 4: Conclusion. Summarize evidence from paragraphs 2 and 3; reassert the opinion expressed in the introduction.

   Include with your essay the line graph, bar graph and pie chart you created showing the data from Figure 7–4 on page 155.

6. a) Work in groups to choose one of the following topics for discussion.
   - What creates successful families?
   - Are families becoming more or less important than they were in the past?
   - Should parents stay together for the sake of the children?
   b) Present your conclusions to the class.

Groups, Cliques and Social Behaviour

In This Chapter

- How and why do people form groups?

- To what sort of groups do people belong?

- How do groups influence their members' behaviour?

- How do leaders affect a group?

Key Terms

social group

crowd

primary group

secondary groups

network

roles

norms

sanctions

clique

leadership

Families are one kind of grouping that human beings form, but people belong to other groups as well. For example, you probably have a specific group of friends, and you might belong to a sports team or a drama group. Most often these are beneficial arrangements, though not always.

Which groups in your life tend to do the following? Discuss the groups you identify with the class.

- are concerned about your best interests

- are interested in what you can do for the group

- are primarily interested in one aspect of your life

- encourage you to do your best

- expect you to be involved with the group for the rest of your life

- expect you to be on your best behaviour

- insist that you fulfill obligations

- provide a group in which to relax

- provide moral support when you have problems

- provide rewards for work done

Are there any groups that tempt you to act against your own better judgment?

Types of Groups

Social Groups, Categories and Crowds

A **social group** refers to two or more people who interact with each other and are aware of having something in common. We belong to some social groups because we were born into them. For example, we were born into our family. We voluntarily join other groups because they provide us with something we need or want.

Social groups meet a variety of needs. Some, such as families and friendships, help satisfy important psychological or social needs such as giving and receiving affection or providing a sense of belonging. Others, such as schools and work groups, help us achieve goals that we could not otherwise accomplish, such as getting an education, making money or producing a product or service. Social groups can provide us with knowledge that would not otherwise be available, help give us a sense of safety and security and help us establish our own social identity as individuals.

A social group is different from a category of people, such as teens, single parents, doctors and so on. A category of people has one thing in common but its members are unaware of each other in a personal sense. For example, you are probably a member of the following categories: students, sons or daughters, employees and teenagers. That does not mean necessarily that you interact or have anything else in common with others of that category.

A social group is also different from a **crowd.** A crowd, such as riders on a bus, may have little or nothing to do with each other even if they are in the same place at the same time. They are simply a collection of people who have come together for a specific purpose: to travel downtown, to shop in the mall, to watch a concert, to express concern for a political policy. A crowd can, on occasion, turn into a group, but only if the people in it begin to relate to each other. A bus caught in traffic, for example, or an elevator trapped between floors, can turn a crowd into a group. You will learn more about crowds in Chapter 10.

Focus Questions

What is a social group?

What are primary and secondary groups?

What are the benefits of networks?

Connections

What role do social groups play in Cooley's theory of the looking-glass self? (See Chapter 6, pages 129–130.)

Figure 8–1

What groups do you belong to? Why? ▼

Primary and Secondary Groups

A **primary group** is a small group whose members have personal, often emotional, relationships with each other. The sociologist Charles Cooley (1864–1929) first named these "primary groups" because they are the first and most important groups in our lives. Typically, individuals spend a great deal of time in primary groups and feel they know the others in those groups well. Primary group members care about each other. They are interested in the whole personality of each member of the group, not just one aspect of it. A family and a small group of friends are examples of primary groups.

Secondary groups are more impersonal and formal than primary groups. Members generally have temporary and short-term relationships. In secondary groups, the individuals judge each other more by what they can do, and what they can offer the organization, than by who they are. A business organization, for example, is mainly concerned with the quality of work of its employees. A school, business organization or athletic team is usually a secondary group.

Figure 8–2

Record two examples for each of these characteristics.

Characteristics of primary and secondary groups

Primary group	Secondary group
• personal relationships	• impersonal and formal relationships
• long-term relationships	• variable, shorter-term relationships
• interested in the person as a whole	• interested in a narrow aspect of the person
• usually face-to-face communication	• often more formal and written communication

Figure 8–3

What benefits and potential problems can electronic networks bring?

Networks

A **network** is a very loose group. Networks connect people who normally would have little interaction with each other. A network can include a large number of people at great distances from each other.

Some network contacts are regular, such as those between friends and acquaintances who keep in touch by telephone or mail. Other network contacts are occasional contacts—perhaps only when someone needs information or a reference. Old school friends, former teachers, people we used to work with and people in clubs and other organizations may be part of our network of acquaintances. People often use networks when looking for a job. Typically, people who are young, well educated and living in urban areas have the most extensive networks.

Information technology, such as the Internet, has dramatically changed the nature of communication between individuals. Through chat groups, Internet users can communicate with others who share similar interests no matter where they live in the world. Consequently, the kinds and extent of networks available to people have greatly increased.

Activities

Understand Ideas

1. Provide a definition and brief example for each of the following terms: *social group, category, crowd, primary group, secondary group.*

2. Review the groups you identified at the start of this chapter (page 164). Categorize each one as primary or secondary.

3. **a)** List all the types of groups identified in the chapter so far.
   b) Explain how a network is different from at least two of these groups.

Think and Evaluate

4. Make a T-chart in your notebook. Label the left side "Pro" and the right side "Con." Then record arguments in response to the following statement: "It is possible to live without groups, as an isolated human being." Use these arguments as the basis for a class debate.

Apply Your Learning

5. Make a chart titled "Personal Involvement with Groups." Divide a page into four sections. In each section, write the name of one group to which you belong. Answer the following questions for each section:
   a) How long have you been a member of this group?
   b) What were the circumstances of your joining this group?
   c) Why do you remain a member of this group? (What needs does the group meet?)
   d) Under what circumstances might you leave this group?
   e) What would prevent you from leaving this group?

6. According to the way a network is described in the text, explain your membership in three networks.

How Groups Shape Behaviour

Focus Questions

How do groups affect the actions of their members?

How do social roles influence behaviour?

Social groups have a powerful impact on our thinking and behaviour. Sociologists have defined several ways in which groups influence the behaviour of their members. For example, groups influence behaviour by assigning their members social **roles**—behaviours that individuals within a group are expected to perform. In a family, a parent is expected to provide economic and emotional support to the children. A new employee in a company is expected to learn the ways of that company, and to respect those who have been there longer. Think of a group to which you belong. What different roles, behaviours and attitudes exist in this group?

Although social roles often provide us with positive models for behaviour, they can also cause problems. A person may continue in a role even when he or she is no longer in the group. A student used to acting in certain ways with friends or family may find that these roles are inappropriate in the school or workplace. Role conflict can occur when a person has to assume two roles that overlap or interfere with each other. A student, for example, may find that family responsibilities interfere with homework.

Norms are the rules within a group that indicate how members should behave. These rules might be formal and written down, or informal and understood by everyone. Following the norms of the group is important if

roles—behaviours that individuals within a group are expected to perform

norms—the rules within a group that indicate how members should behave

sanctions—the means by which the group rewards or punishes members to control their behaviour

Figure 8–4

How do roles, norms and sanctions shape behaviour? Identify each of these in the pictures above.

a member wants to continue as part of that group. Students who consistently refuse to abide by school norms find themselves in difficulty and sometimes outside of the group.

Sanctions are used to encourage or discourage certain kinds of behaviour. Acceptance, good marks and a paycheque are positive sanctions. Rejection, test failures, reprimands and shunning (avoiding or refusing to acknowledge someone) are negative sanctions.

Social scientists have investigated the impact of groups by setting up several kinds of experiments. The three that follow, starting on page 169, are some of the most famous.

SOCIAL SCIENCE *LIVE*

Meeting Norms

Imagine you are meeting someone new at school or at a social gathering. Which of the following topics would you **not** ask about? Why would you not discuss them? Which topics might be suitable in some situations but not in others? Discuss your responses with the class.

1. the weather
2. part-time jobs
3. religion
4. a boyfriend or girlfriend
5. clothes and fashion
6. the person's age
7. sports results
8. how well the person does at school
9. items in the news
10. the person's health
11. food and restaurants
12. how much money the person earns or is given by his or her parents
13. if he or she has any brothers and sisters
14. if he or she has any pets

The Asch Experiment in Group Conformity

In 1952, psychologist Solomon Asch conducted a classic study that revealed the power of groups to shape thinking. In the experiment, all but one member of a small group of students were told the real purpose of the experiment—the study of group conformity. These students were then told that, during the experiment, they were to exert pressure on the one member who had not been told the real purpose of the experiment. The uninformed student believed the experiment was to test visual perception.

All of the students were shown a line and asked to match it to one of the three lines on a card (see Figure 8–5). On the first few trials everyone in the group answered correctly. The informed members then began to answer incorrectly but confidently, as they had been instructed. The uninformed student, who was the last to answer, looked concerned and uncomfortable when the wrong answers were given. That student could either answer correctly or conform to the group by answering incorrectly. What would you have done?

Asch found that one-third of all subjects chose to conform to the group and answer incorrectly. It appeared that the group had the power to pressure individuals to answer incorrectly because they did not want to be seen as different from the others. Have you ever found yourself in a position where group pressure made you consider making a decision that you felt was wrong?

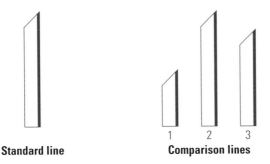

Standard line   1   2   3
                                        Comparison lines

CASE STUDY

1. What did Asch want to find out in his study?

2. What did the study reveal?

conformity—changing opinions or behaviour to match those of another person or group

Figure 8–5

These are the lines used in the Asch experiment. Which is the same as the standard line? Do you think it would have been easy to give the wrong answer by mistake?

Stanley Milgram's Experiment

Stanley Milgram was a student of Solomon Asch. The purpose of his experiments of 1963 was to test the power of conformity. In Milgram's experiment, a researcher, dressed in a white lab coat, instructed a subject to "teach" pairs of words to a "learner"—someone who was seated out of sight of the "teacher." Whenever the learner made a mistake, he was to receive an electric shock. The severity of the shocks was to increase with each mistake. The levels of shocks were labelled "mild," "intense,"

CASE STUDY

1. What did Milgram want to find out in his experiment?

2. What did the experiment reveal?

"dangerous" and "severe." The "severe" level administered 450 volts and was labelled "XXX." In fact, the learner was not really receiving electrical shocks, but the teacher did not know this. Throughout the experiment, as the shock levels increased, the learner pretended to be in pain. He would moan, beg to be released, scream and then finally become silent.

Milgram found that most teachers continued to administer shocks right up to the most severe level. On occasion they asked the researcher if they should continue administering shocks at such high levels; the teachers continued when the researcher insisted they should. Only a few refused to go to higher levels when the learner begged them to stop.

Milgram then changed the experiment in order to investigate how groups could pressure people to administer shocks. In this experiment, a group of three teachers, two of whom were in on the experiment, were to make the decisions on punishment together. All three were to suggest a shock level whenever the learner made a mistake, and the group would then administer the lowest suggested level. Milgram found that when two group members pressured the third to increase the shock, the group administered shocks three to four times higher than in situations in which the teacher acted alone.

A number of broad conclusions have been reached on the basis of this research. For example, it appears that ordinary people, under certain circumstances, can be convinced to cause harm to others, even if these people are not considered guilty of a crime or antisocial. Comparisons have been made with the ordinary character of Nazi soldiers who participated in the death camps during World War II. The questions arise as to what kinds of actions people could be convinced to take, and why they would take them.

Connections

How ethical was Milgram's experiment? (See Chapter 3, page 45; Chapter 6, pages 113–114.)

Figure 8–6

The Milgram Experiment. The "learner" is strapped into a chair and electrodes are attached to his wrist. Why did "teachers" continue to shock the learner, even when they believed they were causing pain?

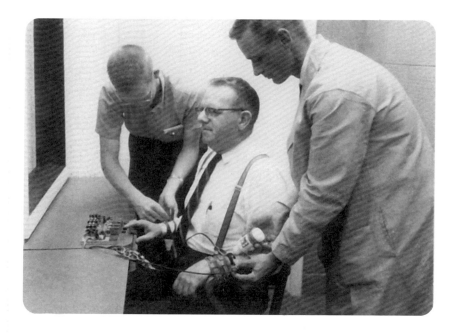

The Zimbardo Experiment

Philip Zimbardo, a social psychologist, studied how roles affect behaviour. He set up a mock prison where students played the roles of prisoners and guards. In his article "Pathology of Imprisonment," Zimbardo described how the roles we play deeply influence our social behaviour:

In an attempt to understand just what it means psychologically to be a prisoner or a prison guard, we created our own prison. We carefully screened over 70 volunteers who answered an ad in a Palo Alto city newspaper and ended up with about two dozen young men who were selected to be part of this study. They were mature, emotionally stable, normal, intelligent college students from middle-class homes throughout the United States and Canada. They appeared to represent the cream of this generation. None had any criminal record and all were relatively homogeneous on many dimensions initially.

Half were arbitrarily designated as prisoners by a flip of a coin, the others as guards. These were the roles they were to play in our simulated prison. The guards were made aware of the potential seriousness and danger of the situation and their own vulnerability. They made up their own formal rules for maintaining law, order and respect, and were generally free to improvise new ones during their eight-hour, three-man shifts. The prisoners were unexpectedly picked up at their homes by a city policeman in a squad car, searched, handcuffed, fingerprinted, booked at the Palo Alto station house and taken blindfolded to our jail. There they were stripped, deloused, put into a uniform, given a number and put into a cell with two other prisoners where they expected to live for the next two weeks. The pay was good ($15 a day) and their motivation was to make money. We observed and recorded on videotape the events that occurred in the prison, and we interviewed and tested the prisoners and guards at various points throughout the study.

At the end of only six days we had to close down our mock prison because what we saw was frightening. It was no longer apparent to most of the subjects

1. What did Zimbardo want to find out in his experiment?

2. What did the experiment reveal?

homogeneous—similar

arbitrarily—randomly

deloused—treated to remove lice

Figure 8–7
A "guard" searches a "prisoner" during the Zimbardo experiment. How do you think each of the men felt during this incident?

Writing a Response Paper

The experiments described in this section have drawn mixed responses from social scientists over the years. Some have argued that these types of experiments are not ethical (see Chapter 3, page 45). Others have argued that the methodology in some of the experiments was flawed. In responding to such studies, there are several clear steps to follow.

Here's How

- What was the purpose of the study described?

- Identify the hypotheses suggested by the research.

- Describe the methods used to conduct the research, as outlined in the text.

- Outline the results of the research. What happened?

- Identify and explain the conclusions reached by the study.

- Respond with your own reactions to what you have read. You might find it useful to start with: "I do understand…" and "I don't understand…".

Practise It

1. Write a one-page response paper to one of the experiments described in this section.

2. Switch papers with a partner who has responded to a different experiment. Evaluate the paper, using the steps above as criteria.

3. Revise your response paper before handing it in or discussing it with a larger group.

---

pathological—severely abnormal

servile—submissive

traumatic—shocking and disturbing

(or to us) where reality ended and their roles began. The majority had indeed become prisoners or guards, no longer able to clearly differentiate between role-playing and self. There were dramatic changes in virtually every aspect of their behaviour, thinking and feeling. In less than a week the experience of imprisonment undid (temporarily) a lifetime of learning; human values were suspended, self-concepts were challenged and the ugliest, most base, pathological side of human nature surfaced. We were horrified because we saw some boys (guards) treat others as if they were despicable animals, taking pleasure in cruelty, while other boys (prisoners) became servile, dehumanized robots who thought only of escape, of their own individual survival and of their mounting hatred for the guards.

We had to release three prisoners in the first four days because they had such acute situational traumatic reactions as hysterical crying, confusion in thinking and severe depression. Others begged to be parolled, and all but three were willing to forfeit all the money they had earned if they could be parolled. By then (the fifth day) they had been so programmed to think of themselves as prisoners that when their request for parole was denied, they returned docilely to their cells. Now, had they been thinking as college students acting in an oppressive experiment, they would have quit once they no longer wanted the $15 a day we used as our only incentive. However, the reality was not quitting an experiment but "being parolled by the parole board from the Stanford County Jail." By the last days, the earlier solidarity among the prisoners (systematically broken by the guards) dissolved into "each man for himself." Finally, when one of their fellows was put in solitary confinement (a small closet) for refusing to eat, the prisoners were given a choice by one of the guards: give up their blankets and the incorrigible prisoner would be let out, or keep their blankets and he would be kept in all night. They voted to keep their blankets and to abandon their brother.

About a third of the guards became tyrannical in their arbitrary use of power, in enjoying their control over other people. They were corrupted by the power of their roles and became quite inventive in their techniques of breaking the spirit of the prisoners and making them feel they were worthless. Some of the guards merely did their jobs as tough but fair correctional officers, and several were good guards from the prisoners' point of view since they did them small favours and were friendly. However, no good guard ever interfered with a command by any of the bad guards; they never intervened on the side of the prisoners, they never told the others to ease off because it was only an experiment, and they never even came to me as prison superintendent or experimenter in charge to complain.

Connections

What impact does the Zimbardo experiment have on our understanding of human behaviour and the nature-nurture debate? (See Chapter 2, page 26; Chapter 4, pages 83–84; Chapter 5, page 106; Chapter 6, pages 116–118.)

Activities

Understand Ideas

1. **a)** Explain the following terms with a definition and an example from your own life: *roles, norms, sanctions.*
   b) With a partner, select one example. Create a short dialogue to demonstrate the term as used in your example.
2. Create one flow chart for each of the three case studies. Follow the example below. Make a personal statement that explains whether you think the conclusions are justified.

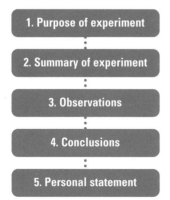

1. **Purpose of experiment**

2. **Summary of experiment**

3. **Observations**

4. **Conclusions**

5. **Personal statement**

3. What general conclusions can be drawn from these experiments? What other questions do these conclusions raise? (See Skill Focus, page 24.)

Think and Evaluate

4. How do you think you would have behaved in the Zimbardo experiment if you were a prisoner or a guard? Would you have conformed to the expected behaviour of your role?

Apply Your Learning

5. **a)** Exchange your Personal Involvement with Groups chart (page 167) with a partner. Review your partner's chart and ask for clarification if necessary.
   b) Explain your partner's involvement in one group to the class.
   c) Is there a common underlying reason people are influenced by groups? Write your answer in a paragraph, making specific reference to three separate student presentations. (See Skill Focus, page 115.)

6. What are the norms of your social science classroom? In other words, what behaviour is expected of those who attend that class? Make a list of what you see as expected behaviours. Compare your list with others in the class.

7. Explain what sanctions are available in any group (e.g., family or in school) to which you belong. What does the group, or members of the group, do when individuals do not conform to expected behaviour?

clique—an exclusive group that includes a small number of chosen members

Cliques: An Important Group

Think about your friends, the people you hang out with, those outside your family with whom you spend the most time. Are they a group of between two and twelve individuals? Are they generally of the same sex and approximately the same age? Do you tend to participate together in the same activities such as having lunch, engaging in the same extracurricular activities or going out on the weekend? If you answered "yes" to most or all of these questions, then sociologists would say that you belong to a **clique** (pronounced "cleek").

Why do people belong to cliques? Through cliques, people find others who share their values, ideas and activities. Cliques provide a way to form close friendships as most people in a clique know each other very well and spend significant amounts of time together. They often engage in a variety of activities and discussions with the other members of their clique.

Cliques change over time. The group of close friends that exists in the primary grades will often become a different clique by high school. After graduation, some close friendships will continue, while others will not. In college, in the workplace or in other areas of adult life, new cliques will form.

Figure 8–8

Why do people belong to particular cliques or larger groups such as gangs? What cliques exist in your school?

Why Do Gangs Form?

Sometimes cliques encourage antisocial behaviour. You can probably think of times when peer pressure has tempted you to do something against your better judgment. Many teens have had this experience, but in some extreme cases the effect of the clique goes further. Sometimes cliques develop into gangs, and sometimes those gangs become violent. Why do gangs form and who tends to join?

Clearly, joining a gang is a personal choice, but generally, it has been found that young people with antisocial behaviour have learned their attitudes in their families, where there is often a hostile relationship between parent and child. These young people gravitate toward others who have had similar experiences. The values of the group then shape their behaviour, and they engage in activities that conflict with society's norms.

Some sociologists believe that such young people may join gangs because they are looking for the close relationships that are denied to them at home. They may feel that they can build a relationship with people who have had similar experiences. However, studies show that, even though members of gangs spend significant periods of time with each other, they do not often describe their relationships as emotionally close. Some psychologists believe that gang members are hoping to gain the power and recognition they do not get in their families, or from society at large. Some anthropologists have suggested that young people are attracted by the sense of anonymity (not being easily identified) found within gangs, which allows them to do as they please.

Which of these reasons do you think are evident in the following article entitled "The Swarm" by John Barber?

At 15, Kevin does not go to school. Two years ago, after his father abandoned his family, Kevin's mother took out her frustrations on him. The abuse was mutual, often violent. Children's Aid became involved. Now his mother is gone and Kevin has moved back in with his father.

His real family is one he found on the street.... "Most kids got involved 'cause of their family situation," he says matter-of-factly.... "You hang around together and form a family. It's a proper family, it gives you security. When you're with everyone else you get a sense of power; you get respect."

How much respect you get depends on how bad you are. Everybody "plays bad" these days. "You name it, we do every kind of crime practically. Assault, grand theft, petty theft, larceny, fraud, B-and-Es, sexual assault.... When you're in a gang you go crazy. You'd be surprised. They get crazy. You see this burning in their eyes. They love to fight." Kevin's nose was broken by one of his own confederates when he started an unauthorized war with another gang.

Kevin looks up.... He makes eye contact for the first time. There's a secret he wants to share, a dirty little secret that would ruin him if it ever got out. "You talk to any gang guy, I don't care how bad he is, deep down he's soft. But you have to play bad so people will leave you alone. You have to make a name so people don't bug you."

What Do You Think?

1. List three reasons given by social scientists to suggest why young people join gangs. Find an example to support each argument in the article.

2. Can a group be an effective support for someone who has had a difficult family life? Explain with reference to various groups.

3. If you could give Kevin some advice, what would it be?

Several social factors shape cliques that are formed in adolescence. These cliques tend to be made up of individuals of a similar age, probably because they are in the same school grade. In early adolescence, cliques are often made up of people of the same sex. Young men and women have different interests at this age and, consequently, they spend time trying to define their gender roles. Research from the United States suggests that members of cliques often come from the same social class and tend to be from the same ethnic group. Do you think that Canadian findings would be the same?

What draws individuals toward certain cliques? Sociologists have found several common characteristics among teen cliques. Teens and their friends often share attitudes about school and educational plans. Someone who intends to go to university, for example, will probably be part of a clique whose members have similar plans. Cliques also tend to form around certain kinds of music, dress, leisure activities and other behaviours. For example, "jocks" and "punks" would probably not belong to the same clique. Dress, attitude and behaviour are indications of how involved teens are in teen culture.

Connections

As a type of peer group, how can a clique act as an agent of socialization? (See Chapter 6, page 121.)

How Do Cliques Influence Behaviour?

Cliques serve a number of important functions. They help young people develop interpersonal relationships and learn how to relate to others. Cliques can help teens feel good about themselves by creating a supportive environment. In this kind of environment, the self-esteem and confidence of members can grow. In a clique, individuals can also investigate interests they may have in common such as sports, academic goals or other interest. While these particular interests may not last, they provide a learning experience for a period of time.

Activities

Understand Ideas

1. Define the term *clique*, and give an example.

2. List the social and personal factors that influence the cliques to which people belong.

Apply Your Learning

3. **a)** Describe some of the cliques that exist in your school. Record how members identify themselves, the places they go and some of their activities.

b) Identify three social and three personal factors that describe one of these cliques— perhaps one to which you belong.

c) Create a symbol that represents this clique.

4. As a class, discuss to what degree, if at all, gangs are present in your community. What characteristics identify them as gangs? (See Skill Focus, page 43.)

Leadership in Groups

Leaders emerge from groups, large or small. A leader is someone who is consistently able to influence the behaviour of others. The kind of leader a group has depends on the nature of the group. Formal organizations will have one kind of leadership while small, family groups will have another.

Kinds of Leadership

Sociologists have described two main kinds of leadership. **Instrumental leadership** organizes a group in pursuit of certain goals. An instrumental leader defines the goals and determines ways to achieve them. Political leaders and leaders of organizations, for example, need to be able to organize groups in this way.

Expressive leadership creates harmony and solidarity among group members. An expressive leader keeps morale high. He or she is usually well liked by group members.

Groups often start out believing that one leader can fulfill both of these roles. Eventually, however, members tend to divide their loyalties between the leader they believe will provide instrumental leadership and the leader they think will provide expressive leadership.

Leadership styles can vary. **Authoritarian leaders** simply give orders. This form of leadership is effective in emergencies when speed and efficiency outweigh other considerations. For example, authoritarian leadership works well in military situations, police forces and in hospital emergency rooms. **Democratic leaders** attempt to win consensus on goals and on courses of action. Democratic leaders are effective if there is disagreement over goals and methods or concerns for individual rights. Democratic leadership is effective in teaching group members to take

Focus Questions

How do leaders affect social behaviour?

What makes an effective leader?

Connections

Does a person's choice of leadership style reflect his or her personality type? (See Chapter 6, pages 130–133.)

Figure 8–9
This social-work student volunteers 12 hours a week to counsel young people in Winnipeg. What kind of leader is she likely to be?

What's Your Leadership Style?

What kind of leader do you think you might be? To find out, respond to the following statement according to the way you would behave if you were leader of a group. Record your answers in your notebook: A = always, S = sometimes, N = never.

1. I would give members complete freedom to do what they want.

2. I am friendly and approachable.

3. I want to be the one who speaks for the group.

4. I like to keep the work moving quickly.

5. I dislike waiting for people to catch up to me.

6. I would act without consulting others.

7. I like to solve problems without help.

8. Lots of detail doesn't bother me.

9. I appreciate help from others.

10. I would encourage the group to set its own pace.

11. I would have the group vote on decisions.

12. I would work hard to get promoted.

Answers

Count **1** for A answers in questions 3, 4, 5, 6, 7 and 12, for S answer in question 2, and for N answers in questions 1, 2, 8, 9, 10 and 11. Count **2** for all S answers except in question 2. Count **3** for all remaining answers. Your total will reflect your leadership style.

If you scored low (1–12), your leadership style is more authoritarian. You give direction. You make all the decisions and don't "waste time" interacting with the team. This kind of leadership works well in crisis situations but you could work on recognizing the experience and knowledge of team members when making decisions.

If you scored in the middle (13–24), your leadership style is more democratic. You encourage team participation in decision making, and you acknowledge team members' expertise and opinions. However, you must be able to make a final decision when necessary.

If you scored high (24–36), your leadership style is more laissez-faire. You are a hands-off leader who gives responsibility to the team but expects results. If you identified responsibilities and roles for team members, the team could go a long way in meeting the goals of the group.

responsibility for actions and decisions. **Laissez-faire leaders** make little attempt to direct or organize the group, which functions mostly on its own. This kind of leadership may be less effective in promoting group goals than other types of leadership.

Characteristics of Leaders

While leadership styles can vary, there are several common characteristics found in leaders. Most leaders have a strong sense of achievement, a high energy level and the ability to make firm decisions. Leaders are usually self-confident, creative and highly motivated by the desire to be in charge and to exercise authority over others. They are often flexible, recognizing that different situations require different actions. Leaders are also familiar with the activities of the group and its goals.

Effective leaders inspire people to be part of the group or mission. Political leaders such as India's Mahatma Gandhi, American President John F. Kennedy, Prime Minister Pierre Trudeau, British Prime Minister Margaret Thatcher, South African President Nelson Mandela and American civil rights leader Martin Luther King were charismatic leaders who attracted devout and enthusiastic followers. Such leaders often have a clear vision of what the future should be.

charismatic leader—a leader who has the ability to inspire followers with great enthusiasm and commitment

While charismatic leaders like Martin Luther King can bring about tremendous changes for the good, others do not always have such a positive goal. Adolf Hitler, Germany's leader during World War II, and Jim Jones, leader of the People's Temple cult (see Chapter 10), were able to attract followers to believe in much more sinister and destructive goals.

Figure 8-10

Some of history's charismatic leaders. Left: Pierre Trudeau; middle: Martin Luther King; right: Indira Gandhi (former Prime Minister of India).

Activities

Think and Evaluate

1. Think of a leader you know. This person might be a team captain, leader of the school council or leader of a fundraising drive.

   a) What kind of leader is the person you have chosen—instrumental or expressive?

   b) Which of the characteristics of leadership does this person show. Give some specific examples.

Apply Your Learning

2. Work in a group. Think of a group situation in which a leader would be present. Prepare skits to demonstrate the three styles of leadership described in the text. Present your skits so that members of the class can identify each style.

Key Points

- Social groups take several forms such as primary and secondary groups and networks. All groups have a powerful impact on our thinking and actions. Groups use roles, norms and sanctions to influence behaviour.

- Cliques are an important kind of group. Throughout our lives, but most importantly in adolescence, cliques are important because they help us understand how we relate to others through the sharing of values, ideas and activities.

- Leadership is another element of group influence. There are several kinds of leadership that allow effective leaders to provide meaning and purpose to the actions of their followers.

Activities

Understand Ideas

1. **a)** Create an outline that records the major headings of this chapter. Follow this example:

   Types of Groups
       Social Groups, Categories and Crowds
       Primary and Secondary groups

   b) What role does conformity play in each of these areas of social behaviour?

Think and Evaluate

2. How does being part of a network influence your view of yourself? Give some specific examples based on networks you have identified earlier in the chapter.

Apply Your Learning

3. Consider your own family. Analyze how you are a part of that social group. Ask yourself:

   a) What am I expected to do, and be, in that group?
   b) What is my position or status in that group?
   c) In what ways am I an important part of the group?
   d) What happens when a family member does something the rest of the group doesn't like?

   Make a web, with you in the centre surrounded by four circles that include your answers to the questions. (See Skill Focus, page 125.)

Research and Communicate

4. Use observational techniques to identify the roles, norms and sanctions that occur in a group with which you are familiar. Study your own friendship groups, your family or your social science class. (See Skill Focus, page 13.)

5. What cliques exist in your community? Find two newspaper articles that discuss cliques or gangs as social groups. Identify and describe their characteristics.

6. Research a historical or current leader of interest to you. What characteristics enabled this person to become a leader?

Chapter

9

Formal Organizations

(P) rimary social groups such as family and friends shape our behaviour and our thinking in many ways. However, these are not the only social groups that affect us. We are also part of secondary groups—the formal social organizations that influence our lives. In fact, most of the world in which we learn and work is made up of formal organizations. Consider this story:

The band that got lucky

Thousands of young people across Canada belong to bands. Very few ever become famous. How b4-4, the boy-band trio, managed to get signed to major label was a case of determination, bravery and right-place, right-time luck.

In search of some free publicity, image-savvy twins Ryan and Daniel Kowarsky, 20, and best friend Ohad Einbinder, 18, were on their way to pop a loonie at the famed MuchMusic Speaker's Corner booth.

As it turned out, they didn't quite make it there. Instead, a different let's-get-noticed tactic was suggested.

The trio decided, on the spur of the moment, to stop by at a record company. As they were trying to persuade the receptionist to let them in, two executives walked past. They invited the trio to play for them, and then offered the band a contract on the spot.

"It's so amazing, we're soooo lucky," Ryan Kowarsky says. "We're living a dream right now. It's such an adrenalin rush to get up and say, 'I can't wait to go to work.' This is what we want to do. Music, music, music, all the time."

- Why did the band want to go to a record company?

- In what ways would the record company be able to help the band?

- Why would the band members probably not be able to help themselves in the same way?

In This Chapter

- What is a formal organization?

- What purposes do formal organizations serve?

- What is a bureaucracy?

- How do bureaucracies differ from other organizations?

- How do formal organizations affect our behaviour?

Key Terms

formal organizations

bureaucracies

specialization

hierarchy of offices

rules and regulations

technical competence

impersonality

formal communication

red tape

collective

181

What Are Formal Organizations?

For most of human history small primary groups, such as the family, have fulfilled most human needs. Secondary social groups, or **formal organizations,** are more recent. While formal organizations have existed in some societies for hundreds of years, they have only become common in Canadian society during the last century.

A formal organization is a large group of people organized in a certain way so that they can achieve a specific goal efficiently. Schools, churches, or governments are all examples of formal organizations. Schools are organized to provide education in an efficient manner; churches aim to provide spiritual leadership; and government organizations attempt to meet the specific needs of communities or the nation as a whole. The relationships between people in these groups is usually more formal than in families or groups of friends. These kinds of relationships are described as secondary group relationships.

Consider the formal organizations to which you belong. You are a student of a school, of course, but you might also belong to the student council, another type of formal organization. You might also belong to a religious organization or have a part-time job in a formal organization. In each case, the organization you belong to has a purpose, and you have reasons for belonging to it.

Figure 9–1

Formal organizations change over time. What formal organization is shown in these photos? How has this type of organization remained the same over time? In what ways has it changed?

Types of Formal Organizations

Sociologist Amitai Etzioni identified three types of formal organizations. The **utilitarian organization** is one that we join because we need the service that organization offers. We join a business in order to make money or earn a living; we go to a hospital to get medical treatment; and we attend a school in order to get an education or special training.

People join **normative organizations** in order to pursue goals they think are worthwhile. Voluntary organizations such as the Scouts or the

utilitarian—practical or useful

normative—related to norms, or the rules and expectations of society that guide our behaviour

Observing Communication

How can we tell if groups exhibit primary or secondary relationships? One way is by observing the ways they communicate. Observe the differences in communication within the groups you encounter during the course of one day. If possible, include the following situations:

- members of your family speaking with each other

- a group of friends discussing topics that interest them

- teachers and members of the administration addressing a group of students

- teachers talking with one or two students outside of class

- a customer being greeted by an employee of a fast-food outlet, a cashier at a department store, or a bank teller

Record the differences you see. What differences other than communication help to distinguish the two types of groups?

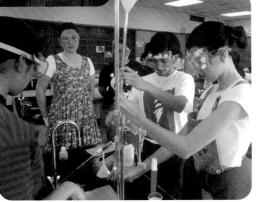

Red Cross are examples of normative organizations. Political parties and churches are also included in this kind of organization.

Coercive organizations, however, are those that we belong to without any choice. A prison or a mental institution is an example of a coercive organization. Such organizations tend to control or shape behaviour in very rigid ways. Rules are strictly enforced, and joining or leaving the organization is generally not a matter of choice.

Figure 9–2

What types of formal organizations are shown here? What details help you identify these organizations?

coercive—inclined to force or restrain

Structures of Formal Organizations

The structure of formal, or secondary, social organizations can vary. Small organizations, such as fitness clubs or church groups, usually have a simple or flat structure that consists of a supervisor or coach and a number of members. Larger organizations, such as communications or entertainment companies, or even your own school, will likely have a complex, or tall, structure (see Figure 9–3). The structure of large organizations is more complex because they require a division of labour in order to accomplish their tasks. For example, when you order fries or a salad at most drive-through restaurants, one person takes your order, another cooks the food, another packages it and so on. No one person does the entire job. In a large company, there may be several levels of managers, each one with a greater degree of responsibility.

When you become a member of a formal organization, it is important that you understand the structure of that organization. If you don't, you may end up behaving in a way that is regarded as inappropriate by others in that organization. It is especially important to recognize who is in a position of authority. If you started a new job and you immediately began to treat your boss as a friend rather than as a figure of authority, your boss and the other employees would probably find your behaviour unacceptable. While more personal relationships may develop over time, it is best to understand the specialized roles that individuals play in the organization and to behave accordingly.

division of labour—one large task divided into different jobs with people trained to perform their own job

Figure 9–3

Types of organizational structures. What are some organizations that might have the structures shown?

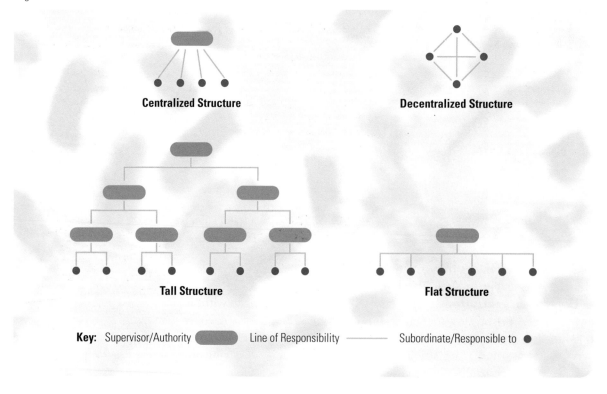

Centralized Structure

Decentralized Structure

Tall Structure

Flat Structure

Key: Supervisor/Authority ⬭ Line of Responsibility —— Subordinate/Responsible to ●

A Formal Organization: Warner Music Canada

Warner Music Canada produces and sells music by some of the world's top recording artists. The Canadian company is one of the many branches of Warner Music, whose headquarters are in New York. Warner Music has offices around the world, from Europe to Australia and from Hong Kong to South Africa. In each of these locations, the company records local musicians and distributes music from other parts of the world. The organization is evidence that music is truly an international language.

In each branch, the company is divided into several departments, including Operations, Human Resources, Marketing, Sales and Distribution, and Information Services (the computer department). "These departments are the same as you find in any retail-based business," says Alan Fletcher, Director of Strategic Marketing at Warner Music Canada. "If you were in the soap business, you would still go through more or less the same stages: you have to do research, you have to manufacture your product, and you have to sell it. And you have to make a profit."

"The main difference in the music business is the emphasis placed on promotion," Fletcher maintains. Marketing and promoting is a large part of what makes a new CD successful. Fletcher is quick to point out, though, that not every CD is a big money-earner. "Only about one in a thousand new albums is really successful," he says. "The majority of new releases in the U.S. sell only about 2000 copies, whereas a release by a superstar might sell 7 million or more copies."

1. What is the purpose of this formal organization?

2. How is the organization set up to produce and market goods more efficiently?

3. Would you like to be part of an organization like Warner Music? Explain.

retail-based business—a business that depends on selling its product in stores

Figure 9–4

From song to CD: The process

The Big Break: People in the A & R (Artists and Repertoire) Department actively seek new music. They might visit clubs, go to concerts, or listen to tapes and CDs that have been sent in by recording artists or their agents. When they find an artist with potential, they offer a recording contract.

The Recording Process: Warner Music does not have its own recording studios. The artists and their managers find a producer and a studio that meets their needs. The company might work together with the artist and producer to make the best recording possible.

Mastering and Manufacturing: The master CD is used to manufacture the CDs that will be shipped to the stores. Warner Music does not have its own manufacturing plant, but some record companies do. Warner Music has the master reproduced at a plant it chooses to provide the service.

Marketing: Even while the recording and manufacturing processes are going on, the marketing department is working to create the graphics that will appear on the CD and to make a marketing plan of how the CD will be promoted and sold.

Promotions: The first song recorded for the CD is produced as a single, and given to the promotions department about six weeks before the album will be released. The promotions staff will work to get the single played on radio stations, to set up media interviews with the artist or band, and to prepare displays in the stores.

Sales: The sales force sells CDs to record and book stores. The sales representatives start booking orders for the new CD for record stores even before the new album is released.

Figure 9–5

Alan Fletcher, Director of Strategic Marketing at Warner Music shows off some of the company's CDs that have "gone gold." An album that sells more than 50 000 copies is said to have "gone gold," more than 100 000 copies has "gone platinum" and more than a million copies has "gone diamond."

Warner Music Canada has eight regional offices across the country, as well as several other satellite offices run out of staff members' homes. These regional offices play a large part in the distribution of CDs, especially when it comes to launching new albums at the same time across the country.

While the music industry has been hugely successful around the world, it is changing in important ways. "We have always relied on retail sales," says Alan Fletcher, "but this is a changing and exciting time. We are becoming used to having music instantly, without having to buy it. Music is used on TV commercials and on video games. If you have satellite TV in your home, you could have up to 45 channels of digital music 24 hours a day with no commercials. And you can download music from various sites on the Internet without going to buy it. It's likely that these changes will soon affect the way a company like Warner Music operates."

Despite these changes, Fletcher says that the skills needed to work in the music industry are similar to those needed in many other kinds of work. "If you want to work in a recording studio, you need the technical training. But for the most part, what you need most are basic skills," he advises. "Basic math and accounting skills, computer skills, and the readiness to update your skills constantly. Excellent communication skills are vital as well, because you are working with people all the time—from dealing with recording artists to working with people in the office to selling CDs to a store. And, of course, you need to be passionately interested in music." Warner Music runs an internship program, which allows students to work for the company as part of their school program. Fletcher believes this is an invaluable way to gain experience and to learn more about the industry.

People at Warner Music work hard. For many of them, the working day is not limited to the hours between 9:00 and 5:00. People in some departments have regular business hours, but others do a full day's work and then have shows, concerts or other events to attend at night. This is a high-powered industry and staff need energy and commitment.

Yet there are many rewards. Trying to meet common goals has created strong bonds among the workers. "This company has a strong family feeling," Fletcher

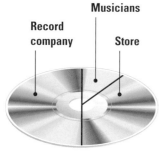

Figure 9–6

Who makes money when you buy a CD? A large portion of what you pay goes to the formal organizations that produce, distribute and sell the CD.

notes. "And this is such an exciting industry. When I first started working in it, I couldn't believe that I was being paid to do something I loved to do anyway. But that is the secret of success, I think. Focus hard on what you love to do, find out where your strengths are and then do the best you can."

Activities

Understand Ideas

1. **a)** Which of the following social groups are formal social organizations? Discuss your answers with a classmate.
   - nursery school
   - a religious congregation
   - high school
   - a group of neighbourhood friends
   - a school team
   - college
   - a fast-food restaurant
   - a family
   - a large business organization

   b) Give two ways in which formal organizations differ from primary groups. Use examples from Warner Music to support your answer.

2. Referring to the text, pick three types of formal organizations and complete a three-column chart with the following headings: Type of Formal Organization; Reasons We Join or Need Organization; Example of Organization.

Think and Evaluate

3. **a)** Identify the four kinds of structures organizations may have.
   b) Suggest reasons why an organization would have one or another kind of structure.

4. If you are a member of a formal organization, why is it important to understand your own role in relation to the roles of others?

Apply Your Learning

5. Brainstorm all of the formal social organizations members of the class have come into contact with over the last week. Make a chart that indicates the names of the organizations, why you came into contact with them, what their purposes are (what human needs they meet), and the impact of the contact on you.

6. Choose your favourite song or CD of the moment. Show how it is a product of a formal organization, using the information from the Warner Music case study as a guide.

Bureaucracies

Have you ever tried to get information on applying for a driver's licence or about a specific course from a university or college? Have you ever returned something you bought at a large store? Did you get what you wanted immediately or did you have to go through several people before you found someone who could help you? In all of these examples, you would have been dealing with a bureaucracy. **Bureaucracies** are the most complex kind of formal organizations. They have been specifically designed to perform numerous tasks as efficiently as possible, yet dealing with them can often be frustrating. This is because bureaucracies are usually large with many formal rules and regulations, and each person has a specific task to do. If you approach the wrong person, he or she must refer

Focus Questions

What is a bureaucracy?

How does a bureaucracy differ from a small group?

Who has authority in a bureaucracy?

Writing a Social Science Report

We can learn more about the organizations around us by conducting a sociological inquiry in the form of a social science report.

Here's How

1. **Define the research problem.** For example, you could take the question in Social Science Live on page 183: "How can we tell if groups exhibit primary or secondary relationships?"

2. **Review the literature.** To answer the question above, you might review what Chapter 8 said about primary groups and what this chapter says about formal organizations.

3. **Develop a hypothesis.** To answer your research problem, you might hypothesize that one way to tell a formal organization from a primary group is to observe the way people communicate in each type of situation.

4. **Design your research.** Make a plan of action for testing your hypothesis. You might observe

people in a variety of different situations to see if their style of communication differs and, if so, what it says about each type of group.

5. **Gather your data.** You collect your information by carrying out your plan of action.

6. **Analyze your data.** Write a brief description of what you have observed.

7. **Draw conclusions.** Based on the data you have collected, what can you conclude about communication in different social groups? Can you tell a formal organization by the kind of communication used? If so, how?

Practise It

Based on your observations from the Social Science Live task on page 183, write a social science report on communication in formal organizations and smaller primary groups, following the steps outlined above.

---

you to the person trained to deal with your problem or question. With many highly complex tasks to be accomplished in society today, bureaucracies have become common and widespread.

In the nineteenth century, the German sociologist Max Weber studied bureaucracies to find how they worked. He identified six major traits they all have in common. One important trait is **specialization.** Each individual is expected to complete specific tasks that are set by the organization, usually in writing. With this division of labour, workers are not expected to perform tasks assigned to others.

hierarchy—the ranking of authority from higher to lower

Within a bureaucracy, there is a **hierarchy of offices,** which means each person works in an office with other people. Together, they are all responsible for some aspect of the overall organization. For example, in a company that sells computers, one department may be responsible for sales, another for advertising and a third for shipping. Within this organization, some workers have more authority than others. Each department in the computer company would probably be supervised by a manager. In turn, this manager would be supervised by someone higher up in the

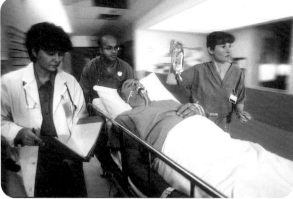

Figure 9–7
Bureaucracies and other formal organizations often require their members to wear uniforms or to adhere to a dress code. What purposes do uniforms or dress codes serve?

organization, and so on. Some offices may follow the centralized model, where everyone is monitored by one individual or group (see Figure 9–3), but a tall structure is more common, with several levels of offices that are monitored by several levels of officials.

Rules and regulations are also a characteristic of bureaucracies. These rules lay out the responsibilities of each person and each department and indicate how workers are to deal with others in the bureaucracy, as well as with the public. Rules also set out the procedures to follow if someone does not obey the rules.

If you are hired to work in a bureaucracy, you are expected to have the **technical competence**—the education, knowledge, skills and experience to do the job. You will probably have to fill out an application and go through an interview for the job. If you are successful in getting the job, your performance may be monitored regularly to see if you are ready to advance to a new position.

Another characteristic of bureaucracies is **impersonality.** Rules are more important than the personal wishes or whims of the individuals who work there. The impersonal aspect of bureaucracies can be frustrating

Connections

What part do roles and norms play in the structure of bureaucracies? (See Chapter 8, pages 167–168).

Figure 9–8

Choose a small group to which you belong. Show how it is different from a bureaucracy, using the points here as a guide. Be sure to give examples to support your answer.

Differences between bureaucracies and small groups	
Bureaucracies	**Small groups**
• members engage in specialized activities	• members engage in many similar activities
• hierarchy clearly defined	• hierarchy informal or non-existent
• rules and regulations clearly defined	• rules and regulations informal
• membership based on technical competence; performance is monitored	• membership variable or based on personal criteria
• relationships generally secondary (some primary relationships may develop)	• relationships are personal and primary
• communication is often formal and in writing	• communication is casual; face to face
• task-oriented focus	• person-oriented focus

Connections

In a bureaucracy, how important is conformity? (See Chapter 8, page 169.)

at times, but it also has some advantages. When the same rules are applied to everyone, there is a greater chance of fair treatment. In your school, for example, the rules for attendance, grades and behaviour are the same for all students. Everyone has to obey them. Special treatment or favouritism is not an accepted part of the bureaucratic way of doing things.

The final characteristic of bureaucracies is a reliance on **formal, written communication.** People in a bureaucracy obviously communicate verbally, but written files that keep a record of communication are necessary when dealing with a large number of people. Written communication ensures that services are provided and that everyone has received equal treatment. If your wallet is stolen and you report the theft to the police, you will give the officer all the detailed information about what was in your wallet. If the officer doesn't record this information in a file, then no one else at the station will know anything about your case. If you call the station the next day to get an update, no one will be able to help you because there is no record of your first call, and the information hasn't been communicated.

How would you describe the difference between bureaucracies and personal groups such as friends and family? Compare your answers with the chart in Figure 9–8.

Authority in Bureaucracies

If you have a part-time job and your boss instructs you to show up for work at a certain time, why do you do what your boss says? If your coach wants you to play a certain position on the team, or your chemistry teacher tells you not to add one chemical to another, why do you obey the instructions? What is the basis of your boss's or teacher's authority? Max Weber studied the question of authority and came to the following conclusions.

How Is Your School Organized?

Imagine if your school had no rules, no principals, no attendance records and no report cards. Students could show up for class whenever they want and teachers could come and go as they please. Would this kind of system be pure bliss or total chaos? Most schools are complex organizations with rules and regulations that help them run efficiently. What about your school? Work in groups of four or five and carry out the following research.

Specialization: Interview at least five people in your school who have specialized jobs. Ask them to describe what they are expected to do and how they know what their job description is.

Hierarchy of offices: Find out if there is a hierarchy of offices in your school. Ask representatives of each office if they are responsible to another office and if so, in what ways? Ask how they could move to a different job in the organization, or get a promotion.

Rules and regulations: What rules guide behaviour of people employed at the school? Are these written rules about behaviour or are the rules simply understood? Are there special rules for the way employees deal with each other? With parents? With students? What is the procedure if an employee fails to follow the rules of behaviour? What rules govern student behaviour in your school? Is everyone aware of these rules?

Technical competence: Interview individuals who hold different positions in the school. Find out what training and qualifications are needed for their position. How is their performance monitored? What further training or experience is needed if they want to be promoted to another position?

Impersonality: Find out the rules for students in your school. Do the rules ensure fair treatment to all students? If so, how? What is the procedure for grading and evaluating student work? What rules govern failure to attend class or behaviour that is considered wrong?

Formal written communication: Interview five members of the school to find out what written files these employees are required to produce as part of their job? Who receives the files once they are completed? Why are these files important? How long are they kept?

Informal social groups: Make a list of several informal groups in your school. How are these groups organized? Where do they meet? What departments do they involve? How important are these groups to the individuals involved?

Combine the results of this research to develop a portrait of your school. Does the school aim to provide the best education? Did you find any problems in the way your school is run? How could these problems be corrected? To what degree does your school act as a formal organization, even as a bureaucracy? To what degree are informal, small group relations also important?

We tend to obey people who are seen as having traditional authority to tell us what to do. For example, people may accept the right of a king or queen to rule or of a religious leader to guide them. Your parents or aunts and uncles have traditional authority; therefore it is considered wrong to disobey them.

We also tend to obey people we see as charismatic—leaders who appear to have special charm, character or wisdom. Even those who disagree with the views of a charismatic leader will often recognize the influence he or

Figure 9–9

What authority is held by the people shown here? Why do we tend to recognize or obey them?

Connections

What type of leadership style would be most effective in a bureaucratic organization? (See Chapter 8, pages 177–178.)

informal structure—relationships that develop naturally among co-workers

she has in getting people to obey. This kind of leadership is sometimes seen in relationships at school. Think of your group of friends. Is there one person who can easily convince the rest of the group to do something? Do you and your other friends look to this person for leadership? What is it that gives this person his or her charismatic authority?

Finally, we tend to obey people who hold power within a formal organization or bureaucracy. These people have achieved a leadership position through the rules of the organization. You might become a leader in an organization by virtue of your education and training or because you have worked there a long time and have greater seniority. In most cases, the rules for becoming a leader in an organization of this sort are clear to everyone. We tend to respect these leaders because they have been promoted as a result of their qualifications and not just because they are popular.

Personal Relationships in Bureaucracies

In every formal organization or bureaucracy, small groups of people come to relate to each other in a more personal way. Sometimes supervisors are concerned that informal structures and friendships in a bureaucracy keep people from doing their work properly. Yet some studies show that this is often not the case.

A group of sociologists studied employees at the Western Electric Company, looking for ways to encourage them to work harder. They discovered that worker output was determined not only by official company rules but also by informal norms or conduct within small groups. For example, the workers put pressure on each other to pull their weight and to do their jobs properly. They tended to monitor each other on the amount of time taken for lunch, the number of breaks taken and many other aspects of the job. The researchers also discovered that employees often developed their own rules that were a strong guide to behaviour even though they were not written down. For example, the workers would not "squeal" to superiors about certain problems they were having. In some cases, relationships among workers extended beyond "on the job" expectations. Many employees spent time together during coffee breaks or lunch or even after work, and friendships sometimes developed. These examples show that, despite the formal rules of a bureaucracy, personal factors also have an important role to play on the job. Some research suggests that this kind of casual interaction at work encourages people to help each other and get the job done. Informal relationships at work can also make time spent at work more interesting and worthwhile.

Activities

Understand Ideas

1. What is a bureaucracy? Why are bureaucracies necessary?

2. List the three types of authority in a formal organization. Provide a real-life example to demonstrate your understanding.

3. a) What is the informal structure of formal organizations and bureaucracies?
   b) What are the advantages and potential problems of informal structures in organizations?

Think and Evaluate

4. In a bureaucracy, each person is required to complete specific tasks. Identify and explain one benefit and one drawback of this aspect of bureaucracy.

5. List three ways in which an employee's performance is monitored in a bureaucracy. Do you agree or disagree with performance monitoring? Give reasons for your view.

6. a) In your opinion, what motivates workers to monitor each other?
   b) Under what circumstances would you "squeal" on a co-worker?

7. a) Work in groups of four to find out what the organizational leaders in your school think are important leadership qualities. Each group member should interview one of the following: a member of the school administration, a department head, a teacher and a member of the student council. (See Skill Focus, page 12.)
   b) In your group, draw up a profile of an effective leader in a large social organization, based on your findings.

Apply Your Learning

8. What kinds of authority would be used in each of the following: family, religious institution, school, large business organization, the government (e.g., the prime minister), a group of high school friends, a clique and your part-time job? In each case, give reasons for your choice.

inefficiency—failure to make the best of time and resources

incompetence—inability to perform a particular task

Figure 9–10

Cartoonist Scott Adams is known for poking fun at bureaucracies. The language of a bureaucracy is often jargon— specialized words or expressions that match specialized work. Sometimes employees use jargon to make themselves and their work seem more important. Jargon is one of the characteristics of the red tape that can make dealing with bureaucracies a frustrating experience.

Assessing Bureaucracies

Bureaucracies are needed to meet the needs of large numbers of people. Health care, education, transportation and defence are all vital to our modern way of life, and bureaucracies provide these services. Large corporations such as telecommunications companies or clothing manufacturers could not deliver their products and services efficiently without formal organization. With large organizations, however, there are bound to be problems. One of the biggest problems bureaucracies face is inefficiency, which can be caused in a number of ways.

Inefficiency is often caused by **red tape**—endless amount of documentation and attention to detail: You need more documentation. You didn't fill out the right form. You don't have proper identification. You need another signature. It is at times like these that bureaucratic procedures can hinder rather than help to meet the tasks the organization is set up to do. A bureaucracy can become inefficient when people in it lose sight of the overall goal and get caught up in the rules and procedures.

Bureaucracies are also inefficient when information does not flow clearly from the people at the top of the organization down to those who must perform the task. If this is the case, people may not have proper instructions for getting their job done or they may not fully understand the purpose or overall goal of what they are doing.

Some sociologists have poked fun at the way bureaucracies operate. Lawrence Peter came up with the theory that individuals in organizations tend to be promoted until they reach a level where they no longer do the job well. They are not promoted any further, but they remain in their jobs. This means that many jobs are filled by people who are not competent to do them. The theory that people rise to their level of incompetence is called the Peter Principle. Bureaucracies continue to function, says Peter, only because there are enough people in the organization who have not reached their level of incompetence and can still perform their jobs well.

Northcote Parkinson believed that work always expands to fill the time available for its completion. If workers are given two days to do one day's work, they will take two days to finish the task. Think of a school assignment. Suppose you are given five days to work on the project. On the

DILBERT reprinted by permission of United Feature Syndicate, Inc.

fourth day, the teacher gives you another five days to work on it. Would you finish the project in five days or would you take the extra five days to work on it? According to Parkinson's Law, you would take as much time as you were given to complete the task, even if it could be done in less time.

The following case study examines some of the advantages and disadvantages of a formal organization that is familiar to most of us.

Grocery Shopping: Then and Now

Many people believe that the switch from small family-run grocery stores, popular years ago, to the large supermarkets of today offers benefits such as convenience, speed of shopping, greater product selection and so on. But few stop to consider what has been lost. Is this move to formal organizations and bureaucracies always an indication of progress? What do you think?

The other day Bev and I went grocery shopping. We stopped in the meat department, choosing from an immense array of cuts continually being topped up by green-coated employees pushing huge meat-bins. My mind wandered. It usually does under such circumstances.

I remembered one summer, as a boy of ten or eleven, working in my grandparents' small town grocery store. My grandparents had owned and worked in the store all their lives, raising a family of four boys and living a financially comfortable life. When I knew them, and worked in the store, they were already in their late sixties or early seventies and still going strong.

That summer I worked for the sum of a dollar a day; honestly, that was what it was. I was saving up to buy a new bicycle, one with curvy handlebars and gears.

CASE STUDY

1. Explain why a modern grocery store can be considered a formal organization.

2. What are some of the advantages of modern grocery stores over traditional family-run stores?

3. What are some of the disadvantages?

Figure 9–11

In what ways do these two stores illustrate the difference between traditional groups, based on primary group relationships, and formal social organizations based on secondary group relationships? Account for the changes.

My memories of working in the store are mellow ones. My grandparents worked five and a half days a week, taking Thursday afternoons and Sundays off. Yet the days in the store, except for Saturdays when the farmers from the surrounding area came in to shop, were fairly leisurely.

The morning began by putting the flowers out at the front of the store. Boxes were then brought in from the back to stock the shelves. Then my grandmother would answer the phone as grocery orders came in from those who could not get down to the store. Customers would come in to the store with lists, and sit on the high wrought-iron chairs while my grandmother bustled about the store, gathering the items. All this was accompanied by a constant chatter about family, town gossip and the next church picnic. My grandfather would come out from the back of the store to chat, and tell a joke, most of which he didn't understand but enjoyed telling anyway.

At lunch he would go home, two blocks away, to have some lunch. Then in the afternoon he would return to the store, load the "orders" onto the pick-up truck. If I was lucky, and the day was a slow one, I would go with him to deliver the boxes of groceries to mothers looking after kids, or to older people who could not easily get down to the store. Of course, some time was needed to gossip about the family.

Later in the afternoon my grandfather would drive out of town to surrounding farms to pick up fresh produce: asparagus, tomatoes and strawberries in season.

Of course my grandmother was left to look after the store all day, although she didn't seem to mind. The store closed at six, and sometimes I would go back with them to their house on Ste. Marie Street for supper, which included some of the fresh asparagus, and strawberries for dessert.

I wakened from my reverie of times past to the reality of the supermarket on a Saturday morning by a not-so-gentle push from someone's shopping cart. The butcher had just finished filling the pork-chop tray to the brim. A fast trip to the green grocer section. Alas, no asparagus. Push the button by the side of the door where fruit and vegetables appear. A young man, a student working weekends no doubt, goes back to check if there is any. Reappears after a few minutes with some bundles of the delicious green veggie.

An interminable lineup at the checkout. Finally, a woman pushes my groceries over the electronic price with amazing speed. Soon I gather, we will do even this electronic chore ourselves and pay by card before leaving. We box our own groceries, push them out to the car and return our basket for the quarter. Glad to be out of the madhouse of frantic shoppers.

Has life improved? No question we have a greater selection than ever before. The supermarket I shopped in was at least ten times the size of my grandparents' store. The prices are cheaper than they used to be in the old days, what with mass buying and distribution.

Yet I can't help wondering, with all the efficiency, has something been lost? What has happened to the personal touch, the inquiry about family and friends? What's happened to the ease of shopping, physically and emotionally? What has happened to the service? I picked it from the shelves, carried it to the check-out, set it out, packed it up, carried it out and delivered it. The supermarket took my money. I guess progress has its costs.

Connections

What does this case study reveal about the writer's psychological needs? According to Maslow's hierarchy, which of the writer's needs were met more effectively by the traditional family store? (See Chapter 4, page 81.)

Unit 2: Social Groups and Organization

Reforming Bureaucratic Organizations

Many suggestions have been made in recent years to make complex organizations and bureaucracies more effective. Some researchers suggest that the specialized jobs and hierarchy of bureaucracies are outdated. A strict division of labour was appropriate in the past when most workers were relatively unskilled. Today, however, employees tend to be better educated and more capable of doing a wider variety of tasks. Some companies have experimented with new roles for their employees, allowing them to work in self-managed teams and become involved in planning goals for the organization. The result? These companies found that employees became more motivated and more productive, and they were less likely to be absent from work. This kind of employee involvement also resulted in fewer employees leaving to work elsewhere.

Technology is another change affecting bureaucracies. Many employees can now work from home, communicating through e-mail and faxes. Working at home gives employees greater flexibility, and many are also highly motivated by this work style.

Figure 9–12

Although bureaucracies everywhere share many features, there are also differences. How do you think workers here are coping with the problems of bureaucracies? What can you tell about attitudes towards formal organizations in these countries?

Japanese office workers do morning exercises.

Employees at this Volkswagen factory in Germany work only four days a week in an effort to cut costs while preserving jobs.

Customers of a Swedish café find a comfortable place to work with their laptops.

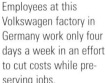

Figure 9-13
The kibbutz is a form of collective common in Israel. Members have their own homes, but often work and eat collectively.

The Collective

One alternative to the bureaucratic style is a **collective.** Collectives are often created by volunteers or part-time workers who are involved in community projects such as alternative schools, small newspapers, health clinics or community action movements.

The collective differs from the bureaucratic structure in several ways. In a collective there is little division of labour, and members contribute to a variety of jobs. Authority in the collective derives from group consensus or general agreement, not from a managerial hierarchy (see the decentralized model in Figure 9–3). Members of a collective value individual initiative more than following rules, and the status of members depends more on personal qualities than on official titles. Collectives tend to function best if they are small. Members need to have face-to-face communication regularly, especially for decision making. Sometimes an organization begins as a collective and then becomes more bureaucratic as it grows, so that members are assigned specific tasks and written records are kept.

Connections

Which leadership style would collectives prefer? (See Chapter 8, pages 177–178.)

Activities

Understand Ideas

1. In your own words, explain two potential problems faced by both employees and customers of bureaucracies.

2. What suggestions have been made to improve the functioning of formal organizations and bureaucracies?

3. What effects is technology having on the reformation of bureaucracies?

Think and Evaluate

4. It is usually difficult to introduce change of any sort into a bureaucracy. Why do you think this is so? What might be some of the results?

5. Identify four differences between a bureaucracy and a collective.

Research and Communicate

6. a) Using the Internet, research an on-line shopping network. What options does this site offer that are different from a traditional shopping experience?

b) Do you prefer the traditional shopping experience or shopping on-line? Write a paragraph explaining your selection. Give at least three reasons for your choice. (See Skill Focus, page 115.)

Key Points

- Formal social organizations are large, secondary groups that are organized to achieve specific goals as efficiently as possible. These organizations may be utilitarian, normative or coercive.

- The ultimate formal social organization is the bureaucracy, first studied in detail by sociologist Max Weber. Formal organizations and bureaucracies perform tasks that are seen as crucial to society, such as educating all young people or providing goods and services of standardized quality to a whole population. Weber recognized six major traits of bureaucracy: specialization, hierarchy, rules and regulations, technical competence, impersonal interaction and formal, written communication.

- Bureaucracies seek to be efficient but often fall short of this goal. Some people believe that the effectiveness of bureaucracies can be improved if people are encouraged to do different tasks and are allowed to participate in the decision-making process.

- It is important to recognize how formal organizations operate. You will probably belong to several during your lifetime. Knowing how they work, or how they are supposed to work, can help you become more effective in dealing with them.

Activities

Understand Ideas

1. List at least five ways in which bureaucracies and formal organizations play a role in our lives.

2. Why are there more bureaucracies and social organizations today than there were 20 or 30 years ago? Consider government bureaucracies (such as the Ministry of Education or Ministry of Health and Welfare) as well as industries and businesses (such as chains of supermarkets, car manufacturers or department stores).

Think and Evaluate

3. Are there alternatives to large bureaucracies? Would it be possible to develop an organization, such as a school, a bicycle manufacturing plant or fast-food chain, where bureaucratic aspects were not present? How would you ensure that the job got done with more personal, small-group interactions? How would you structure decision making and communication so that information was shared and used effectively? Work with a partner to answer these questions. Make a list or chart of your proposals and post it on the bulletin board.

Apply Your Learning

4. **a)** Define *red tape*.
   b) Describe a case in which you, personally, have experienced red tape. Identify who was involved, what happened and how the red tape was eventually eliminated.

Research and Communicate

5. **a)** Spend time in a social organization that interests you. It may be a club you are thinking of joining, a local business or a volunteer or community group. Observe and make notes on the interactions of people in the organization. Find out how the work gets done, how employees feel about their jobs, and how the organization is structured. If possible, interview key members of the organization.
   b) Write a social science report of your findings. (See Skill Focus, page 188.)

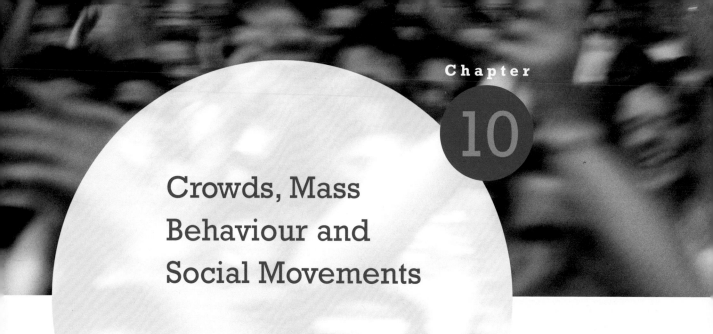

Crowds, Mass Behaviour and Social Movements

In This Chapter

- What are some of the circumstances in which people behave collectively?

- What forms does collective behaviour take?

- How can collective behaviour influence our society?

Key Terms

collective behaviour

casual crowd

expressive crowds

acting crowd

mob

riot

mass behaviour

rumour

gossip

public opinion

panic

mass hysteria

fashion and fad

social movement

Our lives are shaped by many groups. We are clearly part of groups such as families, cliques and larger social organizations, but we also live with and relate to people in other ways. Read the following account and, as a class, discuss the questions that follow.

One night in June 1992 Paul Semple, a 22-year-old photography student, and his two roommates were watching a movie in their Toronto apartment. When they heard screams, they looked out of the window to see a couple and their 11-year-old daughter being violently attacked by four men. Semple and his roommates rushed down into the street to help the victims. They were joined by a neighbour armed with a baseball bat and, together, they chased the attackers. But Semple became separated and was cornered by the attackers. He was stabbed and then kicked and punched. He died of his injuries.

- Were Semple and his roommates right to get involved? Why or why not?

- Do you think Semple might have acted differently had he been alone? Explain.

- Why do people sometimes try not to get involved in incidents they see on the street?

- What would you have done in this situation?

Collective Behaviour

Have you recently attended a school assembly or a music concert? Do you ever find yourself listening to, or passing on, a juicy bit of gossip about a friend or acquaintance? Do your clothes reflect the latest fashions? Have you ever joined with others to support or protest some public cause or political idea? If so, you have engaged in collective behaviour.

Collective behaviour is a broad term that refers to the ways people act in crowds, social movements or across an entire culture or society. Collective behaviour is usually spontaneous and may be unpredictable, as anyone who has been part of a violent demonstration can attest. Collective behaviour can be localized—for example, in a crowd where people gather together in the same place at the same time—or it can be dispersed. Examples of dispersed collective behaviour are rumours, gossip, fashions and fads.

In some cases, collective behaviour can be irrational and even dangerous. Crowds can suddenly turn ugly. Panic and mass hysteria may sweep through a group or a whole community, causing chaos. A charismatic leader can convince followers to perform acts they would never have attempted on their own. Because reactions from crowds are not easily predictable, sociologists have difficulty studying the phenomenon of collective behaviour.

Collective behaviour differs from the small primary groups and the formal social organizations in our lives. Family relationships and friendships usually last a long time. Even organizations may provide us with companionship and other rewards. By contrast, we often engage in collective behaviour with people we hardly know, or never meet, and these interactions are usually short-lived.

Focus Questions

What is collective behaviour?

What are some of the characteristics of collective behaviour?

localized—in one place

dispersed—scattered, spread over a wide area

hysteria—excessive and uncontrollable emotion

Figure 10–1

What do these forms of collective behaviour have in common?

CASE STUDY

1. What was the People's Temple Cult?

2. Why did Jim Jones have such a strong hold on his followers?

cult—a group, usually with religious or spiritual beliefs, that is organized around a charismatic leader

The People's Temple

One extreme example of the irrational behaviour of crowds was the action taken by the People's Temple, a cult in California founded by a charismatic leader named Jim Jones. In 1977, the cult moved to a remote location in Guyana, a small country in South America. The cult called the new location Jonestown. Here, Jones exerted complete control over his followers.

In 1978 a member of the United States Congress went to Jonestown to investigate charges that people were being held against their will. When the congressman and four others tried to leave the cult, they were ambushed and killed. That night, vats of poisoned fruit drink were brought out and cult members lined up to take it. Those who refused to drink the liquid were forced to do so. Over 900 people died.

How could so many people be persuaded to act in this way? Psychologists suggest that people almost always join cults like the People's Temple because they are dissatisfied with their lives and have difficulty coping. A cult seems to offer answers to important questions about the meaning of life. It also provides members with a sense of identity; they may feel relieved to turn over their problems and surrender their individuality to a charismatic leader.

Extreme cults organize life in a rigid way, carefully controlling information from outside. Members' lives are so regulated that they have little opportunity to think freely or critically. Lack of sleep and strict control of food are also used to break down their resistance. The combination of the strength of the group and the weakness of outside influences can be very powerful.

Activities

Understand Ideas

1. **a)** Name three forms of collective behaviour.
   b) Classify these three forms as either negative or positive. Write one sentence to justify each classification.

2. Give four reasons why people join cults.

Think and Evaluate

3. Collective behaviour is generally less predictable than behaviour in primary groups or formal social organizations. Why do you think this is the case?

4. Do you think you could be influenced to join a cult? What criteria would you use to determine if an organization is a cult?

Apply Your Learning

5. **a)** Make a list of all the social situations you have been involved in over the last three days. Divide the list into the following categories: family; friends; encounter in a social organization (e.g., a school, store or religious institution); a crowd of people (e.g., on the street, in a mall or at an assembly).
   b) Describe your activities in any three of the social situations. Did any group influence your behaviour? If so, how?

6. What collective behaviour do you engage in most frequently? List three factors that demonstrate you are engaging in collective behaviour.

Crowds

Focus Questions

What is a crowd?

How do people behave in different types of crowds?

As you saw in Chapter 8, a **crowd** is a group of people temporarily gathered together. You have, no doubt, been part of several crowds recently. How do you think being in a crowd affected your behaviour? As part of a crowd, would you have done things that you would not otherwise have done? Sociologists classify crowds into the following four main types.

The Casual Crowd

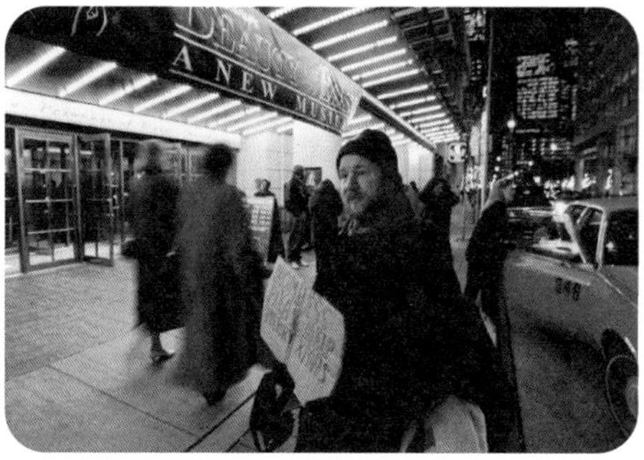

Figure 10–2
Under what circumstances would someone be more likely to get assistance—from one or two passersby or from a large crowd? Why?

The most common type of crowd is a **casual crowd,** a loose collection of people who react very little to each other. In fact, they may go out of their way not to have anything to do with others in the crowd. People in a store, on the street or at a bus stop are examples of casual crowds.

One undesirable aspect of casual crowds is bystander apathy, the unwillingness of members of a crowd to get involved when help is needed. This type of indifference is typically associated with big cities. One Canadian research team put a small child alone in various locations in Ontario and instructed her to ask passersby for the time, directions and other assistance. People in downtown Toronto gave the child the least help, while those in the suburbs gave somewhat more. Passersby in a small Ontario town were even more willing to help the child. Another experiment showed that there was a better chance of one or two people coming to someone's assistance than a large crowd. Why? It may be that people in a crowd think someone else will help. In addition, individuals in a crowd may not want to draw attention to themselves.

The case studies that follow show differing responses to similar, violent situations.

Kitty Genovese

CASE STUDY

1. **Why was Kitty Genovese ignored?**
2. **How do you react to her story?**

Late one evening in March 1964, Kitty Genovese, a 28-year-old New York woman, was coming home from work. She was attacked close to her apartment building. She screamed for help and struggled with her attacker. The assailant stabbed her twice and fled. Genovese was left crawling along the street, trying to make it to the safety of her building.

She continued to scream for help, but no one came to her rescue. At one point, Genovese called out to someone by name, but he passed by and did nothing. No one even called the police. Over the next hour the attacker returned twice more, stabbing her again. She died at the foot of the stairs to the entrance of her apartment building.

Police investigations revealed that at least 38 people in the surrounding buildings heard or saw the attack but failed to react. Interviews with these people later revealed that they were not necessarily uncaring. In fact many were concerned and angry over what had happened but did not want to get involved. Some people had even pulled down their blinds and turned up the volume on their television sets so they could not see or hear what was going on.

CASE STUDY

1. How did Reginald Denny's situation differ from that of Kitty Genovese?

2. Given the situation, are you surprised at the response? Why or why not?

Reginald Denny

In May 1992, a trucker named Reginald Denny unknowingly drove his truck into the midst of a riot in the city of Los Angeles. Rioters stopped the truck. They pulled Denny from his truck and beat him. He was also shot in the leg and left lying on the street.

Denny's attack was recorded by a television camera in a helicopter overhead and broadcast live. Shocked by what they were seeing, four viewers drove to the intersection where Denny lay. They managed to drive him out of danger and get him to a hospital.

Figure 10–3

The Los Angeles District Attorney points to a photograph of a suspect in the beating of Reginald Denny. The panels at the side show scenes recorded by the television camera. How would you have felt had you seen Denny being beaten live on television?

The Conventional Crowd

A **conventional crowd** is a group of people who have gathered for a specific event such as a school assembly, a movie or a wedding. People in conventional crowds usually conform to norms that are generally considered appropriate to the situation; however, expected behaviour varies from one conventional crowd to another. In some school assemblies, for example, you are expected to applaud politely. However, let's say the school basketball team had just won a big championship. In this case, students at the assembly might be expected to show more enthusiasm.

Rules of Crowd Behaviour

Sometimes, the rules for behaviour in a particular situation are unclear. What is your opinion of the following tips for moviegoers? Do you agree with the author about appropriate behaviour in movie theatres? Would you add or delete anything?

- If you just can't live without that licorice, kindly open the package and take the candy out before the movie starts.

- Before you start gorging yourself, remember that you're supposedly here to watch a movie—not have dinner.

- When you find yourself foraging for the last kernel of popcorn, stop it! That's all there is. It's gone and no amount of paper scratching can bring it back.

- Don't try to impress the audience or your companion by (loudly) recognizing every bit actor on the screen. We know who they are, too.

- If you get the urge to laugh when there's nothing funny to laugh at, catch yourself. We all know you're doing this on purpose.

- If the movie theatre is empty—please don't find it necessary to sit next to me! Take advantage of the space—spread out!

- If you think you can save seats for your friends by draping coats over more than two chairs, fine. But don't expect me to protect and patrol your territory while you head out for snacks.

- When you're at the concession stand, and you're tempted to buy a jumbo combo offer—remember your New Year's resolution.

- If you're tempted to impress your companion with your knowledge of the film industry—remember, we watch "Movie Television," too.

- And when the movie's over, pretend it's garbage day—and take your trash out with you.

Work with a partner or in a small group. Think of a social situation in which certain rules of behaviour might apply. Examples include riding an elevator, using public transit, lining up to pay for a purchase. Write a set of rules for that situation, following the model above.

The Expressive Crowd

At a baseball game, crowds cheer and boo. At a rock concert, they shout and whistle. At a political rally they chant and wave banners. **Expressive crowds** such as these gather at events that have emotional appeal. People join expressive crowds because they are excited by what might happen.

The presence of hundreds or thousands of people contributes to a sense of excitement in these crowds. People display their feelings by clapping, cheering, jumping up and down or waving banners. The centre of influence of an expressive crowd—the speaker or band for example—may direct the crowd to do something by speaking or gesturing to them. Effective speakers and performers know how to work the crowd to get enthusiastic responses.

Raves: A Dangerous Form of Collective Behaviour?

Before you decide on your response to this question, read the following information.

What is a rave?

A rave is a large dance party. In the early 1990s, raves attracted a few hundred people. Ravers would find a large empty space, break in, set up speakers for loud music and dance until the police arrived. Gradually, promoters began setting up raves more formally. They would rent warehouses or similar spaces and charge people to attend. By the end of the 1990s, raves in Canadian cities were regularly attracting up to 10 000 people or more.

Why are ravers a subculture?

Raves have several distinctive features and ravers follow certain codes of behaviour. They often dance through the night to electronic "techno" music and wave glow sticks. They wear particular kinds of clothing and exchange small gifts and candy. Ravers also frown on alcohol. Some, however, use "rave drugs," especially a powerful stimulant known as Ecstasy, which can be very dangerous.

Why do raves attract so many people?

Some sociologists think that ravers enjoy the sense of community. Here is a different view from an article in *Maclean's* called "Rave Fever" by Susan Oh and Ruth Atherley.

Sociologist Tim Weber notes that today's teens are looking for positive experiences to offset the comparatively stressful climate they've grown up in. "I was surprised at the number of kids in high school who saw raves as mini-vacations away from daily stressors. Some enjoyed being allowed to act like small children, doing things like wearing costumes, eating candy and playing with toys." They are the generation that grew up with latchkey-ism, AIDS, the dominance of clothing brands and the pressure to start planning a career during adolescence.

Should raves be banned?

In 1994, the British government passed a law that outlawed raves. Some Canadians think that similar laws should be passed here. Between April 1998 and April 2000, at least 14 Canadians died after using Ecstasy at raves, and many more became sick from rave drugs. Critics say the large crowds are drawing many drug dealers, some of whom are selling even more lethal substances than Ecstasy. In addition, illegal overcrowding and lack of running water put ravers at risk. Water is essential to control body heat generated by dancing and rave drugs, and without it, the kidneys and liver can fail.

Other people argue that raves are a positive experience for many participants. They say that only a minority use drugs, and most ravers enjoy an evening of dancing without alcohol or violence. Many of them suggest that it would be better to regulate raves than to ban them completely, and to impose rules that cover water, security and crowding. Police would have to enforce these regulations and clamp down on drug dealing.

What Do You Think?

1. How can raves be dangerous?

2. List three arguments for and against banning raves.

3. Do you think raves pose a danger? What do you think should be done?

The Acting Crowd

An **acting crowd** is fuelled by a single purpose. The crowd may have a political or social goal in mind. An acting crowd may behave aggressively, by rushing the doors of a political institution, or it may behave affectionately, by trying to get closer to a person or group. In either case, an acting crowd can become dangerous.

People in acting crowds often think in simple and divisive terms. They may believe they are clearly right while those who oppose them are clearly wrong. As a result, reasoned arguments are not usually successful in directing these crowds. Emotional appeals, on the other hand, can be very effective. Consequently, these crowds can be vulnerable—as history has shown—to unscrupulous leaders who appeal to people's emotions in order to achieve their own goals.

When an acting crowd turns violent, it can become a **mob,** a highly emotional crowd that pursues some violent or destructive goal. Mobs may attack people or property but they tend to form and break up quickly. In 1985, a conventional crowd assembled to watch the European Cup Final soccer match between Italy and England. As the game was starting, however, English fans began to taunt Italian fans in adjacent stands. Both sides began to throw bottles. The English fans then surged toward the Italians. People tried to scramble over a wall to escape the violence. The wall collapsed under the weight of the fans and within minutes, 39 people were dead and 400 injured.

A frenzied crowd without any particular purpose or goal is a **riot.** People in a riot are unorganized, emotional and often aggressive. A riot may be made up of a number of mobs pursuing specific goals. It may form as a result of a particular incident that has left people angry or excited. Rioters indulge in apparently random violence. They may destroy or set fire to buildings, loot stores or attack people. Some individuals might join a riot simply to take advantage of a chaotic situation to loot and vandalize.

Connections

Is the emotional behaviour demonstrated by a mob or a riot the product of nature, nurture or the unconscious desires of the id? (See Chapter 4, pages 75–76 and pages 83–84.)

Figure 10–4
What kind of crowd is shown here?

Activities

Understand Ideas

1. **a)** Make a chart that identifies and compares the main elements of an expressive crowd, acting crowd, mob and riot.

   b) Summarize the essential differences between each of these crowds.

2. What conditions can lead to bystander apathy?

Think and Evaluate

3. **a)** Compare the case studies of Kitty Genovese and Reginald Denny using the following questions:
   - What was happening to the victim?
   - What different courses of action did bystanders take?
   - Why do you think the bystanders reacted differently in each case?
   - What hypotheses for study might these two cases suggest?

   b) How would you react if you were a witness to the cases described above? Why?

4. Do a PMI (Plus, Minus, Interesting) chart on expressive and acting crowds. Record three points in each category for each type of crowd.

Apply Your Learning

5. Decide which of the following situations justify or require action from bystanders. What action should they take?
   a) an individual being swarmed by a group in a mall
   b) a parent using physical violence, such as spanking or slapping a child in public
   c) a police officer being threatened by two attackers
   d) a police officer beating someone
   e) an individual being physically threatened by an attacker
   f) someone in serious danger, but assistance could mean injury or death to the bystander

6. Assume you are organizing a large sports or social event at your school. How would you organize the event in order to avoid potentially dangerous actions from expressive and acting crowds?

Research and Communicate

7. Have you ever been part of an acting crowd? Write a short description of what happened and how you felt.

Mass Behaviour

Sometimes even people who are not in the same geographical place can engage in collective behaviour. This kind of behaviour is known as **mass behaviour** and it can involve people who are widely dispersed. While ideas, feelings and calls for action can be communicated directly to a crowd, mass behaviour relies on personal communication between individuals. The media are also used to promote mass behaviour. Examples of mass behaviour are rumours, gossip, public opinion, panic and mass hysteria. The term also includes fashions and fads.

As communication over long distances continues to improve, so does our ability to engage in mass behaviour. Before the invention of the telephone, for example, rumours spread more slowly and over a much smaller geographical area. Radio and television have helped shape public opinion on controversial issues. Through mass media, fashions and fads have spread around the world. More recently, the Internet has become an important vehicle for mass behaviour by making information—and misinformation—available to hundreds or even thousands of people in any geographical location in seconds.

Rumour and Gossip

Rumour is unsupported information that people spread informally, often by word of mouth. Rumours often spread in a climate of uncertainty, when people are wondering what is going to happen. Workers who fear layoffs, for example, will be open to rumours if they don't get enough information about their situation. Rumours tend to change as they spread, and are difficult to stop once they begin. Usually only clear and convincing information will put a stop to rumours.

Gossip is a particular form of rumour that deals with personal information about an individual or small group. Gossip can be a form of social control. Knowing that people are talking about you may make you change the way you act. Having a juicy item of gossip to pass along can also give an individual more power in a group. Those who gossip too often, however, sometimes find this tactic backfires, and their own reputation suffers.

Public Opinion

Widespread attitudes about specific issues such as air pollution, gun control, immigration, health care, the role of women or public education are known as **public opinion.** Issues that are of concern to the public may vary, depending upon what is important in the lives of individuals, the coverage of the issue by the media and the political importance of the issue at the time.

While public opinion can exert a strong influence over government actions and policies, it can also be manipulated to serve specific ends. Television and other media have an enormous effect on the way the public perceives an issue. Individuals who have access to the media, such as political leaders, can also influence the way an issue is perceived. In some cases, groups may use propaganda to woo the public into adopting a particular opinion on an issue.

Figure 10–5

Rumours can be quite serious in wartime, as this poster from World War II illustrates. Even in peacetime, unchecked rumours can lower morale and poison the atmosphere of a workplace or community. In times of uncertainty, rumours can help people focus their frustration or anxiety on a particular cause.

manipulated—skilfully managed for a particular purpose

propaganda—systematic efforts to influence public opinion, often through lies or distorted information

Panic and Mass Hysteria

Connections

What are the similarities and differences between panic or mass hysteria and anxiety disorders? (See Chapter 5, pages 101–102.)

Panic is a form of collective behaviour that causes people to react to a threat in an emotional, irrational and sometimes self-destructive way. People trapped in a burning building, for example, may panic and act in ways that hamper everyone's escape. A closely related phenomenon is **mass hysteria,** or collective hysteria, when people respond to an event with irrational and frantic behaviour. Mass hysteria differs from panic in that the people caught up in mass hysteria have little or no direct contact with each other. Mass hysteria and panic can be caused by an actual event, an imagined one or even a rumour. The important point is that people think the event has occurred or is about to happen.

War of the Worlds

CASE STUDY

1. What was the act of mass hysteria in this case?

2. Why did people react in this way?

3. Do you think a similar response to a broadcast could happen today? Explain.

A classic case of mass hysteria took place in the United States in 1938 when H.G. Wells' novel, *War of the Worlds,* was broadcast over the radio. The story, about an invasion from Mars, was presented as simulated news reports that were interspersed with music. At various times throughout the broadcast, an announcer identified the program as a dramatization of a fictitious story.

Millions of listeners, however, believed the events were actually taking place. Many phoned their friends and family to warn them of the invasion. Other listeners jumped into their cars and fled. Some people hid in rural areas for days until they ventured forth to discover what had happened.

It has been suggested that many people reacted the way they did because they were already fearful of events in Europe at the time. In 1938, the world was on the brink of World War II. Because people were already nervous, they reacted emotionally and took drastic action.

Figure 10–7
Which decades do you think are shown in these photos? How can you tell?

Fashion and Fads

A **fashion** is a social pattern adopted by a large number of people, usually for a fairly short period of time. Fashions exist in clothing, hairstyles and music, and in articles such as furniture, cars and even computers.

In traditional societies, social customs and necessity influence fashions. Consequently, fashions change slowly in these societies. In modern industrial societies, however, fashions change more rapidly. People in these societies are less tied to traditional ways of life. They expect change. Many people also use fashions to make a statement about their ability to acquire the newest and best products. The media also play a part in people's decisions regarding fashions. Mass advertising constantly promotes the newest products, while magazines and television programs show people using and wearing the latest fashions. Many consumers model themselves on such media images.

New fashions often begin with the most affluent people in society—those who have the means to purchase the newest items. Gradually, imitations of these fashions are produced that are more affordable to the general public. By that time, however, the wealthy are buying the very latest in fashions that only they can afford.

A **fad** is a social pattern that people follow briefly, but enthusiastically. Fads appear and disappear more quickly than fashions. While a fashion may become part of the cultural mainstream, fads are often outside the cultural norms and they may appear strange to some people. Blue jeans, for example, originated as a fashion in the mining camps of the Gold Rush during the mid-1800s. They have since become a central part of mainstream culture. Pet rocks, in contrast, were a fad that disappeared quickly. But some fads do remain, such as frisbees and video games, and other fads, such as bungee jumping, introduce new behaviour rather than material objects.

Connections

What role does conformity play in the success of fashion and fads? (See Chapter 8, page 169.)

Activities

Understand Ideas

1. What are the differences between panic and mass hysteria?

2. a) What is the difference between a fashion and a fad?
  b) List four examples of technology that has allowed the media to influence mass behaviour.

3. Identify the main difference between rumours, gossip and public opinion.

Think and Evaluate

4. a) What criteria would you use to assess if mass hysteria is taking place?
  b) How would you react if you found yourself in a situation of mass hysteria?

5. a) Are fashions and fads socially useful?
  b) What is the role of affluent people and the media in determining fads and fashion?

c) What problems do you see in a society where fads and fashions are important?

6. a) What social purposes, if any, do rumours, gossip and public opinion serve?
  b) Suggest three negative effects of rumours and gossip.
  c) What steps could be taken to prevent rumours and gossip?
  d) How would you decide when not to listen to rumours and gossip?

Apply Your Learning

7. a) Provide a photograph or drawing of you at your fashionable best. Be prepared to share this picture with the class.
  b) Making specific reference to the picture, explain what fashion statement you are making. Why is this statement important to you?

Social Movements

A **social movement** is a form of collective behaviour by people who are promoting or resisting changes to some aspect of society. One social movement might promote changes to the educational system, for example, while another might try to prevent a waste site from being built in a certain area. Social movements may promote equal treatment of men and women in the workplace or an end to pollution of the environment. Social movements can have broad-based goals aimed at changing society in fundamental ways. Political movements are an example of this kind of social movement. Social movements are usually more organized and longer lasting than other kinds of collective behaviour. In societies such as Canada's, there is a great diversity of opinion, which gives rise to many different social movements.

Figure 10–8

Are there any social movements in which you would like to be involved? If so, which ones? Why?

Making Comparisons

Social scientists compare subjects of study to help them understand the characteristics of those subjects and make judgments when necessary. A comparison can also be a useful way of organizing information that has been collected.

Here's How

- First identify criteria that can be used in your comparison. For example, if you were comparing an expressive crowd and an acting crowd, you might use the following criteria: Type, Purpose, Typical behaviour, Example in text, Example in own experience.

- Identify similarities in any relevant criteria.

- Identify differences in any relevant criteria.

- Draw a conclusion from the comparison. For example, a comparison of an expressive crowd and an acting crowd might suggest that the latter is more likely to become violent than the former.

The diagram below is a useful tool when comparing and contrasting.

Practise It

1. Compare two or more of the following forms of collective behaviour: crowds, mass behaviour, social movements.

2. In three or four sentences, write a conclusion based on your comparison.

Subject 1 _____   Subject 2 _____

How Alike?

Criteria   _____
            _____
            _____
            _____

How Different?

Criteria

Conclusion: _____

Types of Social Movements

Sociologists ask two main questions about social movements: Who will be affected by the social movement? And how much change is the movement seeking? Using these criteria, sociologists can divide social movements into three main categories.

Social movements in the first category are those that seek an alternative or a change in a narrow segment of the population. Mothers Against Drunk Driving (MADD) is an example of an alternative social movement. The second category is made up of social movements that seek limited change, but encompass the whole society. They wish to reform society, pointing it in a new direction or trying to return it to some previous form. A debate over the death penalty would be an example of this kind of social movement if both sides of the issue were trying to win approval for their point of view. Social movements in the third category are revolutionary. They try to change the basic structure of society. The change would have an impact on every member of the society. The separatist movement in Quebec is an example of this kind of social movement.

Theories of Social Movements

Social scientists have developed several theories to explain why and how social movements arise. **Deprivation theory** holds that social movements are started by people who feel deprived in some way. They may feel they lack adequate income, safe working conditions, equal rights or other needs. Organizations fighting against poverty or for Aboriginal rights, for example, argue that people who are poor or are members of First Nations are deprived of rights to which they are entitled.

Mass society theory suggests that some social movements appeal to people who feel socially isolated and insignificant. Social movements provide these people with a sense of belonging, power and importance. The rise of neo-Nazi movements and other supremacist groups in the later part of the twentieth century can be seen, in part, as examples of mass society theory.

Social concern theory states that social movements occur when a social institution or benefit is threatened by change. For example, a social movement might develop, seeking to preserve a system of public education if this system were threatened by change.

Structural strain theory helps to explain movements that aim to bring fundamental, even revolutionary change to a society. In order for this kind of movement to occur, there must be significant problems within a society, and people must feel deprived as a result of these problems. People must also have a plan of action to solve such problems. When these factors are present, the stage is set for some specific event to trigger social action. Action then spreads throughout the society, usually in the form of demonstrations, rallies, the distribution of leaflets and more

Figure 10–9

In the 1990s, Aboriginal groups across the country became more militant in demanding their rights to land, resources and better living conditions. Matthew Coon Come heads the Assembly of First Nations which represents Aboriginal groups in their negotiations with the federal government.

Figure 10–10

People from East and West Berlin combined forces to tear down the wall that had divided them for decades.

organizing. Eventually, social control breaks down in the face of the pressure for change.

The way Eastern European countries gained independence from the former Soviet Union is an example of structural strain theory. During the 1980s, many opponents of the communist government in the Soviet Union believed that democracy was the solution to the country's economic and social problems. When Mikhail Gorbachev, leader of the Soviet Union, introduced economic and social reforms in 1985, these reforms triggered a wave of demonstrations, protests and social unrest throughout countries in Eastern Europe. These activities culminated in the tearing down of the Berlin Wall in 1989 and the breaking up of the Soviet Union in 1991.

culminated—reached a point of intensity and completion

Activities

Understand Ideas

1. **a)** What is a social movement?
   b) What kinds of social movements are there?

2. Why do people join social movements?

Apply Your Learning

3. Survey the newspapers over an assigned period of time. Find articles about three social movements. What do they want to accomplish? What is your position on these social movements?

Research and Communicate

4. What social movement would you like to start? Provide a description of the movement and identify what kind it would be. Explain the purpose of the movement and describe how you propose to achieve its goals.

5. Research a social movement of interest to you. It might be concerned with a specific issue, such as animal rights or the environment. Alternatively, it might be a movement that aims to change society in a major way, such as the Quebec separatist movement, or a new political party. What are the goals of the movement? How is it achieving these goals? What do you think its effect will be? Be prepared to present your findings to the class. (See Skill Focus, page 97.)

Key Points

- Collective behaviour is the result of large groups of people acting spontaneously and for a brief period. Those involved may be in the same place or dispersed throughout a society. Collective behaviour is an important influence in our lives, and it has become more so through the influence of mass media.

- There are several forms of collective behaviour. Crowds, mobs and riots involve collective behaviour of groups that are in the same place at the same time. Rumour and gossip, fads and fashions and public opinion are forms of collective behaviour that involve people who may never meet.

- Social movements are an important form of collective behaviour. Different theories explain why and when social movements arise, including deprivation theory, mass society theory, social concern theory and structural strain theory.

- Each of these forms of collective behaviour influences us in different ways. Overall, however, their influence is not as long lasting or predictable as that of small groups and social organizations.

Activities

Understand Ideas

1. Create an outline of this chapter. Use the given headings, sub-headings and key words in bold. For each section, answer the general questions: "What is the main idea?"

2. Using your outline, reflect on what you have learned about crowds, mass behaviour and social movements. Write three paragraphs that summarize your learning about each main topic. In each paragraph, make specific references to words that appear in the headings, sub-headings and key words.

Think and Evaluate

3. Consider the following situation: You are a first-year college or university student. You are approached in the Student Centre by two other students, one male and one female. They invite you to a "social" the following evening. What questions should you ask them before accepting or declining the invitation? Record a minimum of five questions.

Apply Your Learning

4. **a)** Compare the four kinds of crowds described in the chapter. (See Skill Focus, page 213.)

   b) Record a personal crowd experience. Follow this outline:

   Paragraph 1: Identify or classify this crowd as one of the four types described in the chapter.

   Paragraph 2: Explain the most important thing you learned about crowds from your experience. Would you change your behaviour in this situation if you could?

Research and Communicate

5. Conduct observational research on a crowd using the following headings: Type of crowd being researched; Questions to be investigated; Description of the actions of the crowd; Interactions between people; Kinds of emotions expressed by the crowd; General observations and conclusions about the crowd. Submit a report on your findings. (See Skill Focus, page 188.)

Chapter 11

Culture and Discrimination

I n this unit, we have looked at various types of groups. Cultures, too, are a type of group. Investigate some of the ways culture can influence our outlook by following these steps:

- Individually, draw a pair of eyeglasses on a sheet of paper. In words, or with small symbols, answer the following questions in the lenses:

  What is your country of birth?
  How many sisters or brothers do you have?
  What languages are spoken in your home or family other than English?
  What are the occupations of one or two people in your family?

- Exchange your drawing with a partner. Note the differences.

- As a class discuss:

  How might some of these differences influence the way people see the world?
  What can happen if we believe that everyone sees things the same way?
  Your discussion might include the following terms: *perceptions, assumptions, conflict* and *respect for differences.*

- In a one-paragraph personal response, answer the following questions: "What did you learn about how different people see the same thing? How did you feel when someone had a different point of view? How can you help others see your point of view?

Adapted from *Tribes: A New Way of Learning and Being Together,* Jeanne Gibbs

In This Chapter

- What is the difference between a society and a culture?

- In what ways can a society respond to cultural groups?

- What challenges and opportunities does a multicultural society face?

- What causes prejudice and discrimination?

Key Terms

society

culture

social institutions

segregation

assimilation

multiculturalism

prejudice

stereotypes

discrimination

systemic discrimination

harassment

racism

sexism

ageism

genocide

Society and Culture

In this unit, we have learned about some of the ways in which people form groups. Taken together, all of these groups contribute to our society. A **society** is a group of people in a particular geographic area who share the same rules and laws. A society survives by using agreed-upon ways to meet its needs and solve its problems. Societies come in many shapes and sizes. A society can be made up of a small group of people cast away on a desert island, an isolated village in northern Ontario or a whole country such as Canada.

The groups in our society also contribute to our culture. How do society and culture differ? As you saw in Chapter 2, a **culture** is the set of ideas, beliefs and behaviours that is handed down from one generation to the next. If you moved to another country, you would take your Canadian culture with you in the form of your learned beliefs, values and behaviours. You would not, however, take Canadian society with you. When you leave a society, you leave behind many of the "social" ways of doing things. For example, you must obey the laws of the country you are in, even though some aspects of the new society may conflict with your cultural values and ideas.

A society may consist of people of the same culture or it may be made up of a number of cultures. Canadian society is made up of several cultures. Canada's original inhabitants were the First Nations. Then came French and English settlers. In time, other immigrants came to Canada, each bringing new cultural ideas and ways to add to Canadian society. In the late 1800s, Irish immigrants came to Canada to escape famine and starvation, Japanese and Chinese immigrants came to work on the railroads and immigrants from central and eastern Europe carved out farms

Figure 11–1

In what ways are culture and society different?

Figure 11–2

Does your family or someone you know appear in this chart?

Immigrants to Canada by place of birth			
Place of birth	**Before 1961**	**1971–1980**	**1991–1996**
United States	45 050	74 015	29 025
Central and South America	6 370	67 470	76 335
Caribbean and Bermuda	8 390	96 025	57 315
United Kingdom	265 580	132 950	25 420
Europe excluding the UK	687 780	223 750	172 060
Africa	4 945	58 150	76 260
West-Central Asia and the Middle East	4 975	30 980	82 050
Asia (including Eastern, South-east and Southern Asia)	27 605	297 395	510 660
Oceania and Other	4 250	15 420	9 875

on the prairies. After World War II, Canada's population increased significantly, as immigrants came mainly from Europe, seeking a new life after the horrors of the war. These immigrants helped to build Canada's growing cities. From the 1970s to the present, people have immigrated to Canada from all parts of the world, including Asia, South America, the Middle East, the Caribbean and Africa.

How Societies Function

A society sets out methods for meeting the needs of its population. The methods are known as **social institutions.** Publicly funded schooling is one Canadian institution—a way in which Canadian society meets the need to educate its population. Our health care needs, too, are met through health and medical institutions. If we are sick, we go to a doctor, or to a hospital. A concert or a hockey game is a social institution that fulfills our need for fun and excitement.

Social institutions can change over time, to meet the changing needs of society. For example, before education was made compulsory in the nineteenth century, children often learned by working alongside family members, or in one-room schoolhouses that were quite different from classrooms of today.

Figure 11–3

Societies are set up in order to meet human needs. Specific social institutions meet specific needs. Can you think of other human needs not included on this chart? What social institutions have formed to meet those needs in Canada? ▼

Human needs and institutions		
Human needs	**Institution**	**Canadian examples**
• providing and distributing material goods such as food, clothing and shelter	economic system	• privately owned businesses • government corporations • trade unions • families
• transmitting and developing culture and knowledge	education system	• schools • universities • mass media • family
• making social decisions • dealing with other countries • enforcing laws	political system	• federal, provincial, municipal governments • judicial system • police
• answering ethical questions • meeting spiritual needs	religious systems	• churches, synagogues and mosques • philosophic and spiritual groups
• reproduction and child care	family schools	• nuclear and other family types • nurseries • schools • hospitals

Social institutions are sometimes informal and understood by the society in general, without being set in law. For instance, we usually expect our families to provide us with food, clothing and other material goods and skills that we need to survive. At other times, these needs are met by more formal structures or institutions such as social service agencies, which are set by law. Figure 11–3 illustrates a number of social institutions in Canada and the needs they fulfill. You will be learning more about institutions in Canadian society in later chapters in this book.

Activities

Understand Ideas

1. Record the definitions of *society* and *culture*.

2. Examine the table in Figure 11–2.
   a) What three groups accounted for the highest number of immigrants before 1961? Use an atlas to name four countries that would be included in these categories.
   b) What three groups on the chart accounted for the highest percentage of immigrants in the 1990s? Use an atlas to name three countries that would be included in these categories.
   c) How have immigration patterns changed since the first half of the twentieth century? What factors can you think of that might account for this change?

Think and Evaluate

3. a) In note form, write five points that support the following statement: "It is possible for several cultures to exist in one society but it is not possible for several societies to exist in one culture."
   b) Write five points that oppose the statement.
   c) In a well-developed paragraph, using the information from either part a) or b) above, argue the case either for or against the statement.

4. a) Select one social institution and predict five changes that might happen to this institution in the future.
   b) Share your predictions with a partner. Be prepared to present one example to the class.

Focus Questions

What is a minority group?

How do minority groups relate to the rest of society?

minority groups—relatively small groups of people who differ somewhat from most others in their society

Cultures Within a Society

How can various cultures live together within one society? Over time, three approaches have emerged: segregation, assimilation and multiculturalism.

In some societies, members of minority groups live, work and go to school separately from the rest of society. This approach is known as **segregation.** Groups sometimes segregate themselves voluntarily, as a way of preserving their culture. For example, old order Mennonites prefer to live in separate communities where they can practise their religion and way of life. In other cases, however, segregation can be imposed on a group, even though members of the group have no desire to be separated from the mainstream. This was the case in World War II, when Japanese-Canadians were segregated in camps in the British Columbia interior because they were considered enemy aliens.

Figure 11–4

Amish farmers work together to build a new home in Pennsylvania, USA. Like Mennonites, the Amish reject many of the trappings of modern life and keep themselves apart from the rest of society. Their own sense of community is very strong.

Connections

Why would a dominant culture be considered an agent of socialization? (See Chapter 6, pages 123–125.)

A policy of **assimilation,** in contrast, encourages minority cultures to adopt the ways of the dominant society. The United States, for example, has traditionally encouraged immigrants to give up their language, culture and ways of doing things in order to become "American." This approach has the benefit of creating a strong national identity, which is shared by all citizens.

Sometimes groups are pressured to assimilate into a dominant culture. Until the 1970s, this was the case in Canada, where the government tried to force First Nations to assimilate and adopt a more European lifestyle. Members of First Nations were restricted to reserves where it was difficult to maintain their traditional culture and way of life. First Nations children were forcibly removed from their families and placed in residential schools, located far from their homes. The children were forbidden to speak their own languages and practise their religious beliefs. The government also banned First Nations' religious ceremonies, such as the sun dance and the pot-latch. The potlach was an elaborate gathering that included singing, dancing, speeches and gift-giving. The ceremony was a vital part of First Nations' economy and helped form allegiances among clans.

Figure 11–5

Dancers at a potlatch ceremony in a Haida village in 1902. The potlatch was an elaborate gath-ering, often attended by large numbers of people.

The government believed that assimilation was in the best interests of both Canadian society and the people of the First Nations themselves. The government finally aban-doned the policy but, by that time, much damage had been done to First Nations cultures. Today, many First Nations are experiencing a cultural renewal, and generations that were denied access to their traditional culture are rediscov-ering their heritage.

cultural pluralism—a form of society in which many diverse cultures are fully accepted

Since 1971, Canada has adopted an official policy of cultural pluralism or **multiculturalism.** Under this model, different cultures are encouraged to retain their distinct characteristics, ideas and beliefs within the larger society.

Supporters of multiculturalism say that everyone benefits from the new ideas and innovation this kind of mixed society provides. Moreover, being exposed to different cultures encourages us all to be more tolerant and enriches our lives. Yet living in a multicultural society also presents challenges. Some people feel that Canada's sense of national identity is weakened because we encourage many diverse cultures. Others, including some immigrants, claim that encouraging newcomers to retain their culture actually isolates them from the rest of Canadian society.

culture conflict—conflicting demands of traditional family background and the values and lifestyle of a new homeland

Trying to balance two cultures can also be stressful for families that have recently arrived in Canada. Younger people usually adapt more quickly to a new society. Their adjustment can, however, lead to culture conflict—competing demands on young people from their family on one hand and from outside groups on the other. Parents may expect their children to conform to traditional ways while friends and other acquaintances urge these young people to adopt new ways of doing things. Despite these challenges, many Canadian immigrants have adjusted well to life in Canada and are making successful contributions to their new society. Which of these views are presented in the following article?

CASE STUDY

1. Explain the conflict felt by many young Korean-Canadians.

2. Do you think there is an easy way to deal with this conflict? Give reasons for your view.

A Challenge for Korean-Canadians

Cathy Lee may seem like a typical university student. She dates people she likes, enjoys spending time with her friends and loves to sample different ethnic cuisine. Her Korean parents, however, insist that she obey Korean customs. They want her to date Koreans, have Korean friends and eat Korean food.

This kind of conflict is typical of the struggles that many young Korean-Canadians face. They feel a strong need to retain their Korean heritage, but there is also a need to integrate into Canadian society.

"Having a Korean background means being tied to a community of others like yourself," says David Kim, 20, who is a Queen's University student. "The members of the community share similar experiences, language and mutual friends."

Having a shared set of beliefs also means sharing common values. One important value in the culture is respect for elders.

"In Canadian society, when parents make a mistake, children are taught to tell them they are wrong," comments Kenneth Khang, 52, who is executive manager at the Korean-Canadian Cultural Association. "But in the Korean culture, we are taught to respect elders whether they are right or wrong. Korean-Canadian young people acknowledge the great sacrifice made by their parents. They understand their parents' dedication and the priority given to them as children."

From "Balancing Heritage with Canadian Culture" by Caroline Choi

For many youths, preserving the Korean culture is one way of saying thank you for their parents' sacrifices. It's also vital for the survival of that culture within the mosaic of Canada. Simon Park, 22, a commerce major at Queen's University, says this survival is fundamentally important.

"We should not be ashamed of our cultural heritage," he says. "If we forget where our cultural roots lie, then we lose a great part of who we are."

Figure 11–6
The fact that Canadian society is officially multicultural does not mean that all immigrants will choose to retain every aspect of their original culture. Some are eager to assimilate into mainstream society, while others preserve certain aspects of their culture.

Activities

Understand Ideas

1. a) Use a dictionary to define the word *mnemonic.*
b) Create a mnemonic device using the first letters of the three words for the main ways in which societies can accommodate minorities.
c) Create a three-column chart to record the main features of each of these three ways.

Think and Evaluate

2. a) Read the following quotation. Then, in your own words, explain what the speaker is trying to communicate.
"I did not come here to be labelled as an ethnic or a member of the multicultural community, or to be coddled with preferential treatment, nurtured with special grants and then to sit on the sidelines and watch the world go by. I came here to be a member of the mainstream of the Canadian society."
Rais Khan, professor of political science, University of Winnipeg.
b) Does this quote support segregation, assimilation or multiculturalism?
c) Write a one-page response to the quotation.
- Agree or disagree with the speaker's point of view.
- Explain your point of view by referring to your own thoughts and feelings.
- Make at least one direct and specific reference to the quote.

d) Exchange responses with a peer. Write a one-paragraph peer response beginning with one of the following phrases:
- An idea that I connect with is…
- I learned that you…

3. a) Record three problems and three challenges faced by the younger generation in recent immigrant families.
b) Which do you think is the most significant problem? Which do you think is the most significant challenge? Explain.
c) Are the problems and challenges faced by the younger generation in recent immigrant families simply the problems of growing up, or are they shaped by cultural background? Explain your views in a paragraph.

Research and Communicate

4. Make a KWL chart (What I *know,* What I *want* to know, What I *learned).*
a) Review the text information on Canada's policy of multiculturalism by completing the **K** part of the KWL chart. Record at least three points.
b) To complete the **W** section, identify three things you want to know about the policy of multiculturalism.
c) Using the Internet, research one of your questions. Record five things you have learned in the **L** section.

egalitarian—equal rights and opportunity for everyone

Prejudice and Discrimination

Multiculturalism is just one of many policies Canada has adopted to protect the different groups within society. The Canadian Charter of Rights and Freedoms and human rights laws also aim to establish an egalitarian society—one in which everyone can be treated equally, regardless of age, sex, physical capabilities, religion or ethnic background. Truly egalitarian societies are rare, however, and the reality is that different groups often have to struggle against prejudice and discrimination.

Prejudice can be defined as an unfavourable belief or judgment about members of a group, without the knowledge or experience needed to make such a judgment. Although we can be prejudiced in favour of something or someone, prejudices often reflect a negative attitude about a group or a situation. Prejudices are often based on **stereotypes**—simplified beliefs based on judging all members of a group by the behaviours of a few. People who hold stereotypes ignore the reality that each one of us is an individual. When a stereotype is applied to us, our individuality is taken away. We are seen as part of some group—teenagers, men, women, the elderly, the unemployed or a particular ethnic group—with a list of characteristics that is supposed to apply to us, regardless of our individual personalities.

Have you ever felt that you were being treated unfairly—perhaps in a store or restaurant, because of your age or the way you were dressed? If so, then you were probably experiencing prejudice. Have you ever looked at an older person and made a judgment about how that person thinks or is likely to act without knowing him or her personally? Then you probably have a stereotype about older people that affects your attitudes and actions.

Prejudice often leads to **discrimination,** a set of actions that societies or individuals take against particular groups of people because of their race, gender or other common characteristic. Discrimination usually

Figure 11–7

We often make judgments based on physical differences, gender or age that reveal prejudice and can lead to discrimination.

Canadian Values

Values are the fundamental standards that people in a culture hold as desirable. Do Canadians share some common values? In 1990–1991, 400 000 Canadians were asked to answer the question, "What does it mean to you to be Canadian?" Their responses expressed their sense of what sets Canada apart from other people and countries. Here are the values they identified as being typically Canadian:

- a belief in equality and fairness in a democratic society

- a belief in consultation and dialogue

- a belief in the importance of accommodation and tolerance

- support for diversity

- compassion and generosity

- an attachment to Canada's natural beauty

- commitment to freedom, peace and non-violent change in world affairs

Survey students in your school to find out what values they think are typically Canadian. After you have compiled your results, compare them with the list of values above. How closely did your research agree with that of the 1991 survey? How can you account for any differences?

---

denies the members of such a group their rights or privileges, goods or services, opportunities or an equal place in society. An individual may not have access to jobs, safety, education or political rights simply because he or she is a member of a particular group.

Types of Discrimination

Some forms of discrimination are supported by laws or widely practised and supported by regulations. This type of discrimination is known as institutional or **systemic discrimination.** Discrimination exists within the institutions that provide for the needs of members of the society.

Systemic discrimination has occurred in many places. In South Africa, the government policy of apartheid, or separation, meant that people were treated differently depending on the colour of their skin. Prior to 1993, people who were not white South Africans were not allowed to live in certain places, to use certain facilities, to receive equal pay or to have equal rights before the law. In the United States, until the 1960s, laws in the southern states also enforced the separation of whites and non-whites in schools, restaurants and other public facilities.

There have been many examples of systemic discrimination in Canadian history as well. Here are some of the most notable:

- The Indian Act ensured that members of First Nations were treated differently from other members of society. For example, until 1982, if an

> **Connections**
>
> How can gender socialization prevent access to certain opportunities? (See Chapter 6, pages 124–125.)

systemic discrimination—any act of discrimination that is supported by official or unofficial laws

Understanding Value Statements

A value statement expresses a person's feelings about what is right, wrong, good, bad, important or worthless. A value statement is different from a factual statement. It is important to recognize value statements, so that we can evaluate opinions rather than accepting them as fact. Sometimes a value statement can reveal the speaker's prejudice.

Here's How

1. Factual statements describe things that actually exist or have actually happened. They can often be backed up with records and statistics.

2. Value statements reflect the attitudes of the speaker. If you can sensibly add "Some people think" to the start of the statement, it probably reflects values rather than fact.

Practise It

1. Classify the following as value statements or factual statements:
   - Statistics show that Canada's population is aging.
   - Teenagers make a lot of noise.
   - Canadians believe in equal and fair treatment for all.
   - Canada is an officially multicultural society.
   - Young people tend to adapt more quickly than older people to a new culture.
   - Canada's policy of multiculturalism is better than the American policy of assimilation.

2. Review the case study on Korean-Canadians. Identify at least two factual statements and two value statements.

Aboriginal woman married a non-Aboriginal man, she had to give up her Indian status and rights. This law, however, did not apply to Aboriginal men.

- During the 1800s, African-Canadian children in Ontario were not allowed to attend school, even though their parents paid school taxes.

- In the early 1900s Chinese immigrants had to pay a special "head tax" to enter Canada.

- Canadian women were not allowed to vote in federal elections until 1918. Women won the right to vote in all provinces only in 1940.

Connections

In what ways could cliques bring about unofficial discrimination? (See Chapter 8, pages 174 and 176.)

Unofficial discrimination occurs when individuals or organizations discriminate against people even when doing so is against the law. A property owner, for example, might refuse to rent an apartment to a young person, or an employer might fire an older employee. Discrimination in the form of verbal or physical attacks is known as **harassment.**

As you have seen, segregation can be a form of discrimination, as it was in the case of Japanese-Canadians in World War II. An even more severe form of discrimination is **genocide**—the widespread killing of members of a particular group. Sadly, there are many examples of genocide in human history, several of them during and after World War II.

Relocation of Japanese-Canadians from Vancouver during World War II

Graves of genocide victims in the African country of Rwanda, 1996

Figure 11–8
At its worst, prejudice can lead to massive acts of discrimination against large groups of people.

Who Suffers?

Discrimination can be directed against any group. Usually discrimination takes place against those who have less influence, status or power in a society. It may also be based on traditional values that have remained widespread even though times have changed. When discrimination is based on prejudice and stereotypes, there is no rational reason for it. For example, people who have a disability may experience discrimination in accessing public services, or in finding jobs, even though they are fully qualified. Some studies indicate that people whose appearance varies from the norm may be passed over for promotion more frequently than others. People who stutter are often dealt with impatiently.

Three of the most common forms of discrimination in our society are racism, sexism and ageism.

Racism is a specific form of discrimination directed toward members of any racial or cultural group. Sociologists have identified three assumptions held by racists:

- They assume that a number of important human abilities and social traits are hereditary rather than learned.

- They believe that human groups differ in their possession of traits such as intelligence.

- They assume that hereditary differences between groups of people make some groups superior to others.

Sexism and **ageism** are forms of discrimination practised against people of a specific gender or age. "Men don't make good primary school teachers because they aren't as nurturing as females" is an example of a sexist comment. This assumption is not supported by research. "People over 40 don't understand teenagers" is an ageist comment. Although some people over 40 may not understand teenagers, others do.

Can Schools Perpetuate Prejudice and Discrimination?

The socializing agents that shape who we are include family, peers, media, education and religious institutions. If any of these agents practise prejudice or discrimination, we could be affected by their attitudes. Institutions such as schools also impart values such as self-discipline, responsibility, turn-taking and sharing. But do they also impart less positive values?

Any institution that has the ability to socialize people also has the power to perpetuate myths and stereotypes that lead to prejudice and discrimination. All social institutions and organizations are made up of people. Therefore, it is possible for them to reflect the biases of any group or individual. In many cases, however, prejudice can be hidden in an institution such as a school.

Consider the following examples.

Example 1

In the 1990s, Philippe Rushton, a psychology professor at the University of Western Ontario, published a study claiming that intelligence is based on race. Other researchers were quick to point out that Rushton's methodology was faulty. Furthermore, the media revealed that his work was funded by a known white supremacy group.

- What is the potential relationship between the research and the research funding?

- If Rushton had not been discredited, what might have been the consequences in all levels of the Canadian education system?

Example 2

According to a Statistics Canada report issued in September 2000, women make up the majority of full-time undergraduate students in most university departments. Nevertheless, they make up only a minority of the full-time enrollment in math and science faculties.

- It is generally accepted that there is no biological reason for one group to be better at math or science than another. What factors might then explain the low enrollment of women in math and science faculties?

Example 3

Canada's educational system has at various times both streamed and de-streamed students, often by academic ability. Supporters of streaming say that it is difficult to teach 30 or more students at the same time if they have a wide range of abilities. Critics of streaming argue that this approach labels students and does not allow some of them to reach their full potential.

- What connection might there be between streaming and the potential for prejudice and/or discrimination?

What Do You Think?

1. Work in a group of at least six students. Divide into three smaller groups or pairs, each focusing on one of the examples above. Prepare a response to the question(s) at the end of your example.

2. Present your example and responses to the group.

3. Then discuss: Do you agree that schools can perpetuate prejudice and discrimination? If so, what can be done to counteract this tendency? Alternatively, are schools more likely to counteract prejudice and discrimination? If so, how?

What Do Jokes Say About Prejudice?

Sometimes jokes can be cruel about a specific group. Do such jokes reveal prejudices? Respond to the following questions in your notebook or on a sheet of paper. Write **A** for Agree, **U** for Unsure and **D** for Disagree. Then discuss your ideas with others in your class. Listen to their thoughts, and decide whether you should adjust your own thinking.

1. Jokes are just for fun. No harm is done by sexist or racist jokes.

2. Jokes about a specific group are often based on stereotypes.

3. It's a free country. People should be able to say what they want.

4. There isn't anything you can do to stop people from telling racist or sexist jokes.

5. People don't mind if you make a joke about them based on a stereotype of their culture.

6. You would not mind if someone made fun of your culture.

7. It's okay if members of a group tell a joke about themselves.

8. If people don't speak up, it means they don't mind hearing racist or sexist jokes.

9. You have to have a thick skin in this world. You shouldn't mind a joke being told about your group.

10. Jokes that rely on stereotypes can create prejudices and discrimination by encouraging people to make fun of a particular group.

Activities

Understand Ideas

1. **a)** Define *stereotype* and *prejudice*. Which is primarily based on feelings and which on ideas?
   b) What is the difference between prejudice and discrimination?

Think and Evaluate

2. In social organizations, such as your school or in a place of business, individuals have different, often unequal, rights and privileges. You have no doubt noticed that your teachers occupy a different position in the school than do students. Is this discrimination? Why or why not?

Apply Your Learning

3. Reread the section on discrimination in the text. Using the guidelines in the Skill Focus on page 226, write one value statement and one factual statement to describe **a)** systemic discrimination; **b)** unofficial discrimination.

Research and Communicate

4. A group of students is sitting around at lunch when one of them tells a racist joke. Some people laugh; others look embarrassed. No one makes any critical comments. What can you do? Work with a partner or small group to list at least four options. Decide which option would be the best, and explain why.

What Causes Prejudice?

Sociologists and psychologists have proposed many theories to explain prejudice. Some theories focus on social causes—how prejudices are learned from others. Other theories examine the psychological roots of prejudice.

Social Learning Theory

Attitudes and beliefs are the result of socialization, of living within and learning from the surrounding society. It is not surprising, therefore, that prejudiced attitudes and beliefs are also the result of socialization and learning. When we are small children, the ideas and behaviours of parents, peers and others can have a particularly long-lasting impact. As children grow up, other social influences such as friends, neighbours and even schools may reinforce prejudicial attitudes. For example, until recent years school textbooks often showed minority cultures in negative ways, or ignored them altogether. This treatment of minorities tended to strengthen any existing prejudices learned in the family. Television and other media may also teach stereotypical and prejudicial attitudes.

Positive attitudes, as well as negative ones, can be learned. For example, younger people in Canada tend to have more positive attitudes toward immigration and a pluralistic society than do older people.

Figure 11–9

The circle of discrimination. Prejudice and discrimination can set up a vicious circle from which it is difficult to escape. How can you break this cycle? What are the social advantages to eliminating such cycles of discrimination?

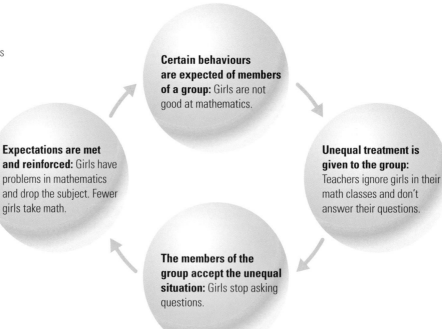

Certain behaviours are expected of members of a group: Girls are not good at mathematics.

Unequal treatment is given to the group: Teachers ignore girls in their math classes and don't answer their questions.

The members of the group accept the unequal situation: Girls stop asking questions.

Expectations are met and reinforced: Girls have problems in mathematics and drop the subject. Fewer girls take math.

77% of the respondents believe that different ethnic groups should try to adapt to the value system and way of life of the majority in Canadian society. However, 18% thought these groups should maintain their differences.

50% believe that relations between different racial and ethnic groups are "excellent" or "good," but an equal number felt relations were "only fair" or "poor."

25% felt that there is "a great deal of racism" in Canadian society, and 60% felt there was "some racism." However, only 13% thought racism was a very serious problem in Canada.

50% believe that the unwillingness of Canadians to accept diversity is a greater barrier to community than the unwillingness of ethnic groups to adapt to Canadian society. About 43% felt that the unwillingness of ethnic groups to adapt was a greater barrier than a lack of acceptance of diversity.

Figure 11–10

How do Canadians feel about their multicultural society? A Decima research poll on the subject showed these statistics. Would you expect the responses to differ if the survey was given to youths rather than only to people 18 and older?

Social-Economic Theories of Prejudice

Other theories look to social groups and economic conditions as factors that contribute to prejudice. During an economic recession, people who fear they might lose their jobs could develop more negative views of immigration, believing that immigrants pose a threat to their job security. When people react this way, immigrants become scapegoats—people who are blamed unfairly for certain problems or difficulties in society.

Psychological Theories of Prejudice

Even when they are raised in a society where there is generally very little prejudice, some individuals become extreme racists. They might feel great hostility toward people who are different, and they might even become aggressive or join racist organizations. Researchers have tried to understand the psychological basis of the more extreme forms of prejudice. Research shows that some people become prejudiced out of fear and suspicion of people who seem different. These differences may call into question their own ways of doing things and threaten their self-esteem. An insecure person may find it comforting to believe that members of some other group are inferior.

One psychological theory suggests that racism stems from frustration in life, such as failure to achieve a better job or standard of living. This frustration is expressed as hostility against those who are socially less powerful. Another theory suggests that some people are more inclined to be prejudiced by virtue of their personality. Someone with an authoritarian personality is concerned primarily with power. People with this personality usually oversimplify situations, dividing the world into good and bad, right and wrong, black and white. Obedience to rules and laws is very important to people with authoritarian personalities, and they believe in

Connections

How can public opinion be manipulated into creating scapegoats, applying stereotypes or spreading hostility, fear and suspicion? (See Chapter 10, page 209.)

Ugandan immigrants become Canadian citizens

Figure 11–11

The policy of multiculturalism encourages Canadians to celebrate cultural differences rather than fear them.

Korean dancing team at a multicultural festival, Dartmouth, Nova Scotia

Pakistan-India cricket match, Toronto, Ontario

the natural authority of dominant social groups. They are often ethnocentric, that is, they see their own race or ethnic group as superior to others. As a result, they often find scapegoats to blame for personal problems.

People who exhibit these traits might have had parents who punished them severely and demanded obedience. These parents might have taught their children that the world is a dangerous place and that it is acceptable to release aggression against certain groups.

Focus Questions

What can be done to minimize prejudice?

When is contact between groups most effective?

Dealing with Prejudice and Discrimination

Social scientists have found that, under certain conditions, increased contact between social groups can minimize prejudice. People who do not know each other have less chance of understanding one another. Ignorance may lead to stereotypes and hostility. However, when people interact directly, they see others as individuals rather than simply as members of a group.

Identifying Bias

All materials, whether written or visual, are shaped by the point of view of the creator. When the point of view excludes some ideas or is prejudicial toward particular groups, it is **biased**—slanted in favour of a particular position, often a prejudiced position. To determine bias, it is important to recognize the point of view of the speaker, writer or producer.

Here's How

There are several questions that help to determine whether materials contain bias:

- Are certain groups portrayed in a simplified or stereotypical way, or even ignored altogether?

- Are certain people, situations or products shown or described as all good or as completely bad?

- Are particular groups portrayed as limited to certain jobs and activities?

- What value judgments are evident?

- Are there opinions or facts that have been omitted?

- Through whose eyes is the material being viewed?

Practise It

1. Television situation comedies often portray people in terms of stereotypes. Watch one sitcom of your choice, and make note of any stereotyped characters in it. Identify the specific aspects of the character that you feel are stereotyped.

2. Share your information with others in the class.

Contact also enables people to see similarities between themselves and the members of other groups. Differences sometimes disappear as two groups begin to imitate each other. In studies of integrated housing, workplaces, schools and camps, it was found that contact led to friendly relations and positive feelings.

Contact between groups is most effective when the members of each group are of equal status in income, occupation and roles within the group. The contact should be of a favourable and pleasant nature. Having a mutual goal that requires co-operation and interdependence is often the best way to overcome barriers.

Education can also help to reduce prejudice. Courses that provide information about different social groups and encourage group interaction help individuals identify prejudice and take action against it. Education also helps individuals develop logical methods of approaching social issues. Putting different groups together in schools is another way of fighting prejudice.

mutual goal—shared goal or aim for which both parties must work together

Figure 11–12

Insecure people may try to improve their position by joining racist organizations. To change this kind of prejudice, it is often necessary to find other ways to raise the individual's self-esteem.

Activities

Understand Ideas

1. Use a concept map to identify the main ideas for the following theories of prejudice: social learning, social-economic, psychological. (See Skill Focus, page 125.)

Think and Evaluate

2. How can you decide if someone is prejudiced? Write at least four criteria.

3. **a)** List five things you, as an individual, can do to combat prejudice and discrimination.
   b) How many of these ideas do you already practise? What specific actions could you take to do more?

4. Name one person, either a public figure or an individual you know, whom you see as a role model for fighting discrimination and prejudice in society. Explain why you chose this person, and how he or she has inspired you.

Apply Your Learning

5. In small groups, discuss experiences you have had with prejudice or discrimination. (See Skill Focus, page 43.) Choose one of these incidents, and develop a short dramatic sketch that illustrates the situation, why it happened and how people responded or should respond to it. Present your sketch to the class.

Research and Communicate

6. Use magazine and newspaper pictures or your own sketches to make a collage illustrating one of the following themes:
   a) causes of prejudice and discrimination
   b) the feelings of those suffering from prejudice and discrimination
   c) the social and economic consequences of prejudice and discrimination
   d) what can be done to deal with prejudice and discrimination

Key Points

- Society and culture have distinct meanings to social scientists. While culture stays with you wherever you go, a society exists in a specific geographic location. When you move to another society, you must adapt to some extent to the way things are done.

- Social institutions help societies meet the needs of their members; they also vary over time and in different places.

- Three ways in which societies can choose to deal with different cultures are segregation, assimilation and multiculturalism.

- Prejudice implies negative attitudes toward and stereotyped ideas about the members of a particular group in society. Discrimination refers to the actions taken by individuals or society that are based on prejudice. Despite laws to the contrary, Canadian society is not free from discrimination against minority groups.

- Education and increased contact with diverse groups can reduce prejudice in society.

Activities

Understand Ideas

1. In what ways do multiculturalism and segregation overlap in their treatment of minorities? In what ways are these approaches different?

Think and Evaluate

2. **a)** Review the chart of social institutions in Figure 11–3. Why are family and schools grouped together?
   b) Separate family and schools as institutions. Identify the basic needs met by each.

c) "Family and schools are closely linked and cannot be separated as institutions." Write a paragraph agreeing or disagreeing with this statement. Provide three reasons to support your opinion.

Apply Your Learning

3. **a)** Identify several ways in which you have chosen to be influenced by other cultures. Think of fashions, ideas, food, clothing, people and music.
   b) How have the media influenced your choices? Using the Skill Focus on page 233, identify bias in the media, either for or against the cultural preferences you have adopted.

4. Explain the difference between culture and society. Describe one identifying feature of your culture and one of your society.

Research and Communicate

5. Write an essay outlining how the absence of prejudice and discrimination could benefit society. Use the following outline:

Paragraph 1: Introduction. Define the terms *prejudice* and *discrimination*, acknowledge the negative effects of both and list three reasons why society would benefit from their absence.

Paragraph 2: List three negative effects of prejudice on society, and provide evidence to support your points. Explain your information.

Paragraph 3: Follow the outline given for paragraph 2, but focus on discrimination.

Paragraph 4: Begin with "Society would benefit from the absence of prejudice and discrimination because…" and include three reasons to support this statement. Explain your information.

Paragraph 5: Summarize the main ideas, concluding opinions and/or questions.

Unit 2: Build Your Research and Inquiry Skills

1. Finding a Partner

Issues
- What characteristics are important in a marriage partner?

Inquiry and Analysis
- Survey a range of people in your class to see what characteristics they think are important in a marriage partner.
- Record the results in a questionnaire similar to the one below. List up to 15 characteristics. You might want to consider the following: trustworthy, dependable, considerate, affectionate, physically attractive, ambitious, shares interests and hobbies, likes children, careful with money, likes to spend money.
- Score each response this way: Very important = 2; Not very important = 1; Not at all important = 0.
- Determine which characteristics members of the class consider most important. Tabulate responses by males and females separately.

Characteristics	Very important	Somewhat important	Not at all important
trustworthy			
dependable			

Communication
- Present your findings in statistical form.
- Make charts or graphs to show your findings.

SKILL REVIEW: **Using Statistics, page 147; Making and Reading Graphs, page 155.**

2. Our Social Behaviour

Issues
- How do norms affect the way we interact with each other on a daily basis?
- How do we react when a norm is not followed?

Inquiry and Analysis
- Work in a group to conduct the following experiment over the course of the day:
  - Choose some group members to conduct the experiment and some group members to serve as the control group.
  - Members of the experimental group: Every time you meet someone who says "How are you" or a similar phrase of greeting, stop and tell that person how you are. Notice how each person responds.
  - Members of the control group: Behave as you normally do when people greet you, but notice how people typically behave when they greet each other in this way.

SKILL REVIEW: **Conducting an Experiment, page 9.**

Communication
- Share your findings with the group. Discuss why people reacted as they did. Take notes of the discussion.
- Write a social science report to explain your experiment and the conclusions you have drawn.

SKILL REVIEW: **Group Discussions, page 43; Writing a Social Science Report, page 188.**

3. Cliques and Crowds in Your School

Issues
- What cliques exist in your school?
- What crowds exist in your school?
- How do we identify cliques and crowds?

Inquiry and Analysis

- Review the text information on cliques and crowds. For the purposes of this activity, a clique can be defined as a group of people who spend most of their time together. A crowd is a group that can be identified by a particular style, a set of interests and perhaps ways of dress. For example, "jocks" might be one crowd.
- Interview a number of people, selected at random. Find out what cliques, or crowds, they identify in your school. Ask how they recognize a clique or a crowd. Be sure to prepare your questions in advance and to record their answers.

SKILL REVIEW: **Conducting an Interview, page 12.**

Communicate

- Discuss your findings with the class. What are the benefits and drawbacks of cliques and crowds?
- As a class, develop a master chart of the cliques and crowds that exist in your school. Does everyone agree with the items on this list? What are the distinguishing characteristics of these two groups?
- Make an organizer to compare cliques and crowds, based on your findings.

SKILL REVIEW: **Making Comparisons, page 213.**

4. Collective Behaviour

Issues

- What fashion or fad is currently popular?
- How does it influence you or people you know?

Inquiry and Analysis

- Use the inquiry model to investigate a fad or fashion in your school. You might ask a question such as, Why are many students wearing...?
- Use observation and interviews to find out answers to the following: What is the origin of the fad or fashion? What is its appeal? Who tends to follow it? How long will it last? What does it tell you about the values and ideas of your culture?

SKILL REVIEW: **The Inquiry Model, page 6; Conducting an Interview, page 12; Conducting Observation Research, page 13; Raising Questions, page 24.**

Communication

- Write a report of your findings under the following headings: Question, Hypothesis, Supporting evidence, Conclusion, Questions for further research.

5. Prejudice and Discrimination

Issues

- What forms of prejudice and discrimination are most prevalent in your community?
- Why do these forms of prejudice and discrimination exist?
- What can be done about them?

Inquiry and Analysis

- Identify a particular form of prejudice or discrimination that exists in your community. Consider discrimination based on age, gender, race, physical characteristics or background.
- Explain who experiences the prejudice and discrimination, who tends to be prejudiced and to discriminate, and what attitudes and feelings both groups have.
- Provide evidence to support your view.

Communication

- Discuss your examples and evidence with a group.
- Use brainstorming techniques to develop methods to deal with prejudice and discrimination.
- Present these methods to the class, and ask for feedback and suggestions.
- Write a short article on how to deal with prejudice and discrimination with the intention of getting it published in the school or community newspaper.

SKILL REVIEW: **Group Discussions, page 43; Thinking Creatively, page 64.**

Unit 2: Demonstrate Your Learning

Task 2–1: The Groups in Our Lives

Background Information

We live our lives in groups and spend most of our waking hours in one group context or another—our families, our circles of friends, the people we work with or the classmates we go to school with. We define ourselves in terms of groups: "I am a Canadian," "I am a high-school student," "I am an Ontarian." Many of the most important changes in our lives result from changing groups—leaving home, going to university, getting a job—and membership in new groups often leads to changes in our attitudes and values.

Which groups are part of your life? In what ways do these groups influence you? Which groups do you believe have the greatest impact on your life? These are the primary questions governing this performance task.

Your Task

In this task, you will

- conduct a study of the groups to which you or someone you know well belongs; you will
  - identify the groups to which you or your subject belongs
  - examine what kinds of groups they are
  - explain why you or your subject belongs to these groups
  - draw conclusions, based on your research, about why people are attracted to various social groups
- draw on the theories of anthropologists, psychologists and sociologists outlined in this unit and apply research and inquiry skills to conduct your study
- present your findings in the form of a social science report

Review What You Know

1. Review the kinds of groups discussed in this unit and the ways in which these groups function. Be sure you understand the following terms:
- family (page 145)
- social groups (page 165)
- primary groups (page 166)
- secondary groups (page 166)
- cliques (page 177)
- crowds (page 203)
- mass behaviour (page 208)
- culture (page 218)
- society (page 218)

Think and Inquire

2. Decide on a subject for your investigation. It could be you or someone you know.

3. State the question(s) that will guide your inquiry. Use the questions in "Your Task" above as a guide.
4. Formulate your hypothesis.
5. Set up a research plan that will allow you to investigate the influence of the social groups on you or your subject. If you are planning to focus on yourself, you will probably use observation research. If you plan to focus on someone you know, you will probably use interviews and observation. Be prepared to defend your choice of research method.
6. Gather the information you need. Include quotes from individuals to illustrate your findings, where appropriate.
7. Record your findings carefully, analyze your data and draw conclusions.

SKILL REVIEW: **The Inquiry Model, page 6; Conducting an Interview, page 12; Conducting Observation Research, page 13; Raising Questions, page 24.**

Communicate Your Ideas

8. Write a social science report of your investigation.

SKILL REVIEW: **Writing a Social Science Report, page 188.**

Apply Your Skills

9. In completing this task, you will demonstrate the following skills:
- reviewing concepts
- organizing ideas
- applying ideas
- interviewing
- conducting observation research
- writing a social science report

Criteria for Assessment

Social Science Report

Introduction
- states the issue or question
- states position and hypothesis

Description of Research Plan
- outlines steps in the research
- describes reasons for choosing this method of research

Collection of Data
- organizes observations and findings
- describes observations and findings fully
- provides quotes to illustrate observations and findings

Analysis
- discusses observations and findings in an organized manner
- draws specific conclusions about aspects of the research
- makes connections between the findings and ideas beyond the research

Conclusion
- briefly summarizes the research and its findings
- reaches general conclusions
- indicates further questions for research

Unit 2: Demonstrate Your Learning
Task 2–2: The Group and I

Background Information

There are several kinds of groups in our lives. Sociologists identify primary and secondary groups as two important distinctions. Family and close friends are primary groups. Within these groups, personal concerns are taken into account, and the individual as a whole is considered important.

We also live within larger groups, where secondary relationships play a role. For example, you go to a school where you interact with teachers and classmates; you may have, or will be part of, a job situation where secondary relationships are paramount. Although these interactions may include primary relationships, it is the secondary group that will dominate in these situations. You will also encounter secondary relationships when you buy something from a department store, contact a government agency or belong to a political organization. We should recognize when we are dealing with one type of group or another. We should also understand how we can, and should, relate to both of these groups.

In this task, you will focus on one group that is particularly important to you. You will identify the kind of group it is and how this group has influenced your thoughts and behaviour. From this research, you will be able to determine how you will react to group influence in the future.

Your Task

In this task, you will

- use information presented in this unit and the inquiry skills you have developed to observe, describe and analyze a group—one to which you or someone you know belongs
- investigate the following aspects of the group:
  - whether it is primary or secondary
  - its norms (the expected ways of acting in the group)
  - the roles that are performed within the group (the parts different people play)
  - the sanctions imposed on members (what happens when people fail to conform to group expectations)
- present your findings in the form of an oral presentation or a concept map

Review What You Know

1. Review the information about groups in this unit. Be sure you understand the following terms:
- primary groups (page 166)
- secondary groups (page 166)
- norms (page 167)
- roles (page 167)
- sanctions (page 168)

Think and Inquire

2. In consultation with your teacher, decide whether you will prepare an oral presentation or a concept map.
3. Decide which group will be the focus of your study.
4. Identify the central question[s] that will guide your research. Use the questions listed under "Your Task" as a guide.
5. Formulate a hypothesis.

6. Decide which research methods you will use to conduct your research. Observation, interviewing and conducting a sample survey could all be used for this task.

7. Conduct your research. Gather and record your data carefully. Analyze the results and draw conclusions.

SKILL REVIEW: **The Inquiry Model, page 6; Conducting a Sample Survey, page 11; Conducting an Interview, page 12; Conducting Observation Research, page 13.**

Communicate Your Ideas

8. If you are preparing an oral presentation, outline the aim of your research, your hypothesis, your research plan, your findings and your conclusions. If you are making a concept map, place the group you have studied in the centre and show how it is connected to the various aspects you have discovered in your investigation.

SKILL REVIEW: **Making an Oral Presentation, page 338; Organizing Ideas with Concept Maps, page 125.**

Apply Your Skills

9. In completing this task, you will demonstrate the following skills:
- reviewing concepts
- organizing ideas
- applying ideas
- interviewing
- making an oral presentation
- organizing ideas in a concept map

Criteria for Assessment

Oral Presentation
Content
- introduces the topic
- organizes the information, including issue or question, hypothesis, description of research plan, description of findings, analysis of findings and conclusion drawn
- explains the information clearly

Preparation
- appears well rehearsed
- uses appropriate tone and language
- uses appropriate visuals in an effective manner
- encourages discussion by using prepared questions

Delivery
- speaks clearly and loudly
- speaks at a steady pace and varies voice
- makes eye contact with audience members
- shows enthusiasm for the subject
- presents with appropriate posture, manner and gestures

Concept Map
Content
- identifies the main idea in the centre of the map
- identifies appropriate related topics
- draws appropriate links between the main topic and related topics
- draws appropriate links between related topics
- includes brief details for each topic
- writes brief explanations on linking lines to explain connections between topics

Presentation
- includes a heading
- provides drawings and labels that are clear and neat
- uses colour effectively to highlight connections

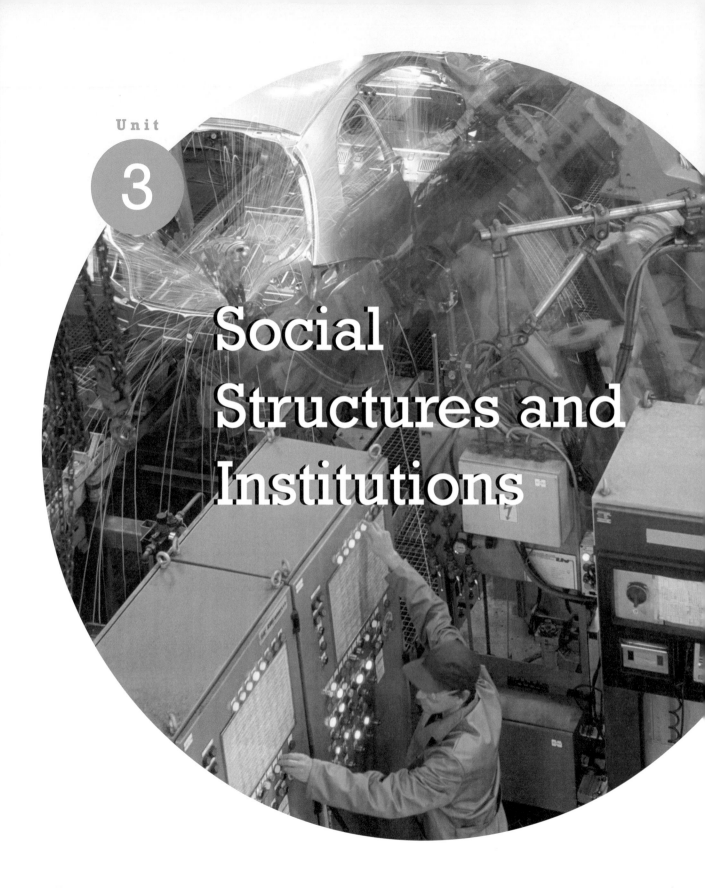

Social Structures and Institutions

Unit Overview

In Unit 1, the methods and ideas of the social sciences were introduced along with the major question, How can anthropology, psychology and sociology help us understand ourselves as individual human beings and as members of society? In Unit 2, the social sciences were directed specifically toward understanding the groups and organization of human society.

In Unit 3, the social sciences will focus on another major theme—the social structures and institutions that human beings develop not only to survive but also to improve their quality of life. Think, for a moment, how society provides you with food, shelter, companionship, education, entertainment and security. People in all societies create social structures and institutions in order to meet these needs.

Anthropology, Psychology and Sociology in This Unit

Although human needs are similar all over the world, how they are actually fulfilled varies from one culture to another. Anthropology can help us understand such variation and the reasons for it. In this unit, an anthropological approach will be used to examine and compare how young people are educated around the world, how work is performed in different places, how social control is ensured and how our lives are affected by technology.

The psychologist's point of view will explore the impact of social institutions on individuals. How are people's thoughts and actions influenced by their level of prosperity, by the education they receive, by the kind of work they do and by the way they spend their leisure time? What is the effect of change and technology on human mental processes and individual behaviour?

Through the eyes of the sociologist you will investigate the nature of social classes, social structures and institutions in Canadian society. What can we find out about our schools, our workforce, our prisons and laws, our health-care system as well as the information technology that has become such an important part of our lives? How do we think about, and give meaning to, these structures and institutions? What other factors shape our social world?

Unit Expectations

- Which social institutions are common to a variety of cultures?

- How do social institutions function in different cultures?

- What are some of the recent changes in work and education, and what impact do these changes have on Canadian society?

Chapter Topics

Chapter 12: Education and Schools

Chapter 13: The World of Work

Chapter 14: Social Classes and Poverty in Canada

Chapter 15: Deviance and Social Control

Chapter 16: Recreation and Health

Chapter 17: Culture, Communication and Computers

Research, Inquiry and Communication Skills

Writing an Essay

Documenting Sources

Conducting a Seminar

Debating

Writing a Position Paper

Making an Oral Presentation

Content Analysis

Assessing Internet Information

Chapter 12

Education and Schools

In This Chapter

- How does education vary in different societies?

- What changes are occurring in education?

- How do changes in society affect education?

- What direction will education take in the future?

Key Terms

education

traditional societies

contemporary societies

intended goals of education

unintended goals of education

hidden curriculum

meritocracy

streaming

education gap

employability skills

distance education

lifelong learning

Society provides formal training to its members, especially to children and youth, through education. It is likely that you have received formal education for the last decade and will continue to do so for a few more years. It is also likely that your education will be a lifelong pursuit, as you may return to school from time to time for further job training or other learning.

But how do you define *education*? Examine the following list of activities. Which activities would you define as educational? Discuss the list with your group. Then list at least three activities of your own, explaining why they are educational.

- special-interest courses (art, woodworking, sewing, sign language, etc.)

- a first-aid course

- team sports

- correspondence courses through a university

- home schooling

- poetry and literary readings

- summer camp

- after-school religion classes

- on-the-job training program

- learning to play an instrument

- karate lessons

- volunteer community services

- participating in a co-op program at a university

What Is Education?

Focus Questions

How does education vary from one society to another?

How does a society's economy affect its level of education?

Education can be defined as the different ways a society conveys knowledge to its members. This knowledge can include facts and job skills, as well as cultural norms and values. Although **traditional societies** may have schools, most education takes place within the family and immediate social group. Knowledge and important skills are passed down from parents to children, generation to generation. In **contemporary societies,** such as ours, formal education usually takes place in schools rather than in homes or in small groups. Different factors affect the educational system in contemporary societies. One factor is rapid change, especially in science and technology. Another is the wide variety of specialized skills that are needed in the workforce. A third factor is the complex social structures and organizations within which we live. Formal education is one of the major social institutions in contemporary societies.

traditional societies— societies with little dependence upon scientific or technological development

contemporary societies— changing societies, dependent upon industry and advanced technology

The following case studies of traditional Inuit and contemporary Japanese education illustrate the wide variation of education that exists. Each society must make decisions about what it considers necessary to teach its youth. These are important decisions for a number of reasons. If, for example, young people do not learn the knowledge, skills and attitudes of their society, they will not be able to function as successful adults within that society. And if they cannot function successfully, the society as a whole will suffer. Since each of these societies has its own customs, social structures and institutions, the process of education is unique to that society.

Education in Two Societies

A Traditional Society

The following passage is from Farley Mowat's book, *People of the Deer*. The passage describes a traditional childhood among the Inuit people living west of Hudson Bay in the mid-twentieth century. Much of the traditional Inuit lifestyle and educational system Mowat described in his book in 1951 has disappeared.

CASE STUDY

1. **Would traditional Inuit ways of learning work in Canada today?**

2. **Would Japanese forms of education work in our society?**

…The children live their lives free of all restraint except that which they themselves impose; and they are at least as well-behaved as any child anywhere. By the time a child is three, it is already aware of the general pattern of its life. Kunee, at the age of five, was already an accomplished woman of the People, yet Kunee had never been taught what she must do. She was simply observant and imitative, as most children are, and she saw what others did and longed to do as well by herself.

The children's work is also their play. At night, when the adults are asleep or resting on the ledge, no voice is raised to chide the girl children, who remain active until the dawn, keeping the fire alive under the cooking pot and concocting broths and stews, not with toy things, but with the real equipment which will

chide—scold

Figure 12–1

Modern Inuit children play baseball at a whaling camp. In what ways do you think the education of these young people is similar to and different from the education described by Mowat?

be theirs in maturity. No regimen or hard routine is laid upon them. When they are sleepy, they sleep. When they are hungry, they may always eat, if there is food. If they wish to play, no one will halt them and give them petty tasks to do, for in their play they learn more of life than can be taught by tongues and by training.

Suppose a youth, a ten-year-old boy, decides he will become a great hunter overnight. He is not scolded and sent sulkily to bed for his foolish presumption, nor do his parents condescend to his childish fantasy. Instead his father gravely spends the evening preparing a miniature bow which is not a toy, but an efficient weapon on a reduced scale. The bow is made with love, then it is given to the boy, and he sets out for his distant hunting ground with the time-honoured words of luck ringing in his ears. There is no distinction, and this lack of distinction is not a pretense, it is perfectly real. The boy will be a hunter? Very well then, he shall be a hunter—not a boy with a toy bow. When he returns at last with hunger gnawing at his stomach, he is greeted as gravely as if he were his father. The whole camp wishes to hear of his hunt, and he can expect the same ridicule at failure, or the same praise if he managed to kill a little bird, which would come upon a full-grown man. So he plays, and learns, under no shadow of parental disapproval, and under no restraint of fear.

Education in Japan

In the article, "Japan's Kyoiku Mamas," author Marlise Simons describes a very different educational system from that of the Inuit of Hudson Bay.

Thirteen-year-old Naoko Matsuo has just returned from school to her home in suburban Yokohama, Japan. Instead of dropping off her books and beginning an afternoon of fun, she settles in to do her homework. Several hours later, Naoko's mother reminds her that it is time to leave for the juku, or "cram school," that she attends for three hours three evenings a week. Mother and daughter travel four stops on the subway to downtown Yokohama and climb to the second floor of an office building where Naoko joins dozens of other girls and boys for intensive training in Japanese, English, math and science.

Tuition at the juku consumes several hundred dollars of the Matsuo family's monthly income. But they recognize the realities of the Japanese educational system, and consider this investment a necessity. The extra hours in the classroom will soon pay off when Naoko takes a national examination to determine her school placement. Three years later, she will face another hurdle with the high-school placement exam; this test, once again, will determine the quality of her education. Then will come the final challenge: earning admission to an exclusive national university, a prize won by the one-third of Japanese students who perform best on this examination. Stumbling in the race that is Naoko's next five years will mean learning to settle for less. Like most other Japanese families, the Matsuos are convinced that one cannot work too hard or begin too early to prepare for university admission.

Economic Development and Education

Schooling in any society is closely tied to that society's level of economic development.

Hunting and gathering societies did not have systems of formal education. Children gained knowledge of their culture and learned the necessary skills of survival by observing and imitating their parents and other adults. **Agricultural societies,** which include most of the world's population today, have limited schooling, with an emphasis on practical skills and traditional tasks. The opportunity to study science, literature, art history or other subjects is available only to those families that can afford to pay for further education. Canada was in this stage of economic and educational development during the nineteenth and early twentieth centuries. In today's low-income agricultural countries, the majority of people receive little formal education. **Industrial societies** are high-income societies where education for everyone is a priority. Workers need basic skills in reading, writing and arithmetic in order to work in industrial production. Therefore, industrial societies set up schools (formal institutions) to educate the youth.

In **post-industrial societies** more jobs are found in the field of information technology and service industries than in industrial production. Problem solving and decision making are important skills in post-industrial societies. Consequently, higher levels of education are needed than in industrial societies, and people regularly go back to school to upgrade and renew their skills.

Figure 12–2

What impact does a society's economic system have on its education? ▼

High school in Japan

Village education in Somalia

Visiting scholar at Eton, an exclusive private school in Britain

Writing an Essay

The essence of an essay is the gathering of ideas to present a written description or argument in support of a point of view or position. Your ideas should be supported by research and organized in an effective way to convince others of their worth.

Here's How

1. Identify the task. Find out what is required from your teacher or the assignment outline. Identify what is expected in terms of length, style, organization and research required.

2. Choose a topic. First and foremost, choose a topic that interests you. Be sure that the topic meets the requirements of the assignment and that you can complete it in the time and with the resources available to you.

3. Research the topic. Find out if there are particular sources recommended for the topic. Gather resources from the library, Internet and other sources. Read and make notes on the most general sources to begin with. Begin to develop an idea of questions and points of view related to the topic. Organize your notes. (See the Skill Focus on Gathering and Recording Information on page 73.)

4. Plan the essay. Begin to develop your own point of view about the topic. Determine what is the main point you want to make. State this in one or two sentences. This will become your thesis statement. Gather and organize the information and evidence that support and oppose your thesis.

5. Write the essay. While organization and style can vary, there are several elements of effective essays:

- **Introduction:** The first paragraph introduces the topic, the major question or issue and the thesis statement. It also usually includes a statement of how the evidence supporting the thesis will be organized.
- **Body of essay:** Major arguments, supported by evidence, are organized into paragraphs. Paragraphs should be organized to present evidence in the most effective way. (See also the Skill Focus on Writing a Paragraph on page 115.) Be sure to use correct grammar and spelling.
- **Conclusion:** The final paragraph sums up major arguments and restates the thesis position.
- **Appearance and format:** The cover page should include the title of the essay and your name centred in the top third of the page. The name of the course, instructor and date should be centred in the bottom third of the page. Type on the pages should be double-spaced with a 2.5-cm margin.

Practise It

Write an essay describing what you think are the most important goals of Canadian education. Follow the steps above. Be sure to support your views with suitable evidence.

Activities

Understand Ideas

1. Define education and provide an example from both traditional and contemporary society.

2. a) In his description of a traditional Inuit childhood, what does Farley Mowat mean when he writes, "the children's work is also their play"?

b) What does this description say about the education of the Inuit?

3. a) What is the *juku*?

b) Why do most Japanese students consider *juku* a necessary investment?

Think and Evaluate

4. Create a chart to compare education in modern Japan with that of the traditional Inuit under the following categories:
- purpose of education
- methods used to educate the young
- teachers
- social structures within which education takes place
- similarities and differences between Canadian education and that of the Japanese and the Inuit

5. What do you think would be the result if, for some reason, education did not occur for a generation in a society such as ours, or such as that of the Inuit?

6. Canadian students, like Japanese students, should be required to take a national examination to determine secondary-school placement. Do you agree or disagree? Give three reasons to support your position.

Apply Your Learning

7. Review the two case studies, traditional and Japanese education systems. Which one of the two learning environments appeals to you? Provide three reasons to explain your choice.

Research and Communicate

8. Interview someone who was educated in a period or culture different from your own. Prepare interview questions regarding the experience of being educated in that system, the subjects and topics considered important, the teaching and learning methods used, how learning was tested or evaluated and how that system is different from your own.

Education in Canada

The Goals of Education

Why are you going to school? What prompts you to spend 12 or more years of your life in a classroom? For the first few years, you had little choice and didn't think about these questions very much. By this point in your life, however, you have choices since most young Canadians are not required by law to attend school after the age of 16. However, it is very likely that you will continue your education for some time to come. No doubt, you have a number of reasons for extending your formal education. Generally, the goals of education can be broken into two categories: intended goals and unintended goals.

The **intended goals of education** are to transmit knowledge, skills and behaviour to young people. The knowledge may be traditional or

What purposes should education serve?

What are the intended and unintended goals of education in Canada?

How has education in Canada changed over generations?

more modern. For example, communication skills such as reading, writing and discussion have always been taught in schools and are skills considered crucial in our society. At the same time, new ideas in the sciences, mathematics, social studies and arts and humanities are also conveyed through schools. Specific job-oriented skills are often taught in post-secondary schools, such as community colleges or universities.

Through school, individuals may also discover special talents. Students with an aptitude for music, art, mathematics or technology, for example, are often encouraged to continue their studies in this field. In this way, society provides opportunities for young people to select and prepare for a career or vocation or further develop a special interest.

Figure 12–3

What do you think should be the major goals of education? Why?

Schooling also helps young people identify and develop values and ideals that are shared in their society, which contributes to social unity. This goal is especially important in communities whose population is socially diverse. For example, multiculturalism is an important part of Canadian society and while students are encouraged to develop a sense of Canadian nationalism, they are also taught to accommodate a wide variety of cultural groups. At the same time, because ideas and cultures are so diverse in Canadian society, there is often a wide range of opinions about how young people should be socialized. For example, some parents want to see their children firmly disciplined while others prefer a more relaxed approach to teaching children how to behave.

Educational systems may also provide a society with hidden benefits, or **unintended goals.** These services have often been called the **hidden curriculum.** The provision of child-care facilities for working parents is one of the most obvious benefits of educational institutions. Schools are also a place where adolescence is prolonged in order to keep young people out of

the job market for as long as possible. Schools provide a social centre where young people can meet others and establish personal relationships. Young people often meet their future business acquaintances and marriage partners in school. School is also a place where young people can learn values that a society deems important. Students can learn the value of co-operation with others or develop work-related skills such as how to organize information or accept responsibility. They also learn how to operate within a complex organization—the school—which helps prepare them for complex organizations in the work world.

A Historical Look at Canadian Education

Many of the Aboriginal peoples who lived in Canada for centuries were hunters and gatherers, and their children were educated by parents or family. During the early period of European settlement, prior to the mid-nineteenth century, it was rare for children to attend school. Wealthy families might have sent their children for private tutoring to learn how to read and write. By the middle of the nineteenth century, however, most Western nations, including Canada, were establishing free public education for everyone, although not everyone took advantage of it. As society began to industrialize, basic literacy, communication and mathematics skills were necessary and more children began going to school, at least for a few years. Few students went beyond grade 8, however, and many learned only to read and write. As late as 1920, only 7 percent of children stayed in school after grade 8. By comparison, in 1996, 90 percent continued their education after grade 8.

During the twentieth century, the length of time Canadians spent in school increased steadily. Today, a growing number of young people go to college, university or other post-secondary training. In the years between 1988 and 1994, for example, Canada's population grew by 8.8 percent while full-time post-secondary enrolment grew by 18.1 percent. During this period, Canada had the highest level of university enrolment of all countries in the OECD (Organization for Economic Cooperation and Development).

As you will see in the following chapter, Canada's economy has been changing, and this change calls for educational institutions to adapt to new demands of the workforce. Canadians today remain in school longer and return to school regularly over the course of their lives. Technological training is a priority in the public education systems as well as in private organizations, but employers also value employees with an education in the liberal arts and humanities because their education has provided them with skills in reasoning and decision making.

Figure 12–4
A one-room schoolhouse in Lipton, Saskatchewan, 1915

1. What purposes did education serve in each of these cases?

2. How would you describe each society?

Changes in Education and Society

Case One Once the crops had been brought in by late September or October, young boys and girls returned to school—a one-room schoolhouse in the middle of farming country. The teacher was a young woman who had recently graduated from high school and had taken one year at teachers' college. The school held about 40 pupils ranging in age from 5 to about 14. Many of the students would not attend class in early spring because they had to help with plowing and planting. The curriculum consisted primarily of reading, writing and arithmetic although some geography, history and science were also taught. The teacher would teach one small group at a time, while the others worked from their books. Most students left school at the age of 12 or 13 and began to work at home or on neighbouring farms.

Case Two Most students completed their primary education and continued on to secondary school. The age when students left school had risen to 16 and most young people completed their high-school education. Secondary schools had become large organizations, with one or two thousand students and up to a hundred teachers. Students took a variety of courses, each taught by a specialist in the field. Some were traditional subjects such as Latin, Greek, English literature, history, mathematics and science. Other courses such as home economics, physical education, health and art were oriented toward life skills and leisure. An increasing number of courses such as keyboarding, technical training and bookkeeping, were aimed at preparing students for the workplace. The method of teaching and learning was based mainly on memorization, and textbooks were the primary source of information. Most students entered the workforce after completing high school. Only about 5 percent went on to post-secondary education.

Case Three Formal education for most young people continued until they were in their 20s and included post-secondary education. Some post-secondary education was geared toward skill development and career training, especially in technical college. Other education focused on careers in the social services, such as social work or management skills. Still other post-secondary education took place in the universities where theoretical as well as practical approaches to knowledge were taught. Adults of all ages returned to school in order to keep up with advances in their occupations, or to develop knowledge in new areas. Teaching and learning methods focused on the abilities of students to work independently. Students studied how to solve problems and make sound decisions. Research was often done using a variety of sources available in libraries and on the Internet.

Connections

Why can changes in education be considered a form of cultural adaptation? (See Chapter 2, pages 35–38.)

What Should Schools Do?

In the changing modern world, we cannot be absolutely sure what knowledge or skills will be important in the next 10 or 20 years. As a result, it is difficult to know what and how schools should teach. There are many conflicting ideas of what the focus of education should be. What is your opinion?

A. Look at the list of possible goals below. In your notebook, classify each goal according to whether you think it is "very important," "somewhat important" or "not very important." Then identify which courses you have taken in the past two years that have helped you to develop in each of the areas. What conclusions can you draw?

1. developing personal and social skills

2. developing a positive self-image

3. providing job training

4. teaching basic physical and biological science

5. teaching critical or creative thinking

6. teaching decision making

7. teaching general knowledge about cultures and their history

8. teaching how to use leisure time

9. teaching legal and democratic obligations

10. teaching mathematical skills

11. teaching reading, writing and communication skills

B. Rank the following subjects from most to least important. Discuss your results with your classmates, and provide reasons for your opinions.

- Computer skills

- Foreign languages

- Geography

- Mathematics

- History

- Science

Now compare your ranking with the results of a Canadian poll shown below. Respondents were asked which of the subjects were absolutely necessary.

- Mathematics: 83%

- Computer skills: 64%

- Science: 38%

- Geography: 37%

- History: 36%

- Foreign languages: 20%

Activities

Understand Ideas

1. What are two intended benefits you have received from your education? What are two unintended benefits?

2. In the three cases identified in this section, which one is an example of an agricultural society? An industrial society? A post-industrial society?

Think and Evaluate

3. List five criteria you would use to assess an education system. In what order would you rank these criteria?

4. In the twenty-first century, technological training is more important than the study of English literature, history and philosophy. Do you agree or

disagree with this statement? Provide three reasons to support your thinking.

5. In what areas of your life or in which organizations other than school are you learning important knowledge and skills? What are you learning in each of these situations? Consider your family, friendship groups, clubs and social groups, teams and sports, part-time jobs and religious organizations.

Apply Your Learning

6. Write a scenario of what you think education will be like 50 years from now. How will education be related to the economy? In your scenario include the following: what students will learn, why certain subjects will be taught, what social needs will be met and what teaching methods will be used in formal education.

Research and Communicate

7. Interview someone who is taking a college or university degree in a field you find interesting and may want to pursue yourself. Find out why this person is taking this particular degree, what kinds of courses are required, how these courses compare with those in secondary school, what the job prospects are for people who graduate in this area of study and what methods of teaching, learning and assessment are used. (See Skill Focus, page 12.)

8. Interview four different teachers to find out what their predictions for education are in the future. Make a list of their observations. Compare your list with other students in your class. What are the similarities in the findings? How do the findings differ?

Focus Questions

Does education help solve problems of inequality?

How does education deal with gender issues?

What problems and challenges do Canadian schools face today?

Issues in Education

Because schools have become central social institutions, the issues they face are of great importance. Are all students given a fair opportunity, regardless of their background or gender? How should schools control students who are undisciplined? What can be done about violence in our schools? And what about those students who drop out or fail to reach academic goals?

Schools and Social Equality

In Canada, schools are seen as a place where young people with talent are recognized and encouraged to succeed. Students are rewarded according to their ability and talents. This reward system, called a **meritocracy,** is an important aspect of education because it is seen to be fair to all students. A meritocracy contributes to the general well-being of an institution because it is based on fairness.

Some researchers, however, question whether the current system of education provides equal opportunity for all students. Does background, social class or ethnic origin prevent some students from achieving the merit and rewards they deserve? Research shows that social class has a strong bearing on a person's chances of attending university. For example, a person is more likely to attend university or college if his or her parents are white-collar workers with a post-secondary education. Many studies also show that children of more affluent families tend to stay in school longer. High tuition fees can prevent poorer students from having the same opportunity to continue their education as students from wealthier

meritocracy—a social system where rewards are based on a person's ability and talent

social class—division of society into different categories, depending on income or job

white-collar workers—employees performing non-manual work, e.g., professional, clerical, or administrative

families. Even with the increase in the number of universities in the latter part of the twentieth century, affordability remains a problem for many students. Social class is not the only barrier students may face in furthering their education. Educators are not indifferent to the social background, race, ethnicity or gender of their students and they may discriminate against students on these bases, even if they are unaware of their attitudes or actions.

Some researchers who have studied the issue of equal opportunity in schooling believe that the practice of **streaming** in education is part of the problem. Through streaming, students are put into different programs or courses at an early stage of their education. The courses they take may or may not prepare them for higher education. Critics of streaming argue that young people from lower social-economic backgrounds, or those who have recently immigrated, are often encouraged to take programs that do not lead to higher education. In light of these criticisms, some schools are cautious about streaming. Many teachers, however, support streaming because it means their classes will be made up of students who share common characteristics. Parents, too, often support streaming because it allows their children to be instructed in classes with students who are more competent in those subjects. Streaming can also have an important impact on student self-perception. Young people who spend years in higher streams tend to see themselves as bright and able whereas those in lower streams may develop lower self-esteem.

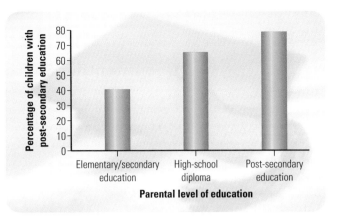

Figure 12–5
The likelihood of studying at the post-secondary level is greater for students if one of their parents has a post-secondary education.

Education and Gender

"The vast majority of girls will make homemaking a career, [although] they may for a limited period engage in some other occupation." This quote, from a report by the Ontario Royal Commission on Education, was published in 1950. A revolution has taken place since these words were written. Today, the average woman with children works outside the home for approximately 30 years of her life, and both men and women spend almost an equal number of years working outside the home. In other words, everyone—man or woman—needs education for employment.

Do women and men benefit equally from education? Traditionally, men received more education than women. However, the **education gap** between women and men has been closing. In 1971, only 3 percent of all women aged 15 and over had a university degree. By 1981 that figure had doubled to 6 percent and by 1996 it was 12 percent. Some female students, however, remain reluctant to study subjects that have been traditionally dominated by male students.

Connections

In which faculties are women still under-represented? Why? (See Chapter 11, page 228.)

Documenting Sources

When writing an essay, it is important to let the reader know the sources of your information. Documenting your sources assures the reader that your information is credible. Acknowledging your sources prevents plagiarism—presenting someone else's work as if it were your own.

Here's How

1. Use **footnotes** (at the bottom of the page) or **endnotes** (at the end of the essay) to give the source of quotations and ideas you have taken from others. Use a small number at the end of the quotation.[1] In the note, follow the example below. Cite the author, title, city of publication, publisher, date of publication and page. Follow the punctuation in the example.

> 1. Wayne Sproule, *Our Social World* (Toronto: Prentice Hall, 2001), 67.

If you cite the source again in the same essay, you may use a short notation:

> 2. Sproule, 78.

2. Prepare a **reference list** or a **bibliography** that lists all of the works you consulted in your research, even if you have not used them in your footnotes or endnotes. Put your bibliography separately on the last page of your essay.

List the entries alphabetically by the author's last name. If there is no author, list the source by the first significant word in the title.

A book:
Sproule, Wayne. *Our Social World.* Toronto, Prentice Hall, 2001.

An article in a journal:
Steinmetz, Lisa, "90210: Life Imitates Television," *National Geographic*, Volume 198, Number 5 (November 2000), pp. 126–130.

An essay in an anthology:
Finnegan, Judith. "Sociological Understanding and Common Sense," *Sociology: Making Sense of Society*, ed., John Marsh (Harlow, Essex: Prentice Hall, 2000), p. 5.

Sources found on the Internet should include the author of the Web page (if stated), title, URL and date posted (if stated).

Practise It

Return to the essay you wrote in response to the Skill Focus on page 248. Add notes and a bibliography to your essay.

Walnut Cove

Figure 12–6
All essays must give proper credit to the work of others.

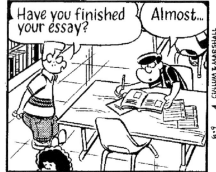

Moreover, some studies have looked at the different ways in which male and female students are treated in classrooms. One study indicates that male students receive more attention from teachers and are given more time to talk in the classroom. Some schools have attempted to provide equal opportunity to all students by setting up separate classes for male and female students in subjects such as mathematics.

Discipline in Schools

Many Canadians believe that schools should teach personal discipline, but that the job is not being done properly. They feel that some students behave in a manner that shows little regard for other people's rights or property. Some of the most common discipline problems in our schools today include

- students who display a disdain for learning by being rude to teachers or challenging their authority

- students who disrupt the classroom or in some way interfere with the education of themselves and others

- students who do not attend class

The discipline issue that has been the focus of most media attention in recent years is violence in the schools. In the past five years, there have been a number of cases of beatings and knifings in Canadian schools. In April 1999, at a school in Taber, Alberta, a student shot and killed 17-year-old Jason Lang. The killing came a week after two students at Columbine high school in Colorado shot and killed 14 students and a teacher and wounded 23 others before killing themselves.

Such cases are exceptional, yet students, parents and teachers have become increasingly concerned about weapons being brought into schools, violent bullying and gang conflicts. Many Canadian schools have implemented a "zero tolerance" approach to violence, so that a student who commits a violent act on school property will be suspended, expelled or turned over to the police. Do you agree that the lack of discipline is a problem in schools today? Is so, what can be done about it?

Corporal Punishment

In 1879, a Toronto headmaster, F.S. Spence was fined $3 for tying down and beating 10-year-old Letitia Wright for leaving school without permission. The problem wasn't that the beating had occurred. The problem, according to those of the time, was that Letitia was a girl. The Toronto board chairman explained that it was a mistake to beat girls because "their nature was so peculiar and so very different from boys that whipping did them no good; and neither could one reason with them as with boys."

Figure 12–7

What trend do you see here? What factors do you think contribute to this trend?

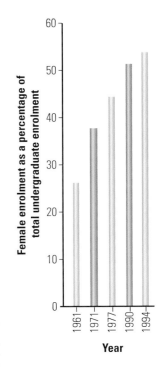

CASE STUDY

1. How serious is the problem of discipline in Canadian schools today?

2. How should breaches of discipline be handled?

Another problem was that the beating had left welts on her back. There was no question, however, that the beating was necessary, since, according to the school board, Letitia was "disobedient, defiant and impertinent" and had once stolen a pair of mittens. Corporal, or physical punishment was necessary for proper discipline in the schools, they said. The board said that in future, however, teachers would be disciplined if their floggings left marks.

Over the course of the twentieth century, corporal punishment in schools was used less and less. By the 1970s, some students were still being strapped, although several boards of education were dropping the use of the strap altogether. Today, a number of countries have banned the use of corporal punishment in schools, among them Sweden, Denmark, Finland, Norway and Austria. Although most boards in Canada today do not allow the use of the strap, it is still a legal option. Section 43 of the Criminal Code allows "using force in the way of correction toward a pupil or child….if the force does not exceed what is reasonable under the circumstances."

Connections

Is corporal punishment a form of child abuse? Why or why not? (See Chapter 6, page 120.)

Dropping Out

While the rate of students completing secondary and post-secondary school has increased steadily over the last few decades, the number of students quitting or dropping out of school before completing a high-school diploma is a problem that concerns many Canadians. Twenty-seven percent of Canadian high-school students drop out before graduation, about the same as the percentage in the United States. However, this rate is much higher than the 15 percent rate for other industrial nations.

Students who drop out might come from any kind of background but studies suggest that the average high-school dropout is more likely to

- have had lower grade averages

- come from a single-parent household

- have parents with lower education

- have failed a grade in elementary school

- have worked more than 20 hours per week during the final school year

- use alcohol (regularly) and drugs

Dropping out leaves young people ill-equipped for the workforce and at high risk for poverty. School dropouts are more likely to be unemployed (34 percent) than are graduates (23 percent). Faced with this reality, many of those who leave school return to the classroom at a later time to complete their education.

Average annual earnings by education and gender, 1995		
Educational Attainment	Women	Men
Less than Grade 9	$ 20 637	$ 29 634
Some Secondary School	$ 21 971	$ 33 735
Secondary School Graduate	$ 25 760	$ 35 650
Some Post-Secondary	$ 27 399	$ 37 859
Post-Secondary Certificate	$ 28 840	$ 39 710
University Degree	$ 42 584	$ 55 976

Figure 12–8

What appears to be the relationship between education, employment and income?

Source: Statistics Canada, 1996.

Academic Standards

Some Canadians have expressed concerns about Canada's academic standards and the overall quality of our educational experience. They feel many Canadian graduates lack certain skills that are in high demand in the current job market. Their concerns have been heightened on occasions when Canadian students have appeared to do poorly in international mathematics tests involving a number of countries. The business community and the media have criticized Canada's public school system for the poor results of its students.

A number of suggestions have been made to improve Canada's academic standings, including more standardized testing; fewer school boards and teachers for better efficiency; vouchers that would allow students and families to shop for their choice of schools; privatization of schools; partnerships between corporations and schools; corporate sponsorship of various programs; and harmonization with educational practices in the United States. These suggestions continue to be debated, and it is difficult to determine at this point whether such changes would, in fact, improve education.

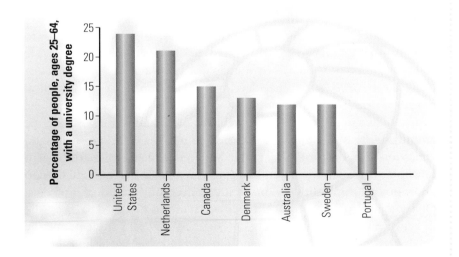

Figure 12–9

University degrees in a global perspective

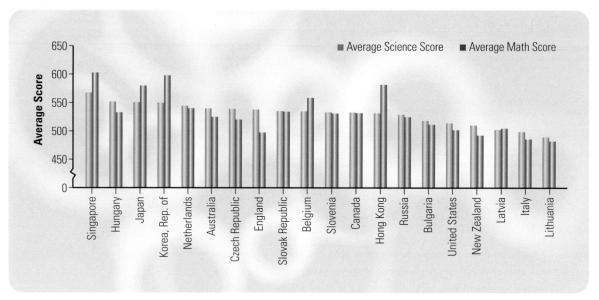

Figure 12–10

Top 20 science and math average test scores, 13-year-old students, 1999. What do these international statistics reveal about academic standards in different countries? What questions should be asked about such statistics?

Focus Questions

What are the current trends in education?

What direction is education taking?

Connections

How can education help reduce prejudice in a diverse society? (See Chapter 11, pages 232–233).

The Future of Education

Where is education going in the future? Some people would like to see Canada's educational system concentrate more on the basics, such as reading, writing and memorization of material. Canada's diverse society, however, presents some unique challenges to educators. Given the large number of immigrants, some people believe that our education system should guarantee equal access and participation to everyone, regardless of his or her background.

In addition, the workforce of the future may need more than the basics in order to cope in a world in which technology has changed almost every aspect of our lives. The challenge for Canada's education system will be to keep pace with this change and adapt to new demands in our society.

The Conference Board of Canada, in its report *Understanding Employability Skills*, states that developing common sense and practical judgment should be a focus of education today. It believes that the demands of the workplace are changing rapidly and these skills are the **employability skills** that will help people transfer their knowledge and education from one work situation to another. Students will need to learn how to use their knowledge and skills in new situations. They will need to know how to think critically, make sound decisions and solve problems. One study of 20 companies and 5 universities was designed to assess the fit between the skill development of Canadian university students and the needs of corporations. The skills most in demand were not technical skills,

Is Distance Learning the School of the Future?

People who live in remote areas might not have the same access to education as do people who live in cities. They might have to travel away from home to school or college, far from their families and at great cost. **Distance education** may help to solve this educational inequality in the future.

Each school day, high-school students Beverly Collier, Jennifer Freake and Holly Stinson head off to attend classes at Lakewood Academy in Glenwood, Newfoundland. They spend some of their time in the regular classroom, but they also take some of their classes with students in other schools that might be many kilometres away. Their school does not offer Chemistry and Advanced Mathematics, because of low enrolment, so the school instead enrolled the three students in distance education programs for these courses.

Every second day, the students work from a specially equipped classroom, where they go on-line with other students in rural communities to take classes. An instructor at a different location teaches them through an audio-conference system and a "telewriter," which works as an electronic blackboard. The instructor is able to transmit graphics and freehand writing or sketches during a session. The students are able to ask questions, observe problem-solving activities conducted by the instructor, and use the telewriter to demonstrate solutions they have developed. In addition, they can interact with other students at other locations. In this way, the classes are completely interactive. The students can also fax work samples back and forth, and complete assignments and laboratory work during off-line classes. Each school has a staff member who acts as a distance education coordinator. The coordinator at Lakewood supervises the chemistry labs, oversees exams and tests, distributes assignments and handles any problems that arise with equipment. Holly,

Jennifer and Beverly agree that the program has many benefits:

> We feel that distance education has allowed us to develop the ability to work independently and efficiently. Through the program, we have learned good work and study habits. We also feel that the distance education classes have prepared us for post-secondary education.

Newfoundland's Telemedicine and Educational Resources Agency (TETRA) provides the network used to link the students with the rest of the "class" and the instructor. Hospitals and other health services, colleges and universities also use TETRA services. The first TETRA course was offered to 13 remote schools. In 1997, about 1100 students in 78 different locations received part of their high-school program through the services. The programs produced by TETRA are recognized as being among the most innovative in the world.

In the future, distance programs will provide "open learning," with opportunities for the learners to study at the time, pace and place of their choosing. Students will be able to use distance programs to accumulate all the credits they need for high-school graduation. As the system develops, Beverly, Jennifer and Holly will likely look back on themselves as pioneers in their field.

From *Atlantic Canada in the Global Community* by Jim Crewe et al.

What Do You Think?

1. Make an organizer to compare distance learning with learning in the classroom.

2. What do you think the role of each kind of learning will be in the future? Make some predictions, giving reasons for these trends.

3. Would distance learning be useful in your school? Are there other applications for this service, other than rural or remote settings?

Figure 12–11

Lifelong learning also takes place after retirement. What are the benefits of continuing your education after you have finished working?

such as using the computer, but skills such as the ability to integrate and use information, adapt to change, take reasonable risks, conceptualize the future, show leadership and be able to manage conflict.

Lifelong learning is another key to success, according to some researchers. Less than half of the Canadian workforce will be in traditional full-time jobs within the next decade, they say. Therefore, educators must teach students how to continue to learn throughout their lives. This kind of learning will mean upgrading and improving current skills, taking courses to learn new skills and keeping up with technological change.

In the future, it is also likely that we will have alternatives to education in schools. The growing use of computers and the Internet mean that, increasingly, people can access courses on-line and at home. A range of university courses are now run electronically with little or no physical contact between the teacher and student. It is possible that other institutions, such as business organizations, will also play a role in educating the young. In the past, businesses have expected schools to prepare students for employment. In recent years, however, businesses have become more involved in providing educational materials to schools. Some educators fear that educational material from private corporations will promote those corporations and interfere with a student's ability to think independently and critically. Others welcome the additional materials and support, especially as schools operate on tight budgets.

Activities

Understand Ideas

1. **a)** Make a chart summarizing the issues faced by schools in Canada, as outlined in the text. Use the following headings: Issue, Problems caused, Example(s).

   b) Identify two or three other issues to add to the chart.

Think and Evaluate

2. Why is it important in a society such as ours that education be a meritocracy, an institution that recognizes and rewards merit in many different forms?

Apply Your Learning

3. Do you think your education has been affected by gender bias? If so, how?

4. **a)** Do you think your school has discipline problems? If so, what are they?

   b) How do you think these problems should be handled?

Research and Communicate

5. Observe how male and female students are treated by teachers in various classes. You may wish to use unstructured observation, or use structured observation with a checklist. For example, are male or female students asked to respond to teacher questions more often? Who takes leadership roles in various classes?

6. Using a survey questionnaire, identify career goals of male and female students in your school. Are there significant differences? If so, how would you describe them?

Key Points

- Education is an institution that exists in all societies because children need to learn the ways of their culture to be successful within it.

- Although traditional societies may have schools, they usually rely on families to pass on the necessary skills and knowledge for survival. In contemporary societies, education has evolved into a formal institution.

- There is a relationship between the economy of a society and the educational system. Canada has gone through a number of economic stages. Today, in the information age, education is also adapting to a new economy.

- The intended goals of education include the transmission of knowledge, socialization, social unity and recognition of special talents. The unintended goals include providing child care, keeping adolescents out of the job market and teaching social attitudes and values.

- A meritocracy serves an important function of education because it is seen to be fair, rewarding students according to their ability.

- Some of the problems in the Canadian educational system include discipline, violence, the drop-out rate and lower academic standards in comparison with international standards.

- The Canadian education system is undergoing a series of changes, based on our economy and our society. Issues include employability skills, life-long learning and alternatives to schools.

Activities

Understand Ideas

1. What causes education systems to change? How has new technology changed the way students are educated?

Think and Evaluate

2. Do you think criticisms of Canada's education system are justified? Use the criteria you developed for Activity 3 on page 253. Be sure to support your opinion with evidence gathered from the chapter and your own experience.

Apply Your Learning

3. A close friend has just informed you that he or she plans to drop out of school this year. What reasons would you give to persuade your friend to stay in school?

4. Review the list of goals for education today in Social Science Live on page 253. Create five new goals you would like to see your school incorporate into the curriculum. Write two reasons why these goals are important to have. Be prepared to defend your list in class.

Research and Communicate

5. How would you design the secondary school of the future? What courses should be compulsory? What teaching and learning methods would you use? How would you address some of the issues identified in this chapter? Write an essay answering these questions. (See Skill Focus on pages 248 and 256.)

6. a) How are decisions made in your school? Interview school administrators to find out. Ask the following questions: What role do principals, assistant principals and superintendants have in decision making? What role do parents play? Do students have a voice? What provincial laws influence decision making?

b) Do you agree with your school's decision-making process? If so, why? If not, how do you think decisions about education should be made?

The World of Work

In This Chapter

- What is work?
- How is the nature of work changing?
- How do changing work patterns affect our lives?
- What changes are occurring in the role of women in the workforce?
- How is conflict addressed in the workplace?

Key Terms

work

economy

goods

services

industrial economy

post-industrial economy

manufacturing sector

service sector

globalization

collective bargaining

gender segregation

Almost everyone works. But what people do, and how they think about their work, varies from one individual and one culture to another. Start your exploration of the world of work by reviewing the list of jobs below.

teacher	computer programmer	truck driver
nurse	engineer	fashion designer
pharmacist	construction worker	software designer
factory worker	physiotherapist	business analyst
financial planner	plumber	interior designer
firefighter	cleric	waiter
politician	artist	writer
dancer	counsellor	film producer
police officer	marine biologist	salesperson
doctor	nuclear physicist	actor
lawyer	accountant	tool and dye maker

- Choose one job that interests you. With the approval of your teacher, you may select a job that is not on the list.

- Explain your interest in the job you have chosen.

- Are you prepared to spend a minimum of five years doing this type of work?

- How would this work affect your lifestyle?

- In your view, how might this job change within the next 20 years?

What Is Work?

Focus Questions

What is work?

Why do people work?

At home, at school or at a social occasion, people are constantly asking each other, "What are you going to do with your life?" or "What do you do for a living?" The usual reply to such questions is to mention a profession or a specific job: "I plan to be an architect," or "I sell computers." Work is an important part of our lives. It determines what we do for the greater part of our day; it also reveals a great deal about who we are and about the lives we lead. For many people, work is a means to an end, permitting them to acquire the necessary and desirable things in life. For some, the goal is to make as much money with as little effort as possible. For others, it is a goal in itself, something to do just for the satisfaction of doing it.

In this chapter, we will define **work** as paid employment in the labour force, unpaid chores in the home as well as volunteer services in the community. What work do you enjoy doing? What work do you do because you must? What kind of work do you want to do in the future?

Figure 13–1

What different types of work are illustrated here? How do you view each of these activities?

From Early Times to the Industrial Age

Focus Questions

What are goods and services?

What are the various types of economies?

How is work tied to the economy of a society?

How has the Canadian economy changed over time?

How has industrialization affected quality of life?

Understanding the kinds of work a society performs requires knowing the economy. The **economy** is the social institution that organizes how goods and services are produced, distributed and consumed. **Goods** are material items such as food, clothing or shelter. **Services** are activities that benefit others such as the work of physicians, police officers and teachers.

In Chapter 2, we learned that anthropologists identify the way various cultures around the world adapt over time and give rise to very different economies. In the earliest economy, hunting and gathering, small groups of people wandered in search of game or wild plants; work was done when needed in order to survive. Later, other economies emerged. In this chapter, we will focus on the work performed in three types of economies: agricultural, industrial and post-industrial.

Agricultural Economy

About 10 000 years ago, an agricultural revolution took place as people learned to plant crops and domesticate animals to provide a more certain and stable existence. With the growing availability of food, people began to assume specialized economic roles such as making crafts, designing tools, constructing dwellings and governing the group. At this time, work life became more distinct from family life, although production still occurred close to home. Pioneer Canada, for example, was such a society.

CASE STUDY

1. How did agricultural work shape people's lives in the early twentieth century?

2. How were gender roles defined on the farm?

3. How important was children's work on the family farm?

Figure 13–2

How has agriculture in Canada changed over time? How will these changes affect the future of the family farm?

Farming in Pioneer Canada

At the dawn of the twentieth century, Alexander Muterer, his wife, Nicholas, and their three children were a typical Canadian farm family. Chores started at dawn, continued past dusk year round and involved the children at an early age. The Muterers produced all their own food, clothing, farm implements, animal feed and entertainment, without the aid of electricity, indoor plumbing, telephone, TV, washing machine or automobile.

Like many farmers of their era, the Muterers were prosperous, independent producers of cash crops, with their own dairy and cattle herds, hens and pigs, and horses for working the fields and for transportation. A lot of their work revolved around animals; they experienced a closeness to nature and to the creatures they cared for, a closeness that would disappear for many people as the century progressed.

Every day, the girls helped their mother prepare a hearty breakfast: porridge with milk and brown sugar; eggs and uncured bacon called "side pork" butchered from the family's own pigs; toast from homemade bread, and tea. Nicholas served Alexander first, while she ate last. She looked after everyone and sometimes didn't sit down until the others had finished eating.

From autumn to early summer, the children walked almost 2 kilometres to and from school; in winter, if the roads were bad, they were transported by horse and sleigh. Home from school, the boys worked in the barn; the girls did house and garden chores, canning and preserving, washing clothes by hand and ironing.

From "Life on the Family Farm" by Judy Steed

Industrial Economy

About 200 years ago, the Industrial Revolution brought about an **industrial economy.** With the aid of technology, non-human energy sources such as steam and coal were harnessed, moving work from homes to factories and allowing societies to mass-produce goods such as clothing, tools and furniture. Work became highly mechanized, and fewer jobs required heavy physical labour. However, in order to specialize but still maintain ever-increasing quantities, factory production required both machines and people. Machines and workers performed single tasks over and over, making small contributions to the finished product instead of creating an entire product from start to finish. As a result, skilled workers, such as spinners and weavers in the cotton industry, found themselves out of work; most people became employees rather than independent workers.

mass-produce—using a mechanical process to make large quantities of a standardized product

Many other social changes came about in the industrial economy. Large cities grew up around factories that were built in locations suited for gathering raw materials and shipping finished products. Workers moved to the city, looking for employment. Without legislation or planning, early cities became crowded, and factory conditions were harsh and sometimes dangerous. In the early days of industrialization, wages were low and poverty was widespread. It was not until the late nineteenth and early twentieth centuries that government legislation and labour unions improved wages and working conditions.

The ability to make products in mass quantities meant that goods had to be sold to a larger market, not just to local communities. Goods produced in one location could now be shipped across the country and all over the world. The need to obtain raw materials and export manufactured goods resulted in new and improved methods of transportation. Railways, steamships and canals were built in the nineteenth century, trucks and airplanes in the twentieth century. Even the measurement of time was revolutionized—coordinating expensive equipment and labour required careful attention to timing and scheduling. The clock became the governor of lives, prominent in every factory. While pre-industrial societies measured time by the seasons or the position of the sun, now it was measured precisely by the hands of the clock.

Figure 13–3

Factory in Brantford, Ontario, 1899. What signs of the Industrial Revolution are evident in this photograph?

Work in Twentieth-Century Canada

Industry continued to thrive in the middle of the twentieth century. By the 1950s in Canada, manufacturing had become a crucial part of the economy. Such development changed the nature of work. In many industries, a few large companies started to replace several small companies. For example, at the beginning of the century, there were dozens of small companies making automobiles. By the late twentieth century, only three corporations dominated the automobile industry in North America: General Motors, Ford and Chrysler.

Other changes occurred as well. As companies grew, more employees performed managerial and administrative work, adding to the complexity of organizations by creating new jobs. People were needed to manage operations, to buy and sell goods, and to keep employee records. As we discussed in Chapter 9, organizations started to introduce more rules and regulations, developing bureaucracies to deal with increasing specialization.

Some changes improved conditions for employees in the industrial system. Workers formed labour unions to represent their interests in negotiations with factory owners. Governments in Canada and in other Western nations passed laws to improve working conditions, set minimum wages, outlaw child labour and ensure safety in the workplace. Also, standards of living and quality of life improved as goods and services became more accessible. Today many people in industrial nations enjoy quality education and health care, adequate housing, safe food and water, and an abundance of consumer goods such as appliances, televisions and computers.

Connections

Do bureaucracies improve or hamper efficiency? (See Chapter 9, pages 187–197.)

CASE STUDY

1. Why were these workers afraid to leave their employers?

2. What were some of the conditions that had worsened since the beginning of the Depression?

3. Why were companies able to get away with violating existing labour laws?

Surviving the Great Depression

During the Depression of the 1930s, working conditions worsened partly because men, women and even children, desperate to keep their jobs at all costs, were willing to put up with the most appalling circumstances. The following excerpts from Pierre Berton's book, *The Great Depression*, provide snapshots of workers' lives at that time.

Eleanor Hamel, a 25 year-old seamstress, had gone to work at the age of 13. It was, of course, illegal. The minimum age was 16, but nobody paid any attention to that. Miss Hamel made seven dollars a week at Rubins, and when she asked for ten dollars she was denied it. When she threatened to go to Fashion Craft, the foreman told her that she would be blacklisted in the community. It was well known that anyone who quit one firm could get no work elsewhere.

Another seamstress, 23-year-old Berthe Nolin, was paid six dollars for an official 55-hour week. Actually, she worked much longer. Her day began at 7 a.m. and was supposed to end at 6 p.m., with an hour for lunch. But she often worked until 10:20 p.m., although the foreman punched her card at 6:15 to maintain the fiction that the company was obeying the 55-hour law. Because of these long evening hours, Berthe and her fellow workers often went without supper. The Minimum Wage Board winked at this and at similar infractions.

All told of being bullied, threatened and nagged to speed up their work so that they would produce enough goods to earn the minimum wage, saving Eaton's the cost of making up the difference. Mrs. Wells had worked for Eaton's for 18 years sewing skirts, blouses and dresses. "You had no time to get up and have a drink of water...or look at anybody; you just went on working. And, of course, they expected you to make more than you really could." Mrs. Wells' daughter, Winnifred, was so tired at night that she couldn't eat her supper. Before the Depression, she had been supplied with a stool while examining dresses. But after 1933, when the stools were removed, no examiner was allowed even that brief rest. Miss Wells was on her feet the whole day, so tired that she dreaded getting on the streetcar when she went home "because if I sat down I could not get up again, my legs would be so stiff." Yet, her take-home pay was less than half what it had been in 1929.

Activities

Understand Ideas

1. How does the definition of work vary according to the type of economy?

2. Create a concept map to explain the basic elements of an industrial economy.

3. How did industrialism in the twentieth century change the structure of organizations?

Think and Evaluate

4. Why do people work?

5. What is the value of non-paid work? Provide some examples of this type of work.

Apply Your Learning

6. **a)** What household chores are you required to do?
   b) Are you compensated for your work? If not, would you be more inclined to do it if you were? Why or why not?

7. **a)** Why is a clock a symbol of industrialization?
   b) Given a choice, would you prefer to have your time managed by the clock and the calendar, or by the sun and the seasons? Provide two reasons to support your answer.

Research and Communicate

8. As a class, research and debate ONE of the following issues: The family farm in Western Canada will disappear in favour of "mass production" agriculture; OR Communities in Atlantic Canada will survive in spite of the depletion of cod stocks.

9. **a)** Using resources such as the library, newspaper articles, magazines and the Internet, gather information about the impact of technology in Canadian society.
   b) Complete a PMI (Plus, Minus, Interesting) based on the information you have gathered. Be sure to include at least five points in each column.
   c) Display your PMI and share your findings with the class.

10. The case study excerpt about the Great Depression states that Eleanor Hamel started to work in a factory at the age of 13. Was it common practice at that time to hire children and teenagers to work in factories? If so, were they subjected to the same working conditions as adults? Investigate this topic and record your findings in a social science report. Be sure to follow the guidelines in Chapter 9, Writing a Social Science Report (page 188).

Focus Questions

How is the nature of work changing?

What brought about the information revolution?

What types of work are increasingly in demand?

What is globalization?

Post-industrial Economy

During the second half of the twentieth century, Canada was beginning to change from an industrial to a **post-industrial economy,** shifting from a system based primarily on manufacturing to one based on service work and the extensive use of information technology. Between 1961 and 1991, the proportion of people working in manufacturing fell from 24.7 percent to 16.5 percent. Meanwhile, in the information field and service industries, the percentage rose from 58.2 percent in 1961 to 75.0 percent in 1991. The proportion of workers in management and clerical positions has also grown significantly. Computer programmers, writers, financial analysts, advertising executives, architects and consultants are considered typical workers in the post-industrial era. Other service industries expanded in such areas as health care, education, sales and finances.

Work in the New Economy

Due to rapid advances in technology, the post-industrial economy is often referred to as the information revolution or the electronic age. Computers and the Internet have the astounding capability of not only sending data around the world but also allowing individuals to interact with the information. As a result, the nature of work is being shaped by computer technology.

What kinds of work will be created in this "new economy"? Because we are still in the middle of the post-industrial revolution, it is difficult to predict the outcome. However, some trends are appearing. For example, manufacturing jobs are declining. During the 1990s, industries laid off employees from the **manufacturing sector**—jobs related to the large-scale production of material goods. Many of these workers were not called back. Why? The answer is computer technology, which was partly

Figure 13–4
How do these top 10 occupational areas reflect Canada's changing economy?

Top 10 occupational areas in Canada
1. Sales and service
2. Business, finance and administration
3. Trade, transport and equipment
4. Management
5. Processing, manufacturing and utilities
6. Social science, education, government services and religion
7. Health
8. Natural and applied sciences
9. Primary industry (agriculture, animal husbandry, forestry and mining)
10. Art, culture, recreation and sports

responsible for reducing the workforce at some companies by as much as 40 percent! In its early stages, technology tends to reduce the number of lower-skilled jobs, creating only a few highly skilled jobs in their place. Over time, more individuals are hired for their knowledge of electronics and computer technology in order to meet the growing need for those who can build, service and repair both hardware and software.

The **service sector,** jobs related to industries that provide services to the public, offers a wide range of employment opportunities. These jobs include traditional services such as transportation, retail, hospitality, banking, and advertising as well as other expanding services such as finance, investment and business consulting, communications, utilities, health care, education and public relations. Some of these service occupations, especially in the information industry, call for a high degree of education and skill. Other positions, such as waiter or cashier, will require less formal training and more in-house training. Although economists and sociologists cannot predict which will be more in demand— technical skills or service skills—they do agree that workers in all fields must have good communication skills and must be comfortable with information technology.

hardware—the mechanical, electronic or structural parts of a computer

software—the standard programming procedures and specific programs provided by a computer system

hospitality—the hotel and restaurant industry

in-house training—coaching and practice provided on the job

Globalization

Canadian theorist Marshall McLuhan wrote about popular culture and the influence of electronic media. As far back as the 1960s, he popularized the concept of the "global village"—the idea that the world is becoming one large community with interconnected needs and services. How right he was! Lower trade barriers now allow goods to move more easily from one nation to another; companies are becoming international by merging and by selling their products in other parts of the world; and decision making can occur anywhere at any time with the aid of fax, e-mail and video-link technology.

Globalization is the attempt to make goods and services available on a worldwide basis by offering customers a standard product that appeals to tastes in different societies and cultures. The impact of globalization on Canadian workers is dramatic— they must compete with labour and corporations, not only in North America but all over the world. Because some products can be manufactured more cheaply elsewhere, unskilled or semi-skilled job opportunities in Canada are becoming rare. The demand for higher-level skills means that education and training is essential for Canadian workers to be successful in the job market.

Figure 13–5

McDonald's restaurant in Beijing, China. In the global economy, companies try to produce a standard product that has some degree of flexibility. For example, in China, McDonald's burgers are made of beef or pork, but in India they are made of lamb to accommodate the dietary customs of the country.

Pieces of a Puzzle

The more you learn about yourself, the easier it will be to choose the type of work you would like to do. Rank the following values and preferences in order of importance to you. Then discuss your ranking with the class. Work as quickly as you can—be spontaneous!

- Challenging work and sense of accomplishment
- Full use of skills and abilities
- Good working relationship with manager
- Sufficient time for personal life
- Opportunity for advancement
- Training opportunities to improve or learn new skills
- Working with co-operative people
- Living in a desirable area
- Freedom to adopt your own approach to the job
- Recognition for good work
- Opportunity for high earnings
- Employment security
- Good fringe benefits
- Good physical working conditions

Anthropology, psychology and sociology are all social sciences that explore your needs and values. Gather the results from some of the activities you have already completed:

- your culture diagram in Chapter 2 (page 19)
- your current location on Maslow's hierarchy of needs in Chapter 4 (Activity 5c, page 81)
- your vulnerability to stress in Chapter 5 (Social Science Live, page 93)
- your results from Jung's personality self-assessment in Chapter 6 (page 133)
- your top five values from the ranking exercise you have just completed

When you put the pieces of the puzzle together, what do you see? What conclusions can you draw about the type of work you would like to do? Share your findings with a partner.

Activities

Understand Ideas

1. What are the main characteristics of work in the post-industrial economy?

2. Create a chart to compare the similarities and differences between the industrial and post-industrial economies.

Think and Evaluate

3. Develop a concept map to show ways in which the post-industrial economy might worsen or improve working conditions.

Apply Your Learning

4. What preparations can you make to take advantage of the post-industrial economy?

Research and Communicate

5. What jobs are available in the post-industrial economy of today? Use statistical data to identify job opportunities that are growing.

6. Arrange an interview with someone in a post-industrial, or "new economy" business. Find out what skills and education this business requires.

7. Research career opportunities that interest you. Are jobs in this area on the increase or decrease? Interview people who work in this field to find out more about this type of career and its future.

Work Trends in Canada Today

Focus Questions

What are the current trends of employment in Canada?

How do these trends affect workers and employers?

How do changing work trends affect the rate of unemployment?

What role have unions played in the workplace?

Part-time Work

The shift to a post-industrial economy with a growing service base has brought changes in the way workers are hired. Temporary and part-time employment increased from 13 percent in 1980 to nearly 20 percent of Canadian workers in 2001. Many of these employees tend to be younger workers and women. Employers sometimes prefer part-time or temporary workers because they do not have to pay benefits or time-and-a-half for overtime. In addition, part-timers offer flexibility by filling in for absent workers or providing an immediate response to short-term increases in work flow.

Some people prefer part-time or temporary employment. Students can schedule their work around their classes. Those with family responsibilities can work staggered hours to manage their time more effectively. Many part-time employees, however, would prefer full-time work. In 1994, 5.4 percent of all workers compared to only 2.3 percent in 1981 were working part-time because they could not find full-time employment.

Home Offices

New technology and the Internet now allow some employees to work almost anywhere without having to be in the same building, or even in the same city. Many people are choosing to work at home, blurring the line between "the office" and "home." Home offices offer the benefit of greater flexibility, allowing workers to balance family responsibilities with careers. Other advantages include the convenience of casual dress and no travel time. However, many of those who work from their homes find that they are putting in longer hours than they would at the office.

Figure 13–6

Home offices allow workers greater flexibility to balance family responsibilities with work.

Self-employment

Many people like to be their own boss. Or do they? Do you see yourself working for someone else or becoming an entrepreneur—a person who owns, organizes and manages an independent business? In recent years, self-employment has become a growing trend partly because of the recession in the early 1990s. Many experienced employees were laid off; unable to find work, they started their own businesses. Electronic communication has made working independently a lot easier. Computers, faxes and e-mail allow individuals to run their businesses and sell their services from the home.

recession—a period of at least six consecutive months of decreased prosperity associated with a decline in production and employment

Most entrepreneurs today are small business owners, such as self-employed workers in the construction industry providing services such as carpentry, plumbing, painting and renovating. Professionals such as accountants, financial advisers and lawyers also run their own businesses. In the information and communications sector, self-employed individuals offer services such as writing, researching, designing, editing and word processing.

What are the advantages to self-employment? Firstly, there are no rigid hours or routines to keep and no supervisors or managers to answer to. Secondly, a successful business can sometimes generate higher earnings than a regular salary. However, self-employment also presents challenges. Fluctuations in the economy, such as recessions, can ruin small businesses. In addition, self-employed workers do not have benefits such as pensions or health care; they must purchase these benefits themselves. Also, working independently requires the initiative to find clients and the self-discipline to complete projects on time.

CASE STUDY

1. Why is the number of entrepreneurs increasing?

2. What criteria are used in selecting the winners of the Young Entrepreneur Award?

3. In what ways do you think these winners met the Bank's criteria?

Young Entrepreneurs

In the last 20 years, the number of self-employed people in Canada has been increasing rapidly. One reason for this could be the growing lack of traditional, full-time positions. On the other hand, economists note that many younger people prefer the flexibility and independence often associated with self-employment.

The Young Entrepreneur Awards, offered by the Business Development Bank of Canada, highlight the accomplishments of Canadian entrepreneurs aged 30 and under. One winner from each province and territory is chosen based on a selection of criteria including company growth, involvement in the new economy, innovation, community work and expert performance. Some of the 1999 Young Entrepreneur Award winners included the following:

Kirt Eliza Kootoo Ejesiak, 30, is the president of Uqsiq Communications Inc. in Iqaluit, Nunavut. His visual communications and graphic design company is the only entirely Inuit-managed firm specializing in the communications needs of Inuit organizations.

Ariel Shlien, 30, and Ron Shlien, 28, of Montreal, Quebec, created their company called The Mad Science Group, which sends enthusiastic scientists around the world to schools, children's camps, community centres, parties and scout troops to engage children's curiosity in the study of science. The company has enjoyed outstanding success, opening 115 franchises in 17 different countries and reaching over 30 million children through their various programs.

Dave Zakutin, aged 27, is president of Zakutin Technologies Incorporated. His Waterloo, Ontario, company produces and sells the Radar Ball, a unique baseball that can time the speed of a pitch. His Radar Ball has been so successful that most major league baseball clubs now use it for pitcher training.

From *Young Builders of the New Economy—In the Spotlight* by Business Development Bank of Canada

Unemployment

There is always some unemployment in society, for several reasons. Some individuals cannot work because of disability or illness. Some people move from one location to seek employment in another. Others take a break from the workforce to go back to school, to stay home with children, to travel or to change careers. For reasons such as these, unemployment levels in Canada rarely fall below 5 percent.

High unemployment may occur for reasons related to the economy as a whole. During a recession, businesses downsize to cut expenses. For example, in the recession that occurred in Canada during the early 1990s, the unemployment rate soared to over 11 percent. Unemployment can also increase when workers' skills do not match new positions created by reorganization or technology. For instance, many individuals who lost their jobs during the 1990s were victims of the changing nature of work in the new post-industrial society.

Unemployment also rises when resources become depleted or prices for certain exports drop dramatically. For example, when disappearing cod stocks in Newfoundland forced the government to suspend fishing in the area, many fishers lost their livelihoods. Even now that some fishing is permitted, the diminished supply of cod is still hurting the fishing industry. In the West, when the price of grain is low, and the cost of running a farm is high, many farmers cannot produce harvests profitable enough to keep their family farms. When the price of oil rises, industries that depend on fuel, such as auto manufacturing, trucking and air travel, have trouble meeting their expenses and may have to cut costs by laying off workers.

Unemployment can be devastating to individuals and their families. Work is not only a financial necessity in our society, but it is often how people define themselves. Losing one's job can threaten both financial security and self-image. In some cases, retraining or personal initiative will lead to new job opportunities; in other cases, for workers who have spent a lifetime in a particular field or industry, retraining can be painful and finding work may be more difficult.

downsize—lay off workers to cut costs

Connections

Why are employability skills so crucial for workers who depend on natural resources for their livelihoods? (See Chapter 12, page 260.)

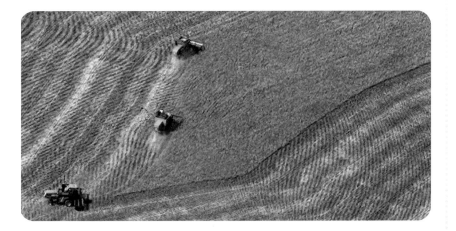

Figure 13–7
Unemployment often rises when world demand for natural resources such as wheat, lumber or oil falls.

Connections

What type of social movement do you think led to the development of unions? (See Chapter 10, page 214.)

Unions

Unions are organizations that represent the workers' point of view to the employer. They developed in response to the social conditions created by the industrial economy of the nineteenth and twentieth centuries. Their purpose was to raise wages, improve working conditions, reduce hours of work, ensure job security and help employees gain more control over how the work was done. These objectives are relevant even today. In fact, union goals in 1900 appear surprisingly modern:

- free compulsory education

- an eight-hour working day

- government inspection of all industry

- public ownership of utilities such as electricity, buses and streetcars

- abolition of child labour under the age of 14

- a living wage and improved working conditions

- protection of the Lord's Day (Sunday) as a day of rest

- recognition of a union's right to negotiate with an employer on behalf of all workers

The first unions in Canada were formed in the 1830s. Since then, various crafts, services, factory jobs, professions and government positions have become unionized. In Canada today, one-third of non-agricultural workers are members of a union. Women in Canada have increased their participation so that by 1990 they constituted 43 percent of union membership.

Today, unions leaders continue to represent workers by meeting with employers to negotiate contracts about wages and working conditions. This process of representation and negotiation is called **collective bargaining.** The steps in the collective bargaining process are shown in Figure 13–8.

Figure 13–8

Steps in the collective bargaining process

Negotiations: Representatives of the union and the employer meet to negotiate wages, hours, benefits, grievance procedures, hiring and firing methods and other working conditions.

Mediation: If the two sides cannot agree, a neutral party can be called in to help them overcome their differences.

Strike: If negotiations or mediations do not lead to agreement, workers may refuse to continue working. They picket the place of work.

Lock-out: The employer may close the place of business if continuing negotiations do not reach agreement.

Arbitration: If the union and the employer cannot reach an agreement, both sides may agree to have a neutral party make a decision.

Contract: Both the union representative and the employer sign a formal written agreement about wages and conditions. A contract usually lasts at least one to two years.

Will You Have a Job?

Will there be enough work to keep everyone employed? New kinds of training and education will certainly be necessary to provide workers with the skills required to find employment in our post-industrial society.

By the end of the decade, less than half the workforce in the industrialized world will have full-time jobs. The rest will be part-timers, temporary workers or those who are unemployed. The relentless march toward productivity and corporate efficiency is already creating a split society of "insiders and outsiders," says Charles Handy, a management professor at the London Business School and author of the critically acclaimed book *The Age of Unreason*. The "insiders" will be highly paid, knowledgeable decision-makers working in head offices. The "outsiders" will be contract workers or part of a flexible workforce that will depend for their living on whatever work is tossed their way.

Society has an obligation to help the underemployed find what they're good at by reinventing the education system. "We have to make people feel clever; we have to believe that if we invest in their education, we'll find that everyone is intelligent at something, whether it's music or sports or languages."

His advice to young people contemplating a future career? "I would tell them to think about customers, not about jobs" because steady jobs will be hard to find. Handy is not ready to condemn modern capitalism to the ashbin, but he does say we need to question the raison d'être [reason for being] of the system. "A society should be measured not by how it earns its money, but how it spends it. We've spent many years boasting about how we made money, but we've created a world where work was god and consumption was the measure of success. We forgot to consider what would happen to people who didn't have access to that consumption."

From "More Part-timers Than Full-timers by Decade's End" by Peter Hadekel

What Do You Think?

1. What are the major predictions about the future of work presented in this article?

2. How can we prepare for the possibilities it describes?

3. What role do you think government and society should have in dealing with this situation?

Figure 13-9
Checking the job bank at a Human Resources Centre. Why does the federal government operate these job banks?

Understand Ideas

1. Why are temporary and part-time jobs increasing?

2. In what ways does new technology influence work? Provide three examples to support your answer.

3. Why do you think self-employment is increasing in the post-industrial economy?

4. Why does unemployment rarely fall below 5 percent?

Think and Evaluate

5. Part-time workers are predominantly young people and women. Why does this situation exist? Do you think that this situation is the worker's choice or the employer's preference?

6. **a)** Create a chart to list the advantages and disadvantages of self-employment.

   b) Compare and contrast self-employment in the pre-industrial period and the post-industrial period. Record at least two similarities and two differences.

Apply Your Learning

7. You are applying for a part-time job in the restaurant business. One section of the application asks you to explain your philosophy of customer service.

   a) Prepare for a mock interview by completing this section of the "application."

   b) With a partner, role-play the interview. As the applicant, hand your "application" to the "interviewer" and discuss your philosophy. Be prepared to answer questions and feel free to share your values and opinions. As the interviewer, ask questions about the importance of customer service.

   c) Switch roles so that everyone has a chance to play the applicant.

Research and Communicate

8. Interview someone you know who works for a large corporation. Find out about the work involved, the concerns that person has and the benefits of the job.

9. Search for a newspaper or magazine article about a current or recent labour dispute. Is the article written impartially or from the employer's or the union's point of view? Referring to your article and Figure 13–8, which step of the collective bargaining process are the two parties at? Follow this dispute to its conclusion by collecting subsequent articles. Note the steps involved and how long the process takes. Report the final outcome to the class.

Focus Questions

How is the role of women changing?

What is gender segregation and how does it affect all employees?

How is conflict addressed in the workplace?

Women and Work

Changes in the Role of Women

Anthropologists and sociologists have discovered that in all societies, women, men and sometimes children, have worked. In some societies they shared the same kinds of work; in others, roles were determined by gender. In the last half of the twentieth century, a revolution occurred in the type of work performed by women and in their participation in the labour force. As we saw in Chapter 7, such changes have had a significant impact on marriage roles and the family.

Women continue to work in the home but are increasingly doing jobs that are paid and performed outside the home. At the beginning of the twentieth century, about 14 percent of women were working outside the home; by 1991 this figure was 60 percent. While women made up only 15 percent of the total labour force at the beginning of the twentieth century, by the end of the century they composed 45 percent of the workforce. Also, more married women are in the labour force than ever before. Until the 1960s, a typical woman working outside the home was unmarried. In 1941 fewer than 5 percent of married women were in the labour force, whereas by 1991 the figure was 63 percent.

Several factors led to this revolutionary change in the role of women in the workforce. Firstly, the Canadian economy expanded its service sector, creating more job opportunities for everyone. Secondly, from the 1960s on, more women than ever before graduated to enter professions such as teaching, medicine and law. Thirdly, families started having fewer children, so women, who traditionally stayed home to care for children, devoted fewer years to full-time child care. Finally, the increasing financial pressure on families changed dramatically. In the 1950s, one middle-class wage earner could support a family comfortably. Now most families must have two wage earners to maintain their desired standard of living.

Connections

How have changes in the role of women in the workplace affected the role of women in the family? (See Chapter 7, page 154.)

Gender Segregation and Work

It is no surprise that education and the world of work are closely related. In Chapter 12, we discussed the education gap between men and women. Just as the education gap has been narrowing in recent years, so have the differences between men and women in the workforce. Not only have more women entered the workforce, but they are also participating in a wider range of occupations. Where teaching and nursing were considered two of the few acceptable jobs for women, Canadian women are now entering many new fields. Nevertheless, **gender segregation** still occurs, with a concentration of men and women in different occupations.

Figure 13–10

Three Canadian women who have helped to break down gender segregation. Left to right: Manon Rheaume, former NHL hockey player; Kim Campbell, Canada's first woman prime minister; Roberta Bondar, Canada's first woman astronaut.

Job segregation by gender has important consequences. For example, about 30 percent of Canadian women are employed in clerical occupations and another 16 percent in service occupations. Men, on the other hand, are more often employed in manufacturing, construction and transportation, and tend to hold more managerial and administrative positions

Figure 13–11

This table compares the number of men and women in each job category as well as their average earnings in the 10 highest-paying and the 10 lowest-paying occupations in Canada in 1995. Does it surprise you to learn that women consistently earn less than men?

Men and women in the Canadian workforce, 1995

	Number of Workers		Average Earnings	
	Men	**Women**	**Men**	**Women**
All occupations	**4 514 850**	**2 998 940**	**$42 288**	**$30 130**
Total: 10 highest-paying occupations	**158 795**	**38 940**	**$99 605**	**$64 716**
Judges	1 360	405	$128 791	$117 707
Specialist physicians	9 345	3 220	$137 019	$86 086
General practitioners and family physicians	16 055	5 615	$116 750	$81 512
Dentists	6 995	1 535	$109 187	$71 587
Senior managers in goods production, utilities, transportation and construction	32 625	2 880	$102 971	$58 463
Senior managers in finance, communications and other business services	19 190	3 860	$104 715	$71 270
Lawyers and Quebec notaries	32 305	12 080	$89 353	$60 930
Senior managers in trade, broadcasting and other services	24 610	4 060	$84 237	$48 651
Primary production managers (except agriculture)	6 670	405	$78 421	$48 479
Securities agents, investment dealers and traders	9 640	4 880	$90 391	$47 323
Total: 10 lowest-paying occupations	**49 810**	**181 105**	**$18 640**	**$15 146**
Sewing machine operators	2 490	27 750	$20 664	$17 340
Cashiers	9 025	47 110	$20 557	16 977
Ironing, pressing, and finishing occupations	9 90	2 375	$19 297	$16 499
Artisans and craftspersons	2 840	3 040	$20 555	$13 565
Bartenders	7 080	8 495	$18 899	$14 940
Harvesting labourers	525	605	$18 683	$14 465
Service station attendants	8 630	2 175	$16 520	$14 947
Food-service counter attendants and food preparers	5 550	16 680	$17 912	$14 681
Food and beverage servers	11 940	38 250	$18 192	$13 861
Babysitters, nannies and parents' helpers	740	34 625	$15 106	$12 662

Source: Statistics Canada

than women. These facts are crucial because the jobs generally held by women tend to bring lower pay, fewer opportunities and less responsibility and authority. Figure 13–11 shows that a significant wage gap still exists between men and women, even when they perform exactly the same work. Women earn less—even in jobs that have traditionally been held by women.

Within large organizations, many women feel they are achieving equal opportunities to advance. However, there is a long way to go. A 1994 survey by Statistics Canada showed that 40 percent of men but only 25 percent of women described themselves as supervisors. An analysis of the top 300 Canadian companies found that women were less likely to hold senior management positions or to serve on the board of directors. The "glass ceiling," the invisible barrier that prevents women from advancing, is still in effect although progress is slowly being made.

Connections

What, if any, is the relationship between the education gap and the wage gap? (See Chapter 12, page 255.)

Tawney Meiorin Wins Her Case

Female employees struggling to gain a foothold in non-traditional jobs are often faced with a situation known as "equality with a vengeance." The argument goes something like this: If you want to work in traditionally male jobs, fine. We'll treat everyone exactly the same. And if the end result of this approach is that no women survive in the job, tough luck.

It is becoming increasingly clear in the context of modern employment law that this argument will no longer wash. Real equality includes the idea that reasonable accommodations must be made to ensure that everyone truly has the opportunity to participate.

A case argued in a British Columbia court illustrates this point. Tawney Meiorin lost her job as a forest firefighter with the British Columbia government in 1994. It wasn't because the 29-year-old firefighter could not do the job. She had worked on the initial attack crew in the Golden Forest District for three years without any apparent shortcomings. Her only fault was that she was unable to pass a physical fitness requirement imposed in 1994. In particular, she failed to pass a 2.5-kilometre running test by 49 seconds. Forest firefighters were required to complete the course in 11 minutes or less. Notwithstanding her previous performances she was now considered "physically unqualified to carry out the work required."

After losing her job, Meiorin filed a grievance through the government employees' union, calling into question the fairness of the fitness test as a job requirement. The government argued that the test was administered equally to all employees and the same standard applied to everyone. The government also claimed that any attempt to lower the standards would seriously compromise the safety of both male and female crew members and undermine their forest-firefighting efforts.

Arbitrator Mervin Chertkow was not convinced by this reasoning. The bottom line was that the test had the effect of excluding a large proportion of female candidates. It was telling that only 35 percent of women passed the fitness test,

CASE STUDY

1. Why did Tawney Meiorin believe she had been treated unfairly?

2. What was the government's position regarding testing standards?

3. What was the arbitrator's final conclusion?

4. On what basis did the Supreme Court reach its decision?

grievance—complaint

arbitrator—a person appointed to settle a dispute and impose a decision

Figure 13–12

Tawney Meiorin after winning her case

compared with 65 percent to 70 percent of men. This outcome arose, not because more women tend to be out of shape, but because there are physiological differences in aerobic capacity between men and women. Even with training, most women could not meet the new standard.

Women were clearly disadvantaged by the fitness test, which had the effect of barring most of them from forest-firefighting jobs. As a result, the arbitrator ordered the government to give Meiorin her job back. He left it to the government and the union to work out how the fitness test should be revised to be fair for both sexes.

From "Female Firefighter Seeks Equity" by Jonathan Eaton

The British Columbia government appealed the arbitrator's decision, but almost two years later, in 1999, the Supreme Court of Canada ruled in Meiorin's favour. The Court found that the B.C. Government's testing standard discriminated on the basis of sex, and that it could not be justified as a legitimate occupational requirement.

Responding to Workplace Diversity

visible minority—a group whose physical appearance indicates that it is not a member of the majority

Although women are not a minority in the general population, they are still considered a "visible minority" in the workplace. However, Canada's labour force has undergone a transformation—over the last 25 years the number and proportion of women and other visible minorities entering the workforce has increased significantly. As a result, employers are starting to recognize the importance of altering the workplace and its policies to address the needs and concerns of working women and other minorities. For example, some employers are offering flexible work hours, daycare facilities on company premises or the option of working at home.

With respect to discrimination in the workplace, the Supreme Court decision in the Meiorin firefighter case has ground-breaking significance. It sets out new legal principles and establishes an obligation on the part of the employer to accommodate the diverse needs and abilities of its employees. This decision will be applied by other courts when they consider claims of discrimination in relation to all workplace rules, standards and practices.

Connections

What can be done to reduce discrimination in the workplace? (See Chapter 11, pages 232–233.)

Equally important is the need for employers to resolve conflicts that arise from social differences among employees. In every province in Canada, employees are protected by a human rights code that states that harassment related to gender, race or ethnicity will not be tolerated. For example, the Ontario Human Rights Code defines harassment as "engaging in a course of vexatious comment or conduct that is known, or ought reasonably to be known, to be unwelcome." Employers recognize that they must provide a safe environment. As soon as they become aware that someone is being harassed, they are legally obliged to take action to deal with the situation.

vexatious—annoying

Conducting a Seminar

A seminar is a meeting about a set topic, attended by a group of participants and led by a designated person. The purpose is to investigate a topic or resolve an issue.

Here's How

1. Prepare for the seminar:
   - Choose a leader who will gather information in order to determine the major topics and questions to be discussed. The leader will also prepare and distribute materials beforehand for participants to read.
   - The participants prepare for the seminar by reading assigned materials and considering the questions prepared by the leader.

2. Conduct the seminar:
   - The leader presents an outline of the topic.
   - The leader takes a position on the topic and invites group members to respond to the information presented or the questions raised.
   - The leader ensures that all group members have the opportunity to express opinions.
   - Participants discuss the information, issues and points of view.
   - The leader brings the discussion to a close by identifying major ideas and by summarizing points of view.

Try It

1. Work in groups of four or five to conduct a seminar on the role of women in the workplace. Be sure to consider the following questions: What obstacles do women face in seeking non-traditional jobs? What are the advantages to having jobs open to either sex? What jobs continue to be largely restricted to either men or women? Why are they restricted?

2. Present your seminar's conclusions to the class.

Activities

Understand Ideas

1. Why does the number of women in the labour force continue to rise?

2. **a)** What is the "glass ceiling"? Provide examples to illustrate your definition.

   b) Why does the glass ceiling still exist?

Think and Evaluate

3. Referring to the case study entitled Tawney Meiorin Wins Her Case (page 281), explain what impact you think the decision of the Supreme Court of Canada will have on other similar instances of "equality with a vengeance"?

Apply Your Learning

4. Describe a situation in which you have experienced gender discrimination. If you have never experienced this situation before, interview someone who has and share what you have learned with the class.

Research and Communicate

5. Interview several working women. To what extent do they feel they have the same job opportunities as men? To what extent do they feel that their opportunities are limited because they are women? Report your findings to the class.

Key Points

- The economy of a society is the social institution that organizes how goods and services are produced, distributed and consumed.

- The kind of work we do is shaped by the culture and the economy in which we live; those economies include hunting and gathering, agricultural, industrial or post-industrial.

- Canada has shifted from an industrial economy based on manufactured goods to a post-industrial economy based on services and information technology.

- Rapid advances in computer technology have led to a computer and information revolution that continues to shape the nature of work.

- The role of women in the workforce has undergone a transformation—the number and proportion of employed women have increased significantly.

- Gender segregation is still occurring in the workplace despite the movement of women into non-traditional types of work.

Activities

Understand Ideas

1. Design a chart to show the positive and negative effects of industrialization on employee working conditions.

2. With a partner, discuss the personal repercussions of being unemployed.

3. How are women and other visible minorities protected from harassment in the workplace?

Think and Evaluate

4. **a)** How would you design your home office?
   b) What do you believe would be the benefits and drawbacks of working at home?

5. In your opinion, why do women earn less than men?

Apply Your Learning

6. If you wanted to compete for the Young Entrepreneur Award, what business venture would you launch? What resources could you consult to find out more about starting your own business?

7. In groups of five or six, conduct a seminar on the following topic: Does gender segregation exist in your school? Examine possible gender segregation among teachers and students. For example, are certain subjects more likely to be taught by male or female teachers? Is participation on the student council or in school sports segregated by gender? Are certain subjects more likely to be chosen by male or female students? If gender segregation does exist, what can be done about it? Be sure to follow the guidelines in the Skill Focus on Conducting a Seminar (page 283).

Research and Communicate

8. **a)** Review the Skill Focus in Chapter 4, Gathering and Recording Information (page 73). Gather information that either supports or opposes the idea that advancing technology contributes to rising unemployment.
   b) As a class, debate the issue, with both sides presenting facts and examples to support your views.

9. Review the Skill Focus in Chapter 12, Writing an Essay (page 248). Follow these guidelines to write an essay that will address the following question: Do labour unions effectively represent the Canadian workforce in the twenty-first century?

Social Class and Poverty in Canada

E very society has some way to structure how people get financial rewards and other benefits. In some societies access to wealth is based upon who you are: your family or class background. In others it is based upon the talents and abilities of the individual. Whatever the case, access to wealth can affect the way we live and the opportunities that are open to us. The list below shows benefits that many people in Canada consider important. In your opinion, which of these are essential? Which, if you did not possess them, would you consider a sign of poverty? Which of them could be considered a sign of wealth?

- a balanced diet
- adequate clothing
- housing with electricity, heat, running water and privacy
- household appliances such as a stove, refrigerator and washing machine
- medical and dental care
- opportunity to complete education
- recreation and cultural activities
- transportation, public or private
- employment opportunities
- economic security during old age and periods of ill health
- communication facilities such as telephone, radio, television, computer

What do you think influences wealth and poverty in Canada? What are the effects of wealth or poverty on individuals and groups? What can and should be done about variations in wealth?

In This Chapter

- What social classes exist in Canada?
- How is poverty defined and which groups in Canada are most likely to suffer from poverty?
- What impact does poverty have on a society?
- What steps are being taken to try and address the problem of poverty in Canada?

Key Terms

social classes

ascribed status

achieved status

wealthy upper class

middle class

working class

poverty

Low-income Cut-off (LICO)

working poor

homeless

child poverty

The Economy and Social Class

In every society there are groups of people who receive more benefits or have more influence and power than other groups. These groups are often divided into **social classes.** There are a number of criteria used to define each class, such as income, influence, lifestyle, education and type of work. Other factors can determine a person's social class. In traditional East Indian society, for example, people were born into classes called castes. A person's social status was based upon his or her caste and it was not possible to change one's caste. For the most part, only certain jobs were available to members of each caste. A person's class can also be based on gender, race, age or inherited social class. Status based on these criteria is known as **ascribed status**—status that is assigned to an individual at birth or through aging.

ascribed—recognized as belonging to

Social Class in Canada

In Canada, many people believe that a person's social status is based largely upon **achieved** rather than ascribed characteristics, that is, we earn our rewards through personal merit, effort and hard work. These people believe that Canada is a meritocracy. Some Canadians, however, question whether social status can truly be determined by an individual's personal effort. One basic assumption in a meritocracy, for example, is that everyone begins with an equal opportunity. It may be more difficult, however, to advance economically and achieve a higher status for someone who is born into a poor family. Students from poorer families may have more difficulty continuing their education because of financial hardship or lack of encouragement from family members. Moreover, certain groups in Canadian society may, through no fault of their own, be assigned an ascribed status that prevents them from getting the best jobs, or earning the highest pay. Young people, women, Aboriginal people, people from different ethnic groups, older people or those with disabilities are often at a disadvantage simply because of who they are.

Generally, however, Canadians do not widely recognize different social classes. Most Canadians, when asked, describe themselves simply as middle class. To discuss social class seems to go against the democratic view of social equality. Different social classes are generally not reflected in the media or in public discussion. Yet in everyday life, most people recognize the differences in attitudes and cultural behaviour of people from varying income brackets and social backgrounds. In order to examine society more closely, sociologists have identified four major social classes: the wealthy upper class, the middle class, the working class and the poor. Although the distinction between these groups is not always clear, these labels provide a framework for discussing social groupings in most western societies, including Canada.

Connections

How does conflict theory view the way social classes interact? (See Chapter 6, page 112.)

The Wealthy Upper Class

The **wealthy upper class** in Canada makes up about 3 to 5 percent of the population. Much of the income of this class derives from inherited wealth, although some members of the upper class have earned their fortunes. In 1996, each of the 50 richest individuals and families in Canada were worth at least $145 million.

Members of the upper class usually go to the most expensive and highly respected schools and universities. In these schools, they often make contact with others of their social class, which gives them the advantage of a network of influential connections. Later, many work as top executives in large corporations or as senior government officials. Their positions give them a great deal of influence in and control over the economy and politics. Research into the lifestyles of the rich in Canada indicate that they are often not well known and they tend to lead lives away from media attention. Many rich Canadian families use their wealth to endow universities, museums and theatres and to subsidize a variety of cultural activities.

Figure 14–1

Home in Laval, Québec, bought by singer Celine Dion for $7.8 million. Dion also bought three neighbouring properties. In Canada, wealth is concentrated in the hands of a few.

Individual	Source of Wealth	Wealth (in billions)
Kenneth Thomson	Publishing, information distribution	$23.5
Irving family	Oil, shipping, lumber, media	$6.2
Bombardier family	Aerospace, manufacturing	$6.0
Galen Weston	Retail, groceries, real estate	$5.35
Gururaj Deshpande	Optical network components	$5.05
Charles Bronfman	Alcohol, entertainment	$4.95
David/Cliff Lede	Fibre optics, construction	$4.6
Jeff Skoll	Internet	$3.85
Ted Rogers	Cable TV, media/communications	$3.0
Ted Mathews	Telecommunications	$2.8

Source: *Canadian Business,* August 07, 2000.

Figure 14–2

The ten richest families in Canada

The Middle Class

Sociologists vary in their definition of **middle class.** Some sociologists determine middle class by a person's income and the kinds of goods and services he or she can afford. Other sociologists define the middle class by the type of work a person does and the degree of control he or she has over financial and human resources. Traditionally, middle-class work involved the professions such as medicine or law. After the Industrial Revolution in the late eighteenth century, however, the middle class expanded to include office managers and employees, factory owners and others who benefited financially from the industrial age and who could afford a better lifestyle.

In the late twentieth century, higher attendance at universities and colleges increased entry into many professional and business occupations, which brought further growth in the middle class. Because most middle-class people work in offices or a similar environment, they are also called "white-collar" workers.

The middle class in Canada includes about 40 to 50 percent of the population. This group has considerable influence on culture in Canada and in North America in general. Television and other mass media, for example, are largely aimed at a middle-class audience because this class represents a widespread and powerful group of viewers and consumers. Most popular television sitcoms assume middle-class values and lifestyles in an attempt to attract this large market.

The Working Class

The **working class,** like the middle class, is also a product of industrialization. During the Industrial Revolution, many countries underwent a massive shift from an agricultural-based economy to an industrial-based one. Many people moved from rural areas to the cities to work in large factories. Karl Marx (1818–1883) was a German philosopher and economist who studied the new industrial society and the role of workers in that society. Marx defined the "working class" as people who sold their labour to owners of factories for wages. Today, Marx's definition is probably too narrow, since almost everybody works for someone else. A more current definition of working class has more to do with the kind of work a person does. People who work in factories or at manual labour, such as technicians, mechanics or tradespeople would fall under the definition of working class. These workers are also known as "blue-collar" workers. Some working-class jobs require little formal training while other jobs demand a high degree of technical schooling and expertise. Traditionally, working-class jobs paid less than middle-class ones, although this is not always the case today. A

Figure 14–3

We live in a consumer society where many of us expect to have money to buy material goods on a regular basis. However, a significant number of Canadians can afford only to meet their basic needs, and some cannot afford even that.

Unit 3: Social Structures and Institutions

Poverty Quiz #1

Many Canadians are unaware of the extent of poverty in Canada, particularly among certain groups. In your notebook, answer the following questions honestly. Check your answers with Figure 14–11, Poverty: Facts and Myths, on page 300.

1. What are the chances that you could experience poverty in your lifetime?
   a) 1 in 8   **b)** 1 in 4   **c)** 1 in 3
   d) 1 in 2

2. According to Statistics Canada, what percent of Canadian children were considered poor in 1995?
   a) 11.5%   **b)** 15.3%   **c)** 21.0%
   d) 24.3%

3. What percent of unattached women live in poverty?
   a) 25.8%   **b)** 36.5%   **c)** 44.4%
   d) 57.4%

4. How prevalent is welfare fraud in a large province like Ontario as a percentage of total welfare budgets?
   a) 2–4%   **b)** 5–8%   **c)** 10–12%
   d) 20–28%

5. The world's richest 358 people have the combined wealth of how many of the world's poorest people?
   a) 400 000   **b)** 1.5 million   **c)** 500 million
   d) 2.3 billion

skilled technician, for example, may earn more than an office worker. About 30 percent of Canada's population could be classified as working class.

At one time in Europe and North America, people from different classes could be identified by the clothes they wore or the lifestyle they led. For example, working-class men often wore caps while middle-class men wore fedoras and suits as a sign of their class. In today's society, there is little visible distinction between social classes, as most people buy from the same stores, wear the same style clothes and often take part in the same cultural activities.

The lines between classes are blurred in other ways as well. Working-class families may live in modest neighbourhoods, but they still enjoy many of the consumer goods available to the middle class. Their children often go to university or trade schools as do the children of middle-class families. Scholarships and student-loan programs have allowed many working-class children to join the professions or highly skilled vocations.

The Poor

The poor make up about 20 percent of the Canadian population. Low income makes life unstable and insecure for poor individuals and families. Some poor people earn just enough to buy the necessities of life. Others cannot get better work because of a disability, lack of training, age or family responsibilities.

Connections

What is the relationship between poverty, unemployment and the dropout rate? (See Chapter 12, page 258.)

Poor people have many disadvantages in society. They are unable to acquire the goods and services that other Canadians accept as their right. They often live in less desirable housing or neighbourhoods. In all parts of the country there are poor people who sometimes go hungry. In large cities, poor people are usually separated into rental housing in poorer neighbourhoods. The poor are also less able to rise above their circumstances than the working class, due to lack of resources. Government reductions in social assistance in the last few years have made it even more difficult for poor people to move out of their situations. In many cases, attempts to improve their situation by taking on part-time or low-paying jobs has meant cuts in welfare payments, and the loss of medical and other benefits.

Poverty often passes from one generation to another. Children from poor families may leave school before they acquire the necessary skills to get a good job. Some marry young and have children before completing their education. In turn, their children may be unable to complete their formal education because of lack of financial support or encouragement.

Activities

Understand Ideas

1. What social and economic classes have been identified in Canadian society? What are the characteristics of each? Make a table to record your answer.

2. **a)** What is the difference between ascribed and achieved social status?
   b) How does the idea of ascribed and achieved characteristics help explain wealth and poverty?

Think and Evaluate

3. Why is it often difficult to identify different social classes in Canada?

4. To what degree, if at all, do these categories of social and economic classes match your own perceptions of Canadian society?

Research and Communicate

5. How are the working class and middle class products of the Industrial Revolution?

Focus Questions

How is poverty defined in Canada?

What groups are among the poorest in Canada?

deprivation—lacking advantages, opportunities or basic necessities

What Is Poverty?

When we refer to someone as being poor, what exactly do we mean? One way to define poverty is to ask what benefits people consider necessities in a society. Those who do not possess these benefits are then defined as poor. This type of poverty is known as **absolute poverty,** the deprivation of resources that are considered essential. You reviewed the benefits that many Canadians believe are important at the start of this chapter. Which benefits did you consider essential?

Another way to understand poverty is to consider how wealth is distributed. This way of defining poverty is called **relative poverty,** measuring the deprivation of some people against those who have more.

Statistics Canada uses a system of measuring relative poverty called the **Low-income Cut-off (LICO)** line. By using this measurement, Statistics Canada can determine what percentage of Canada's population can be classified as poor. The first step in determining the LICO is to find out what percentage of a family's income is spent on food, clothing and shelter. This percentage is based on pre-tax income, that is, income before taxes have been deducted. Research shows that the average family spends about 35 percent of its pre-tax income on these three basic necessities, with the largest portion being spent on housing. Because poor families have less income, a greater percentage of that income is spent on these necessities. Families that spend 55 percent of their income on food, clothing and shelter are classified as living below the LICO line. These families are considered poor because they have very little income left to pay for other necessities. Using this calculation, over 5 million Canadians—17.5 percent of the Canadian population—had incomes below the LICO in 1997. See Figure 14–6 on page 294 for a breakdown of the groups of people in Canada who live below the LICO line.

The Working Poor

More than half of all low-income families have some kind of employment. However, most of these people earn just enough to buy the necessities of life. These people are called the **working poor,** because even though they work, they are not earning enough money to prevent them from being poor. Many of the working poor have jobs below their skill level, or are doing part-time or seasonal work. Canadians working for minimum wage are usually working poor. In some cases, well-qualified individuals find there is no demand for their particular skills, and they are forced to take jobs that pay minimum wage—the lowest wage that someone can legally be paid. In other cases, people who have been trained professionally in other countries find that their accreditation is not recognized in Canada, and they must start again at the bottom of the economic ladder.

Because they are employed, the working poor often miss out on benefits and programs that are meant to help the unemployed. At the same time, they enjoy few if any of the consumer goods that are available to the majority of Canadians. They often must work long hours just to get by, making it difficult for them to look for better employment.

The Homeless

A significant number of poor people are also **homeless.** Some of the homeless are young people who run away from home because they have been abused or because

Figure 14–4

Minimum wage service jobs are often called McJobs, although they are not limited to fast-food restaurants. The number of working poor appears to be growing because low-paying and part-time jobs are increasing faster than other kinds of jobs.

they cannot get along with their parents. Others are unskilled or unemployed older people looking for work in the city. Some homeless people are alcoholic or drug dependant. About one-third of people who are homeless have a mental illness.

In recent years, a new group has joined the ranks of homeless in Canada—families. Families now make up about a third of all the homeless. Some families live on the streets because the family's wage earner has been put out of work. Some families have been forced out of apartments because of increases in rent. Still others cannot pay the rent or mortgage because their wages are too low.

The number of homeless people on Canadian streets has caused public concern, especially during the winter. However, little concerted action has been taken. Hostels, shelters, food banks and churches provide some help where the homeless can find a bed and a meal, and sometimes emotional support, as the first-hand account of Jeremy Hudson in the case study below reveals. However, long-term solutions to the problem of homelessness have not been found.

concerted—serious

CASE STUDY

1. Why did Jeremy Hudson leave home?

2. What were the difficulties he encountered?

3. What helped him get his life back on track?

Life on the Streets

I am 17 years old. I lived on the streets for nine months and experienced things that no teenager should.

The story begins in my hometown of Ottawa where I lived with my stepmother and father. A year ago, we had a horrible argument and I was kicked out. Since Ottawa doesn't have many shelters, I stayed at the Salvation Army for a couple of months. It wasn't the most pleasant place, but I counted myself lucky to have a roof over my head.

I then decided to pick up and move to Montreal. There was no real reason except that I was drawn by the culture and it was time for a change of scenery. With two friends, I planned to hitchhike and start a new life in a new town….

panhandling—begging for money from passersby

Once in Montreal, I spent my days panhandling, but I didn't do very well. So, I decided to work for my money. Most days, I would play my guitar or drums, but sometimes I would take all the pennies I had collected and make them into towers. I displayed my penny sculptures and hoped passersby would be impressed and spare me some change.

I also spent a lot of time job hunting, but employers said they were looking for people with at least high school education. I didn't have much to offer.

Only two shelters in Montreal would accept teens. One would let me stay one night a week, while the other would offer me shelter there one out of every 10 days. Often I had nowhere to sleep. Sometimes I would curl up in my sleeping bag in a park. Rain and snow were the worst; I would wander around the city all night, searching for somewhere warm and dry.

I also developed a drug problem. I became addicted to mescaline and wasted what little money I had. Using drugs made me constantly depressed and helpless.

I witnessed a lot of violence and was often in fear for my life. One night I saw two people chasing someone down the dark, deserted alley I was sleeping in.

Next, I heard a shot ring out and the hurried footsteps of the gunmen fleeing the scene.

I had never felt so afraid.

After a few more months in Montreal, I discovered that my biological mother was living in Toronto. Although I hadn't spoken to her for seven years, I really wanted to try and rebuild our relationship.

I phoned up my stepmother in Ottawa, and she agreed to pay for my bus ticket. That night, I was on my way.

Upon arriving at the Toronto bus station, I asked somebody if he knew of any shelters nearby. That's when I learned of Covenant House.

Covenant House wasn't at all what I had expected. I thought it would be like all the others—dirty with drunken people wandering all over the place. But the floors were clean and the beds were made. What surprised me the most, however, was the number of kids staying there.

Soon I got in touch with my biological mother, who was happy to hear from me. I found out that when I was living in Montreal, she had called Ottawa to see how I was doing. My stepmom told her everything was fine.

The people at Covenant House have done more for me than I could have ever imagined. Besides providing me with the basics of life, the volunteers also offered me the emotional support I needed. I'm even continuing my high school education at Contact Alternative School. When I graduate, I plan to study music and art. I've learned that no matter how much help street people get from outside sources, the only person who can really make a difference is the individual. At Covenant House, I've grown stronger and more optimistic. And I've started to make something positive out of my life.

Figure 14–5
Jeremy Hudson found that life on the streets is extremely hard.

From "Gimme Shelter, Please" by Jeremy Hudson

In Jeremy's case, he was lucky to eventually get enough help from volunteer organizations to get him off the street and back in school. Others are not so fortunate.

Activities

Understand Ideas

1. **a)** Write your own definition of poverty.
   b) How does Statistics Canada define poverty? According to this definition, how many Canadians are poor?

2. Why are some people referred to as the working poor?

3. What causes some Canadians to live on the streets?

Research and Communicate

4. Interview a number of people in your school to find out how they define poverty. How do their views differ from those identified in the text?

5. Develop a list of goods and services you believe are necessary for you and people in your region to have. Develop a second list of goods and services that many people want but which you do not consider necessities. Find out how much

income, before taxes and other deductions, you need to acquire these goods and services.

6. a) Go the Ontario Ministry of Labour's Web site to determine the current minimum wage.

b) Complete the following exercise to determine if you could live on this wage: Calculate your weekly salary based on a 40-hour week.

Deduct 55% for rent, groceries and clothes, 20% for monthly bills (i.e., heat, electricity, telephone) and 10% for transportation. What is left?

c) What could you buy with this amount over the course of a week? Are there necessities you would do without? Explain.

Focus Questions

Who are the people who make up Canada's poor?

What are some of the most commonly held myths about the poor?

Who Is at Risk of Poverty?

Defining who is poor in Canada can help us better understand the nature of poverty and its causes. The following are some groups that are at a particularly high risk of being poor.

- Young people in Canada face a difficult time getting a decent job. Many newly created jobs are in the poorer paying service industries where minimum wage is common. Minimum wage does not provide enough income for someone to live above the poverty line. Many young people survive by returning to their parents' home for a period of time to save on rent. Some younger people have difficulty finding employment because they lack skills required for the information age. New technology has created the need for new employee skills. Young people without specialized training are at a disadvantage.

discrepancy—difference

- Single-parent families, on average, have one-third the income of two-parent families. One obvious reason for the discrepancy is that there is only one potential earner in the family, who often must also provide child care. Another reason is that single parents may not have acquired the skills or training necessary to get a good job. Single-parent families headed by women are at a definite disadvantage. They are more likely

Figure 14–6

Poverty statistics based on the Low-income Cut-off line

	1991	1993	1995	1997
All Persons	16.5	18.0	17.8	17.5
Young Families	36.5	41.1	43.5	42.8
Female Single-Parent Families	60.3	59.0	56.8	56.0
Children	18.9	21.3	21.0	19.8
All Seniors	21.9	22.8	18.7	18.7
Youth (24 and under)	57.5	61.7	65.9	60.7
Men	40.7	39.0	28.7	33.3
Women	54.2	56.4	50.6	49.1

Source: Statistics Canada, 1999.

Unit 3: Social Structures and Institutions

to have low incomes than any other family type. Over 50 percent of these families are poor.

- Women, in general, are at a greater risk of being poor than men, whether they are single, with or without children. Women have a 49 percent chance of being poor, compared to 33 percent of men.

- In times of economic recession, older workers face an increased risk of unemployment as companies look for ways to save money. One way to make savings is to lay off older workers who may be earning more than their younger colleagues and have fewer years of service left to offer the company. In other cases, companies see younger workers as having more up-to-date skills—though this may not always be true. Older workers often have problems finding new jobs because many companies prefer to hire young employees they can train. Younger, less-experienced workers are also willing to work for lower wages. However, older workers have more family responsibilities, so more people may suffer economic hardships as a result of older-worker unemployment.

- Almost one-fifth of Canadians over the age of 65 live below the poverty line. The risk of poverty is greatest for older women who are on their own. Most seniors have left the workforce and are dependent on a government or private pension for income. While the cost of living continues to go up, their income does not. The dream of an early retirement spent on a southern beach becomes a reality for only a small proportion of the population.

- Canadian census statistics show that people of working age with disabilities have a 50 percent greater chance of having a low income when compared with all Canadians in the same age group. In many cases, the only barrier to working faced by people with disabilities is discrimination.

- Children have little or no control over their social or financial circumstances. Those who live in poverty are poor because their parents are poor. This makes children vulnerable if their parents fit into any categories already mentioned.

- Poverty rates can be higher in certain regions of the country. Usually this higher rate of poverty is due to unemployment caused by seasonal work or low-paying jobs. For example, many areas of Newfoundland and Nova Scotia have traditionally relied on the fishing industry for employment. In winter, when the weather makes it impossible to fish, many people are out of work. The situation worsened with the decline of fish stocks, and people are often no longer able to make a reasonable living. In northern Canada, unemployment is often high because there can be long periods of little or no industrial development.

Connections

Why are women at greater risk of being poor than men? (See Chapter 11, pages 224–227; Chapter 13, pages 279–281.)

Figure 14–7

Children in Davis Inlet, Labrador. Northern communities in Newfoundland and Labrador are among the poorest in Canada. There are few opportunities for employment, and facilities for housing, health care, education and recreation are inadequate. As a result, substance abuse and a high suicide rate have plagued these communities.

SOCIAL SCIENCE
LIVE

Poverty Quiz #2

The following are some commonly held beliefs about poverty. Which of these statements, if any, do you believe to be true? Why?

- Poverty is the fault of the individual.
- The poor do not want to work.
- Poor people do not pay taxes.
- Welfare rates are too generous.
- Poor people need to be taught basic life skills such as budgeting.

- The welfare system is rife with cheating and fraud.
- Poor families are poor because they have too many children.
- We cannot afford the social programs needed to eliminate poverty.

Check your answers with the information in Figure 14–11, Poverty: Facts and Myths, page 300.

Activities

Understand Ideas

1. **a)** Identify several major social groups who are at risk of being poor.
   b) For each of these explain why they are at an increased risk of being poor.

Think and Evaluate

2. Examine the information in Figure 14–6.
   a) What is the trend for young families? How would you explain why this trend exists?
   b) What is the trend for youth? Why do you think the figures are so high?
   c) How do the statistics for women compare with those for men? What accounts for the differences?

3. Young people who live on the street have alternatives to begging for money: They could get jobs, regardless of how menial, and pay for their own food and shelter. Do you agree with this opinion? Why or why not? Discuss.

Research and Communicate

4. Find a recent article about someone who is or was homeless. Write a summary of the person's situation and how he or she became homeless. Now make a list of suggestions you would make to improve this person's situation. Present your case to the class.

Focus Questions

What are the physical and psychological effects of poverty on individuals?

How does poverty affect a society?

What are the attitudes of most Canadians regarding poverty?

The Impact of Poverty

Poverty often has a negative impact on a person's heath. People who are homeless tend to be sick more often and have shorter lifespans than other groups in society. Poor people often do not eat nutritiously. They are often forced to buy cheaper foods, such as macaroni, bread or potatoes, at the expense of milk, meat and vegetables. This diet can be harmful in the long run, particularly for children. Lack of nutritious food affects a child's growth, mental development and energy level and, consequently, he or she may not do as well in school as children from higher-income families.

Children from poor families are also less likely to stay in school to complete high school or to attend higher education, because their families often cannot afford tuition fees. In addition, poor children may not receive as much encouragement from teachers and others. In addition to its physical effects, poverty exacts a frightening psychological toll on its victims. Long-term poverty can destroy an individual's sense of hope and initiative. The inability to improve one's situation may lead to a feeling of resignation about the future, anger and sometimes a desire to escape. Family break-ups and substance abuse can be the result.

The Effect on Society

Poverty also affects society as a whole. Failure to educate a large portion of a society, for example, lowers the skill level of that society, making it less competitive in the global economy. An uneducated workforce is a disadvantage to everyone because it slows down economic growth, thus reducing a society's overall wealth. Poor health brought on by poverty is also a drain on the medical and social resources of a society.

Poverty may also lead to social unrest. In recent years, Canadians have seen protest marches by the poor, and by organizations working to improve the condition of the poor. Most often, however, poor people have little option but to try to improve their situation on their own.

Figure 14–8

A Calgary police officer examines a makeshift shelter in a city park, before dismantling it along with some 20 other shelters nearby. Why do some people demand that such camps be dismantled? What options are open to those who lose their makeshift homes?

Attitudes to Poverty

Canadians generally want to see poverty reduced or eliminated. Most find the sight of homeless people or poor children troubling. Opinions vary, however, as to how people become poor. About half of Canadians believe that poverty is largely self-inflicted, and that anyone who is willing to work hard can improve his or her situation. These people believe that a healthy economy is fundamental in raising the standard of living for everyone. This theory is known as the trickle-down effect because it suggests that wealth will filter down from the wealthy, who have the power to create jobs, to the poor, who benefit from the employment opportunities.

Other Canadians are of the opinion that poverty is often the result of economic circumstances and usually not the fault of an individual. People who hold this opinion generally support government programs directed at helping the poorest members of society. They also support a more equitable distribution of wealth through taxation and other means.

equitable—fair or equal

While no society has managed to eliminate poverty, some have succeeded in reducing its effects considerably. In Finland, for example, the rate of homeless people has been cut in half in less than ten years because its government provides minimal housing to all citizens. Tackling poverty, however, requires agreement on the root causes of poverty and a willingness to invest in solutions.

What Is Canada Doing to Fight Poverty?

Canada's social welfare system has been built up over the course of the twentieth century. Included in this system are employment insurance for those who are temporarily out of work and social assistance (welfare) for

Figure 14–9
Volunteers sort contributions at a food bank. Is eliminating poverty the responsibility of individuals like these, or is it a collective responsibility that should be addressed by government?

those who need longer-term support, such as single parents without work and those with disabilities that prevent them from working. Traditionally, Canada has had a strong commitment to maintaining its social welfare system. More recently, however, governments have tried to cut their mounting costs, and there has been a move to reduce the amount of assistance people can receive and the length of time they can receive it.

Canada's taxation system redistributes wealth to some degree. Higher incomes are taxed at a higher rate than lower incomes, and revenue from those taxes are used, in part, to fund social benefits. This kind of taxation is called a progressive tax system.

Our laws are also aimed at preventing certain action that can contribute to poverty. For example, racial or sexual discrimination in the workplace is an offence. The law also makes it difficult for employers to lay off workers without good reason. Minimum hourly wage rates set by the provincial governments guarantee all workers a subsistence level paycheque. Labour unions also fight to improve income levels, job security, benefits and workplace safety. Food banks, shelters and charities also help provide the poor and homeless with basic needs, but these places are usually staffed by volunteers and they depend on private donations for survival.

Connections

Has Canada's movement toward globalization helped or hindered the fight against poverty? Why? (See Chapter 13, page 271.)

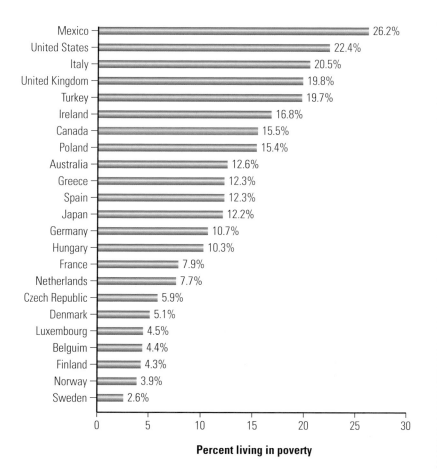

Percent living in poverty

Figure 14–10

According to this study by the UN organization UNICEF, more than 15 percent of Canadian children are living in poverty. Does Canada's position on this chart surprise you? Why or why not? Do you think Canada is doing what it should to fight poverty?

Poverty: Facts and Myths

Facts

1. The Economic Council of Canada estimates that one in three Canadians will experience poverty at some point in their working careers.

2. According to the National Anti-Poverty Organization, a Canadian non-profit organization aimed at improving conditions for the poor,
21 percent of children were considered poor in 1995.

3. Unequal wages between the sexes, and increasing need for a two-income household, contributes to 44.4 percent of all unattached women living in poverty, compared to 34 percent of men.

4. It would take the combined wealth of 2.3 billion of the globe's poorest individuals to equal the combined wealth of the globe's 358 richest. That means that these 358 people control almost half of the world's wealth.

Source: United Nations, 1996

Myths

Poverty is the failure of the individual.
Reality: Many workers have lost their jobs for reasons beyond their control, and cannot find work because it is unavailable. Many people are on welfare because they are unable to provide for themselves, often due to some personal or economic crisis.

The poor do not want to work.
Reality: Most poor people do work full or part time—over 60 percent of those heading poor families, over 70 percent of poor unattached individuals.

Poor people do not pay taxes.
Reality: In Ontario poor people pay about $160 million in income taxes. People on welfare pay sales tax, GST and property taxes.

Welfare rates are too generous.
Reality: All welfare rates are below the poverty line. The highest rates are 20 percent below the line, the lowest are 76 percent below the line.

Poor people need to be taught basic life skills like budgeting.
Reality: Many live far below the poverty line and spend most of their income on basic needs.

Those who feed and clothe a family on a limited income already have budgeting skills.

The welfare system is rife with cheating and fraud.
Reality: A national auditing firm estimated that fraud amounted to about 3 percent of the Ontario welfare budget. On the other hand, income tax fraud has been estimated at about 29 percent.

Poor families are poor because they have too many children.
Reality: Most poor families have either no children, or one or two children. Fifteen percent have 3 or more children under the age of 18.

We cannot afford the social programs needed to eliminate poverty.
Reality: Canada is more prosperous than any European country, yet it spends less on social security and income support measures than countries in Europe do. Western European countries such as France and Germany provide more income and employment supports to families with children.

Source: National Anti-Poverty Organization

Figure 14–11
Check your answers to Poverty Quiz #1 and Poverty Quiz #2 with the information above.

A Lucky Escape

CASE STUDY

1. Why is Carroll Barrett poor?

2. How does she feel about her situation?

3. How did Barrett get help and what might have happened to her without this help?

In some cases, innovative solutions are being tried to give individuals a chance to pull themselves out of the vicious cycle of poverty. The following case study is one example of an innovative approach to a common problem.

It's a routine Tuesday night at Carroll Barrett's. Dinner is on the table by 7, the earliest she can get it there after the 75-minute commute from her job to her apartment, with a loop to pick up her two girls at day care. It's all a lifetime away from last fall, when Carroll found herself doing something she had never imagined could happen to someone like her: She called the city's family-shelter department to tell them she and her daughters would be homeless as of Oct. 6, and would need a place to live....

A clerical employee for the past nine years, the product of a solidly working-class family, she teeters on the border between the many house-comfortable Canadians and those who struggle to maintain a secure place to live. As she said five months after her call to family-shelter services, "I make about $31,000 a year so I'm not quite on the bread line."

But Carroll illustrates just how far the floodwaters of Canada's housing problem have risen: They've inundated those living on sidewalks and in shelters; now they're threatening even those like her, who not so long ago would have been happily settled in good apartments or even their own homes.

Carroll's problems started May 14, 1998, the day her common-law husband moved out and back to his parents, leaving behind a newborn and a 3-year-old, and a pile of debts. She spent the summer alternating between depression and thinking about which bills she couldn't pay. Then her car breathed its last and she had to buy another used one to get to her job. As a result, she missed her $754.96 rent payment in August. She couldn't catch up and in late September, her landlord ordered her to be out by Oct. 6.

By then, she was so drained, she started to think it might be easier just to give up, to go straight to the last resort—one of the Kingston Road motels that have become Toronto's emergency shelter system for families. But Family Services suggested she call Nicole Sequin, a contact for the experimental rent bank being tried by Toronto's shelter, housing and support division.

"Carroll was who we thought would be the typical person we could help," says Sequin.

It was difficult for Carroll to ask for the help. The way she'd always seen things, she's not from that kind of a family. Her mother and father have both worked hard their whole lives at the kinds of jobs that aren't glamorous, but keep cities running, just like Carroll's. The three girls in the family put themselves through college and university.

"I'd never accepted a penny of government help. So it was humbling. But not humiliating." *(Continue on page 303.)*

inundated—overwhelmed or flooded

Figure 14–12

Carroll Barrett earns a regular income in her office job at a university, yet she considers herself lucky that she and her daughters have escaped being homeless.

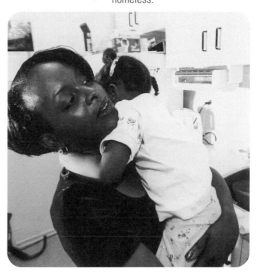

Debating

A debate is a formal argument between opposing individuals or teams. The aim is to convince the listeners that one side is right and the other is wrong. The topic of a debate is stated very clearly, often in the format "Be it resolved that…" One side accepts the resolution as stated while the other denies the statement. Debating skills include the use of logic (rational thinking) and rhetoric (the art of persuasion).

Here's How

1. **Prepare:** Gather the facts, evidence, arguments and illustrations that support the position you plan to take. At the same time, gather information about opposing points of view, so that you can rebut your opponents' arguments. Prepare brief notes outlining the points you want to get across.

2. **Debate:** Follow this format:

   • The chairperson states the topic in the form of a resolution, for example: "Be it resolved that the federal and provincial governments should increase social spending in order to eliminate poverty in Canada."

   • The chairperson introduces the speakers, then explains the rules and time limits. The number of speakers and allotted times may vary, but a possible sequence for a debate is shown in Figure 14–13.

   • Check the criteria for evaluation, and use them as a guideline for presenting your ideas.

3. **Evaluate:** Sometimes a judge decides which side has won a debate, but in many cases the audience decides which side has made the most effective case. Use the criteria on the following page to make your decision. For each one, use the following scale:

Well done: 4
Good: 3
Acceptable: 2
Poor: 1

Figure 14–13

Possible sequence for a debate with three speakers per side

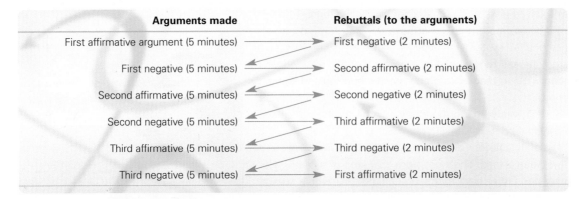

Arguments made	Rebuttals (to the arguments)
First affirmative argument (5 minutes)	First negative (2 minutes)
First negative (5 minutes)	Second affirmative (2 minutes)
Second affirmative (5 minutes)	Second negative (2 minutes)
Second negative (5 minutes)	Third affirmative (2 minutes)
Third affirmative (5 minutes)	Third negative (2 minutes)
Third negative (5 minutes)	First affirmative (2 minutes)

Criteria for Evaluation

- Understanding: Debaters showed understanding of the questions and knowledge of the major points.

- Planning: Debaters carefully planned their strategy and presented and organized their case.

- Clarity: Speeches and rebuttals were organized to make each point clearly.

- Proof: Evidence and examples accompanied each argument.

- Persuasiveness: Ideas were expressed clearly, effectively and with enthusiasm.

- Rebuttal: Opposing ideas were consistently and effectively rebutted.

Practise It

Some Canadians believe that governments should increase social spending on employment insurance, welfare and housing subsidies to help people in need to avoid poverty. Others believe that such spending simply encourages people to rely on handouts, and that it would be better for governments to stimulate the economy to create jobs for more people. Formulate a clear topic on this issue and hold a class debate.

Carroll got a $778 loan to cover her rent arrears, and started repaying $77 a month. In August, the debt was clear.

Carroll got help because Canadians are starting to recognize that the epidemic of homelessness and housing instability is not a temporary downturn but a persistent condition that needs new strategies of prevention and treatment.

From "Homeless Threat Haunts Families on the Edge" by Frances Bula

---

How Do We Compare?

How does Canada rate against other countries in fighting poverty? According to a UNICEF report that looked at **child poverty** rates in 23 developed nations, Canada had the seventh highest level of child poverty. Its 15.5 percent child poverty rate is better than that of Mexico (26.2 percent) and the United States (22.4 percent), but much worse than that of countries such as Sweden, Norway and Finland, with rates that vary from 2.6 to 4.3 percent. (See Figure 14–10 on page 299.)

The UN defines families as being in relative poverty if their income is less than half of the national median. According to the report, a child living in a single-parent household in Canada has a 52 percent chance of being poor, compared with just 7 percent in Finland. The report concludes that, "In the Nordic countries, the low levels of child poverty reflect the high levels of investment in family policies."

Should we be doing more to fight poverty, particularly child poverty? In light of the UN statistics, many Canadians would agree that Canada could do much more to provide assistance to its poor. Whether or not these measures would be effective remains to be seen.

median—midpoint of a range of numbers.

Nordic countries—countries in northwest Europe including Finland, Norway and Sweden

Sweden

United States

Kenya

Figure 14–14

Child poverty exists in wealthy countries such as the United States, although most rich countries have programs to address the problem. At the same time, many children we might consider poor, such as the Kenyan boys and girls shown here, are well taken care of.

Activities

Understand Ideas

1. Make a web diagram to record the impact of poverty on children, individuals, families and society.

2. What are two ways the Canadian government is dealing with poverty? What other ways are Canadians helping to combat poverty?

Think and Evaluate

3. What practical solutions can you suggest to ensure that parents continue to support their children financially after a separation or divorce? What would the overall effect of such a program be?

4. Explain the statement, "In the Nordic countries, the low levels of child poverty reflect the high levels of investment in family policies."

Apply Your Learning

5. Use what you have learned about the causes of poverty and the categories of people who are more at risk of poverty to design a program to help school children who are poor. You may choose to focus on prevention or assisting this group directly.

Research and Communicate

6. Arrange an interview with someone who works at a food bank. Ask the following questions:

   a) Who donates to food banks?
   b) What kinds of food are donated?
   c) Does the food bank ever run out of food?
   d) What time of the year is the busiest for food banks? Why?
   e) How does the food bank advertise for more donations?

Key Points

- Every society is divided into social groups that are based on either ascribed status or personal achievement.

- Most Canadians view their society as a meritocracy where skill and personal initiative can be rewarded. Some people, however, don't receive the benefit they deserve because of factors such as background, age, gender or ethnicity, or because they have a disability.

- Sociologists in Western societies have identified four social classes: the wealthy upper class, the middle class, the working class and the poor. These classifications are only a guide, as the division between classes is often difficult to determine.

- Canada is one of the wealthiest nations in the world, yet 20 percent of Canadians suffer from poverty. In certain groups, such as single-parent families, poverty rates are much higher than in other groups.

- Although Canadians are concerned about the problems of poverty, they have different attitudes as to what should be done to help reduce poverty. Some people believe individual effort and a thriving economy are needed to help solve the problem of poverty. Others believe that Canadian society has an obligation to provide help for those who are poor.

- Employment insurance, social assistance and progressive taxation policies are methods used by Canadian governments to help alleviate poverty. Food banks and shelters are other ways of helping the poor, but these methods are short term and depend mostly on volunteers and donations.

Activities

Understand Ideas

1. Describe Canadian attitudes toward poverty.

2. Describe Canada's welfare system. Who benefits from it? Why are attitudes about it changing?

3. Why are food banks a short-term solution to poverty?

Think and Evaluate

4. Do you know any television shows based on the lives of working-class people? Do these shows have a wide appeal? Why or why not?

5. Why is wealth often associated with power?

Apply Your Learning

6. Debate: Be it resolved that Canada is a meritocracy. Canadians earn their financial and social benefits; they don't inherit them. (See Skill Focus, page 302.)

Research and Communicate

7. **a)** Purchase a newspaper that is sold to support homeless people. Write an analysis of the paper that looks at headlines, front page articles, editorials, photographs and other articles. Present your analysis to the class.

   b) In groups of four, design a newspaper to be sold by homeless people. What sections would you include? What kinds of articles would appear? What other information would you include?

8. Using information in this chapter, write a one-page article for the newspaper you designed in question 7b. You can write about one group (see Figure 14–6), or particular problems and barriers that different groups face. Find a photograph or drawing to illustrate your article.

Deviance and Social Control

In This Chapter

- What defines deviance?
- What causes deviant behaviour?
- What forms of social control are used in Canadian society?
- What are the elements of the criminal justice system?
- Why and how do we punish criminal behaviour?

Key Terms

social norms

folkways

mores

laws

social role

deviance

social control

retribution

deterrence

rehabilitation

recidivism

probation

All social groups and societies expect people to behave in certain ways. At the same time, each person has an individual pattern of behaviour that can, in some cases, conflict with the expectations of society. As a result, groups and societies have methods to ensure that individuals act in a socially acceptable manner. Behaviour in less important situations warrants little social control, but when behaviour has serious consequences, members of the group exert strong social control.

Which of the following behaviours do you think is acceptable? In each case, what reaction would you expect from others?

- In a restaurant, all of your friends order hamburger and fries. You decide to have a hot dog.

- Most people in your group treat each other with respect, but one member of the group gossips constantly and tells lies about the others.

- The school dress code says that all students will wear black trousers or skirts and white shirts. You come to school wearing a red shirt and green pants.

- The line-up at the checkout counter is long, so you walk out without paying for your items.

Social Norms

From early on, we are taught to behave in a particular way in certain social situations. Sociologists and cultural anthropologists use the term **social norms** to refer to social expectations that guide people's behaviour. Some social norms are common across a society. In Canada, we drive on the right side of the road, while in Britain, the norm is to drive on the left side. Other social norms vary from group to group and from society to society. If you transfer to a new school, you will find that some procedures are handled differently. In a new job, you must strive to learn the norms governing behaviour in that position.

Levels of Social Norms

Sociologists identify three levels of social norms, depending on the degree of formality—that is, how explicitly norms are stated and how strictly they are enforced. **Folkways** are informal practices, based on tradition or accepted group behaviours. We expect the person who accidentally bumps into us to say, "Excuse me." **Mores** are more important because they are norms involving moral or ethical judgments. Telling lies or cheating on a test go against important mores in our society. Some mores are so socially important that they are made into **laws,** formal rules enforced by designated individuals within a society. Depending on the culture, laws may or may not be written down. Anthropologists have found that, in most cultures throughout history, what distinguishes a law from a less formal norm is not that the law is recorded, but that it is enforceable by threat of punishment.

Focus Questions

What are social norms?

What are the levels of social norms?

What determines degrees of conformity?

Why do people assume social roles?

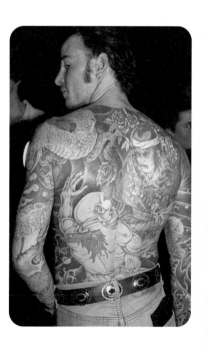

Figure 15–1
Body decoration is an example of a cross-cultural social norm, but some norms vary from one culture to another. What is considered normal in one culture may seem unusual in another.

Norms can also be "prescriptive" or "proscriptive." Prescriptive norms tell us what to do, while proscriptive norms tell us what not to do. Thanking someone for a gift or paying taxes is prescriptive. Not eating with our mouths open or not driving after drinking alcohol is proscriptive. For society to function people must conform to both types of norms most of the time; otherwise, it is too difficult to predict the behaviour of others. We expect the store to stand by its warranty on our new CD player, and we expect our friends to show up when and where we agreed to meet. People may deliberately avoid or stop trusting those who disregard accepted norms. Those who reject more important norms may be charged under the law.

Degrees of Conformity

conformity—behaviour that follows established practice

Each of us is capable of thinking and acting in unique ways. This freedom of thought and expression is not only vital to us as individuals, but also to society, which benefits from the talents, inventions and discoveries of creative people. At the same time, society requires that we maintain a certain degree of conformity. Healthy societies strive to maintain a balance between these two needs.

The group, the situation and the importance of the norm all affect the degree to which an individual conforms. For example, we tolerate our friends wearing a range of clothing, but the military requires members to wear uniforms. Conformity also varies from one society to another. In traditional agricultural societies, everyone had to help plant crops or the community would face starvation. Twentieth-century totalitarian societies such as Nazi Germany demanded total conformity of thought and action. In Western democracies such as Canada, non-conformity is accepted as part of an individualistic society.

Connections

How have experiments helped psychologists discover what people are willing to do to increase their degree of conformity? (See Chapter 8, pages 169–170.)

Social Roles

Norms apply to specific social roles as well as to general social behaviours. As we saw in Chapter 8, a **social role** is a set of expected behaviours and beliefs related to the part one plays in society, such as child, student, friend

Figure 15–2

To what degree do we accept non-conformity?

CATFISH

and store clerk. Anthropologists study the social roles of various cultural groups over time, whereas sociologists study the roles group members assume as part of the socialization process. In your social science class, for example, the teacher plays one social role governed by certain norms, while students play another. We all have many social roles; some we learn to adopt as we go. Unfortunately, we receive no specific training in how to be a parent, a friend or a sister. Other social roles, such as teacher or builder, require formal training as well as practice.

Activities

Understand Ideas

1. Define the following terms and give two examples of each (other than those used in the text):
   - norms
   - folkways
   - mores
   - roles

2. What determines the degree of conformity expected by groups?

Think and Evaluate

3. Categorize each of the following norms as prescriptive or proscriptive:
   - not cheating on your exams
   - minding your own business
   - not taking other people's property without their permission
   - saying "thank you" when someone does something for you
   - shaking hands
   - following a speed limit of 80 km per hour
   - working hard

Apply Your Learning

4. a) List all of the social roles you play in your life.
   b) Pick one social role and identify at least three social norms you must follow in that role. Are these norms folkways, mores or laws?

Research and Communicate

5. a) Choose any group that interests you. Research this group to determine the following:
   - some of the accepted norms of the group
   - the roles different members play
   - the rewards and punishments used by the group to maintain social norms
   b) Report your findings to the class and identify the research methods you used.

Deviant Behaviour

Deviance is behaviour that differs from the social norms of the group and is judged as wrong by members of that group. Such behaviour is a question of degree, ranging from rude table manners to mass murder. Deviance is not the same as diversity: Diversity includes the acceptable range of thought and behaviour within society; deviance is harmful behaviour that goes beyond the bounds of acceptable society. Cooking special foods or wearing certain clothes may be a personal or cultural preference, but it is not deviant. On the other hand, stealing or lying to others could be considered deviant behaviour.

Focus Questions

What is deviant behaviour?

What factors influence society's perception of deviance?

Which theories explain deviant behaviour?

Figure 15–3

What is your opinion of the late Victorian clothing worn by the tennis player on the left? How would she have reacted to the outfit worn by tennis star Serena Williams shown on the right?

Connections

What is the difference between abnormal behaviour and deviant behaviour? (See Chapter 5, page 98.)

What is regarded as deviant varies over time, among cultures and among groups within a culture. For instance, old photographs reveal vast differences in the concept of "acceptable" dress. Most nineteenth-century Canadians believed that glimpsing a woman's leg was shocking and unacceptable. They would have seen the attire worn by many people today as deviant. More recently, an American anthropologist on a Pacific island decided to dress like other women of that culture. The next day, she was reprimanded. She apologized and said that from then on she would wear her blouse. That was not the problem, the women said. She had exposed her calves, a part of the body not to be revealed in that culture.

Further examples of differences among cultures are easy to find. In China, for instance, due to the strict laws about population control, it is now considered deviant to have more than one child per family. In other cultures, large families are seen as a financial asset because children are expected to work in the fields to produce food. In Chapter 2 we saw how the !Kung Bushmen reacted to the behaviour of anthropologist Richard Lee. His overt gift-giving was considered deviant in a culture that prized humility and self-effacement.

Finally, one action may be considered socially acceptable in some situations, but deviant in others within the same culture. For example, in most circumstances we consider it deviant to physically assault another person. However, if the assailant acts in self-defence, fights as a soldier in a war or plays certain team sports such as hockey, his or her physical aggression may be accepted as lawful; it may even be rewarded with medals or trophies. Deviance depends on the norms and roles associated with specific situations and groups.

Causes of Deviance

What causes serious deviant behaviour such as crime? As we have seen in earlier chapters, people once believed that possession by evil spirits was the cause of some deviant behaviour, and that the proper way to deal with this problem was exorcism or, in extreme cases, burning at the stake. More recent theories have focused on biological, psychological and social causes.

Biological Theories

In early modern times, attempts were made to explain deviance biologically. Caesare Lombroso tried to identify criminals by their physical characteristics, while phrenologists believed one's character could be discerned from bumps on the head. Both theories were completely without scientific basis. Today, however, some scientists argue that particular kinds of deviance may be based, not on appearance, but on brain function or genetics. One Danish study found more antisocial behaviour in the children of criminals even when they were raised apart from their biological parents. Most sociologists, however, believe that social, not biological, explanations account for most deviant behaviour. Such diverse points of view reflect the nature-nurture debate we discussed in Unit 1.

Psychological Theories

Psychologists often look at early experiences to understand causes of deviant behaviour. Psychoanalysts suggest that criminals cannot control their aggression, while behavioural psychologists argue that, as children, criminals learned to think and act in certain ways and were rewarded for deviant behaviour. In both cases, psychologists respond by providing treatment. Compulsive theft or alcoholism, for example, often respond well to some of the therapeutic options discussed in Chapter 5.

Psychological research into obsessive behaviour and both mood and personality disorders has demonstrated that psychological problems and personality patterns can certainly account for some instances of deviant behaviour. However, statistics have shown that a large percentage of serious crimes are committed by people whose psychological profiles are normal. As a result, we will now take a closer look at the sociological approach, which focuses on the environment.

Sociological Theories

The sociological approach believes that both biological and psychological views fail to take into account how concepts of right and wrong initially arise and how the social environment influences deviance by attempting to control it. Most sociologists see deviance as a learned response to the environment.

Motivational theorist Robert Merton argued that some people are encouraged to achieve but do not have the tools to succeed, so they use deviant ways to reach their goals. For example, if poor children see wealth as desirable but cannot acquire it, they may turn to illegal means such as

Connections

How did Freud explain aggressive behaviour? (See Chapter 4, page 75.)

Figure 15–4

Paul Bernardo, one of Canada's most notorious murderers. Could his actions have been predicted by his physical characteristics, as Lombroso suggested? Or is Bernardo's deviant behaviour due to heredity, a personality disorder or socialization?

theft. Critics say that the motivation theory does not explain why most people, rich or poor, struggle to succeed in socially accepted ways rather than use deviant methods to achieve their goals. Others point out that criminal behaviour occurs in all social classes, and that wealthy people engage in many types of deviant behaviour, from tax evasion to crimes of passion.

Learning theorists claim that people learn deviant behaviour in the same way they learn acceptable behaviour—from others such as family, friends or co-workers. For example, if you work for a company whose values dictate that profits must be made at any cost, even through unlawful or dishonest means, then you may acquire this belief and act accordingly. Learning theory emphasizes the importance of others in our lives, especially the groups we belong to, since the norms of that group will eventually become our own. On the other hand, critics of this approach point out that we tend to associate with those who support our ideas in the first place.

Control theorists hold the view that people display deviant behaviour if they experience an absence of social control, and if the rewards for such behaviour are more certain than the punishment. One version of this theory suggests that all people occasionally find deviance tempting. But thinking about how others will respond stops some individuals from acting on their impulses; those with weak social bonds or few conventional values may feel free to break the rules. Another version of the control theory states that people with low self-control will try to get what they want quickly and easily without thinking of others. This theory emphasizes the importance of socialization—families teaching children to develop self-control. These children will continue to show self-control as adults because they incorporate what they learn into their daily lives and will not risk losing their social ties.

Labelling theorists examine the effect of automatically defining people in a particular way. Authority figures such as psychiatrists or police officers may assign labels, as will family, friends and co-workers. Calling someone's behaviour "criminal," "immoral" or "mentally ill" may encourage others to treat that person according to the label, whether or not the label is fair. In time, the individual may accept this definition and may actually increase the behaviour associated with the label. For example, research showed that young males who belonged to a gang in a small town were treated more harshly when they came into contact with the law. The townspeople assumed they were bad even when there was no indication of wrongdoing. The gang's subsequent deviant behaviour became a self-fulfilling prophecy.

self-fulfilling prophecy— making something happen because it was expected or foretold

Activities

Understand Ideas

1. Using examples for each, define the three levels of social norms.

2. Explain the difference between deviance and diversity. Provide examples to illustrate the difference.

Think and Evaluate

3. Use examples to show how you would distinguish between deviance and non-conformity.

4. In groups of four or five, rate the deviance of the following activities according to the degree to which they cause harm to society. Use a table with the title "Degrees of Social Harm," and include the following headings: Little, Moderate, Serious. Post your table in the classroom and be prepared to defend your decisions.
   - excessive drinking
   - cheating on income tax
   - smoking cigarettes
   - armed robbery
   - child abuse
   - driving without a licence
   - habitual lying
   - smoking marijuana
   - murder
   - pollution
   - reckless driving
   - sexual assault
   - drug addiction
   - excessive gambling
   - knowingly buying stolen goods
   - mugging someone
   - panhandling
   - treason
   - shoplifting
   - vandalism

Apply Your Learning

5. Identify at least two examples of abnormal behaviour (see Chapter 5) that would also be considered deviant. Choose at least two examples of abnormal behaviour that are not deviant. Explain your choices.

6. You and your friends go the mall.
   a) You witness your best friend stealing a pair of sunglasses. What should you do? If you do not say or do anything, are you complying with deviant behaviour?
   b) What consequences do you recommend for your friend? Explain your answer.

Social Control

Focus Questions

What is social control?

What is the difference between informal and formal social control?

How is the Canadian criminal justice system structured?

If you skip along the sidewalk whistling a happy tune, people may stare at you. If you play loud music late at night, neighbours may complain. In each of these cases, deviant behaviour is met by a reaction that sociologists call social control. **Social control** can be defined as the methods used by society to ensure conformity to social norms. Just as there are many kinds of deviant behaviours, there are many kinds of social control.

Informal Social Control

Most social control occurs informally in everyday interactions with others and through our own sense of right and wrong. This is the most powerful

Figure 15–5

The parents of this 13-year-old boy insisted that he wear a sign in a Regina shopping mall after he was caught shoplifting. Do you think this kind of social control is fair? Would it be effective?

Connections

How is Freud's concept of the superego a form of social control? (See Chapter 4, page 75.)

kind of informal social control. At one time or another, we may have stopped doing something because we wondered, "What would other people think?" Informal social control prevents deviance most effectively when it works through self-control, which often begins with the family. Children learn not to pull the cat's tail and that food is supposed to go into the mouth, not on the floor. As they grow older, they learn how to relate to others and how to behave according to the norms of the culture.

Formal Social Control

Anthropologists have always been interested in the subject of social order in various societies. They have found that laws represent the most formal kind of social control. Historical archaeologists, who study ancient documents, have traced the development of written law through time. It seems that when societies grew and became socially diversified, conflicts had to be resolved more formally. For example, the ancient Romans developed written laws to rule an empire of many different cultures. Roman law was the same for everyone around the Mediterranean world; it was enforced by the Roman courts, administrators and military. From the seventeenth century on, the Ashanti of West Africa also ruled an empire using a legal code based on respect for ancestors.

In modern times, formal social controls play a crucial role in large, complex societies where informal or community controls are no longer effective. In Canada, these responses to deviant behaviour are written down in the form of laws and are applied equally throughout society. If you have ever been given a parking ticket or had your behaviour discussed by a school official, you are aware of the nature of formal social controls. These laws are essential when controlling serious forms of deviance that violate important social values, cause harm to others or threaten the social order. Reactions to these offences are carried out by organizations such as

What Happens If You Rock the Boat?

Try doing something that breaks an informal social norm that is not harmful to you or others. Notice the reactions of those around you. What informal social controls are they using to respond to your actions? Would these controls discourage you from repeating this behaviour? Why or why not?

Here are some ideas to get you started:

- taking up two seats on a crowded bus
- standing too close to people as you talk to them
- walking against the flow of traffic in the hallway or on a busy sidewalk
- standing still in the middle of a busy street, watching the sky
- singing in public
- avoiding people's eyes when you talk to them
- reading a book at a party or other social gathering

Share your experiences by reporting your findings to the class.

police forces, law courts, prisons, psychiatric hospitals, Children's Aid Societies and parole systems.

In Canada, laws are made by parliaments at both the federal and provincial levels. The two major branches of law are criminal law and civil law. Criminal courts handle crimes—actions that are considered serious threats to society as a whole, such as assault, theft or murder. Civil law regulates relations and conflicts between individuals or groups and issues such as marriage, divorce or breach of contract. For example, if someone has a grievance against another citizen or business, he or she can sue in a civil court. At the municipal level, cities and towns make bylaws for local issues such as parking, garbage disposal or smoking in restaurants.

parole systems—the process of releasing and monitoring prisoners before the sentences have expired, on condition of lawful behaviour

assault—a violent physical attack causing bodily harm

breach of contract—the failure to fulfill a legal obligation

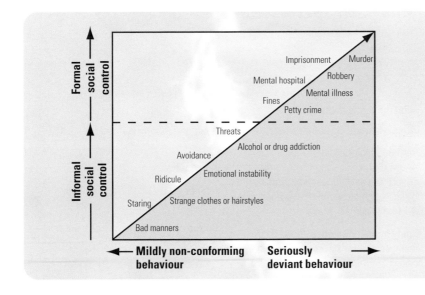

Figure 15–6

This diagram illustrates the types of social control that are used for varying degrees of deviant behaviour. The more serious the deviance, the more formal the social control. Do you think that the social controls shown here are effective?

The Criminal Justice System

The criminal justice system is society's formal response to crime. The major elements of the criminal justice system are the police, the judicial system (courts) and the penal system (prisons). The sociology of law is concerned largely with how each of these branches of criminal justice carries out its role.

The Police

The function of the police is to maintain public order by enforcing the law. Police have the task of recognizing criminal activity, apprehending suspects and turning them over to the judicial system. However, police forces could not possibly monitor the activities of all potential lawbreakers without seriously compromising individual liberty. Also, they have limited

Figure 15–7

These guidelines are used to train police officers in how to respond to a suspect. The inner disk describes the suspect's behaviour, and the outside ring corresponds to the appropriate use of force by an officer.

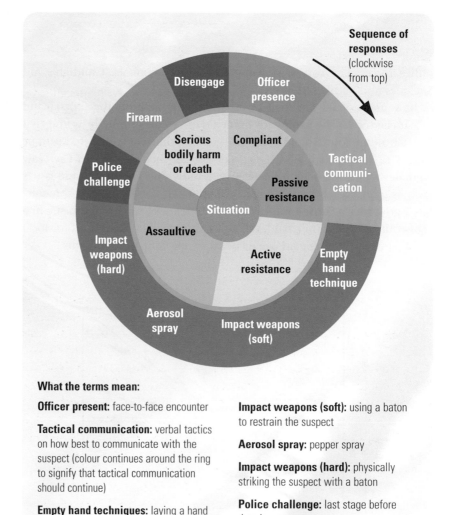

What the terms mean:

Officer present: face-to-face encounter

Tactical communication: verbal tactics on how best to communicate with the suspect (colour continues around the ring to signify that tactical communication should continue)

Empty hand techniques: laying a hand or arm on the suspect, or subduing with hands

Impact weapons (soft): using a baton to restrain the suspect

Aerosol spray: pepper spray

Impact weapons (hard): physically striking the suspect with a baton

Police challenge: last stage before drawing a weapon

resources, so they must direct their efforts in areas that the public feels are the highest priorities. For example, youth gang activity has attracted a lot of attention recently, while at other times the police have focused on drug trafficking or street prostitution.

Because police must often use their discretion in deciding whether to make an arrest, they sometimes come under scrutiny for how they enforce the law and whether they do so in a fair and equitable way. For example, one study showed that police were more likely to make an arrest if a victim demanded it, if they already knew the suspect or if a crowd was gathering. Deciding how to enforce the law is always an important issue in democratic societies. In Canada, the police carry weapons and use force under certain circumstances. If it appears that an officer has used excessive force, he or she may be brought to trial.

Figure 15–8

To the general public, police are often the most obvious kind of formal social control.

The Judicial System

The innocence or guilt of those arrested by police is determined by the courts. All parties involved must follow strict rules of court procedure, a process developed through centuries of constant change. The defendant is considered innocent until proven guilty and has the right to retain a lawyer, to call witnesses and to confront the accuser. The prosecutor in all criminal cases is the monarch (Queen or King), who is represented by Crown lawyers. The defence and the prosecution attempt to convince the court that the accused person is, or is not, guilty as charged. The role of the judge is to see that legal procedures are followed. The judge or jury will determine if the evidence warrants a guilty verdict.

Despite these careful precautions, several cases of people who have been wrongly convicted have come to light in the past few years. Donald Marshall served 11 years for murder in a federal penitentiary until he was cleared and released in 1983. David Milgaard was imprisoned for 22 years for a murder he did not commit. Milgaard was finally released in 1992 by the Supreme Court of Canada, but was not fully cleared until five years later when DNA testing proved his innocence. For many, these cases reinforce arguments against restoring capital punishment, which was abolished in Canada on July 14, 1976. On that date, federal lawmakers replaced capital punishment with a life sentence of 25 years without the possibility of parole. By comparison, capital punishment in the United States is determined by state laws, not federal law. The United States is the only Western industrialized society that still routinely executes serious offenders.

Another issue that concerns people about the court system is the fact that a disproportionate number of Aboriginal people occupy Canadian prisons. Aboriginals make up just 3 percent of the general population but 12 to17 percent of the prison population. These figures cause some individuals to raise the issue of possible bias. They question whether the police are more likely to arrest Aboriginal suspects and whether judges are

DNA testing—analyzing material that carries genetic information to the cell; this procedure can eliminate the accused as a suspect

capital punishment—death penalty for a capital offence such as murder

bias—stemming from prejudice, an unfair act or policy that prevents impartial judgment

Figure 15–9

An Aboriginal healing circle meets to discuss an appropriate response to a 20-year-old shoplifter. How does this approach compare with the one shown in Figure 15–5 (page 314)?

Connections

What can be done to eliminate possible bias in the criminal justice system? (See Chapter 11, pages 232–233.)

more apt to find them guilty. Because of these concerns, efforts are being made to find alternatives to prison sentences. Many Aboriginal communities form healing circles where victims, elders, judges, lawyers and other concerned members of the community gather to decide how to help both victims and offenders in the healing process. This method of social control also determines penalties and encourages offenders to make amends and to change their behaviour.

The Penal System

Those found guilty of a criminal offence may face a range of consequences: a suspended sentence (no penalty imposed), community work or imprisonment. Sentencing can be imposed to punish or rehabilitate the offender, or to protect society. The following section looks more closely at the goals and types of punishment used in the Canadian criminal justice system.

Activities

Understand Ideas

1. Provide examples to show how you would distinguish between informal and formal social controls.

2. Draw a concept map to illustrate the elements of the Canadian criminal justice system.

Think and Evaluate

3. Why do you think police activities are subject to such close attention by society? Do you believe that the police warrant such intense scrutiny? Why or why not?

Research and Evaluate

4. Conduct an informal poll among people your age to determine their degree of confidence in the Canadian justice system—police, courts and prisons. What areas do they think need improvement? Do they feel that bias exists in the system? Compare your results.

5. Visit a courtroom and observe a trial in session. Prepare a written report of your observations including whatever information you can gather about the charge, the accused, the witnesses, the evidence you heard and the judge's options for sentencing. (See Skill Focus, page 13.)

Punishment and Its Goals

Until modern times, punishments handed out by formal courts and judges were often extreme. Police forces were usually small and unable to catch many criminals, so it was hoped that harsh and public punishment would prevent further crime. In eighteenth- and nineteenth-century England, public hanging was a common way to deal with more than a hundred offences, including pickpocketing. Ironically, the crowds at public hangings often lost wallets and purses, as pickpockets took advantage of the large gathering of people whose attention was elsewhere.

Debates about appropriate punishments for crimes are based on assumptions about the purpose of punishment. For example, if punishment is aimed at social protection, its goal is to ensure the safety of society by removing offenders from the community. Sometimes repeat offenders can be kept in prison indefinitely. In most cases, however, they are released after serving a portion of their sentence. Early release, which some people fear actually threatens the safety of the community, usually depends on the offence and the behaviour of the prisoner while serving time.

Protecting members of society, however, is not the only reason for punishing offenders. Another reason is **retribution,** the belief that a wrong done by an individual should be met with an equivalent form of suffering—"an eye for an eye." Victims' rights groups insist that the current justice system does not take the issue of punishment seriously enough, so some people use retribution to justify a return to the death penalty for murder. Supporters of the death penalty believe that it serves another purpose as well—**deterrence,** the attempt to prevent further criminal behaviour through punishment. In general, deterrence focuses on setting an example to discourage criminals from re-offending and to prevent others from committing similar crimes. Some societies still perform executions publicly as a deterrent to others.

Rehabilitation is the view that the offender can be brought back into society through education, therapy or a positive, supportive environment. The goal of rehabilitation arose in the nineteenth century when social scientists realized the effects of social conditions on human behaviour. Many sociologists and psychologists still believe that criminal behaviour is the result of unfavourable childhood experiences. As critics of the prison system, they argue that instead of offering prisoners the opportunity to rehabilitate, incarceration may even encourage them to re-offend once they are released. This view is shared by members of the Aboriginal community who emphasize rehabilitation as an important goal in the Aboriginal healing circles mentioned in the previous section on page 318.

Focus Questions

What are the goals of punishment?

Why are young offenders treated differently from adults?

How effective are prisons as a form of social control?

What are the alternatives to prison?

incarceration—imprisonment

Figure 15–10

Locking prisoners into pillories or stocks was a common punishment in earlier times. Why were such punishments carried out in public?

Getting Tough on Youth Crime Doesn't Pay

The following article was written by Michele Landsberg, a well-known newspaper columnist. What position does she take on dealing with youth crime?

Kimberly, 14, a young prostitute who was arrested and is now trying to put her life back together, stands right at the heart of a Canadian contradiction. This vulnerable kid with the street-smart veneer has been "sexually, emotionally and physically abused." She was a street prostitute from the age of 11 and was first dragged before the courts for the theft of a $1.50 ring. From then on, it was a downward spiral of breached probation, group home, running away, more court appearances. In other words: Kimberly, having suffered grievous abuse, was criminalized.

An overwhelming majority of Canadians, when asked, think that we should get really tough on youth crime. Send them to boot camp! Throw away the key. Do the crime, serve the time... Here's the contradiction at the heart of our Canadian conversation on crime: an overwhelming majority of "youth criminals" are the Kimberlys of this world. Who among us, having heard Kimberly's story, would advocate harsh punishments for her?

There is no youth crime wave, as I heard again and again from weary court officials and youth lawyers: almost all the young offenders who come before the courts are there for incredibly petty offences. With boys, the charges often start with a rougher kind of mischief—intimidating classmates, a hallway punch-up, petty drug offences. Quite often, the veneer crumbles in court. Far from "laughing" at the supposedly feeble provisions of the Young Offenders Act, the boys are scared and many cry. Few are accompanied by parents.

Recently, Statistics Canada reported that nearly one-third of sex assault victims are children under 12, and nearly two-thirds are under 18. Many of these are the youngsters who, if they have no family support, rebel, run away and end up in court—often to be ordered back to their abusive homes. They run again, breaking the court order and bingo: they're young offenders. Then what do we do? Punish them more and harder?

We do know what works. There are exciting innovations, elsewhere, in "restorative justice," where victim confronts perpetrator in a non-legal setting. Very early educational enrichment works. Parenting centres, extra school staff for faltering kids, intensive therapy programs all help. Stability helps, but that takes good pay for devoted children's aid and group-home counsellors. Housing and welfare for abused teens, community schools and job training adapted for difficult youth—not headline material, maybe, but it all works.

What Do You Think?

1. What do you think Michele Landsberg believes is the purpose of punishment?

2. Do you agree with the writer's opinion about society's response to youth crime? Why or why not?

3. Write a response to the article from the point of view of someone who wants tougher laws for young offenders. Which of the goals of punishment do you think this person would support?

Youth Crime

Young people who break the law are usually subject to less severe penalties than adults. According to the Young Offenders Act, children under 12 cannot be brought to trial. Those 12 to 17 years of age are tried in youth court, where the maximum penalty is five years in custody. Their identity cannot be published, and imprisonment is seen as the last resort. The principle behind these lighter sentences is that young people are thought to bear less responsibility for their actions because they do not have the experience in making decisions that adults do. Also, because of their youth, they may have a better chance of reforming, especially if they are kept away from older criminals.

However, many citizens' groups have called for tougher laws against youth crime. Some people feel that the law is too lenient to act as a real deterrent. Responding to these concerns, recent changes in the law make it easier to transfer serious cases involving teenagers from youth court to regular court, where they face the same penalties as adults. As an alternative, some jurisdictions have set up facilities called "boot camps," using strict discipline, physical exercise and a regimented daily timetable to reform young offenders. Proponents of boot camps claim that tough punishment will prevent reoccurrence, although the evidence to support this assumption is debatable.

Some psychologists and sociologists believe in exploring more creative solutions. After all, if the source of juvenile crime often lies in the social circumstances of the child's life, they argue, it might be better to focus on rehabilitation rather than on punishment.

Figure 15–11

An inmate at a boot camp scales a wall during obstacle-course training. Do you think boot camps serve as an appropriate and effective punishment for young offenders?

Is Youth Crime on the Rise?

Some people believe that the number of crimes committed by adolescents is increasing. Figure 15–12 on the following page compares adult and youth crime in Canada from 1995 to 1999. What conclusions can you draw from these statistics?

Another interesting way to examine youth-crime statistics is to compare the types of sentences handed down by the courts. In youth court, a sentence is called a disposition. Dispositions can serve as a type of social control, imposing consequences in order to control and, hopefully, change deviant behaviour. Figure 15–13 lists the number of cases heard in Canadian youth courts from 1994 to 1999, according to the type of disposition. Which years had the highest and lowest number of dispositions in total? What kind of disposition was handed down most often?

Connections

How has media attention on school violence influenced our perception of youth crime? (See Chapter 12, page 257.)

Youths and adults charged in criminal incidents, 1995–1999

All offences	1995	1996	1997	1998	1999
Adults	454 465	454 971	429 898	427 608	426 838
Male	376 269	376 236	355 032	352 639	352 540
Female	78 196	78 735	74 868	74 969	74 298
Youths	128 809	128 542	120 208	117 542	111 474
Male	101 407	100 654	93 674	91 116	86 484
Female	27 402	27 888	26 534	26 426	24 990
Violent crime					
Adults	117 409	117 246	115 095	113 498	111 379
Youths	22 441	22 521	22 172	22 195	21 081
Property crime					
Adults	159 128	162 946	147 849	141 246	133 067
Youths	68 105	66 702	58 340	54 104	48 415

Source: Statistics Canada, Catalogue no. 85-205-XIB, CANSIM, Matrices 2198 and 2199, updated November 30, 2000.

Figure 15–12 ▲
Does the information shown here support the popular idea that youth crime is on the rise?

Cases heard by youth courts according to disposition, 1994–1999

Dispositions	Cases in 1994–1995	Cases in 1996–1997	Cases in 1998–1999
All dispositions	76 969	74 797	71 961
Secure custody	11 616	11 772	12 312
Open custody	13 596	13 506	12 857
Probation	35 627	37 960	34 451
Fine	4 472	3 574	4 081
Community service	4 866	4 594	4 988
Absolute discharge	2 413	1 464	1 130
Other dispositions[1]	4 379	1 927	2 142

Figure 15–13 ▶
Which type of disposition do you think is most effective? Why?

[1]Includes restitution, prohibition, compensations, apologies, essays, counselling programs and conditional discharges.

Source: Statistics Canada, Catalogue no. 85-002-XIE, CANSIM, Matrix 8907, 2000.

Prisons as Social Control

Until the early nineteenth century, punishment for crime included imprisonment, hanging or exile to colonies such as the Americas or Australia. In the nineteenth century, more prisons were built as an efficient way to punish, discipline and rehabilitate criminals. They also served as a way to remove dangerous offenders from society. In modern

Unit 3: Social Structures and Institutions

Writing a Position Paper

A position paper is an opportunity to state your point of view about an issue, with the aim of persuading the reader to agree with you.

Here's How

A well-known criminal lawyer was asked to present his position on capital punishment. He replied: "I oppose capital punishment. I oppose it for three main reasons." In this terse opening, he provided his point of view and indicated how he would organize his arguments. He then went on to explain the three reasons, using facts and logical arguments to support them. His approach is the one to follow when writing a position paper.

1. **Introduction**
   - Clearly identify the issue. An issue is a question that has at least two possible answers, for example, "Should Canada reinstate capital punishment?"

   - Determine your point of view or position on the issue. State it simply and clearly.

2. **Body**
   - Find out how much research you are expected to do. Follow the guidelines on page 73.

   - Decide on the main arguments you will use to defend your position. Support each argument with factual evidence, examples or other information. For instance, you might write the following: "There is always the danger of executing the wrong person. Donald Marshall, David Milgaard and Guy Paul Morin were all wrongfully convicted of murder. Had the death penalty been imposed, innocent people would have been executed."

   - If you are using statistics, be sure to review the guidelines on pages 147 and 155.

   - Write your arguments out in a logical and convincing way. Each argument may consist of one or more paragraphs, depending on its complexity. Do not put more than one argument in a paragraph. (See Skill Focus, page 115.)

   - Organize your arguments in the most effective way possible. Sometimes you will choose a logical order based on time or sequence of events. At other times, you may wish to save your best argument for last, for maximum impact. In the case of our example of a paper on capital punishment, you should use your second-best argument first and the other arguments in between.

3. **Conclusion**
   - Conclude with a paragraph that sums up your main arguments and restates your position.

4. **Presentation**
   - Check and correct your grammar, punctuation and spelling.

   - For the body of your paper, use 12-point type, double-spaced with a 2.5-cm margin.

   - Add a cover page with the title and your name centred in the top third of the page, along with the course, teacher and date centred in the bottom third of the page.

Practise It

Choose a controversial issue that grabs your attention and is related to this chapter. You may wish to use the topic of capital punishment as in the example above. Following the guidelines in this Skill Focus, write and submit your position paper.

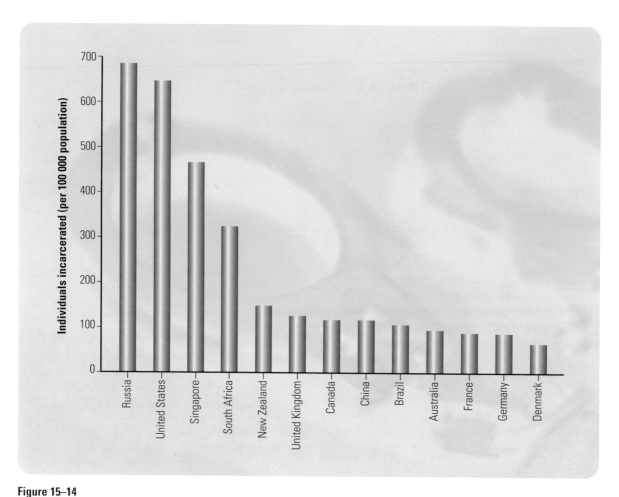

Figure 15–14

An international comparison of incarceration rates, 1997–1998. This graph illustrates the degree to which different countries use prison as a form of social control.

repressive—keeping people under tight control, preventing normal growth and development

times, prison populations have been expanding in many Western nations. As the bar graph in Figure 15–14 shows, in Canada there are about 115 people in prison for every 100 000 adults. Although this is less than one-quarter of the rate in the United States, it is higher than the rate in most European nations. Remember, this increase in prison populations does not necessarily reflect an increase in crime rates; it simply indicates the growing use of prisons as a form of social control.

How effective are prisons in dealing with criminal behaviour? Critics say that prisons are ineffective, inefficient, costly and repressive. By depriving inmates of their liberty, prisons do succeed in exacting retribution and in protecting society from criminals, at least for as long as prisoners are kept in custody. However, the **recidivism** rate, that is, the rate at which criminals repeat their offences and return to prison, can be as high as 80 percent, casting doubt on the deterrent effect of incarceration. Furthermore, critics claim little is done in prisons to prepare inmates to survive and function in society. Others ask why an expensive option like imprisonment is used for non-violent offenders when these individuals could be contributing to society in some way to pay for their actions.

Alternatives to Prison

In Canada, keeping a person in prison for a year costs about $44 000. As governments search for ways to cut public spending, less expensive modes of social control are likely to develop, such as returning criminals to the community while monitoring their every move electronically. As we discussed on page 318, Aboriginal groups are trying to replace prison sentences with healing circles, an approach that focuses on rehabilitation and a healing process for both victim and offender.

Other alternatives to prison sentences also exist, such as those listed in Figure 15–13, which shows disposition options for young offenders. Fines are sometimes levied for traffic violations and minor offences. Community service may replace prison terms for non-violent or first-time offenders who are required to work for a prescribed number of hours in the community, usually at tasks related to the nature of the offence. For example, someone with a conviction for possessing an illegal drug might be sentenced to speak about drugs to young people in schools. **Probation** allows the person convicted of a crime to stay in the community, subject to conditions such as visiting a probation officer and remaining in a certain area. If these conditions are not met, the probation period may be converted into a prison term.

Putting Out the Fires in Their Hearts

Non-violent ways of dealing with criminals have been used in some traditional cultures. Ella Deloria was a Native American anthropologist who grew up on a reserve during the 1890s. She published studies that examined traditional Aboriginal cultures in North America. In this example, a young Sioux murderer is brought before the community to be sentenced.

The angry relatives debated the kind of punishment that would fit the crime while the wise elder listened. After a good while he began to speak: "My Brothers and Cousins, my Sons and Nephews, we have been caused to weep without shame. No wonder we are enraged, for our pride and honour have been grossly violated. Why shouldn't we go out then and give the murderer what he deserves?"

Then, after an ominous pause, he suddenly shifted. "And yet, my Kinsmen, there is a better way!" Slowly and clearly he explained the better way. It was also the hard way, but the only certain way to put out the fire in their hearts and in the murderer's heart as well: "Each of you bring to me the thing you prize the most. These things shall be a token of our intention. We shall give them to the murderer who has hurt us, and he shall thereby become a relative in place of him who is gone. And from now on, he shall be one of us, and our endless concern shall be to regard him as though he were truly our loved one come back to us."

The Slayer was brought to the council not knowing what his fate was going to be, but the council's speaker offered him the sacred pipe saying, "Smoke now with your new relatives, for they have chosen to take you to themselves in place

Connections

Why can some alternatives to prison be considered examples of operant conditioning? (See Chapter 3, page 55.)

CASE STUDY

1. What treatment did the offender receive for his crime?

2. Why did the community deal with the offender in this way?

3. Do you think that this method of social control will help to prevent future crime in the community? Why or why not?

of one who is not here. It is their heart's wish that you shall become one of them: you shall go out and come in without fear. Be confident that their love and compassion which were his are now yours forever." And during that speech, tears trickled down the murderer's face. He had been trapped by loving kinship, and you can be sure that he made an even better relative than many who are related by blood, because he had been bought at such a price.

From *Speaking of Indians* by Ella C. Deloria

Activities

Understand Ideas

1. Identify the major goals of punishment. Provide an example of the type of punishment that could be used to meet each goal.

2. What other factors determine the type of punishment imposed?

Think and Evaluate

3. a) According to your own point of view, rank (in order of importance) the goals of punishment you identified in Activity 1. Provide arguments to support your position.

b) Should the goals of punishment change for violent crimes and for repeat offenders? Why or why not?

4. Do you believe that young offenders who commit serious crimes should be treated more leniently than adult offenders? Defend your view.

Apply Your Learning

5. In groups of four or five, brainstorm the possible kinds of punishment that courts can issue. You may wish to use the Internet to consult the Criminal Code. What appears to be the goal of each of these kinds of punishment?

6. Recent statistics show that youth crime may be decreasing. What could account for this trend?

Research and Communicate

7. As a class, debate this issue: Boot camps are effective ways of reducing youth crime. Review the Skill Focus for conducting a debate in Chapter 14, page 302.

8. Research the success rate of Canadian prisons. Do prisons reform inmates? Which approaches taken by prison officials appear to have some benefit? Document your findings and describe the research methods you used. Be sure to follow the guidelines in the Skill Focus in Chapter 9, Writing a Social Science Report, page 188.

9. Invite a police officer to speak to your class. Prepare questions about the crimes committed in your community and how criminal activity is controlled.

Key Points

- Every society defines certain behaviour as deviant. Deviance reflects the culture and the times, from opposing social norms to committing serious crimes.

- The causes of deviance can be explained by biological, psychological or sociological theories, which tend to favour either the nature or nurture approach.

- Societies deal with deviance in various ways, depending on the culture, the situation and the seriousness of the offence.

- The Canadian criminal justice system consists of the police, the courts and the prisons.

- The nature of punishment depends on its purpose: protection of society, retribution, deterrence or rehabilitation.

- Young offenders are treated differently from adults because some believe that due to their lack of experience, they are less responsible for their actions and may have a better chance of rehabilitation if they are separated from adult offenders.

- Prison is a costly form of social control, and its effectiveness has mixed results. Some alternatives to prison include electronic monitoring, probation and community service.

Activities

Understand Ideas

1. Create a concept map to describe the biological, psychological and sociological theories used to explain the causes of deviant behaviour.

2. Do you think that deviant behaviour is a product of nature or nurture? Be prepared to support your point of view.

Think and Evaluate

3. Which alternative to prison do you believe is most effective? Why? Which goals of punishment would this method address?

4. Refer to the case study about a Sioux community (pages 325–326). Do you think this way of dealing with criminals could be used in Canadian society? Why or why not?

Apply Your Learning

5. a) Obtain a copy of your school's code of behaviour. Complete a PMI (Plus, Minus, Interesting) using a minimum of three points per category.

   b) With a partner, create a revised code of behaviour for your school. Present your code to the class, highlighting the changes you have made. Discuss which social norms you are protecting and which social controls you are using. Does your code include methods of punishment? Why or why not?

Research and Communicate

6. a) When determining the effectiveness of a justice system, what criteria would you use?

   b) Interview a criminal lawyer to investigate the effectiveness of the Canadian justice system, using your criteria as a basis for your discussion. Also ask about possible bias in the police force or in the courts. Prepare your questions in advance and review the guidelines in Chapter 1 for conducting an interview (page 12).

   c) Report your findings to the class.

7. Prepare a position paper on supporting or opposing the electronic monitoring of convicted criminals. Be sure to follow the guidelines of the Skill Focus on page 323, Writing a Position Paper.

Recreation and Health

Key Terms

leisure

recreation

play

sport

health

life expectancy

health-care systems

anorexia nervosa

bulimia

sexually transmitted diseases

euthanasia

he social sciences study all aspects of life, including everyday activities and concerns such as recreation and leisure, play and sports, illness and health. In this chapter we will consider recreation and health. While we investigate each aspect of life independently, we will also show how they are connected in a number of ways.

In which activities do you take part most often? Rank the following from most often to least often. Now divide the activities. Which would you classify as recreation and which as health? Do any of them belong on more than one list?

• playing a sport

• praying privately

• playing computer games

• watching sports

• participating in a hobby

• reading books or magazines

• exercising

• watching television

• spending time with family or friends

• listening to music

In a 1995 survey, 41 percent of Canadians said they played sport for recreation while 93 percent said they relaxed by listening to music. How do these results compare with your and your classmates' activities?

Recreation and Leisure

Most Canadians relax and enjoy themselves during their **leisure** or free time—time away from work, school and family or social responsibilities. **Recreation** is what we do for entertainment and enjoyment in our free time. Some people play a sport, listen to music, go to movies, watch television or spend time with their family and friends. Leisure-time activities and recreation can vary from culture to culture, even from individual to individual. The list of activities at the beginning of this chapter is only a small indication of the many ways people can use their leisure time.

Play

What we do for recreation can also be called **play.** We usually associate play with having fun, but anthropologists have described play as a kind of openness because it involves new and creative ways of doing something. It is possible that play encourages the release of chemicals, such as endorphins, that make us feel good. All mammals play, especially young ones.

Anthropologists suggest several reasons for this behaviour. Their research shows that young animals play because they need to practise their survival skills such as fighting, running and hunting. Similarly, for humans, play can be rehearsal for real-life roles. For example, children often play "house" pretending to be mothers or fathers, or they pretend to work as firefighters, doctors, teachers or other roles they may fill in the future. Play also helps children learn important social skills. When they play games, for instance, they must learn to co-operate with others if they want to be accepted into that game. Play also helps humans develop mentally because it stimulates the imagination. Through games, children are free to express their attitudes and feelings about certain situations. According to some research, play can even help repair developmental problems caused by injury.

Focus Questions

How do Canadians spend their leisure time?

Why is play an important part of our lives?

Connections

Which of Maslow's hierarchy of needs are fulfilled by recreation? (See Chapter 4, page 81.)

Bengal tiger playing with stick

Children participating in the Toy of the Year Awards

Figure 16–1

Whether alone or in groups, humans and other mammals have a need to play.

Sport

Focus Questions

What is sport?

How has sport changed over time in our culture?

How does sport reflect the culture in which it is played?

Connections

How might participating in sports help to alleviate stress? (See Chapter 5, pages 95–96.)

Sport is a particular form of play that requires physical exertion and involves a competition between individuals or teams. The competition is governed by rules that set out the goal of the game and acceptable methods to achieve that goal. For the most part, sport requires skill and endurance. Some players develop superior skills that make them stars and set them apart from other players. Many Canadians are involved in team sports, such as hockey, soccer, basketball and baseball, while others enjoy individual sports such as running, cycling, hiking, skiing or golfing.

Certain people are attracted to sports that are dangerous, even life-threatening, because these activities test their skill, endurance and strength more than other sports. People who engage in sky-diving, mountain climbing, auto racing or hang-gliding often describe their experiences as thrilling and exciting. Some sports even pit humans against animals. In Spain and Portugal, for example, bullfighting is a long-standing sport and cultural tradition. Bullfighters are regarded as courageous and talented athletes. In the North American west, rodeos are popular events that involve traditional activities such as bull riding, calf roping and other challenging skills that were traditionally cowboy activities.

Sport and Culture

In the late nineteenth century amateur sports became popular in schools and universities in many countries, mostly for people in the middle and upper classes. Involvement in sports was seen as a way of building character by developing a sense of fair play, stamina and healthy competition.

Figure 16–2

Bull runners, wearing traditional red-and-white costumes, participate in the annual "running of the bulls" in Pamplona, Spain. Why do you think some people are attracted to this kind of dangerous activity?

Is There Too Much Violence in Sports?

Violence in sports, particularly in team sports, has become a common sight for sport fans in Canada and elsewhere. Some hockey players, soccer players and boxers have been charged with assault as a result of their actions during play. Opinions differ as to how violence in sports should be handled. Some people feel that aggression and violence are part of sport, and players who break the rules and use excessive force should be punished only according to the rules of the game. Other people argue that violence in sports should be treated as violence in society and that violent players should face the penalties set out in the law.

The following letter to the editor appeared in *The Toronto Star* in response to a story about a hockey incident in 1972. Do you agree with this reader's opinion?

I am shocked that your sports columnist Mary Ormsby would think that all Canadians "cheered" when hockey player Bobby Clarke deliberately broke Valerei Kharmalov's ankle during the famous 1972 Canada-Russia series.

Personally, as a Canadian, I was ashamed.

At the time, Kharmalov was arguably the greatest hockey player in the world, and with him on the ice the Canadians may never have prevailed. And it was offensive when instead of finally apologizing, Clarke recently had the audacity to boast (with a smile no less) on national TV that his actions at the time were, in fact, quite deliberate. I wonder what kind of a message he thought he was sending out to all the young hockey players watching.

Many true hockey fans have never respected Bobby Clarke or admired the legendary goon tactics of his Philadelphia Flyers that have permanently scarred "the greatest game on earth."

Far from a hero, Clarke should go down in NHL history as an embarrassment and a disgrace to the hockey community at large.

The following excerpt, from the *Encyclopedia of World Sports*, presents a different view on violence in sports. This view suggests that violence is an inherent part of some sports but excessive violence may be the result of social expectations and financial pressures.

All sports are inherently competitive and hence conducive to aggression and violence; however, in some, such as boxing, rugby, soccer and American football, violence and intimidation in the form of a "play fight" or "mock battle" between two individuals or groups are central ingredients. Such sports involve the socially acceptable, ritualized expression of violence, but just as real battles that take place in war can involve a ritual component, so these mock battles that take place on a sports field can involve elements of, or be transformed into, non-ritual violence. This may occur when, perhaps as a result of social pressures or the financial and prestige rewards involved, people participate too seriously.

What Do You Think?

1. Do you agree with the position taken in the letter to the editor on violence in hockey?

2. Do you think that violence is a necessary part of sports?

3. Do you think that violence in sports is glorified?

4. What should be done when one player deliberately injures another in a sporting event?

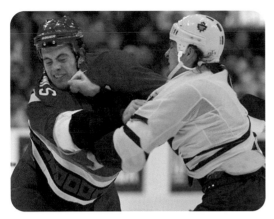

Figure 16–3

Does violence in professional sports reflect or influence basic cultural values? Explain.

The revival of the Olympic games in 1896 was also a boost to amateur sports at that time.

Sport as a major professional institution, with paid players, did not develop until the late nineteenth and early twentieth centuries. Equipment and rules became standardized, and national leagues were set up in such team sports as football, hockey and basketball. During the 1920s, professional sports grew rapidly with the development of mass media, such as radio and movies. By the late twentieth century, televised sporting events raised interest and the economic value of sports to an even greater degree. Today, most professional players are highly paid for their talents. Sport is not just a game to these players; it is work. Coaches, trainers and others who assist the players also work in sports.

Sport often reflects the basic values of the culture in which it is played. For example, English missionaries introduced cricket to the Trobriand Islands in the early twentieth century. By the late twentieth century, the islanders had made it into a different game. In their culture, it had become a substitute for warfare that was played between villages. Instead of 11 players a side, they might have 40, or however many were available to play. The home team always won, but not by much so as not to shame the visitors. People danced and chanted when the players took the field or left it. The chants were comments on current events. The game was accompanied by a ceremonial exchange of food and other goods.

Trobriand Islands—small islands near the island of Papua New Guinea in the south Pacific Ocean

Activities

Understand Ideas

1. Define leisure, recreation and play.

2. a) What are some benefits of play?
   b) Why do humans and other mammals play?

Think and Evaluate

3. All sports are inherently competitive and hence, conducive to aggression and violence. Agree or disagree, giving reasons for your view.

4. What are the social and financial pressures referred to in the quote from the *Encyclopedia of World Sports*?

Research and Communicate

5. a) Ask three children what they play at recess or after school, and why they play the kind of games they do. How do their reasons for play compare with those given in this section?
   b) Ask three of your peers what they consider play. How do they describe play? What reasons do they give for play?
   c) Write a short report describing your findings.

6. Use interview and survey methods to find out how students in your school feel about violence in sport. Report on your findings.

Health

When we speak of **health,** we are usually referring to more than the absence of disease or illness. Health can also refer to a person's physical, mental and social well-being. Social scientists understand that people's health is greatly influenced by society's social conditions.

Health Across Cultures

Social scientists who study the impact of social conditions on the health of a society are known as medical anthropologists. Their research shows that at different periods in history, certain social conditions contributed to certain kinds of illnesses.

- In traditional hunting and gathering cultures, food shortages were a major threat to human health. People were often forced to go for long periods of time without adequate nourishment. Lack of food left people susceptible to infection and injuries. Life was physically very demanding for people in these early societies and few lived past the age of 40. Illnesses were usually treated by a traditional healer, someone seen as having special spiritual powers who used natural remedies to heal the sick.

- As many societies shifted to an agricultural way of life, a regular supply of food became available. People ate better and lived healthier, longer lives. Some agricultural societies, however, had only a narrow range of available food and their diets were often based on one staple such as rice, wheat or potatoes. Only the wealthy could afford a more balanced diet. Infectious diseases became a major cause of illness and death. Some Aboriginal populations in the Americas and elsewhere were completely wiped out by smallpox and other infectious diseases brought over by European explorers and settlers. Aboriginal populations had no immunity against these new diseases, and traditional healing methods failed to stop the spread of these deadly infections.

- During the nineteenth century, as many countries industrialized, overcrowded and filthy living conditions of the working-class neighbourhoods brought on diseases such as typhoid, cholera, diphtheria and tuberculosis. Among poor urban workers in the early period of industrialization, the average **life expectancy** was about 27 years. There was little understanding of the causes of these diseases and few people made the connection between disease and unclean conditions.

In the early 1850s, an English nurse named Florence Nightingale went to help the soldiers who had fought in the Crimean War. She was appalled at the high death rates of wounded soldiers, and at the filth of the hospital. Once she ordered the hospital cleaned up, recovery rates of the injured soldiers soared. By the 1860s medical research discovered that disease was caused and spread by germs developing in unsanitary conditions. Once

staple—chief component

immunity—resistance to infection

life expectancy—the average period that a person might be expected to live under current conditions

Figure 16–4

Life expectancies at birth for selected countries, 1998. Choose one high-ranking country and one low-ranking country. Locate both of these countries in an atlas. From the atlas or an encyclopedia find at least three pieces of data to explain why life expectancy is high in the one country and low in the other.

Life expectancies, 1998

Country	Life Expectancy for Both Sexes (in years)	Country	Life Expectancy for Both Sexes (in years)
Japan	80.0	Costa Rica	75.9
Sweden	79.2	Singapore	78.5
Greece	78.3	Malawi	36.6
Zambia	37.1	Ghana	56.8
Canada	79.2	Germany	77.0
Australia	79.9	Egypt	62.1
Israel	78.4	Ethiopia	40.9
Netherlands	78.0	Haiti	51.4
Pakistan	59.1	Ireland	76.2
United Kingdom	77.2	United States	76.1
France	78.5	Finland	77.2
Kenya	47.6	San Marino	81.4
Spain	77.6	Portugal	75.7

Source: U.S. Census Bureau.

Figure 16–5

A medical worker from the Red Cross inoculates a Rwandan child against measles.

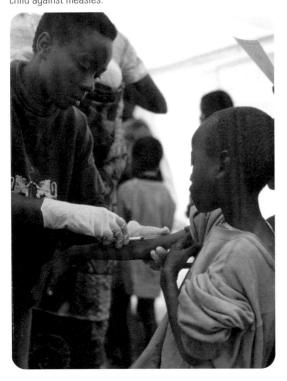

this connection between filth and germs was made, many life-threatening infectious diseases were brought under control through proper sanitation.

During the twentieth century, life expectancy increased steadily in the industrialized nations of the world, including Canada, mostly because of the availability of nutritious food, clean drinking water and proper sanitation. Today, most infectious diseases can be prevented, cured or their progress delayed by medical treatment. The greatest threats to the health of Canadians today are diseases brought on by the environment or by lifestyle, as the article on the next page suggests. Diets high in fats, lack of physical exercise, environmental pollution, smoking, drinking and overexposure to sunlight all contribute to the leading life-threatening illnesses—heart-related diseases and cancer.

In less developed countries, however, poverty remains a major cause of illness. One in five people around the world has a serious illness due to poverty. Life expectancy in the poorest countries in Africa is approximately 40 years. People in these countries suffer from malnutrition, which makes them more susceptible to diseases such as gastroenteritis or measles. In certain parts of Africa, for example, the death rate from measles is a thousand times greater than in North America. Contaminated drinking water also spreads infectious diseases in many developing nations. For example, Schistosomiasis (liver flukes) is a fast-spreading and dangerous parasitic infection spread by snails that live in water.

A Dangerous Lifestyle

Two out of every three Canadians are such couch potatoes they're putting their lives at risk, according to a national health survey. The study found that 63 percent of Canadians were physically active for less than an hour a day. That level of inactivity poses the same health risk as smoking a pack of cigarettes a day, one doctor said.

"Unfortunately we are a nation of sedentary people and we're caught in an unhealthy grip of inertia," said Dr. Nick Busing, president of the College of Family Physicians of Canada, one of the survey's sponsors. He said Canadians must recognize the real physical dangers of the "couch potato" mentality.

The report, also sponsored by the federal and provincial governments, shows that the inactivity of the majority of Canadians is putting them at risk for heart disease, adult-onset diabetes, colon cancer, osteoporosis and depression.

The report found that 25 percent of all deaths due to heart disease in 1993 were a direct result of inactivity and could have been avoided. If Canadians were sufficiently physically active, the savings to the health-care system would be $700 million a year, the report said. "A simple message that any activity is good, but more is better, has got to go out to every Canadian."

Health improvement measures, 1997

	Both Sexes	
	Millions	**Percentage**
Total*	23 420	100
Nothing	12 213	25.1
Increase exercise	6832	29.2
Lose weight	1289	5.5
Improve eating habits	1191	5.1
Quit/reduce smoking	591	2.5
Drink less alcohol	67	0.3
Receive medical treatment	285	1.2
Take vitamins	197	0.8
Other	240	1.0
Not stated	515	2.2

*Population 15 years and older

Source: Statistics Canada, 1997.

gastroenteritis—inflammation of stomach and intestines causing vomiting and diarrhea

CASE STUDY

1. What are the risks involved in having a sedentary lifestyle?

2. How much exercise should a person get in a week?

inertia—a lack of movement

osteoporosis—a condition that causes the bones to become fragile

Figure 16–6

This chart shows the methods Canadians chose to improve their health in 1996–1997. Do you think Canadians are doing enough to improve their fitness?

How Fit Are Canadian Children?

For many Canadians, the lack of fitness among young people has become a serious concern. Do you think fitness is an issue today? Read the following statements. Which of the following do you believe are true?

1. Regular physical activity improves children's mental health, growth and development.

2. The number of Canadian children considered overweight decreased between 1981 and 1996.

3. Regular physical activity has little impact on academic performance.

4. The rate of diabetes among young children is decreasing.

5. Children are 20 percent less active than they were 30 years ago.

6. The average Canadian child watches more than 26 hours of television each week.

7. Percentage of Canadian girls who are overweight is higher than percentage of Canadian boys who are overweight.

8. More students are taken to school and other places by car for convenience and safety.

Answers

1. True. 2. False. Numbers increased by 30% for boys and 24% for girls. 3. False. Physical activity enhances academic performance. 4. False. It is increasing. 5. False. They are 40% less active. 6. True. 7. False. See #2. 8. True.

The Canadian Fitness and Lifestyle Research Institute recommended people do the equivalent of one hour of walking per day, even if it's broken down into 10-minute chunks and consists of alternate activities such as tossing a ball. Those who do more strenuous sweat-breaking exercise would only have to do so three or four times a week to reach the same fitness level. Dr. Andrew Pipe, a physician at the University of Ottawa Heart Institute, said that moderate exertion is enough.

"We are not talking about turning this nation into a team of 30 million marathon runners," he said. "We are urging Canadians of all ages to be active for 30 minutes at least four times a week."

The study found that 66 percent of Canadian women were inactive, compared with 60 percent of men. Two-thirds of children and young people are not active enough to lay a solid foundation for future health and well-being, the study found. It also showed that activity levels increase from east to west, with residents of the Atlantic provinces and Quebec having the lowest levels of healthy activity, and Alberta and British Columbia having the highest. Ontario registered the national average at 63 percent.

From "'Couch Potato' Life Called a Health Risk" by Derek Ferguson

Health Care

Health-care systems have changed drastically in most societies over the past century. At one time, in most industrial countries such as Canada, the

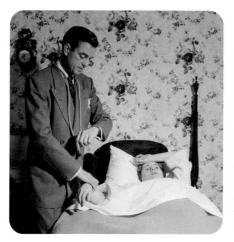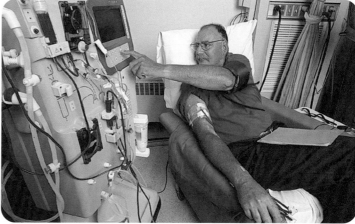

Figure 16–7

Until the 1960s, doctors visited their patients in their homes. Today, many patients are treated in hospitals, where the treatment can be less personal. Scientific discoveries and new technology have greatly improved the treatment of most diseases and illnesses.

family doctor was the mainstay of health care. Doctors usually treated patients at their homes, and a good bed-side manner was important. Information on diseases and medical treatments were limited by today's standards. Hospitals were mostly seen as places where patients went to die.

During the twentieth century, medical discoveries led to treatments and cures that seemed miraculous. Penicillin, the most widely used antibiotic in the world today, for example, was discovered by accident in 1926. Prior to its discovery, a case of pneumonia or a bad throat infection could be life-threatening. The discovery of insulin in 1922, by Canadians Frederick Banting and Charles Best, drastically reduced the number of deaths from diabetes. In the second half of the twentieth century, organ transplants could give people the opportunity to live longer and healthier lives. Laser surgery revolutionized the way surgeons operated. Today, the role of the doctor has changed, with many specializing in a particular area of medicine, such as pediatrics, obstetrics or geriatrics. Many hospitals also specialize in serving particular patients such as cancer patients or children.

pediatrics—field of medicine that specializes in children

obstetrics—field of medicine that specializes in pregnancy and childbirth

geriatrics—field of medicine that specializes in older people

Canada's Health Care

Canada has a **public health-care system,** which means that everyone has access to doctors and hospital facilities, regardless of income. The system is paid for through taxes and health-insurance premiums that are deducted from Canadians' paycheques. The first province to implement a health-insurance program was Saskatchewan, under the leadership of Premier Tommy Douglas in 1948. In the 1960s Prime Minister Lester Pearson implemented the health-insurance program across Canada. Prior to this time, Canadians had to pay for all medical treatment, which was costly, particularly for low-income families. Many people avoided getting medical or hospital treatment because they could not afford it.

Several countries regard Canada's health-care system as a model system because of its accessibility to everyone. In recent years, however, the enormous cost of Canada's health-care system has become a major concern for the government and public alike. The financial strain on hospitals across

Making an Oral Presentation

Many people feel anxious when they have to make an oral presentation. The key to overcoming this anxiety is to prepare the content of the presentation carefully and to practise the delivery often enough to develop more confidence.

Here's How

1. Content

- Select a main topic and divide it into subtopics. Be sure to make your main points clearly and support them with evidence and examples, as you would in a written essay.
- Develop an introduction and conclusion carefully. Start with a strong first statement that will catch the listener's attention. End by reinforcing your main point.

2. Preparation

- Check your timing. Practise the presentation so that you know how long it will take.
- Be sure to use tone and language appropriate to your audience. You might be talking to your classmates, but a presentation requires a fairly formal tone.
- Rehearse the delivery. You do not have to know the material off by heart, but you should it know it well enough to be able to look up from your notes.

- Prepare visual aids, if you need them. Be sure you will have facilities to show the aids you have prepared. Make sure your visuals will be visible from the back of the room. Rehearse using them.

3. Delivery

- Speak clearly and loudly enough to be heard by the people furthest away.
- Pace yourself: don't speak too quickly or too slowly. Don't speak in a monotone; vary your voice.
- Make eye contact with different people in different parts of the room as you speak.
- Show enthusiasm for your subject.
- Don't slouch, pace back and forth, or jingle coins in your pocket. Your posture and mannerisms will affect the way the audience responds to you.

Practise It

Prepare and deliver an oral presentation on the Importance of Recreation. Consider the importance of stress relief, physical fitness and social benefits among the arguments you make.

---

two-tier—having two ranks or levels

the country has caused some people to question whether Canada can afford a publicly funded health-care system. In provinces such as Alberta and Ontario, there has been a movement to allow a wide range of private medical care to exist alongside the public-health system. Supporters of this movement argue that individuals have the right to pay for alternative or extra services if they wish. Critics argue that this will create a two-tier system, in which the wealthy will receive better health care than the rest of Canadians. They argue that Canada cannot afford to dismantle its health-care system. How this issue will be resolved is still to come.

Activities

Understand Ideas

1. Organize the information about health and illness in different societies. Use a chart that has the following headings: Nature of the society, Kinds of illness and disease, Reasons for illness and disease, Treatments available.

2. **a)** What kinds of illness and health problems are common in industrial countries today?
   b) Why are they common?

Think and Evaluate

3. Argue your view:
   a) Should all medical procedures be covered by a national health insurance policy?
   b) Should it be possible for some procedures to be purchased from private services?

Research and Communicate

4. Interview a doctor, nurse or health worker. Find out what kinds of illness and disease they usually treat. How are these illnesses and diseases treated? What do they see as the main challenges of health care in Canada?

5. Prepare a class presentation on the changing role of nurses in the past 100 years. Your research should include information on
   - why nursing was traditionally seen as a female occupation
   - how this perception has changed
   - the various roles of nurses today
   - why some Canadian nurses have gone on strike in the past

Health Issues Today

Focus Questions

What are the major health issues affecting Canadians today?

What are the health risks associated with smoking, drinking and sexually transmitted diseases?

Despite the almost miraculous advances that have been made in the treatment of diseases and illnesses in the past century, there remain serious health problems that are difficult to solve.

Eating Disorders

As you saw in Chapter 5, **anorexia nervosa** and **bulimia** are eating disorders that can lead to serious health problems. People who suffer from anorexia reduce their food intake, use laxatives and induce vomiting to rid the body of food. They may exercise compulsively in an effort to burn off calories. People suffering from bulimia binge-eat, ingesting large amounts of food at a time, then induce vomiting, starve themselves or fast in an attempt to lose any weight they think they have gained. Women, particularly young women, make up 95 percent of anorexics in Canada and men make up 5 percent. About 20 percent of Canadian women have some symptoms of bulimia and 4 percent will suffer from severe bulimia during their lifetime.

What causes eating disorders? Some psychologists believe such disorders are caused by personal problems, anxieties or conflicts an individual may have. They feel that someone with an eating disorder has a distorted view of his or her own body, seeing it as overweight when it may be underweight to the point of serious illness or starvation. An eating disorder, psychologists believe, may be a person's attempt to gain control of his or her world. In their analysis of these problems, sociologists see society as a major contributor, particularly when certain messages are given out by the mass media. Actors and models often project a body image that is not normal and unhealthy. These public figures have an impact on young people who may already be sensitive about their own body image.

Cigarette Smoking

Connections

How can advertising be considered an agent of socialization? (See Chapter 6, page 126.)

Cigarette smoking in Canada has declined drastically in the past 40 years. In 1960, 45 percent of Canadian adults smoked. In 1999, that figure dropped to 23 percent. Much of the decline is the result of medical evidence linking smoking with cancer and heart disease. Even non-smokers exposed to second-hand smoke have a higher rate of smoking-related diseases. Most commercial and public buildings have instituted no-smoking policies. Many people no longer tolerate smoking in their homes. While public pressure and government health warnings have helped reduce the percentage of smokers in Canada, smoking in some groups is actually increasing. Women and young people have become targets for tobacco advertisers because smoking in these two groups is increasing.

Figure 16–8

Do you think health warnings on cigarette packages and posters such as this one discourage people from smoking? Why or why not?

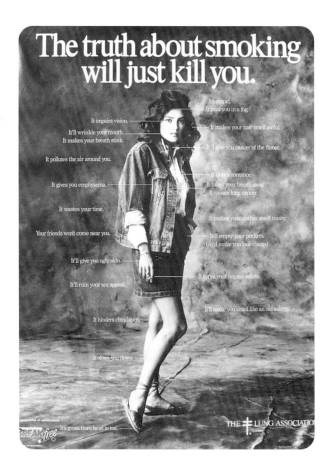

Alcohol and Drug Addiction

The percentage of Canadian adults who drink alcohol has declined since the 1970s, when 65 percent said they drank alcohol at least once a month. By the 1990s, that figure was down to 55 percent. There is, however, wide variation in the amount consumed. Thirty percent of those who drink have fewer than one drink a week, while 42 percent have one to six drinks a week. Seventeen percent have 7 to 13 drinks a week while 11 percent have 14 or more drinks a week.

Alcohol is legally and socially accepted in North American society. It is a part of many social gatherings and celebrations. Nevertheless, alcohol is a drug that, if used in excess, can cause serious problems. People who cannot control their drinking can cause harm to themselves and others on the job, on the roads and in the family. Excessive drinking or alcoholism can also lead to liver damage, heart disease and brain damage.

Until the mid-twentieth century, drugs (other than alcohol) were restricted to very small parts of the population. During the 1960s and 1970s, however, drugs such as marijuana and LSD were used by many young people, even though the drugs were illegal. Since this time, the use of these drugs has decreased significantly, as people became more aware of the physical and psychological harm they could cause. The use of other drugs, however, increased among specific subcultures. During the 1980s, for example, cocaine was used by those who could afford it. Cocaine is addictive, and many people who started out as casual users became addicts. Many were forced to turn to illegal means, such as prostitution or theft, to feed their habit. Crack cocaine, a highly addictive and cheaper form of cocaine, has also become widely used. In the 1990s, a drug called Ecstasy was used by youths, particularly at raves—loud all-night parties.

Figure 16–9

Is there a relationship between age and the amount of alcohol consumed in a week?

Alcohol consumption by age group, 1999

Age	Number of Regular Drinkers (thousands)	Number of Drinks Per Week (%)			
		Less than 1	1 to 6	7 to 13	14 and more
15–17	426	54	27	X	X
18–19	594	35	35	17	X
20–24	1309	28	38	21	12
25–34	2575	28	46	16	10
35–44	3418	23	50	17	10
45–54	2359	25	44	20	11
55–64	1446	24	46	18	12
65–74	864	23	40	24	12
75+	435	23	46	24	8

Source: Statistics Canada, 1999.

How can you tell if some-
one you know is addicted
to alcohol or drugs? (See
Chapter 5, page 107.)

Use of any drug whether it is legal or not, can have serious conse-quences. Some people are unable to control their intake, and they become addicted. Psychologists believe that certain personality and psychological characteristics predispose someone to dependency. For example, in many cases of substance abuse, there is a family history of such abuse. Psychologists are still uncertain whether patterns of abuse are the result of learned behaviour or biological factors, or both. Substance abuse can also be the result of peer pressure. For example, in a social group where heavy drinking is the norm, there is increased likelihood that individual mem-bers of the group will become dependent on alcohol. The following arti-cle focuses on several other dangers.

CASE STUDY

1. Is teenage drinking on the rise?

2. What are the dangers of getting drunk on weekends and at parties?

coma—prolonged unconscious-ness, usually caused by severe injury or excessive use of drugs

From "Teens and Alcohol" by Wojtek Dabrowski

Alcohol Abuse: Some Painful Risks

Noah is like many other teenagers: he goes to school, does his homework and almost every weekend, he likes to knock a few cold ones back with his friends….

In a 1999 survey of elementary and high school students in Ontario, the Centre for Addiction and Mental Health found that 42 percent had five or more drinks on a single occasion in the previous month. That's a significant rise from 30 percent in 1993. And in 1999, about 67 percent of high school students sur-veyed said they had drunk alcohol in the past year.

"The majority of students do drink," says centre researcher Dr. Edward Adlaf. "By and large, it's social locations, parties, other get-togethers. What's more concerning from a public-health perspective is that we've been finding more students involved in heavy-drinking episodes."

But getting loaded on the weekend can be dangerous, says Dr. Karen Leslie, who's in charge of the substance-abuse program at Toronto's Hospital for Sick Children. While most teens probably know about hangovers, there are other risks more painful than just a headache. The liver is responsible for breaking down alcohol in the body, but when it can't cope anymore, it stops working and the entire body begins to shut down. Then, the drinker either vomits or goes into a coma. Or both. Death can result if alcohol levels are high enough, Leslie says.

There's also the issue of doing things while drunk that you'll regret later. Leslie says many teenage drinkers end up in tears, with sexual assaults of young women happening often.

"For a lot of young people, their first sexual experience happens when they're drunk or high," Leslie says, adding that girls don't usually plan ahead to make sure their drinking environment is safe. As for young men, Leslie says the usual bad side-effects of drinking are run-ins with police. "They get caught up in illegal activities that end up getting them charged," she said.

Jen, 17, knows about having too much. "You do stupid things, like embarrass yourself," Jen says.

But on one night Noah didn't know when to say "when." He drank 12 ounces of hard liquor…and was soon dropping his pants in front of coffee-shop windows. He came home with cuts and bruises on his knees from falling over several times. "I have no recollection of that night, whatsoever."

Sexually Transmitted Diseases

Sexually transmitted diseases (STDs) are diseases that are transmitted through sexual contact. These diseases are serious illnesses that, if left untreated, can cause sterility, liver failure, blindness, or death. Gonorrhea, syphilis, herpes, chlamydia and HIV/AIDS are examples of sexually transmitted diseases. These kinds of diseases became a major health issue during the 1960s when the introduction of birth control pills brought about a sexual revolution. Prior to this time, the number of people who had sexual intercourse before marriage was much lower than it is today. The pill helped avoid unwanted pregnancies and premarital sexual activity became much more common. Increased sexual activity resulted in more cases of STDs.

- Most cases of gonorrhea and syphilis can be cured with penicillin although some strains of these diseases remain resistant to treatment. If untreated, gonorrhea can cause sterility. Syphilis can damage major organs and result in blindness, mental disorders and death.

- Although herpes is less serious than gonorrhea and syphilis, it is incurable. A person with herpes may not have any obvious symptoms for a period of time, and then painful genital blisters may appear, accompanied by fever and headache. A pregnant woman with active genital herpes can transmit the disease to her child during delivery. Herpes can be fatal to the baby, and women who suffer from this form of STD usually give birth by cesarean section.

- Chlamydia is one of the most common STDs in North America. It is a bacterial infection that affects men, women and infants. In many cases, the symptoms of chlamydia are difficult to detect and people are often unaware that they are carrying the disease for months or even years. If left untreated, chlamydia can cause permanent damage to the reproductive organs, chronic pain, infertility or sterility, miscarriage, or ectopic pregnancy (a serious condition that can cause the pregnant woman to die). In infants, chlamydia can cause eye, ear and lung infections.

- Human immunodeficiency virus (HIV) is the forerunner to full-blown acquired immune deficiency syndrome (AIDS). HIV is contracted in several common ways: through blood, sexual contact and contaminated needles. HIV is not spread through casual contact with an infected person. You cannot become infected by shaking hands or hugging an infected person. There is no case of the virus being transmitted through coughing and sneezing, or through sharing such items as towels, dishes or telephones. The risk of transmitting HIV through saliva is extremely low. People carrying the HIV virus do not immediately

Figure 16–10

Johanne Decarie (right) contracted HIV through a blood transfusion in 1985. She subsequently passed it on to her daughter Billie Jo (left) in childbirth.

develop AIDS. In fact, most people with the virus show no symptoms for at least a year and they are often unaware they are infected. Within about five years, however, 25 percent of HIV-infected persons will develop AIDS, and most HIV-infected people will develop AIDS eventually.

AIDS is the most serious health threat facing many countries today. Governments and health organizations throughout the world are trying to educate people about the spread of AIDS. In Canada, as in other countries, more and more young people are taking precautions against AIDS and other sexually transmitted diseases. Drugs have also been developed that help treat AIDS, and consequently, prolong the life of an AIDS victim. The young woman described in the following article is using her time to educate others.

1. Why is Trudy Parsons talking to teens in her hometown about AIDS?

2. Why do most sexually active teens not use a condom every time they have sex?

Trudy Parsons, AIDS Activist

The car speeds west along the Trans-Canada Highway as snowflakes swirl from an aluminum-coloured sky. "The worst thing is going home," Trudy Parsons says, huddled in the front passenger's seat, wearing a baggy men's overcoat.

As the car nears Bay Roberts, the Newfoundland outport where she spent her teen years, Parsons, now 22, recalls the wave of panic she felt when she returned to her old high school a year ago. There, in a crowded classroom, her voice quavered as she warned teenagers about the dangers of HIV, which is believed to cause acquired immune deficiency syndrome (AIDS).

Parsons tested positive for the virus three years ago. Now, with another room full of students waiting at her old school, her anxiety again deepens. "I grew up with these people," says Parsons, who works full-time for the Newfoundland AIDS Committee. "My family lives out there—and I fear that they will be judged because of a mistake that I made."

From Newfoundland to British Columbia, Canadian teenagers are struggling with the urgent issue of how to conduct their lives in the shadow of AIDS. Despite nationwide AIDS education campaigns, only 38 percent of sexually active teens across Canada say that they use a condom every time they have sex, according to a *Maclean's* Decima poll. In her work for the AIDS committee, travelling across the province to raise public awareness about the disease, Parsons says that she finds most teens do use condoms, but not all the time. "These kids still think that it is a gay men's disease and they can't get it," she says.

Bay Roberts, a town of 5000, is bordered by a narrow harbour on one side and barren, rocky hills on the other. Parsons remembers teenage life there as dull, but generally happy. She babysat for relatives, sipped beer in the woods on weekends, went to dances. Then, when she was 19, Parsons contracted the HIV infection from a Bay Roberts-area man. He was her third sexual partner. "I wish that I had known someone like me when I was in high school. If I had had the opportunity, maybe things would have turned out differently for me."

Ascension Collegiate's guidance counsellor, Mervin Clarke, says that education campaigns urging teens to use condoms have made an impact. "When teens have sex," he says, "most of them take the correct precautions." But he adds: "There are some who understand the dangers, and still don't protect themselves. They think that they are immortal." It is that kind of attitude that Parsons is fighting.

She leans forward in her chair in the school's guidance office as she speaks. Of slender build, with a mane of thick black hair framing her thin, serious face, she hardly looks older than the two dozen 16- and 17-year-olds who sit in a tight circle around her. They are Ascension's peer counsellors. And Parsons' message has captured their attention. When the bell rings to change classes, the students are reluctant to leave. Tanya Craik, a 16-year-old from Bay Roberts, walks up to Parsons and embraces her. "You see her and you realize that if it can happen to her, it can happen to anybody," says Craik, clutching her school books to her chest. "It's not something you want to think about—but you have to."

Trudy Parsons seems tired but relieved as Bay Roberts disappears in the distance behind her. Because of her own unfamiliarity with the virus, she thought that she had only a year to live when she first learned that she was HIV-positive. And there has been another pleasant surprise: a six-month-old romantic relationship, even though she thought her dating days were over. "I have proven myself wrong on every count," she says. Still, even during her happy moments, despair lurks beneath the surface. Parsons acknowledges that sometimes her work seems futile....

"I'm the only person doing this. And my going to a high school once a year is not going to reinforce anything," she says wearily. "You know you are going to see some of them again, and that it is going to be at the AIDS clinic in St. John's—and it is going to be because they are HIV-positive."

From "Love and Fear in the Age of AIDS" by John Demont

Activities

Understand Ideas

1. What are some of the causes of eating disorders such as anorexia and bulimia?

2. **a)** What are some of the problems related to the abuse of substances such as alcohol, tobacco and other drugs?
   b) Why do some people have a difficult time controlling their intake of these substances?

3. What is the relationship between HIV and AIDS?

Think and Evaluate

4. Thin is in. Do you agree with this statement? Why or why not? Do you think such an attitude is healthy? Give reasons for your view.

5. By increasing the drinking age to 21, the number of teen-related problems with alcohol will be reduced. Discuss.

Research and Communicate

6. What is fetal alcohol syndrome? Research the effects of this problem on children born with this syndrome. What treatment is available for these children?

7. Do library research on the problem of AIDS in Canada. Look for information on
   • prevention of AIDS
   • statistics on the number of people with AIDS in Canada
   • impact of AIDS on people in developing countries

Social Issues

What is euthanasia?

Why is euthanasia becoming a major issue in Canada?

Why is there a problem filling the demand for organ transplants in Canada?

Euthanasia

debilitating—making feeble or disabled

Euthanasia is the willful killing of a person who is suffering from a fatal or extremely debilitating disease. In many cases, the person who is suffering has asked for the right to die because the pain is so intense that he or she can no longer tolerate it. Euthanasia has also been called mercy killing because it is seen as putting people out of their misery. Euthanasia is a highly controversial issue. Some people believe euthanasia is murder, and that anyone who kills another, for whatever reason, should be punished according to the law. Others believe that people who have fatal or incurable diseases should be allowed the right to end their lives if they choose to. Three Canadian cases in particular have heightened the debate about whether euthanasia should be legal. As you read about them, keep in mind the following questions:

- What do these three cases have in common?

- How do they differ?

- Can euthanasia ever be justified? Why or why not?

- Who should decide whether a person has the right to die?

CASE STUDY

1. What is the difference between active and passive euthanasia?

2. How did the court rulings in the two cases affect the lives of Nancy B. and Sue Rodriguez?

Euthanasia: Some Famous Cases

Nancy B. was a 25-year-old quadriplegic. She had Guillain-Barre syndrome, a neurological disorder that attacks the nervous system and paralyses muscles. She couldn't breathe without a respirator. Although many people recover from Guillain-Barre syndrome, Nancy B. had an incurable form of the disease, which would have left her bedridden for the rest of her life. Nancy B. went to court to win the right to have the plug of her respirator pulled out so that she could die naturally. On January 6, 1992, the court ruled that a patient has the right to refuse medical treatment, even if death results. On February 13, 1992, medical staff disconnected Nancy's respirator. She died seven minutes later. Nancy B.'s form of death has been called **passive euthanasia** because disconnecting a machine or withholding a medical procedure allows the patient to die naturally. No extreme or "heroic" measures are taken to save them.

Sue Rodriguez was diagnosed with Lou Gehrig's disease, which causes body functions to deteriorate over a period of time. Rodriguez believed she should have the right to end her life when her condition worsened. She feared, however, that she would not have the physical ability to do so. In 1992, she petitioned the British Columbia courts to allow her permission to commit suicide with the aid of a doctor. Rodriguez was trying to

Figure 16–11

Left: Sue Rodriguez turned to the courts to help end her suffering. Instead of waiting for a natural death, she wanted to die on her own terms and in her own time. Do you agree with the court's decision in the Sue Rodriguez case?

Right: Robert Latimer was eventually convicted of murder and sentenced to life in prison. How would you feel if you were a jury member? How do you think someone with a disability would react to Latimer's conviction?

change the law that prohibited **active euthanasia,** which would include administering a lethal drug, or otherwise assisting in ending the life of a patient. The court refused Rodriguez's request. In 1993 the Supreme Court of Canada also ruled against her. Sue Rodriguez, however, did end her life, with an unknown doctor present. Right-to-die legislation has come before the Canadian parliament a number of times, but it has always been rejected or ignored. A Senate committee in 1997 recommended that a third-degree murder category be legislated, which would impose less severe penalties for cases of compassionate assisted suicide.

The case of **Tracy Latimer** highlighted many of the issues raised by euthanasia, as the following report reveals.

His little girl was in terrible pain and faced a future of further agony. So, on October 24, 1993, Robert Latimer decided to end her suffering. He placed his disabled daughter, Tracy, in the cab of his Chevy pickup, piped in deadly carbon monoxide fumes and waited for several minutes until she stopped breathing. That act sparked a gut-wrenching debate across the country about mercy killing and the rights of the disabled. Latimer has always said he acted out of love for 12-year-old Tracy. "It was no crime," he says simply. "The alternative of leaving a person to suffer is a greater wrong." His decision to end his daughter's life came after a doctor recommended removing her thigh bone to ease her pain. Tracy had already endured operations on her back, hips and legs, and her parents were horrified by the idea of yet another surgery that would leave her leg hanging loosely from her body. Tracy had one of the most severe forms of cerebral palsy. She functioned at the level of a 3-month-old and couldn't walk, talk or feed herself. Advocates for the disabled say a description that stops there dehumanizes Tracy because she was also a person who found pleasure in music, the Jacuzzi, swinging in a hammock, and family bonfires.

"Stripped to its bare essentials, Latimer's position is that a parent has the right to kill a disabled child if that parent decides the child's quality of life no

Connections

What type of social movement would fight for right-to-die legislation? (See Chapter 10, page 214.)

Should Doctors Always Prolong Life?

Medical and scientific advances have made it possible for people to continue living with the support of machinery and other means. Doctors now have the power to decide whether a person's life should be prolonged. How are such decisions made? In small groups, discuss whether life should always be prolonged, bearing in mind the different factors highlighted below.

- **Ethical:** Is it ethical to prolong someone's life artificially? Is it ethical to let a person die when you can keep him or her alive through artificial means?

- **Financial:** Should society spend large amounts of money to keep people alive who may never get better? Should money be an issue when talking about human lives?

- **Quality of life:** Is there a point at which a person's quality of life is so poor that death would be preferable? Does any person have the right to determine at what point someone else's life is not worth living?

- **Medical advances:** Research continues to find cures for many diseases that cannot yet be treated successfully. Should heroic measures be taken to keep people alive in the hope that a cure to their illness will be found? Should people with terminal illnesses be forced to continue to live even if they would rather die?

- **Legal issues:** Will passive euthanasia open the door to other kinds of mercy killings? Should active euthanasia be made legal?

longer warrants its continuation," the Council of Canadians with Disabilities and other groups argue in their impassioned legal brief.

Justice Minister Anne McLellan had said in 1997 she'd consider lowering the mandatory minimum jail time for murder. However, a brief written by her department defends the required sentence, arguing there's no room for case-by-case exemptions. The jurors who convicted Latimer thought there should be. Many were clearly stunned—gasping, even crying—when they learned their verdict meant a life sentence and no parole for 10 years. The trial judge agreed Latimer should receive a rare constitutional exemption, sentencing him to two years less a day—one year in jail, the other confined to his farm. A year later, Saskatchewan's appeal court reversed the trial judge's decision, ruling Latimer must serve at least 10 years in prison.

From "Was Killing Disabled Daughter an Act of Love or Murder?" by Valerie Lawton

Connections

According to those who support the decision to uphold Latimer's sentence, what purpose does his punishment serve? (See Chapter 15, page 319.)

Latimer's case went to the Supreme Court of Canada for a final decision. In January 2001, the Supreme Court ruled that Latimer must serve a life sentence for murder, with no possibility of parole for 10 years. Many Canadians were shocked by the severity of the sentence, believing that Robert Latimer was acting out of love for his daughter. Others welcomed the decision. One member of an organization representing people with disabilities said that, "It is a comfort to know that we are citizens as others and that the law will protect us. We are very relieved."

Organ Transplants

In 1967, Dr. Christiaan Barnard of South Africa performed the first heart transplant. The recipient, Louis Washkansky, died of pneumonia 18 days later. Since then organ transplants have become common hospital procedures and success rates continue to climb. Kidneys, livers, hearts, lungs, pancreases and other organs are regularly donated and transplanted into waiting patients.

The supply of needed organs, however, never meets the demand for these organs. In most cases, organs that are donated come from people who have died. Immediately after someone dies, his or her organs can be kept alive and transplanted into someone else. Many people have informed their family or doctor that, upon death, their organs can be donated to someone else. In many cases, however, when a person dies, the family is too emotional to consider donating his or her organs. In 2000, there were 1540 patients on waiting lists for organ transplants in Ontario alone. In that same year, only 154 donors were available in Ontario. A severe shortage of donated organs has resulted in a black market in donor organs. Some poor people in developing countries sell their organs to people in richer countries. It is believed that 20 to 30 Canadians have bought

transplant—transfer of living tissue or organ from one body to another

black market—the unauthorized selling of officially controlled or rare goods

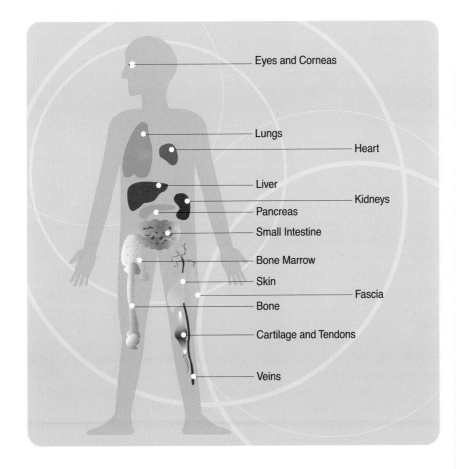

Figure 16–12

Up to 200 people can be helped by one donor. Do you know someone who has received an organ donation? Have you discussed the idea of organ donation with your family members?

Eyes and Corneas

Lungs

Heart

Liver

Kidneys

Pancreas

Small Intestine

Bone Marrow

Skin

Fascia

Bone

Cartilage and Tendons

Veins

organs on the black market, paying from $2000 to $60 000 for an organ. There are moves to make the purchase and sale of human organs a criminal offence, but this practice is currently prohibited only by a provincial regulation, punishable by up to $1000 and six months in jail.

No matter what the source of an organ, a transplant is often a difficult and dramatic event. This report describes the case of one recipient.

CASE STUDY

1. Why did Sarah Goethals receive a new heart?

2. What was the outcome of the operation?

A New Heart for Sarah Goethals

It arrives in a white plastic cooler high in the air like a football trophy by a breathless doctor with a human life in his hands. There is no time to lose.

Upstairs at the Hospital for Sick Children, surgeons are about to slice open the thin, pale chest of a 12-year-old girl. Her name is Sarah Goethals, and this warm July night, her young life hangs suspended. The container is handed to a nurse dressed in green. Quickly, firmly, she lifts the lid. Inside is a plump, peculiar, red-brown mass basted in its own blood, the extracted heart of a young donor whose name no one in this room will ever know.

In another hospital, in another city, a family grieves the loss of their child. But here, at Sick Children's hospital, Sarah lies still and softly breathing, a winner in a macabre and miraculous lottery of life.

It is July 16. Sarah has been on Ontario's heart transplant waiting list, Life Row, for only 75 days—a quick and lucky turnaround. Three months earlier, on a Friday, she suddenly fell ill at school in her tiny hometown of Elm Creek, Manitoba. It didn't seem serious at first; she just felt sick to her stomach and tired. By early Sunday, Sarah's feet began to swell. By evening, she was in the pediatric intensive care unit at the Health Sciences Centre in Winnipeg. The grade 6 pupil had developed dilated cardiomyopathy, a condition that causes the heart to weaken and swell. A transplant was her only hope...

And the thought of a transplant terrified her. Even now, as Sarah is preparing for surgery, the family is confused and fearful.

The operation begins at 9:30 p.m. as an anesthetist places a mask on her face and the young girl quickly loses consciousness. One of the surgeons carefully saws through her breastbone, then divides her chest at the midline revealing Sarah's damaged heart. Everything is carefully synchronized so that once her heart is removed, the new one is immediately put in its place. The new heart is then carefully sewn together in five places. It is at this instant, in Sarah's case it was around 12:30 a.m. last July 16, that a miracle, unthinkable even 40 years ago, begins as another human being's heart beats for the first time in Sarah's body.

But will it work?

Dr. William Williams, the head of cardiovascular surgery, studies the monitor, not speaking. Then he smiles. The heart is working...

Ten days later, Sarah glances over at the heart monitor beside her hospital bed and smiles. She doesn't know whose heart is beating steadily and quietly 93 times a minute inside her. Only that a child slightly smaller than herself died on the evening of July 15, and the family agreed to donate the organs.

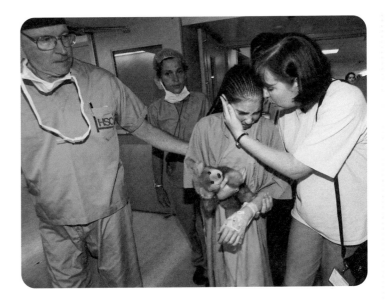

Figure 16–13
Sarah Goethals' mother comforts her, as she is led into the operating room by heart surgeon Dr. William Williams.

The knowledge that other children haven't been as fortunate as her bothers Sarah. "While I was waiting, I met another girl. She's 15 and she's been waiting for a heart since last November. It's really hard for her. I hope she gets her heart soon." Five months later, that other little girl is still waiting.

From "Survival in a Heartbeat" by Patricia Orwen

Activities

Understand Ideas

1. What are the arguments in favour of euthanasia? What are the arguments against it?

2. Why is euthanasia a more widespread social issue than it was in earlier times?

3. What does Canadian law say about euthanasia?

Think and Evaluate

4. What are the differences between the cases of Nancy B., Sue Rodriguez and Tracy Latimer?

5. Write a letter to the editor of a paper, stating how you think the black market in organ donation could be stopped.

Apply Your Learning

6. Develop a survey to help you take an opinion poll on the issue of euthanasia. You want to find out
   - the number of people who oppose all forms of euthanasia
   - the number of people who support euthanasia under some conditions but not others
   - the number of people who support all forms of euthanasia

Survey the students and teachers in your school. Record your findings. Share the results with your class.

7. a) Examine the way that Canadians view death. Include a description and evaluation of the following:
   - acceptance of death
   - burial arrangements
   - funeral arrangements
   - how grief is expressed
   - life insurance
   - religious beliefs

b) What do your conclusions suggest about the Canadian attitude toward death? Write a report describing your findings. (See Skill Focus, page 188.)

Key Points

- Recreation and health are closely connected. Recreation, such as sports, greatly influences a person's physical, emotional and mental health.

- Play is important in children because it helps prepare them for future roles as adults and it teaches them how to co-operate and socialize with others.

- Sport is a particular form of play that involves physical exertion, competition and rules. Sport often reflects the basic values of the society in which it is played.

- Major health problems in Canada are the result of poor eating habits, a sedentary lifestyle and pollution in the environment.

- Eating disorders, sexually transmitted disease, drug abuse and alcoholism are among some of the health problems in Canada today.

- Medical discoveries have led to a significant reduction in infectious diseases, to organ transplants and to the ability to prolong life artificially.

- Euthanasia is a controversial issue that raises questions about whether people who are terminally ill should have the right to decide when and how they will die.

Activities

Understanding Ideas

1. **a)** What illnesses are associated with a poor lifestyle?
   b) How does poor lifestyle in industrialized countries differ from poor lifestyle in less developed countries?

Think and Evaluate

2. Look at the chart on life expectancies (Figure 16–4, page 334). Which eight countries have the highest life expectancy? Which eight have the lowest? What factors contribute to a high life expectancy?

3. Are all sports competitive? What are the benefits of competitive sports? Are there any disadvantages to competitive sports? Explain.

4. A publicly funded health-care system should not pay for smoking-related illnesses. Do you agree or disagree? Discuss.

Apply Your Learning

5. How does play affect learning? Provide an example from your life where you learned something through playing.

6. Make a 5-minute oral presentation on one of these topics using the guidelines on page 338:
   - why eating disorders develop
   - why teens smoke
   - how lifestyle affects eating habits
   - why physical fitness in young children is declining and how it can be improved

Research and Communicate

7. Canadians are becoming more interested in homeopathic or alternative remedies for illnesses and health problems. Define homeopathy. Find an article on a homeopathic treatment for a particular health problem. Write a summary of the kind of treatment the article recommends and why this treatment is recommended. Write your reasons for supporting or not supporting this treatment. Present your report to the class. (See Skill Focus on pages 97 and 323.)

8. Choose one issue from this chapter and create a poster or brochure to educate the public on the issue. Possible topics include the importance of physical fitness, violence in sports, the dangers of drinking and driving and health risks associated with smoking, sexual activity or drug use.

Culture, Communication and Computers

e are living through a revolutionary period in human culture and society. The first stage of this period was the **communication revolution,** the development of radio, film and television. The second stage was the **information revolution,** which began with the development of computer technology. This chapter looks at these two related stages and considers the impact they have had and will have on our lives.

Start by thinking about the role of communications technology in your own life. In your notebook, make a copy of the following chart and use it to record your responses. How often in a week do you use each of the following forms of communication?

	Seldom or Never (0 to 2 times)	Regularly (3 to 7 times)	Often (8 or more times)
Newspapers or magazines			
Radio			
Television			
Books			
Movies			
Telephone			
Fax machine			
Internet			
Other (specify)			

Compare your responses with those of others in the class. What conclusions can you draw about the use of communications technology by your classmates?

In this Chapter

- How do the mass media affect us?

- How are popular culture and mass media related?

- How will information technology affect our lives, education and work?

Key Terms

communication revolution

information revolution

mass media

popular culture

folk culture

elite culture

cultural diffusion

global village

Focus Questions

What are the mass media?

How have the mass media affected our popular culture?

Mass Media

Today we take it for granted that we can learn about the world from newspapers, listen to the radio while driving to a destination or entertain ourselves by watching television or movies. However, at one time, these forms of communication were revolutionary and exciting. Newspapers have been available for centuries, but motion pictures did not arrive until the early 1900s, radio until the 1920s and television in the 1950s. They are all forms of **mass media**—methods of communication that can transmit messages to large numbers of people. Mass communication of this sort is primarily one way, unlike telecommunication devices such as the telephone, which involve a two-way flow of messages. Canadians spend a great deal of time receiving messages from the various mass media. The average Canadian spends about 19 hours a week listening to radio and 23 hours watching television. Women tend to watch television more than men, and seniors more than others. Women over the age of 60 watch television twice as many hours each week as adolescents or children do.

Each of the mass media has some unique features as well. From the beginning, motion pictures have been used largely for entertainment, to tell stories and to amuse. Radio had a wider function. Not only did it entertain with stories, comedies, dramas and music, it also provided regular newscasts and some educational programming. The Canadian government became aware of the power of the radio as a social agent, and in 1929 took control of allocating and approving radio band waves. In its day, radio had a powerful impact on human thought and social awareness. One Toronto radio listener of the 1920s wrote:

Figure 17–1

Radio broadcasts were a very popular form of entertainment in the 1930s and 1940s.

Through it [radio], I have become aware of whole country-sides, which before were merely names on a map. I am finding out how their people think and feel. I am becoming surprisingly familiar with their little mannerisms of speech and accent. I hear about their politics, their civic troubles and their national problems. They have become my neighbours. By radio, this world is being drawn together. We feel closer. A friendly comradeship is developing. We are beginning to know each other, and knowledge destroys prejudice and suspicion, that unholy pair of war makers.

Television was invented in the 1920s and became practical and popular during the 1950s. Every roof sprouted a television antenna and every living room contained a black-and-white television set. Over time, the technology improved with colour, cable, remote control and digital images. The impact of television has been incalculable. From infancy, children spend more waking hours watching television than doing any other single activity. The power of television to shape

ideas and behaviour has been a major concern of social analysts. Of particular concern has been the violence and other anti-social behaviour often portrayed on television.

Popular Culture

Popular culture is culture that is produced and shared through mass media by large numbers of people over wide areas. Images of pop stars, McDonald's hamburgers, Santa Claus and MuchMusic are examples of popular culture; so are the products we buy, the values we hold in common with many others and the way we spend our time. We learn about popular culture from others immediately around us and from the media itself. To some degree, everyone in Canada shares in popular culture. Think of how often you turn on the television set, eat in a fast-food restaurant or buy a pair of blue jeans. Videos, CDs, television and radio broadcasts, movies, magazines and newspapers are all well-known examples of mass media that transmit and help create popular culture.

Figure 17–2
Which cultural icons are shown here? How did the mass media contribute to their popularity?

Elements of Popular Culture
Popular culture came into being during the nineteenth and twentieth centuries. It could not have existed before that, because it depends on the mass production, distribution and consumption of ideas and products

Figure 17–3

The elements of popular culture. How is each stage necessary to the next stage?

Mass production

POPULAR CULTURE

Mass consumption

Mass distribution

Mass communication

Connections

What characteristics does popular culture share with other cultures? (See Chapter 2, pages 27–28.)

through the mass media. It also depends on the existence of a large enough group of people who can afford to be part of it. Popular culture can be compared to two other kinds of culture: folk culture and elite culture.

Folk culture develops within a limited community and is usually communicated orally. It generally has a long history. For example, we participate in folk culture when we take part in the holidays and ceremonies our family has been involved in for generations, or eat the foods prepared according to old family tradition. **Elite culture,** in contrast, is produced for a limited number of people with exclusive, specialized interests. Reading Shakespeare, Confucius and Plato, or looking at the paintings of Leonardo da Vinci and Van Gogh are ways to take part in elite culture. Elite culture changes little over many generations, and participation is limited to those willing and able to learn enough about it to appreciate it.

Popular culture changes more rapidly than folk or elite culture. New clothing, automobiles, computers, songs and slang phrases are constantly emerging. "What's new?" is not an accidental greeting in the age of popular culture. Those who immerse themselves in popular culture are constantly aware of the newest styles, trends and fashions. Popular actors, singers and other media people often communicate new trends over the mass media.

Activities

Understand Ideas

1. **a)** What are the common characteristics that all forms of the mass media share?
   b) What unique characteristics do movies, radio and television have?

2. **a)** What is popular culture?
   b) How is popular culture different from folk culture and elite culture?

3. How do mass media shape popular culture?

Think and Evaluate

4. Why do you think that fame is so fleeting in popular culture?

Research and Communicate

5. **a)** Analyze the lyrics of one current hit song. What cultural message is being communicated?
   b) Share your analysis with a group of four or five classmates. Do others in the group agree with your interpretation? Why or why not?

6. Make a collage showing aspects of popular culture today. Include as many different elements of pop culture as possible. Include such things as clothing styles, car designs, movie stars, popular music groups, etc. Present your collage to the class.

Issues Related to Mass Media

Media Advertising

Advertising that can reach huge audiences is necessary in a society based on the mass production and distribution of goods. Manufacturers and service providers need advertising to convince large numbers of consumers to buy their products. However, mass advertising in itself has little social purpose beyond selling a product or service. In fact, it may convince people to buy products that they do not need, or it may send harmful social messages. Therefore, governments often regulate what is advertised and how it is presented. Cigarettes, for example, can no longer be advertised on Canadian media. Advertising generally discourages people from using their powers of critical thinking. Instead, it tends to appeal to our emotions and to our desire for immediate gratification or distraction. Advertisers often aim to create a feeling around their product or service, rather than encouraging real debate or thought on the part of the consumer. To do this, advertisers use psychology to appeal to our desires and needs.

Techniques Used in Advertisements

The techniques used in advertisements are also used in other forms of propaganda—political speeches or communication aimed at presenting a one-sided or distorted view of a subject. During the twentieth century, governments, businesses and private organizations have used the mass media as an effective way to spread propaganda. It is important to be aware of the techniques used by advertisers and propagandists. On the next two pages are some of the more popular methods of advertising.

Focus Questions

How do advertisers use psychology to appeal to our desires?

How does the concentration of media ownership affect the flow of information?

Connections

According to behavioural psychologists who study the effects of reward and punishment, which media would be more effective, positive or negative advertising? Why? (See Chapter 3, page 55.)

Figure 17–4

Advertisers try to appeal to these emotions in consumers. Do you recognize these techniques when you look at advertisements?

- **Personal Attacks or Name-Calling** By using a bad name for or making fun of a rival product, advertisers try to make people condemn that product without considering the pros and cons. Propagandists use this same technique to discredit other ideas.

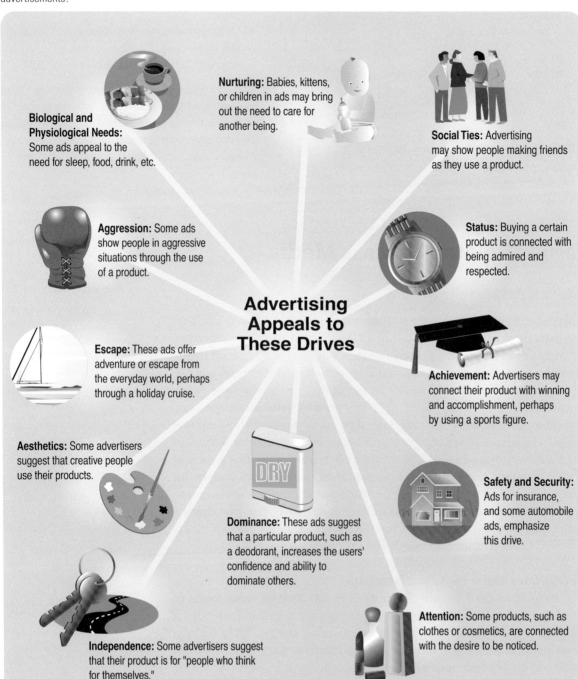

Biological and Physiological Needs: Some ads appeal to the need for sleep, food, drink, etc.

Nurturing: Babies, kittens, or children in ads may bring out the need to care for another being.

Social Ties: Advertising may show people making friends as they use a product.

Aggression: Some ads show people in aggressive situations through the use of a product.

Status: Buying a certain product is connected with being admired and respected.

Advertising Appeals to These Drives

Escape: These ads offer adventure or escape from the everyday world, perhaps through a holiday cruise.

Achievement: Advertisers may connect their product with winning and accomplishment, perhaps by using a sports figure.

Aesthetics: Some advertisers suggest that creative people use their products.

Safety and Security: Ads for insurance, and some automobile ads, emphasize this drive.

Dominance: These ads suggest that a particular product, such as a deodorant, increases the users' confidence and ability to dominate others.

Independence: Some advertisers suggest that their product is for "people who think for themselves."

Attention: Some products, such as clothes or cosmetics, are connected with the desire to be noticed.

- **Generalizing** Many advertisers try to get others to accept an idea or product by associating it with common values. How might words or phrases such as "value for your money," "for the love of Canada," or "a quality product" encourage people to accept a product or idea without checking the evidence?

- **Testimonials** Advertisements often use words of support from a respected person. For example, athletes endorse sports equipment; popular singers and celebrities support politicians in their campaigns.

- **Plain Folks** Advertisers may try to identify themselves or their product with their audience. This is why advertisements often show dramatizations of everyday life in a typical household. Politicians use this technique when they talk about their simple or impoverished childhood, or talk of their love for a particular region of the country.

- **Card Stacking** Frequently, advertisers use the evidence and arguments that support only one product or position while ignoring the rest. In some cases, evidence may even be falsified or distorted; in other cases, it is simply meaningless. For example, an advertisement for a pain reliever may boast that "four out of five doctors surveyed say they recommend Asperbuff to their patients over other leading brands of pain reliever." Perhaps advertisers are not telling you how many doctors they surveyed and how they chose the survey participants.

- **Bandwagon** Advertisers recognize that many people want to be part of a trend. They try to persuade their audiences to accept an idea or product because "everybody's doing it."

Ownership Concentration

Many mass-media outlets are owned and controlled by only a few people and organizations. For example, at the start of the twenty-first century, the Hollinger Corporation controlled 58 of the 104 daily newspapers in Canada. Overall, large newspaper chains control 80 percent of all daily circulation newspapers in Canada. Concentration of control is occurring in many businesses these days, but many people worry when the product is information. Concentration of ownership gives some corporations enormous power over what we see and hear, and even over what we think.

Also worrisome to some analysts is the trend of large media companies merging with other large companies. Often this gives the companies control of several different kinds of mass-media outlets. These companies are so large and contain so many separate divisions that it is difficult for the viewer or consumer to keep track of who owns what. Without this knowledge, it is difficult to judge the objectivity of the information being presented. For example, in 1996 Warner Brothers released the film *Space Jam*, which starred the animated character Bugs Bunny along with NBA

Connections

What is the relationship between ownership concentration and globalization? (See Chapter 13, page 271.)

basketball star Michael Jordan. The film was advertised heavily during NBA games, which were broadcast over the Turner cable network, and it received a favourable review in *Entertainment Weekly* magazine. *Sports Illustrated for Kids* magazine devoted an entire 64-page special collector's edition to the film, with the rationale that it was "no ordinary film." What many people did not realize was that all of these media outlets—Warner Brothers, *Entertainment Weekly*, *Sports Illustrated*, and Turner Broadcasting—were owned by the same parent company.

Supporters of such mergers claim that they are necessary in order to survive the growing costs of providing entertainment and that mergers ultimately serve the consumer better by providing lower prices. They also insist that the companies have an arm's-length relationship with the editorial content of their news and information programming. These arguments have failed to convince many of their critics, however. Writer Naomi Klein puts it this way:

> The mergers [of large entertainment companies] have bred a monster race of slick and safe entertainment caricatures. Through carefully timed releases of movies, magazines, video games, CDs and CD-ROMs, they can now hijack our culture on every front and feed all the profits into the same pockets.

Social Change

Figure 17–5

How can television influence our view of the world?

What kind of reality does television present to its viewers? Most sociologists agree that mass media, such as television, generally reflect fairly conservative social norms, and characters are often presented as stereotypes. For example, while women on television are no longer portrayed exclusively as housewives and mothers as they were in the fifties and sixties, some female characters are still shown to be more interested in relationships than in careers or schooling. They are also more likely than male characters to be shown paying attention to their looks and being complimented on their appearance.

Many people feel that the mass media should use their power to shape social values. If television was more willing to challenge the status quo, changes could happen much more quickly. Most sociologists and other commentators agree, however, that mainstream television does not fulfill such a role. The main goal of television is to attract as many viewers as possible in order to create advertising revenue. It is, therefore, more likely that television will reflect what the majority of viewers want to see, rather than introduce ideas that challenge social norms. Documentaries and educational television, on the other hand, have more freedom to explore ideas and challenge audiences with new views and interpretations.

status quo—how things already are

Is Your Life on Television?

How closely does television mirror your own life? Use the following activity to find out. Compare your family to one portrayed on a television show, and take note of similarities and differences. In your notebook, make a chart like the one below to record your findings. Add any other questions that seem relevant to you.

	My Life	TV Life
Who lives together as a family?		
Where do they live: in the suburbs, in the city, in the country, etc.?		
Where do they live: in a house, an apartment, a condo, etc.?		
What do the kids and/or parents talk about?		
What do the kids and/or parents fight about?		
How do the family members spend their free time?		
On what do they spend their money?		
Who in the family has jobs: one or both parents, some of the older children, other relatives, etc.?		
What is important to the kids?		

Source: Media Awareness Network

Does Television Promote Violence?

Concerns have been raised since the early days of radio about the impact of media violence, especially upon children. Researchers disagree, however, about the exact impact of violent programming on behaviour. Some evidence indicates that violence in the media, especially television, encourages viewers to think and act more violently themselves. Others maintain that the connection is not clear.

Psychologists often use laboratory experiments to explore the link between television and real-life violence. These experiments usually compare two groups: one that watches violent programming and another that watches non-violent programming. Experiments such as these often show

Figure 17–6

What values are projected by television scenes like this one? Do shows like this provoke real-life violence?

that viewing violence results in increased aggressiveness and that those who watch violent programming show less self-discipline and patience in trying to accomplish tasks or deal with others. These effects have been noted in subjects regardless of their personality, age, gender or social background.

Sociologists and psychologists have put forward several theories to explain how television violence may encourage aggression. One is that exposure to violence desensitizes people so they gradually tolerate higher and higher levels. A second theory is that watching violence weakens self-control responses built up by the society. A third theory is that violence, like any other behaviour, is learned and that television violence provides viewers with models for behaviour, showing them how and when to use violence. Yet another theory holds that television violence makes viewers believe that the world is a mean and frightening place, encouraging some people to over-react in uncertain situations.

However, other researchers point out that there are several weaknesses in laboratory experiments. First, people do not usually watch one violent show after another, as they do in the lab. On a typical night, most of us will watch a mixture of programming. Also, subjects in the experiment may assume the experimenter is expecting aggressive behaviour and act accordingly. Finally, critics point out that experimental studies demonstrate only a short-term link between television violence and aggressiveness. The experiments do not account for the effect of negative reactions from parents or peers when children act aggressively. When parents or peers criticize violent behaviour, they counteract the influence of television.

desensitizes—reduces emotional response through repeated exposure

It may also be important to distinguish among different kinds of television violence in order to decide its impact. As we saw in Chapter 3, studies suggest that aggressive behaviour from children will increase as the portrayal of violence becomes more lifelike. For example, children recognize quite early on that cartoons are unrealistic. Crime shows, on the other hand, are closer to reality, and news programs are about real events. It may be that reality-type shows have a greater impact than the cartoon violence used in laboratory experiments. Other evidence indicates that active viewing—discussing the content of television shows critically with others—can help to diminish the effects of violent programming.

Television Violence

One U.S. study monitored a random selection of daytime and evening programs on 23 American cable channels over 20 weeks in 1995. In total, 2500 hours of television programming were included in the study, representing 2693 programs. Some of the study's findings are as follows:

- People who commit violent acts go unpunished in 73 percent of all violent scenes.

- Victims appear unharmed in 47 percent of violent interactions, and 58 percent show no pain.

- Only 16 percent portray the long-term negative effects of violence, such as psychological, financial or emotional harm.

- A total of 25 percent of violent interactions on TV involve handguns.

- Only 4 percent of violent programs emphasize an anti-violence theme.

- Movies are most likely to present violence in realistic settings (85 percent of the time), and to include gory violent scenes (28 percent of the time).

- TV violence is not usually explicit or graphic. Less than 3 percent of violent scenes feature close-ups on the violence, and only 15 percent depict blood.

- Children's programs are the least likely of all genres to show the long-term negative consequences of violence (5 percent of the time), and they frequently portray violence in a humorous context (67 percent of the time).

A follow-up study looked at scenes of violence that were considered to be higher risk than others for children under seven. These included violence in which the perpetrator was attractive, where the violence went unpunished or received minimal consequences, and in which violence was portrayed realistically. It found that on average there were 800 violent scenes that met these criteria in a typical week.

CASE STUDY

1. How much violence is there on television?

2. Is all media violence the same?

3. What is particular about violence on children's programs?

perpetrator—a person who commits a crime

Content Analysis

Content analysis is an approach to analyzing all kinds of communication, from a selection of writing, to a conversation, to an electronic image. It is based on identifying the number of times a particular item occurs in the communication. For example, you might want to know how much and what kinds of violence are shown on television. The findings of content analysis can tell us a great deal about what is important to the communicator.

Here's How

1. **Determine the question and purpose of your research.** For example, you might want to compare the amount of violence in television shows produced in Canada with those produced in the United States.

2. **State your hypothesis.** In our example, it might be that Canadian shows have less violence than American shows.

3. **Describe your research plan or process for gathering information.** In this case, it might be to watch two Canadian shows and two American shows, using a content-analysis checklist to observe and note all instances of violence in these shows.

4. **Develop a content-analysis checklist** (see below). Be sure to develop relevant criteria. In this case, you would need to use criteria that show what you mean by violence.

5. **Count and analyze** the number of instances of the criteria that you have chosen.

6. **Draw conclusions based on your research.** Was your hypothesis supported by the data? What further research needs to be done?

Practise It

Using content analysis, conduct research into an aspect of advertising or television that interests you. Follow the guidelines above.

Content Analysis Checklist

Hypothesis: _____

Communications being analyzed (identify shows or other communication): _____

	Canadian show #1 Date:_____	American show #1 Date:_____	Canadian show #2 Date:_____	American show #2 Date:_____
Verbal anger				
Verbal threats				
Creating fear				
Physical aggression (e.g., pushing or coercion)				
Causing pain or injury				
Causing death				

Activities

Understand Ideas

1. Why is advertising an essential aspect of mass media and popular culture?

2. What concerns are raised about the social norms reflected on television?

3. What kinds of violence affect children most?

Think and Evaluate

4. Do television producers have the ability to shape attitudes and behaviour in positive ways? Do they have a responsibility to try to do so? Explain your response.

5. Look at the list below. How might the portrayal of violence in each case affect a young viewer's understanding of violence and its consequences?
   - The hero, or "good guy," in a show uses violence to solve a problem.
   - The hero, or "good guy," in a show is harmed or killed by a violent act.
   - The violence on the show is not graphic. There are no close-ups of blood or injuries.
   - The violence shown is graphic, with close-ups of blood and injuries.
   - The violence shown is on the news. Images are graphic, but little time is devoted to explaining the background causes or results.

Apply Your Learning

6. Create a chart that lists the pros and cons of advertising. What do you think is the biggest concern for society regarding mass advertising?

7. "Advertising appeals to our emotions and to our desire for immediate gratification."
   a) Bring in clippings from newspapers or magazines to support this view. Share your evidence with the class.
   b) Which techniques shown in Figure 17–4 are evident in each advertisement?

Research and Communicate

8. Debate: "Governments should not regulate advertising." (See Skill Focus, page 302.)

Mass Media and Culture

Focus Questions

How does the mass media help to spread culture?

What are the positive and negative effects of mass media on culture?

As Canadians, we live across a wide geographic area, yet through media such as television, we can share ideas and images from all parts of the country. We are as familiar with social scenes from St. John's and Vancouver as we are with those from Toronto or North Bay. While we may take this cultural familiarity for granted, it was not true of our grandparents' generation. The consequences are both positive and negative. On the one hand, cultural familiarity helps create a common culture, drawing the country together by providing common experiences and knowledge of different parts of the country. On the other hand, if one culture is more dominant than others, it can seriously threaten the local cultures that make up the different regions of Canada.

Cultural Diffusion

In anthropology, **cultural diffusion** is the spreading of cultural ideas or behaviours from an original source to other places. Cultural diffusion can

Figure 17–7

The culture of southern Canada easily travels to northern Canada. Here, Prime Minister Jean Chrétien talks to members of the Inuit community in Iqaluit through telecommunications technology.

occur when people travel or move, carrying their culture with them, but it can also occur much faster electronically. Television is a powerful instrument of cultural diffusion, sending images and messages around the world. For example, northern Inuit communities have been increasingly exposed to southern urban culture since the arrival of television. Urban-based action shows, Hockey Night in Canada and advertisements for useless products, such as air conditioners, have become familiar experiences for northern Canadians. This may be why some young people in the Canadian north suffer from "culture shock" or cultural confusion.

The Canadian government recognized the power of broadcasting in the 1930s when it created the Canadian Broadcasting Corporation (CBC). Part of the CBC's aim is to provide Canadians with relevant news and information, to support and contribute to Canada's culture and to build bridges between communities and regions. However, it is not possible to stop television broadcasts from crossing borders, and Canadians often prefer American broadcasting over their own. For this reason, Canadian content regulations demand that radio stations play at least 35 percent Canadian music. These regulations have helped to create a thriving Canadian music industry. More recently, Canadian politicians have tried to ensure that magazines coming from the United States also have Canadian content.

While American influence has long been seen as a threat to Canadian culture, an even more profound change is occurring today that is bringing all world cultures closer together. In the late nineteenth century, a community was thought of as a small rural group in which everyone knew each other. In the twentieth century, people recognized that cities could also contain neighbourhood communities. Today, we live in the **global village** identified by Marshall McLuhan (see Chapter 13) in which people around the world belong to an international community. We are tied together through mass media, popular culture and improved telecommunications.

There are advantages and disadvantages to the global village. On the one hand, the global village has enabled us to know more about the lives of people from places we might otherwise never see. On the other hand, it has enabled countries of the industrialized world to export their culture and values. Young people around the world listen to British music, yearn for Italian clothes and eat in Chinese restaurants. American culture, in particular, is pervasive, especially in music, movies and books. Many people fear that local cultures are being swamped by the influence of the mass media.

pervasive—becoming widespread

Figure 17–8

The Xingu people, in Brazil, have allowed certain elements of the modern world into the relative isolation of their villages. Do you think they will still be able to maintain their traditional beliefs and lifestyle under the influence of the mass media?

Activities

Understand Ideas

1. Explain the term *cultural diffusion,* and describe how it has changed in the twentieth century.

Think and Evaluate

2. Debate the following resolution: Be it resolved that the development of a global culture through the mass media should be encouraged. (See Skill Focus, page 302.)

Apply Your Learning

3. What influences do you believe shaped your culture?

Research and Communicate

4. a) Find out what rules govern Canadian content on radio, on television and in magazines. Write an essay outlining the details. Document your sources. (See Skill Focus, pages 248 and 256.)

b) Do you agree with these rules? What rules would you add, change or remove?

The Information Revolution

Focus Questions

How has the computer changed the way information is spread?

What are the psychological and social effects of high-tech developments?

The first electronic computer was built in 1946. It had 18 000 vacuum tubes, filled a large room and had less power than your desktop computer. By the late 1970s, computer chips got smaller and it became practical for ordinary people to possess their own computers. By the 1980s many people did. Today, computers are everywhere: on desktops, in cash

Figure 17–9

The early computers of the 1960s were large enough to fill a room. Today, computer technology grows ever smaller and more powerful. What do you predict for the future of this trend?

Connections

How might the sedentary lifestyle associated with using computers affect our health and well-being? (See Chapter 16, pages 335–336.)

registers, at the bank and everywhere else in the social world. They shape our lives in every possible way. In the 1990s, more and more computers were hooked up to other computers via the Internet. Developments in telecommunications and mass media occurred at around the same time. The combination of these new technologies has begun to change how we think and learn, just as the Industrial Revolution changed the way we worked and consumed. Marshall McLuhan maintained: "The industrial machine extended the strength of our muscles; the information age will extend the powers of our minds." What changes has this brave new world of electronics and information created? Some see it as a new golden age in which humans can realize their fullest potential. Others see a darker future, in which humans are subservient to their machines. What do you see for the future?

The pace and sophistication of technological change in the information age are increasing every year. The speed of computers doubles every 18 months. It is hard to assess the implications of a revolution while you are in the middle of it. The situation is changing so quickly that predictions of what society will be like in 50 years—or even a decade from now—are tricky. However, some effects of this unprecedented pace of change and development are already clear.

Psychological Effects

Psychologists agree that all our high-tech wizardry has not made our lives simpler—in fact, technology is actually becoming a source of anxiety and stress for many of us. Rather than creating more leisure time by speeding up the time it takes to complete tasks, technology seems to have increased our workload to the breaking point. We are expected to respond instantly

Assessing Internet Information

The Internet has opened up a vast world of information for anyone doing research. It is important to remember, however, that anybody can have a site on the World Wide Web. As a result, a great deal of information on the Internet is of doubtful value. Of course, the Internet also contains a good deal of useful information, but it is best to find out as much as you can from other sources before using Internet information. When you do begin your research on the Internet, you must assess any Web site you use carefully.

Here's How

1. **Authority:** Are the authors of the site identified? What qualifications do they have? A Web site set up by a university, major institution or government is more likely to have reliable information.

2. **Up-to-date information:** Is the site dated, so you can assess how current it is? Does material on the site need to be updated?

3. **Quality of information:**

   - Does the information appear to be thorough and accurate, based on what you already know about the subject?
   - Is the information clearly organized?

   - Is the information presented with correct spelling, grammar and punctuation?
   - Are references provided for the sources of information quoted on the site?
   - Are links to other sites provided where information can be checked?

4. **Good taste and fairness:**

   - Is the information fair and free of prejudice?
   - Is the language appropriate?
   - Are there any signs that the Web site is distorting information from other sources?

Practise It

1. Work with a partner to draw up a Web Site Assessment Form to use when doing research on the Internet. Base your form on the criteria listed above as well as any other criteria you think are relevant.

2. Review any research you have done on the Internet for this course. Revisit at least two of the sites and evaluate them using your Web Site Assessment Form.

3. Revise your Web Site Assessment Form if necessary and post it on the class bulletin board.

---

to demands for information and to be available at all times by cellular telephone. According to a 1998 Statistics Canada survey, about 21 percent of women and 16 percent of men over 15 experienced time stress. This was up by about 5 percent for both genders over a similar survey in 1992. But some people believe that the Information Age is doing much more to us psychologically than creating stress. They claim that the Internet is radically changing the way we think and process information:

Since the birth of the printing press, humans have emerged in a print-based world where we acquire and absorb information in a linear fashion, for

From "Rewired" by Robert Cribb

example, from the top left-hand corner to the bottom right when reading English. Point A leads to B, which in turn brings us to C. Narratives flow from one event to the next. But today, we are raising the world's first Internet generation in a communications medium that is distinctly non-linear and increasingly non-textual. Hypertext—a method of quickly moving from one electronic document to another on the Web—can instantly transport readers from the opening lines of an Internet site to contextual background on a different site to related pictures in yet another location, all with a couple of clicks....

Today's adults, many of whom did not grow up with computers, are accustomed to processing information in the old, linear way. The question is, will younger generations adapt to this new, disjointed and largely visual approach to information processing? According to one commentator in his forties, "Our grandchildren will have an ease at making meaning from fragments instead of a clearly constructed argument. They're wired differently."

Social Effects

How does the computer affect education? What can you learn from using a computer besides how to use it? Clearly, the computer can provide more information faster than you could acquire it otherwise. But does it teach you how to use the information and be critical of what you find? Does it teach you how to solve important problems in life? No one doubts that computers will increasingly be a part of learning and education in the future. Computers are a powerful tool that can enhance learning in many ways—by providing access to an abundance of information and the ability to connect to schools and other resources around the globe.

Opinions differ, however, as to the exact role that computers and information technology will, or should, play in learning, especially during early childhood. Studies on the effectiveness of computer-based education have so far been inconclusive. While some studies do indicate that computers can enhance learning, others seem to indicate the opposite. And some critics feel that the vast amount of money being spent to provide and maintain computers and Internet access in schools would be better used to fund arts and enrichment programs or to hire more teachers. One writer sums it up this way:

> Childhood learning is primarily a social activity. Young children especially learn at least as much from talking with their teachers and with other students as they do by solving problems on their own....
>
> The fact that computer technology plays an ever-larger role in many aspects of our daily lives does not mean that having children use computers at the earliest possible age is in their best interests. Other forms of learning should take precedence during the early years....Most people can acquire an adequate level of computer competence in a matter of months. Access to computers in high school would give students more than enough experience of the most up-to-date computer applications....

While computers may or may not be appropriate as educational tools for the young, they are a fact of life for older students and adults. The need to constantly upgrade one's skills in information technology will make learning a lifelong activity, as we saw in Chapter 12. Already, older workers are returning to the classroom or taking distance learning courses throughout their working lives.

The development of new computer technology has also had a significant impact on the kinds of work that we do. The speed and accuracy of computer technology have already eliminated thousands of jobs in manufacturing, as factories are equipped with robotics to replace human workers. In white-collar jobs, older workers are finding themselves at a disadvantage when competing next to younger workers who have grown up with computers. Many of those who have lost their jobs have turned to self-employment, working from home via computer, e-mail and fax. And the future may hold more of the same. Some analysts are even predicting that jobs as we know them may disappear entirely, as machines take over more and more low-tech jobs. High-tech companies may decentralize, losing the

Figure 17–11

These children are lucky to have computers in their classroom. But what about the schools, the students or the families who can't afford to buy computers? Will they be left behind? Will social divisions emerge between those who have access to computers and those who do not?

Connections

Why would high-school students take distance learning courses? (See Chapter 12, page 261.)

decentralize—transfer powers away from one central location

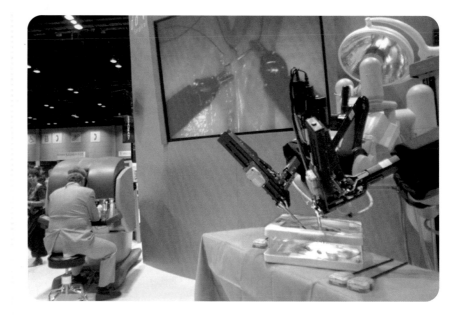

Figure 17–12

This remote-controlled system for performing surgery is operated by a doctor at a work station while three armed robots work at the operating table. Would this type of technology reduce the number of workers during an operation?

overhead costs of maintaining buildings and offices in favour of electronic connections among far-flung individuals working from home.

Socially, are computers creating a world of isolated individuals? According to some analysts, this may be the case. Where mass media, such as television, allowed us to share in common experiences and a popular culture, some critics feel that the Internet may reverse this effect. The Internet is so large that every user has a different experience. This seems to encourage a huge diversity of communities and subcultures that defy control. On-line chat groups, in which individuals converse without ever having to meet, may be weakening social bonds further by reducing face-to-face interaction. In addition, the Internet is notoriously difficult to regulate. Information can be transmitted from anywhere in the world, making it difficult to trace its origin. Thus, the Internet has brought a certain loss of social control, as sites containing hate literature, pornography, and illegal information have become easily accessible to anyone with a computer and Internet access.

However, many others see a positive aspect to the changes brought about by computer technology. The Internet, they point out, is a much more interactive medium than television or any of the other mass media. Rather than passively receiving information from a TV screen, Internet users interact with what they view, moving from site to site at their own discretion and choosing, or even creating their own content. And supporters of the advancements in communications claim that the difficulty in regulating content on the Internet is actually a means of safeguarding democracy. Countries with repressive governments, in which mass media are not free to report information, are hard pressed to keep it from leaking in via the World Wide Web. This can only help to inform and empower the average citizen.

hate literature—material written to promote suspicion and hatred toward a particular group

pornography—sexually explicit material that equates sex with power and violence

empower—to give power to [someone]

Unit 3: Social Structures and Institutions

Will Technology and Humans Coexist in the Future?

Will future anthropologists see humans today as the last stage before the emergence of a new biological-technological species? Is humanity on the verge of an evolutionary change? Even social scientists cannot predict the future. However, others are more willing to go out on a limb. Read the following article by Robert Cribb with a critical eye as you consider how your own future might be shaped by technology.

Welcome to Earth's third millennial birthday.

Everything, from social ethics to the human body to the very nature of love, has been morphed beyond recognition. This is a world of space-age holograms and androids, in-vitro harvested bodies carrying centuries-old minds and strange genetic mixes of human beings, animals and machines...

"Humans 1000 years ago tended to be pretty much like humans (in the second millennium). In the next 1000 years I don't know if those basic aspects of human life will maintain consistency," theorizes medical futurist Katherine Koch. "Do we have babies? Do we die? Is it necessary to live in communities anymore? Are we even still flesh and blood? Science will be able to eliminate any aspect of what used to be real."

"Machine and human intelligence will converge," says James Canton, a noted futurist and author of *Technofutures*. "We're talking about computer brains, the formation of artificial life that will think and have opinions. It's inevitable." Chips are everywhere. Your clothes tell you when it's time for them to be dry-cleaned. Your fridge orders groceries when you're running low on synthetic tomatoes. You are 250 years old, although your body is only 20 years old. It's your third genetically grown physical form, injected with your mind and consciousness when your old ones got tired...

"The concept of personhood—what a human being is—will have expanded to include machines and human-animal hybrids by 3000," suggests Joan Slonczewski, science fiction author and microbiology professor at Ohio's Kenyon College. "Machines will wake up as intelligent, self-aware entities. Machines will be understood as people who are born in factories. We will even fall in love with them."

For Tony Paxton, a professor of molecular and medical genetics at the University of Toronto, it's a disturbing vision. "You can envision that people will be effectively guaranteed healthy, long life spans and that we'll deal with terrible blights of hunger and disease. But the potential misuse of those technologies is dangerous and frightening to consider." Consider, for example, intelligent computers forming a globally interconnected consciousness that decides it might be prudent to destroy its chief rival—us.

Yet for all the potential pitfalls of the distant future, technology also promises to change our lives immeasurably for the better: healing us, improving our minds and bodies and allowing inspiration, rather than wealth, to become our driving motivation. "I see us living longer with greater freedoms and choices to do with as we wish, in a world with a lot more affluence and more time to pursue spiritual, creative, artistic pursuits," Canton says. "It will be almost Utopian."

What Do You Think?

1. Organize the forecasts made in this article. For each forecast, identify the pros and cons for human existence.

2. Which of these predictions do you think seem most likely to occur?

3. Evaluate the credibility of the experts quoted in the article. What do you think they are basing their predictions on?

Figure 17–13

Do you agree that our interaction with technology might eventually make us less human? Why or why not?

Will Technology Redefine Humanity?

Anthropologists have long pondered what makes us human, and the issue has acquired new importance with the invention and rapid development of computer technology. There are those who fear that computers will eventually deny us our humanity. Sociologist and social analyst Neil Postman is one such writer. The computer, he says, tends to lead us to redefine humans as "information processors" and nature itself as information to be processed. We now tend to see ourselves as thinking machines. Once we define ourselves that way, says Postman, our human qualities, such as our emotions and spirituality, become secondary. They become less important than the things that machines do better, such as processing information. Not only do we become machines, he says, but we become inferior to computers. Other social researchers are not concerned about this connection. Some accept that a union of humanity and technology, of biology and mechanics, is inevitable. We already use mechanical parts to repair the body, they say. Why should we not use technology to enhance the mind? And consider this: If genes can be altered through advances in genetic research, will the line between nature and nurture disappear?

Activities

Think and Evaluate

1. For what aspects of learning do you think computers are most useful? What aspects cannot be achieved with computers alone?

2. Do you think hypertext is creating a new way to think? Or is it simply discouraging us from thinking logically? Defend your answer with examples or arguments.

3. Write a response to Neil Postman, in which you agree or disagree with his view of the future.

Apply Your Learning

4. Describe how computers have influenced your education so far. What role are they likely to play in your future education?

5. Summarize the positive and negative effects of the Internet and computers on your social world. Which argument do you believe is most compelling? Why?

Research and Communicate

6. You are an anthropologist in the year 3000. You have just discovered a videotape of a classroom, circa 2000. Describe this ancient culture to your contemporaries, either in an oral presentation, or in a written report. (See Skill Focus, pages 188 and 338.)

7. Interview several of your teachers. Ask them what they think are the advantages and limitations of computers in education.

8. Find out what kind of skills are expected to be in demand in the near future. Why will they be in such demand?

Key Points

- The communication revolution started with the development of film, television and radio. It is now in its second phase with the development of computer technology.

- The mass media have had a powerful impact on us. The original purpose was to entertain, inform and educate. More recently we are realizing that the mass media also help shape ideas and behaviour, and spread popular culture.

- Current issues in mass media include the social effects of advertising, the concentration of ownership of the media, the role the media play in social change, and the amount of violence portrayed by the media.

- The information revolution has begun to change how we think and learn. Technological change is occurring at a rapid pace, with both psychological and social effects. People are, in general, more stressed by the demands placed on them.

- The role of technology in the future is open to debate. It is clear that technology will always be an important part of our lives, but there are those who fear that computers will eventually deny us our humanity.

Activities

Understand Ideas

1. **a)** What is the role of mass advertising?
   b) What concerns can be raised about the influence of mass advertising?

2. What are the concerns about the portrayal of men and women on television?

Think and Evaluate

3. Do you believe there is a strong, moderate or weak link between media violence and aggression? Provide three reasons to support your answer.

4. Develop a rating system for violence in television shows that could be displayed at the beginning of each program. The ratings would be used by parents to determine whether the content was suitable for their children. Each rating should be accompanied by a clear description of the level and kinds of violence it covers.

Apply Your Learning

5. Select a television show that consistently includes violence. Re-write the script to minimize the amount of violence shown. Share your before-and-after script with the class.

6. Find three print ads that use movie stars, sports heroes, musicians or other popular celebrities to endorse the product. Why do you think the companies chose these particular celebrities to sell their products?

Research and Communicate

7. **a)** Watch a sitcom or soap opera. Use content analysis to explain how it portrays a group of your choice, e.g., teens, women, men, the elderly, etc. How does this portrayal shape the attitude of viewers? (See Skill Focus, page 364.)
   b) Write a short plot outline for one program in this series that would help to shape the attitudes of viewers in a positive way.

8. Create a television or magazine advertisement for a fictional product. Identify who you think is most likely to buy the product, and target those consumers in your ad. Use one or more of the techniques discussed in this chapter.

9. Find out who owns your local newspaper(s) and radio station(s). Does the owner also control other media companies? If so, which ones?

Unit 3: Build Your Research and Inquiry Skills

1. Education

Issues

- What are the primary characteristics of education today?
- What purposes do our schools serve?
- What are the challenges for education in the future?

Inquiry and Analysis

- Review information in the text on the purposes of education, existing problems and challenges for the future.
- Make a concept map of education that includes information from the text and your own ideas based on personal experience and concerns.

SKILL REVIEW: Organizing Ideas with Concept Maps, page 125.

Communication

- Prepare either a position paper or a short oral presentation on Future Challenges for Canadian Education.

SKILL REVIEW: Writing a Position Paper, page 323; Making an Oral Presentation, page 338.

2. The World of Work

Issues

- How do people view and do their work today?
- What kinds of work will be most common in the future?

Inquiry and Analysis

- Choose an area of work that interests you.
- Find and interview someone involved in that area of work. Investigate the following topics:
  – the job description of a position in that field
  – how the job has changed over time
  – what the job will be like in the future
  – preparation and training for that particular field
  – rewards and challenges in that type of work
- If possible, get permission to job-shadow someone in that field of work. (Job shadowing means following someone throughout the day to observe how the work is done.)

SKILL REVIEW: Conducting an Interview, page 12.

Communication

- Prepare a description of the job you have chosen, under headings based on the topics above.
- Hold a class job fair in which you present your description and answer questions about the job to interested students.

3. Rich and Poor

Issues

- What kinds of poverty exist in Canada today?
- What contributes to the various types of poverty?
- What is the impact of poverty on those who experience it?
- What is being done to eliminate poverty in Canada?

Inquiry and Analysis

- Gather and organize a portfolio of recent media articles on poverty in Canada.
- Share and trade articles with others in the class.
- Choose one article for further analysis.
- Read the article carefully. Take notes on the major points it makes.

SKILL REVIEW: Analyzing and Judging Information or Ideas, page 97.

Communication

- Write a response paper to the article you have chosen.
- Exchange your article and response with at least one student who has responded to a different

article. Together, list the conclusions you can draw from your articles about the causes of poverty in Canada, who suffers from poverty and what is being done to eliminate it.

SKILL REVIEW: **Writing a Response Paper, page 172.**

4. Social Control

Issues
- What are some of the serious forms of deviant or criminal behaviour in our society?
- What methods of social control are used to deal with them?
- How effective are these methods of social control?

Inquiry and Analysis
- In a group, choose to focus on one of the following forms of deviant behaviour: youth crimes, driving offences, theft, assault or substance abuse.
- For the deviant behaviour you have chosen, find statistics that show its history and current trends.
- Consult the literature in the library and on the Internet to research the psychological or social causes of the behaviour.
- Find out, in the Criminal Code or elsewhere, which social controls for this behaviour are used in Canada and in other countries. How effective are these forms of social control?

SKILL REVIEW: **Gathering and Recording Information, page 73; Using Statistics, page 147; Assessing Internet Information, page 369.**

Communication
- Hold a seminar to discuss the form of deviant behaviour you have chosen.
- Choose someone other than the seminar leader to report your findings to the class.
- Compare your results with those of other groups. Identify and discuss the key issues that have emerged.

SKILL REVIEW: **Conducting a Seminar, page 283.**

5. Culture, Communication and Computers

Issues
- Do the media present biased views of social groups?
- Which groups are most likely to be presented in a biased manner?

Inquiry and Analysis
- Identify bias in at least one form of mass media.
- You may wish to choose advertisements on assorted media (television, radio, magazines, newspapers, billboards, flyers, etc.); television or radio programs; books, magazines, or newspapers; movies, videos or the Internet.
- In your analysis, look for bias against one particular group. For example, you could examine bias based on age, gender, physical appearance, race, culture or social class.

SKILL REVIEW: **Understanding Value Statements, page 226; Identifying Bias, page 233; Content Analysis, page 364.**

Communication
- Prepare an oral report of your findings to present to the class.
- Describe the media, the group, the type of bias you found and its potential effects. Be sure to answer this question: If you were the producer, the writer, the editor or the advertiser, how would you present the same information in an effective but unbiased manner?

SKILL REVIEW: **Making an Oral Presentation, page 338.**

Unit 3: Demonstrate Your Learning
Task 3–1: Comparing Cultures and Institutions

Background Information

Understanding and participating in a culture is an essential part of being human. Culture provides us with the ideas and the materials to fulfill our human needs. Through learning and sharing, we become the people we are, living and thinking the way we do. As members of a culture, we are also part of social structures and institutions that provide ways to meet specific needs such as food, shelter, learning and social order.

Social scientists study cultures, societies and social institutions in order to understand how they influence people. They have found, by closely observing the world around us, that there are many different ways to live. These differences provide great advantages to human beings—they give people ideas about how to change and improve their social and cultural environment. At the same time, cultures share many characteristics. As a result, observing and analyzing two or more cultures can allow social scientists to carefully draw conclusions about cultures overall.

Your Task

In this task, you will
- research and analyze two cultures, focusing on several major social institutions, such as the family, education, work and the economy, social class, social control, recreation and health
- work with three or four students to develop a comparison chart of several cultures
- write an essay in which you compare the two cultures you have researched, with a special focus on the following questions:
  - What are the differences?
  - What are the similarities?
  - What do the similarities tell you about cultures in general?

Review What You Know

1. Review information on culture and social institutions in Chapter 11 (Unit 2) and key ideas from Unit 3. Be sure you understand the following terms:
- ethnography (page 32)
- family (page 145)
- culture (page 218)
- social institutions (page 219)
- education (page 245)
- work (page 265)
- economy (page 265)
- social class (page 286)
- social control (page 313)
- recreation (page 329)
- health (page 333)

Think and Inquire

2. Work in a group to choose two cultures for each student to research and analyze.

3. In your group, determine which categories or aspects of each culture you will use as a focus. Use the institutions listed in "Your Task" as a guide.
4. Choose your method of investigation. If one of the cultures is Canadian, you might choose observation. In most cases, however, it is likely that you will have to conduct your research in the library and on the Internet.
5. Apply the research methods you have chosen and gather information under the selected categories.
6. Work with the members of your group to create a comparison chart. List the categories along one side of the chart and the cultures along the other. Complete the chart with the information you have collected.

SKILL REVIEW: **Analyzing a Culture, page 37; Gathering and Recording Information, page 73; Making Comparisons, page 213.**

Communicate Your Ideas

7. Write an essay comparing the cultures you have researched. Use the categories from your chart as criteria for comparison. Be sure to answer the questions in "Your Task." Document your sources.

SKILL REVIEW: **Writing an Essay, page 248; Documenting Sources, page 256.**

Apply Your Skills

8. In completing this task, you will demonstrate the following skills:
   • discussing issues in a group
   • gathering and recording information
   • analyzing a culture
   • making comparisons
   • writing an essay

Criteria for Assessment

Comparison Chart
   – includes a title
   – shows criteria for comparison
   – identifies selected cultures
   – completes all categories on the chart
   – includes relevant information in all categories
   – presents information neatly

Essay
Introduction
   – states the issue or question
   – states position and hypothesis
Content
   – uses categories in the chart effectively to compare at least two cultures
   – identifies differences and similarities between cultures
   – uses differences and similarities to generalize about cultures as whole
   – organizes arguments in well-structured paragraphs
   – supports arguments with evidence
Conclusion
   – provides a summary of the analysis
   – states the general conclusion
Language and Conventions
   – uses correct grammar
   – uses correct spelling
   – uses footnotes or end notes to document quotations and ideas taken from others
   – includes a bibliography to document sources of information
   – follows convention for format and appearance

Unit 3: Demonstrate Your Learning

Task 3–2: Creating Culture, Society and Institutions

Background Information

As individuals and as members of groups, you influence the society, social institutions and culture around you. Every time you say or do something, you contribute to or alter your culture. But societies and cultures can also be changed deliberately. Futurists often like to predict how our lives will change over time. Fiction writers sometimes create their own utopian worlds—beautiful, imaginary places that are impossibly perfect or ideal. Sometimes they design worlds that are anti-utopian, or ugly and frightening. No doubt you are familiar with stories or movies based on this theme.

There are good reasons for developing social ideas that do not, but could, exist. Such ideas motivate us to improve conditions or to avoid creating situations we would rather not experience. In this task, you will have the opportunity to create your own utopian or anti-utopian society as well as the institutions within it.

Your Task

In this task you will

- develop a society with a number of social institutions, choosing one of the scenarios below as your starting point
- analyze and describe the following aspects of this society:
  - dominant values and ideas
  - family life
  - education system
  - economy and work
  - level of technology
  - social control
- explain why each institution is structured the way it is and how it affects people's thoughts and behaviours
- present your society to the class in one of the following ways: a fictional narrative, a cartoon or comic strip, or a role play

Starting Scenarios

Scenario 1: "Marooned"

Buffeted by torrential rains and hurricane-force winds, the ship began to break up. Panic-stricken passengers lowered lifeboats, jumped over the side and struggled to escape the pull of the sinking ship. Rough seas, rain and the night soon swallowed up the ship, leaving the 15 survivors huddled in the lifeboat. All night they bailed water, desperately trying to keep afloat. By dawn, the wind and waves had subsided. In the distance they could see the dim outline of land and they rowed toward it.

By early afternoon they had reached the shore of a white sandy beach, with palm trees in the background. Pulling the boat ashore, they stepped safely onto the land. On this remote south sea island, they all knew, though none said it, that they would likely be here for a very long time. They would have to develop their own society in order to survive.

Scenario 2: "Lost in Space"

The starship *Endeavour* docked on the spaceport. The crew members looked out onto the newly discovered planet. It was about the same size as Earth. Tests showed its environment was also very much like that of Earth and that the inhabitants were physically similar to humans. Large cities could be seen to exist as well as cultivated areas surrounding these cities. As the crew steered the space taxi to the surface of the planet, they could see crowds awaiting them. They wondered what this society would be like.

Scenario 3: "Journey to the Future"

The time traveller awoke inside the time capsule. The dashboard calendar indicated the year 2100. Groggy from time lag, the time traveller stumbled from the capsule. There to meet her was a representative from the future. While the clothing looked a little strange, the future person had a friendly smile on his face. "Welcome," he said, in strangely accented English. "We have been expecting you. Let me show you our world." Grabbing his pocket-size video camera and palm computer, the traveller from the twenty-first century set out to investigate the future society.

Review What You Know

1. Review the following terms, making sure you understand what they mean:
- family (page 145)
- social groups (page 165)
- culture (page 218)
- society (page 218)
- social institutions (page 219)
- education (page 245)
- work (page 265)
- economy (page 265)
- communication (page 353)
- technology (page 353)

Think and Inquiry

2. Choose one of the scenarios above as a starting point for your fictional society.
3. Decide whether your society will be a utopia, an anti-utopia or a projection of your own society with changes.
4. Decide which institutions you will focus on.
5. In point form, outline the main characteristics of the institutions you have chosen:
- How is each one structured?
- Why is it structured in this way?
- What effect does it have on the thoughts and behaviours of its members?

SKILL REVIEW: **Analyzing a Culture, page 37**

Communicate Your Ideas

6. Decide, in consultation with your teacher, how you wish to present your ideas. Possibilities include a fictional narrative, a cartoon or comic strip, or a role play. If you are working on a role play, you will need to work with a small group.
7. Prepare and present your society in the format you have discussed with your teacher.
8. As a class, discuss the societies that are presented. Identify the positive, negative and interesting features of each.

Apply Your Skills

9. In completing this task, you will demonstrate the following skills:
- applying concepts to new situations
- organizing ideas
- using ideas creatively
- presenting ideas
- writing creatively

Criteria for Assessment

Fictional Narrative, Cartoon or Comic Strip, Role Play
- identifies main institutions
- describes how each institution is structured
- explains why each institution is structured in this way
- shows how people behave within institutions and groups
- creates characters who indicate their thoughts and values
- includes a plot that shows how institutions affect the characters
- provides neat and clear illustrations (for cartoon or comic strip)

Glossary

absolute poverty A level of deprivation whereby people lack resources that society considers essential.

achieved status Recognition that is awarded to an individual because of effort and hard work.

acting crowd A group of people who are fuelled by a single purpose.

ageism A specific form of discrimination directed against members of a certain age, usually seniors.

agents of socialization The types of social contacts or influences people experience.

agricultural economy A way of sustaining a society by planting crops and domesticating animals to provide a more stable existence.

amnesia A partial or total loss of memory.

anorexia nervosa An obsessive-compulsive eating disorder whereby an individual reduces the intake of food, sometimes to the point of starvation.

anthropological linguistics A branch of anthropology that studies changes in language over time, how different languages are related and the meaning language has for people.

anthropology The study of human beings as a species and as members of different cultures.

anthropomorphic Giving human attributes to animals.

applied anthropology A branch of cultural anthropology that uses research results to solve practical problems, such as providing health care or cultivating crops.

archaeology Cultural anthropology of the past, particularly of prehistoric times.

arranged marriage Marriage arranged by family members who view marriage as a union between two families where religious and cultural concerns play a role.

artifacts Objects of historical interest that have been produced or shaped by human craft.

ascribed status Recognition that is assigned to an individual at birth or because of one's age.

assimilation A tendency for members of a minority group to adopt the ways of the dominant society.

authoritarian leader A leader who tells followers what to do.

battered woman syndrome An emotional disorder caused by repeated abuse, resulting in fear, anxiety and a pattern of learned helplessness.

behavioural component The aspect of emotional reactions whereby people express their emotions through actions, body language or facial expressions.

behavioural sciences The scientific study of human behaviour within three disciplines: anthropology, psychology and sociology.

behaviourism The study of observable human reactions to the environment.

bias An unfair act or policy that is rooted in prejudice and prevents impartial judgment.

biological motivation The study of how innate physical desires cause behaviour.

biological theory The attempt to explain deviant behaviour through biology.

bipolar affective disorder A condition marked by extreme mood changes that have two stages: a manic stage and a depressed stage.

blended or reconstituted family Parents with children from one or more previous marriages or unions.

bulimia An eating disorder whereby an individual ingests large amounts of food at a time, and then vomits or fasts in an attempt to lose weight.

bureaucracy A type of organization that employs people in highly specialized positions in order to perform numerous tasks as efficiently as possible.

bystander apathy The unwillingness of members of a crowd to get involved when help is needed.

capital punishment The death penalty.

case study The documented observation of an individual, a situation or a group over a period of time.

casual crowd A loose collection of people who react very little to each other.

census An official count of the population in various categories conducted by the government.

charismatic leader A leader with the ability to inspire followers with great enthusiasm and commitment.

child poverty Deprivation experienced by children of poor families.

civil law The regulation of relations and conflicts between individuals, such as marriage or divorce.

classical conditioning How an individual learns to transfer a natural response from one stimulus to another.

clique An exclusive group that includes a small number of chosen members.

coercive organization An organization, such as a prison, where members belong without choice and where rules are strictly enforced.

cognition The process of acquiring, storing and using knowledge.

cognitive component The aspect of emotional reactions whereby people consciously feel happy, sad, angry or excited.

cognitive development How people learn and use language.

cognitive psychology The study of the mental processes involved in memory, learning and thinking.

collective An organization of volunteers where there is little formal division of labour and where authority derives from group consensus.

collective bargaining The step-by-step process of negotiation between an employer and a union.

collective behaviour The ways people act in crowds, groups, social movements or across an entire society.

collective unconscious The part of the mind that stores and remembers both personal and common cultural experiences.

common-law family An unmarried couple with or without children.

communication revolution The change in human culture and society brought on by the development of radio, film, television and computer technology.

communication-based societies Societies that rely on electronically generated data.

companionate love A relationship in love that is enduring and stable and that is generally based on common interests and goals.

concrete operational stage The level of cognitive development that occurs between the ages of seven and eleven when children can see things from the point of view of others but can only perform tasks that depend on the presence of physical objects.

conditioned response A learned reaction.

conditioning The acquisition of patterns of behaviour in the presence of an environmental stimulus.

conflict theory The view that social classes compete for power and that power, not function, holds a society together.

conformity Behaviour that follows accepted practice.

contemporary society A changing society, dependent on industry and advanced technology.

control theory The idea that deviant behaviour occurs through an absence of social control.

conventional crowd A group of people who have gathered for a specific event and who conform to norms that are considered appropriate to the situation.

conventional roles A division of roles based on the belief that men and women in a marriage have different responsibilities and separate areas of activity.

crowd A large group whose members have little or no interpersonal contact.

cult A group, usually with religious or spiritual beliefs, that is organized around a charismatic leader.

cultural anthropology The study of how culture shapes human ideas and learned behaviour in societies around the world.

cultural conflict Competing demands and influence between the culture of the minority group and the culture of the dominant society.

cultural diffusion The spreading of ideas or behaviours from an original source to other places.

cultural pluralism A form of society in which diverse cultures are fully accepted.

cultural relativism The belief that all cultures should be respected for developing ways to survive and for meeting the challenges of their environment.

culture The shared values, beliefs, behaviours and material objects of a group of people.

decision making A four-step process of choosing a course of action: determining options, evaluating options, making a choice and taking action.

deductive reasoning The use of information to draw conclusions, starting with a general principle that is applied to a specific situation.

defence mechanisms Unconscious mental processes used to protect the ego against shame, anxiety or other unacceptable feelings or thoughts.

delusions False beliefs.

democratic leader A leader who seeks consensus.

deprivation theory The belief that social movements are formed by people who feel deprived in some way.

deterrance The attempt to prevent further criminal behaviour through punishment.

deviance Behaviour that differs from the social norms of the group and that is judged as wrong by members of that group.

dialectical reasoning Reaching a conclusion by combining opposing points of view, showing that different opinions can be compatible.

discrimination A set of actions that societies or individuals take against particular groups of people because of their race, gender or other common characteristic.

distance education The teaching of individuals in remote areas through online courses.

downsize To lay off workers to cut costs.

drives Inner urges to satisfy some basic need.

dual career roles A marriage in which both partners have careers and share household tasks equally.

dysfunctional Emotionally and psychologically impaired.

eating disorder An obsessive-compulsive disorder involving failure to eat, or binge eating followed by purging.

economy The wealth and resources of a community; the production, distribution and consumption of goods and services.

education The ways a society conveys knowledge to its members.

education gap The difference between the amount of education received by male students as opposed to female students.

ego The part of the mind that is most aware and that deals with external reality.

elite culture Culture that is appreciated by a limited number of people with exclusive, specialized interests.

employability skills The skills that will help people transfer their knowledge and education from one work situation to another.

entrepreneur A person who owns, organizes and manages an independent business.

ethics Moral principles or rules of conduct.

ethnocentrism The tendency to judge other cultures by one's own values.

ethnography The in-depth description of a particular

culture, written by an anthropologist who lives with the people he or she is studying.

ethnology The study and comparison of past and contemporary cultures.

eustress Positive stress such as falling in love or working hard on a project that an individual enjoys.

euthanasia The wilful killing of a person who is suffering from a terminal, debilitating or painful disease.

evolution The theory that organisms change structurally and genetically over time, resulting in the gradual development of a new species.

experiment A controlled environment where tests are conducted to determine how one factor is related to another.

expressive crowd A group of people at an emotional event such as a rock concert or a political rally.

expressive leadership A style of leadership that creates harmony or solidity among group members.

extended family Relatives in addition to parents and unmarried children, all living together.

fad A social pattern that people follow briefly but enthusiastically.

fashion A social pattern adopted by a large group of people, usually for a limited period of time.

feminist sociology A sociological approach that studies gender roles in society and gender inequality and discrimination, striving to raise awareness and to bring about change both socially and politically.

folk culture Culture that develops within a limited community and that is usually communicated orally.

folkways Informal practices based on tradition.

formal communication The tendency, especially in bureaucracies, to communicate in writing.

formal operational stage The stage of cognitive development that occurs in adolescence and results in the ability to think abstractly and to imagine alternatives.

formal organizations A large group of people, such as those in a school, business or government, who are organized with the purpose of achieving a specific goal.

free-choice marriage Marriage whereby husband and wife choose their spouse based on personal and emotional compatibility rather than family concerns.

functionalism The belief that mental characteristics develop to allow people to survive and adapt.

gender The social roles and characteristics that a society considers appropriate for a man or woman.

gender segregation The concentration of men and women in different occupations.

general adaptation syndrome A three-stage reaction to stress: alarm, resistance and exhaustion.

generalized anxiety disorder Anxiety that occurs in the mind of an individual without any obvious cause.

genocide The widespread killing of members of a particular group.

global village A term identified by Marshall McLuhan to describe the international community that people from around the world belong to.

globalization Making goods and services available on a worldwide basis by offering a standard product that appeals to tastes in different societies and cultures.

gossip A form of rumour that deals with personal information about an individual or a small group.

hallucinations False but convincing perceptions of objects or events experienced when fully awake.

harassment Discrimination in the form of verbal or physical attacks.

hate literature Material written to promote suspicion and hatred toward a particular group.

health Physical, mental and social well-being.

health-care system The regulation and administration of health-care services, such as hospitalization.

hierarchy of needs The theory held by Maslow that human needs can be arranged in order of priority, beginning with physiological needs such as hunger and progressing to the final stage of self-fulfillment.

hierarchy of offices Ranking positions in an organization in order of dominance or importance.

humanism The emphasis in psychology on the unique quality of human beings, particularly their freedom and potential for personal growth.

hunting and gathering society A society where people move from place to place to obtain food and shelter, and where children learn the skills of survival by observing and imitating their parents and other adults.

hypnosis A condition of being in a sleeplike state, particularly susceptible to suggestions or able to recall forgotten memories.

hypothesis A possible answer to a question and a starting point for further investigation.

id Part of the unconscious mind thought to be responsible for instinctive behaviour such as seeking pleasure and avoiding pain.

inductive reasoning Drawing conclusions by moving from the specific to the general, from observations to conclusions.

industrial economy The change in society that occurred about 200 years ago when non-human energy was harnessed, moving work from homes to factories and allowing people to mass produce goods.

informal structure Relationships that develop naturally among co-workers in an organization.

inquiry model An investigation that follows a five-step procedure: identifying a problem or question, developing a hypothesis, gathering data, analyzing data and drawing conclusions.

instincts Inborn patterns of behaviour that are characteristic of a species.

instrumental leadership A style of leadership that focuses on defining goals and determining ways to achieve them.

intended goals of education The primary purpose of

education to transmit knowledge and skills to students.

interview A dialogue between a questioner and a subject to obtain information.

isolates Children who live with little human contact.

labelling theory The effect of automatically defining people in a particular way.

laws Formal rules enforced by designated individuals within a society.

legal-rational authority Leadership earned out of respect for one's education, experience or seniority.

life expectancy The average period that a person might be expected to live under current conditions.

lifelong learning The belief that educators must teach students how to continue to learn ongoingly.

long-term memory The retention of information for long periods of time.

Low-income Cut-off (LICO) A measurement used to determine what percentage of the population can be classified as poor, that is, those who spend 55 percent or more of their income on food, shelter and clothing.

major depression A mental disorder marked by deep, prolonged unhappiness, anxiety, sleeping problems, changes in appetite and possible suicide attempts.

manufacturing sector The jobs in an industry related to the large-scale production of material goods.

mass behaviour Group behaviour that involves people who are dispersed and that relies on personal communication through mass media or the Internet.

mass hysteria A form of collective behaviour whereby people respond with irrational and frantic behaviour but have little or no direct contact with each other.

mass media The means of communication to a large number of people usually through television, radio or newspapers.

mass produce To use a mechanical process to make large quantities of a standardized product.

mass society theory The belief that social movements arise because people feel isolated and insignificant, and joining a group gives them a sense of belonging and importance.

median Midpoint of a range of numbers.

mediation The process by which a neutral party helps two sides overcome their differences.

memory The capacity to acquire, retain and recall knowledge and skills.

mental health Functioning in a state of mental and emotional well-being.

mental illness The disorderly functioning of the mind.

meritocracy A system of rewarding individuals according to their ability and talents.

minority group A relatively small group of people who differ from members of the dominant society.

mob An acting crowd that becomes violent.

mores Norms involving moral or ethical judgments.

motivation The study of what causes behaviour.

multiculturalism An official policy to encourage different cultures to retain their distinctive characteristics, ideas and beliefs.

natural selection Charles Darwin's theory of evolution that states that organisms change structurally and genetically over time, resulting in the gradual development of new species.

nature-nurture debate The controversy as to whether inherited biological characteristics (nature) or environment and learning (nurture) are more influential in determining human behaviour.

needs Physiological or psychological requirements for one's well-being; conditions that motivate action.

negative reinforcement An event, a situation or a condition that decreases the likelihood that a certain behaviour will recur.

network A group of loosely connected people who decide to make regular or occasional contact for a specific purpose, such as finding information or generating business.

norms The rules within a group that indicate how members should behave.

nuclear family One or two parents and unmarried children living together.

observational learning Acquiring the skills of a new activity by observing people who act as models.

obsessive-compulsive disorder A form of anxiety marked by the tendency to perform an action repeatedly in order to relieve a persistent, unwanted thought.

operant conditioning A type of learning whereby responses to a situation occur before they are triggered by outside events, and their repetition is influenced by rewards or punishments.

panic A form of collective behaviour that causes people to react to a threat in an emotional, irrational and sometimes self-destructive way.

paranoia A mental illness characterized by unwarranted feelings of persecution and jealousy.

parole The process of releasing and monitoring prisoners before a sentence has expired, on condition of lawful behaviour.

participant observation Research through observation and participation in a group's activities.

pathological Severely abnormal.

patriarchal A structure in which the male is seen as the head of the family or organization.

peer group Other people of the same age as a particular person.

perception The process by which sensory signals are selected, organized and interpreted in the brain.

personality A pattern of thinking, feeling and acting that is unique to an individual.

personality disorders Mental disorders that make it difficult for individuals to relate to others, to function normally or to hold a job.

phobia A form of anxiety that involves an intense, irrational fear of certain objects or situations.

physical anthropology The social science that seeks to understand and define the physical or biological nature of human beings.

physical component The aspect of emotional reactions whereby people show physical signs such as tensed muscles or increased body temperature.

popular culture Culture that is produced and shared through mass media by large numbers of people.

pornography Sexually explicit material that equates sex with power and violence.

positive reinforcement An event, a situation or a condition that increases the likelihood that a certain behaviour will recur.

post-industrial economy The shift in the second half of the twentieth century from a system based primarily on manufacturing to one based on services and the extensive use of information technology.

poverty line The income below which people are considered poor.

prejudice An unfavourable belief about members of a group, without the knowledge or experience needed to make a judgment.

pre-operational stage The stage of cognitive development that occurs between ages two and seven when children begin to use language but see things only from their own point of view.

prescriptive norms Accepted standards that indicate what individuals in a society should do.

primary group A small group such as a family or a circle of friends whose members have personal, often emotional, relationships with each other.

probation Allowing a person convicted of a crime to stay in society, subject to conditions such as meeting with a probation officer and remaining in a certain area.

problem solving A process to deal with new situations for which there is no well-established response: define the problem, develop a strategy, carry out the strategy and determine if the solution works.

propaganda Intentionally misleading or distorted information used to manipulate public opinion.

proscriptive norms Accepted standards that indicate what people in society should not do.

psychoanalysis A process whereby patients discuss their background, feelings and experiences with a trained therapist.

psychological theory Explaining deviant behaviour by understanding early childhood experiences.

psychopathic personality A mental disorder marked by a total disregard for the well-being of others and a lack of guilt or remorse after committing a crime.

psychology The scientific study of behaviour and mental processes.

psychosocial Both psychological and social.

public health-care system Universal access to doctors and health-care facilities, regardless of income.

public opinion A widespread attitude about a specific issue that can exert a strong influence over government action or policies.

racism A specific form of discrimination directed toward members of any racial or cultural group.

recidivism The rate at which criminals repeat their offences and return to prison.

rehabilitation The view that the offender can be brought back into society through education, therapy or a positive, supportive environment.

relative poverty A way of defining poverty by measuring the deprivation of some people against the situation of those who have more.

retribution The belief that wrongdoing should be met with an equivalent form of suffering.

riot A frenzied crowd without any particular purpose or goal where people are unorganized, emotional and often aggressive.

roles Behaviours that individuals within a group are expected to perform.

rumour Unsupported information that people spread informally, often by word of mouth.

sample survey A questionnaire designed to obtain information about the thoughts or behaviours of a limited number of people who represent a larger group.

sanctions Rules within a group that encourage or discourage certain kinds of behaviour.

schizophrenia A mental disorder marked by distortion of reality, social withdrawal and disturbances of thought, perception, motor activity and emotions.

secondary groups Impersonal or formal groups such as schools or businesses where individuals are judged by what they can do rather than who they are.

segregation Members of a minority group who live separately from the rest of the society.

self-concept Self-awareness and self-image.

self-employment Owning one's own business.

self-fulfilling prophecy Making something happen because it is expected or foretold.

sensation The process by which sense receptors such as sight, hearing, smell, taste and touch are activated so that signals are transmitted to the brain.

sense of self An awareness of what it is that makes each of us unique.

sensorimotor stage The stage of development that occurs between birth and age two when children experience the world primarily through their senses.

sensory memory Receiving information through each of the senses and selecting what should be retained from all the information received.

service sector Industries that provide services for the public, such as banking, retail or transportation.

sex Biologically male or female.

sexism A form of discrimination directed against members of a particular sex.

sexually transmitted diseases Diseases that are transmitted through sexual contact.

short-term memory The retention of information from the environment for 15 to 20 seconds.

single-parent family A parent with one or more children living together.

social class A group of people who have similar income, influence, lifestyle, education and type of work.

social concern theory The belief that social movements arise when a social institution or benefit is threatened by change.

social control The methods used by society to ensure conformity to social norms.

social groups People who interact with each other and are aware of having something in common.

social institutions Organizations or events that help a society meet the needs of its population.

social motivation The study of how learned, psychological needs, such as praise, can cause behaviour.

social movement The collective behaviour of people who promote or resist changes to society.

social norms The expectations of a society that guide an individual's behaviour.

social psychology The study of individuals within their social and cultural setting.

social role A set of expected behaviours and beliefs related to the part an individual plays in society, such as child, student or friend.

social science The study of human societies and social relationships that focuses on people as individuals and as members of groups.

socialization The process by which people learn what they need to know to become a member of a society.

society A group of people in a particular geographic area who share the same rules and laws.

sociological theory Explaining deviant behaviour as a learned response to the social environment.

sociology The study of people in groups—their relationships and the social structures they develop.

specialization Structuring an organization so that each individual is expected to perform specific tasks.

spousal abuse One partner in a relationship suffers injury or violence at the hands of the other partner.

stereotypes People or situations that conform to preconceived characteristics that allow individuals to make faulty generalizations about an entire group.

stimuli Objects or events that produce a response from a person or other living thing.

streaming Placing students into different programs or courses based on early assessment of their abilities.

stress A physical and psychological response to the environment that test one's ability to cope.

stress cognitive appraisal An individual's appraisal first of a threat that is present, and then of ways to deal with the threat.

structural functionalism The view that segments of a society serve a purpose for the society as a whole.

structural strain theory The idea that social movements arise to bring about revolutionary change when people have a plan of action to deal with significant problems; this action subsequently destroys social controls due to the pressure for change.

structuralism The observation of the inner workings of the mind by conducting experiments on sensation, perception and attention.

structured observation The study of people that begins with a written list of what will be observed.

subculture A group of people who share characteristics of the overall culture but also have important distinctive ideas and behaviours.

substance-related disorders The harmful use of substances such as alcohol or drugs.

superego The part of the mind that is influenced by values and acts as a conscience.

symbolic interactionism The view that people are internally motivated by what they have learned and interpreted, rather than externally motivated by social or economic conditions.

systemic discrimination Discrimination that is widely practised and supported by laws.

traditional society A society with little dependence on scientific or technological development.

unconditioned response An automatic, unlearned reaction.

unconscious mind The part of the mind that people are not always aware of—the source of instincts (id) and conscience (superego).

unintended goals of education Benefits that were not planned for, such as community centres in schools.

union An organization that represents the workers' point of view to the employer.

unofficial discrimination An action of discrimination against individuals even though such an action is against the law.

unstructured observation The study of people without a predetermined idea of what to look for.

utilitarian organization An organization that offers a service to its members.

values The basic and fundamental principles or standards considered worthwhile or desirable.

work Paid employment, unpaid chores and volunteer services.

working poor A group of people who earn wages, but not enough to prevent them from experiencing poverty.

Index

A

absolute poverty, 290
achieved status, 286
acting crowd, 207
active euthanasia, 347
Adler, Alfred, 79
advertising, 357–359
ageism, 227
agents of socialization, 119–126
agricultural cultures, 36
agricultural economy, 266
agricultural societies, 145–146,
      247
AIDS, 343–345
alcohol and drug addiction,
      341–342
anorexia nervosa, 103, 339–340
anthropological linguistics, 32
anthropology, 5, 19
applied anthropology, 31–32
archaeology, 30–31
arranged marriages, 150–151
Asch, Solomon, 169
ascribed status, 286
assimilation, 221
authoritarian leaders, 177

B

Bandura, Albert, 56, 57
Barnard, Christiaan, 349
battered woman syndrome, 159
behavioural component, 83
behaviourism, 42–44
bias, 233
biological theories of deviance,
      311
bipolar affective disorder, 104
blended (reconstituted) family,
      145
blind spot, 47
bulimia, 103, 339–340
bureaucracies
      assessment of, 194–196
      authority in, 190–192

characteristics of, 188–190
defined, 187–188
personal relationships in,
      192–193
reform of, 197–198

C

case study, 8–9
casual crowd, 203
child abuse, 120–121
child poverty, 303
childless family, 145
cigarette smoking, 340
classical conditioning, 53–54
cliques, 174–176
coercive organizations, 183
cognition, 50
cognitive component, 83
cognitive development, 128–129
cognitive psychology, 44–45
collective bargaining, 276
collective behaviour, 201–202, 206
collectives, 198
common-law family, 145
communication-based cultures, 38
communication revolution, 353
companionate love, 87
computers. *See* information
      revolution
concepts, 62–63
conclusions, 7, 16–17
conditioned learning, 53–55
conditioning, 53
conflict theory, 112
contemporary societies, 245
control theories, 312
conventional crowd, 204
conventional roles, 154
Cooley, Charles Horton, 129–130,
      166
criminal justice system, 316–318
crowd, 165, 203–207
cultural anthropology, 19, 29–34
cultural diffusion, 365–366

cultural relativism, 29–30
culture
      agents of socialization,
            123–125
      characteristics of, 27–28
      defined, 5, 26, 218
      and society, 218–223
      and sport, 330–332
      types of, 35–38

D

Dart, Raymond, 20
Darwin, Charles, 20, 42
data, 6–7
data analysis, 14–16
decision making, 65–67
deductive reasoning, 63
defence mechanisms, 78
democratic leaders, 177–178
Denny, Reginald, 204
deprivation theory, 214
deterrence, 319
deviance, 309–312
dialectical reasoning, 64–65
discrimination
      dealing with, 232–233
      defined, 224–225
      schools and, 228
      types of, 225
      victims of, 227
distance learning, 261
divorce, 160–162
dreams, 67, 68–69
dual-career roles, 154
Durkheim, Emile, 112

E

eating disorders, 103, 339–340
economy, 265
education
      academic standards, 259
      in Canada, 251–252
      defined, 245
      discipline in schools, 257–258

life expectancy, 333
lifelong learning, 262
Locke, John, 41
long-term memory, 60–62
looking-glass self, 129–130
love, 86–88, 152–153
Low-income Cut-off (LICO), 291

M

major depression, 104
manufacturing sector, 270–271
marriages, 149–152
Marx, Karl, 112, 288
Maslow, Abraham, 80–81, 132
mass behaviour, 208–211
mass hysteria, 210
mass media
    advertising, 357–359
    as agent of socialization, 126
    and culture, 365–367
    defined, 38, 354–355
    ownership concentration,
        359–360
    social change, 360
    television and violence,
        361–363
mass society theory, 214
maturity, 85
McLuhan, Marshall, 271, 366, 368
Mead, George Herbert, 130
Mead, Margaret, 26–27, 121
memory, 58–62
mental health, 91
mental illness
    anxiety disorders, 101–104
    changing views of, 98–99
    defined, 98
    help for, 108
    mood disorders, 104
    personality disorders, 105–106
    schizophrenic disorders, 105
    statistics, 100–101
    substance-related disorders,
        107–108
meritocracy, 254
Merton, Robert, 311–312
middle class, 287–288

Milgram, Stanley, 169–170
mob, 207
mores, 307
motivation
    biological and social, 72–74
    defined, 72
    and Freud, 74–78
    and Maslow, 80–81
motivational theories, 311–312
multiculturalism, 222

N

Nancy B., 346
nature-nurture debate, 26–27,
    116–118
network, 166
Nightingale, Florence, 333
normative organizations, 182–183
norms, 167–168
nuclear family, 145

O

observational learning, 56–57
obsessive-compulsive disorder,
    102
operant conditioning, 55
opposable thumbs, 23
organ transplants, 349–351

P

panic, 210
Parkinson, Northcote, 194–195
participant observation, 13
passive euthanasia, 346
pastoral cultures, 36
Pavlov, Ivan, 53–54
peer group, 121–122
penal system, 318
perception, 46, 48–50
personality, 127–132
personality disorders, 105–106
Peter, Lawrence, 194
phobia, 101–102
physical anthropology, 19, 20,
    21–25
physical component, 83

Piaget, Jean, 128–129
Pinel, Philippe, 99
play, 329
police, 316–317
popular culture, 355–356
post-industrial economy, 270–271
post-industrial society, 146, 247
Postman, Neil, 374
poverty
    attitudes toward, 298
    in Canada, 303
    child poverty, 303
    definitions of, 290–293
    facts and myths, 300
    fight against, 298–299
    impact of, 296–297
    poor (the), 289–290
    risk of, 294–295
prejudice
    causes of, 230–232
    dealing with, 232–233
    defined, 224
    and jokes, 229
    schools and, 228
primary group, 166
prisons, 322–326
probation, 325
problem solving, 65
psychoanalysis, 42, 76–79
psychological theories of deviance,
    311
psychological theories of
    prejudice, 231–232
psychology, 5–6, 41–45
public health-care system,
    337–338
public opinion, 209
punishment, 319–325

R

racism, 227
raves, 206
reasoning, 63–65
recidivism, 324
recreation, 329
red tape, 194
rehabilitation, 319

Credits

Every effort has been made to trace the ownership of copyright material used in the text. The publisher would be grateful to know of any errors or omissions so that they may be rectified in subsequent editions.

Photographs and Cartoons

p. 2, Chris Arend/Stone; p. 3, Corel Library; p. 4, © Chris Arend/Stone; **Fig. 1–1**, © Graham French/ Masterfile; **Fig. 1–2**, Copyright © firstlight; **Fig. 1–3**, © Tony Frerck/ Stone; **Fig.1–4**, PhotoEdit; **Fig.1–5**, Bill Wittman; **Fig.1–6**, PhotoEdit; **Fig. 1–7**, Bill Wittman; p. 18, Corel Library; p. 19, © Pascal Rondeau/ Stone; **Fig. 2–1**, © David Brill/David L. Brill Photography; **Fig. 2–2**, © Bettman/ CORBIS/MAGMA; **Fig. 2–3**, National Geographic Society; **Fig. 2–4**, © Julie Houck/CORBIS/MAGMA; **Fig. 2–5**, © Bettmann/CORBIS; **Fig. 2–7**, CP (Bernard Brault); **Fig. 2–8**, Corbis/ Sygma; **Fig. 2–9** (l. to r.), © Anthony Bannister, Gallo Images/CORBIS, Anthony Bannister, Gallo Images/ CORBIS; **Fig. 2–10**, © Anthony Bannister, Gallo Images/CORBIS; **Fig. 2–11**, © Sherman Hines/Masterfile; **Fig. 2–12**, © Owen Franken/Bettmann/ CORBIS/MAGMA; p. 39, Corel Library; p. 40, © Jim Corwin/Stone; **Fig. 3–1**, Archives of the History of American Psychology, University of Akron; **Fig. 3–2**, Comstock; **Fig. 3–4**, Wilder Penfield Archives, Montreal Neurological Institute; **Fig. 3–7**, © Bettmann/CORBIS/MAGMA; **Fig. 3–8**, © Leonard Lessin, FBPA/Photo Researchers, Inc.; **Fig. 3–11**, Used with permission of Grolier Publishing Company; **Fig. 3–12**, © firstlight; **Fig. 3–13**, © Moshe Shai/CORBIS/ MAGMA; **Fig. 3–14**, from David Katz, *Animals and Men* (London, Longman, Life Sciences and Medicine Library, 1937); **Fig. 3–15**, © Bettmann/CORBIS; **Fig. 3–16**, CORBIS/MAGMA; **Fig. 3–18**, © Gregg Adams/Stone; **Fig. 3–19**, Coin designs courtesy of the Royal Canadian Mint/Images des pièces, courtoisie de la Monnaie royale canadienne; **Fig. 3–21** (l. to r.), Comstock, CORBIS/MAGMA, CORBIS/MAGMA; **Fig. 3–23**, © Bettmann/CORBIS; p. 70, Corel Library; p. 71, Corel Library; **Fig. 4–1**, © Peter Veit/DRK Photo; **Fig. 4–2**, Bettman/CORBIS; **Fig. 4–5**, Bettman/ CORBIS; **Fig. 4–6**, The Granger Collection, New York; **Fig. 4–7**, CORBIS; p. 84, Dick Hemingway; **Fig. 4–10**, Harlow Primate Laboratory; **Fig. 4–12**, CP (Veronica Henri); p. 89, Corel Library; p. 90, © Tim Flach/Stone; **Fig. 5–3** (l. to r.), CP (Colin Corneau), © David Young-Wolff/Stone; **Fig. 5–4** (clockwise from t. l.), Bill Wittman, CP (Camay Sungu), CP (Boris Spremo); **Fig. 5–5** (l. to r.), American Museum of Natural History, Bettmann/CORBIS/ MAGMA; **Fig. 5–6**, © Stephen Cooper/ Stone; **Fig. 5–8**, CP (Wally Santana); **Fig. 5–9**, CORBIS/MAGMA; **Fig. 5–10**, Bill Wittman; p. 110, Corel Library; p. 111, David Young-Wolff/Stone; **Fig. 6–1**, Bettman/CORBIS/MAGMA; **Fig. 6–2**, The Far Side by Gary Larson © 1986 FarWorks, Inc. Used with permission. All Rights Reserved; **Fig. 6–3**, CP (Ryan Remiorz); **Fig. 6–4**, ADAM@HOME © 2000 by UNIVERSAL PRESS SYNDICATE. Reprinted with permission. All rights reserved; **Fig. 6–5** (clockwise from t.), Bill Wittman, Bill Wittman, Eyewire 052004A, Bill Wittman; **Fig. 6–6**, © Brian Vikander/ CORBIS/MAGMA; **Fig. 6–7** (l. to r.), Dick Hemingway, Maryse Laframboise/ DND; **Fig. 6–8**, © Ranald Mackechnie/ Stone; **Fig. 6–9** (clockwise from t. l.), Dick Hemingway, Bill Wittman, Bill Wittman, Bill Wittman; p. 135, Corel Library; p. 136, © Chris Arend/Stone; p. 138, Corel Library; p. 140, Corel Library; p. 142, Pascal Rondeau/Stone; p. 143, Corel Library; p. 144, Corel Library; **Fig. 7–1**, © Oliver Benn/Stone; **Fig. 7–5**, Copyright © 1996 United Feature Syndicate, Inc.; **Fig. 7–7** (l. to r.), CORBIS, David Cummings, Eye Ubiquitous/CORBIS, CP Photo, CORBIS; **Fig. 7–8**, DigitalVision/ Image Club Graphics; **Fig. 7–11**, Copyright King Features Syndicate.

Reprinted with permission of The Toronto Star Syndicate; **Fig. 7–14**, Copyright © firstlight; p. 163, Corel Library; p. 164, Sylvain Grandadam/ Stone; **Fig. 8–1** (clockwise from t.), Bill Wittman, Bill Wittman, Bill Wittman, Myrleen Ferguson Cate/PhotoEdit; **Fig. 8–3**, Copyright © firstlight; **Fig. 8–4** (l. to r.), Dave Ryan/Image Network, CP (Jeff McIntosh), Bill Wittman; **Fig. 8–6**, © Stanley Milgram/ Alexandra Milgram; **Fig. 8–7**, P.G. Zimbardo, Stanford University, California; **Fig. 8–8** (clockwise from t. r.), © Graham French/Masterfile, Bill Wittman, CP (Paul Chiasson); **Fig. 8–9**, CP (Gerard Kwiatkowski); **Fig. 8–10** (l. to r.), CP (Chuck Mitchell), CP Photo, AP/Wide World Photos; p. 180, Corel Library; p. 181, Corel Library; **Fig. 9–1** (l. to r.), Dick Hemingway, © Graham French/ Masterfile; **Fig. 9–2** (l. to r.), CP (Marianne Helm), Bill Wittman, CP Photo; **Fig. 9–5**, Charles Solomon; **Fig. 9–7** (clockwise from t. r.), © Biran Pieters/Masterfile, CP (Kevin Frayer), Copyright © firstlight, Dick Hemingway; **Fig. 9–9** (l. to r.), Dick Hemingway, CP (Jonathan Hayward); **Fig. 9–10**, Copyright © 1996 by United Feature Syndicate, Inc. All rights reserved; **Fig. 9–11** (l. to r.), Copyright © 1999 Glenbow Archives (NA 1447–25), Dick Hemingway; **Fig. 9–12** (l. to r.), © Michael S. Yamashita/ CORBIS/MAGMA, CP (Christof Stache), © Steve Raymer/CORBIS/ MAGMA; **Fig. 9–13**, © Richard T. Nowitz/CORBIS/MAGMA; p. 199, Corel Library; p. 200, Stefan May/ Stone; **Fig. 10–1** (clockwise from t. r.), Copyright © firstlight, CP (Andrée Pichette), CP (Terry Risicki); **Fig. 10–2**, CP (Phill Snel); **Fig. 10–3**, AP/Wide World Photos; **Fig. 10–4**, CP (Didier Debusschere); **Fig. 10–5**, Toronto Reference Library; **Fig. 10–6**, © 1998 Tri Star Pictures; **Fig. 10–9** (clockwise from t.), © Hulton Getty, © Hulton Getty, © Alex Buckingham/Stone; **Fig. 10–8**, Joel Gordon/Joel Gordon Photography; **Fig. 10–9**, CP (Peter

Extracts, Tables and Diagrams

and based on data from Statistics Canada's database CANSIM, Tables D984702, D984686, D984582 and D984566—Matrix 3472, and *Historical Statistics Canada, 1999*, Catalogue 11–516; **Fig. 7–10**, adapted from "Percentage of Women and Men Performing Selected Household Chores, 1998" <www.statcan.ca/english/Pgdb/People/Families/famil36c.htm> Sept. 28/2000; **Fig. 7–13**, reprinted with permission, John te Linde, Ph.D., The City of Calgary; **p. 157**, from *Modern Woman Magazine*, July/Aug 1998, vol. 6, no. 6, **p. 84**; **Fig. 7–15**, adapted from "Divorce Rates in Canada, 1921–1977" from Statistics Canada publications, *Marriage and Divorces, Vital Statistics*, Vol. 11, Catalogue 84–205; *Divorces, 1989*, Catalogue 82–003S, No. 17; *Lone-parent Families in Canada, 1992*, Catalogue 89–522; *Divorces, Shelf Tables, 1996 and 1997*, Catalogue 84F0213; **p. 171**, Philip G. Zimbardo, Inc., reprinted by permission; from "The Swarm" by John Barber; **p. 206**, excerpt from "Rave Fever" by Susan Oh, from *Maclean's*, April 24, 2000, cover story, reprinted by permission; **Making Comparisons, p. 213**, diagram adapted from *Organizing Thinking, Book 2*, © 1990 Midwest Publications, Critical Thinking Books and Software, reproduced by permission of Critical Thinking Books & Software, 800–458–4849 <www.criticalthinking.com> All Rights Reserved; opening activity, **p. 217**, adapted from *Tribes, A New Way of Learning and Being Together* with permission of author, Jeanne Gibbs, CenterSource Systems, Santa Rosa, CA, © 2000; **Fig. 11–2**, adapted from Statistics Canada's Website <www.statcan.ca/english/Pgdb/People/Population/demo25a.h5m>; **p. 222**, from "A Challenge for Korean-Canadians" by Caroline Choi, from *Toronto Star*, Aug. 11, 1998, F4; **Canadian Values, p. 225**, from Citizens' Forum on Canada's Future Report to the People and Government of Canada, 1991, Privy Council Office, reproduced with the permission of the

Minister of Public Works and Government Services Canada, 2000; **Fig. 11–10**, from the "Decima Research Poll," Canadian Council to Promote Equality and Respect, March 1995; **p. 245**, from *People of the Deer* by Farley Mowat, used by permission, McClelland & Stewart, Ltd., *The Canadian Publishers*; **p. 246**, from "Japan's Kyoiku Mamas" by Marlise Simons in Macionis and Benorkraitis, *Seeing Ourselves, Classic, Contemporary, and Cross Cultural Readings in Sociology*, pp. 281–286, © Pearson Education Inc.; **Fig. 12–5**, from Survey of Labour and Income Dynamics Preliminary Interview (Jan. 1993), taken from *Social Inequality* by Curtis, Grabb and Guppy, Public Works and Government Services; **Fig. 12–7**, Statistics Canada, 1980, *Perspectives Canada III*, Catalogue 11–511, Table 4–11, Statistics Canada 1989, *Advance Statistics of Education, 1989–90*, Catalogue 81–220, Tables 7, 8, Statistics Canada 1993, *Advance Statistics of Education, 1993–94*, Catalogue 81–220, Tables 7, 8; **Fig. 12–8**, Earnings of Men and Women in 1995, Statistics Canada, 1996, Table 3, from *Social Inequality in Canada, Patterns, Problems, and Policies* by James Curtis, Edward Grabb, and Neil Guppy, 1999, p. 203; **p. 261**, published with permission of Breakwater, St. John's; **p. 266**, reprinted with permission—TSS from an article originally published in the *Toronto Star*, March 7, 1999; **p. 268**, from *The Great Depression*, Pierre Berton, 1991, Penguin Books, Toronto; **p. 274**, from *Young Builders of the New Economy—In the Spotlight*, Business Development Bank of Canada; **p. 277**, article by Peter Hadekel, reprinted with permission of *The Gazette* (Montreal); **Fig. 13–11**, from Number of Earners Who Worked Full Year, Full Time in 1995 in the 25 Highest Paying and 25 Lowest Paying Occupations and Their Average Earnings by Sex, for Canada, 1995, Statistics Canada; **p. 282**, reprinted with permission of the author; **Fig. 14–2**, reprinted with per-

mission of *Canadian Business Magazine*; **Poverty Quiz #1, p. 289**, National Anti-Poverty Organization; **p. 292**, reprinted with permission—TSS, copyright, Young People's Press; **Fig. 14–6**, Statistics Canada, Low Income Persons, 1980 to 1997 (Low Income Cut-Offs, 1992 base) Catalogue 13–569–XIB, Survey of Consumer Finances, April 1999; **Poverty Quiz #2, p. 296**, National Anti-Poverty Organization; **p. 301**, reprinted with permission—TSS; **Fig. 15–8**, from Ontario Solicitor General's Office as seen in the *Toronto Star*, Nov. 30, 2000; **p. 320**, reprinted with permission—TSS; **Fig. 15–12**, Statistics Canada Internet Site <www.statcan.ca/English/Pgbd/State/Justice/legal14htm> updated Nov. 20, 2000; **Fig. 15–13**, Statistics Canada Internet Site >www.statcan.ca/English/Pgbd/State/Justice/legal16htm> updated Nov. 20, 2000; **Fig. 15–14**, adapted from "World Prison Population List," Research Findings no. 88, Home Office Research Development and Statistics Directorate (UK); **p. 325**, from *Speaking of Indians* by Ella Deloria; **p. 331**, first excerpt from *Toronto Star*, second excerpt from *The Enclyopedia of World Sport*, David Levinson and Karen Christensen, Berkshire Publishing Group <berkshirepublishing.com> and <iworldsport.com>; **p. 335**, reprinted with permission—TSS; **Fig. 16–9**, adapted from Statistics Canada's Website <www.statcan.ca/english/Pgdb/People/Health/health05b.htm> 1999; **p. 342**, reprinted with permission of the Canadian Press; **p. 344**, from "Love and Fear in the Age of AIDS," John Demont, Feb. 22, 1993, reprinted with permission by *Maclean's* magazine; **p. 347**, reprinted with permission—TSS; **p. 350**, reprinted with permission—TSS; **Assessing Internet Information, p. 369**, from *Making History, The Story of Canada in the 20th Century*, Bain et al., 2000, reprinted with permission by Pearson Education Canada; excerpt **p. 369–370**, reprinted with permission—TSS; **p. 373**, reprinted with permission—TSS.